The Archaeology of Time Travel

Experiencing the Past in the 21st Century

Edited by

**Bodil Petersson
Cornelius Holtorf**

Archaeopress Archaeology

Archaeopress Publishing Ltd
Summertown Pavilion
18-24 Middle Way
Oxford OX2 7LG

www.archaeopress.com

ISBN 978 1 78491 500 1
ISBN 978 1 78491 501 8 (e-Pdf)

© Archaeopress and the individual authors 2017

Economic support for publishing this book has been received from
The Krapperup Foundation
The Hainska Foundation

Cover illustrations are taken from the different texts of the book. See List of Figures for information.

All rights reserved. No part of this book may be reproduced, stored in retrieval system,
or transmitted, in any form or by any means, electronic, mechanical, photocopying or otherwise,
without the prior written permission of the copyright owners.

This book is available direct from Archaeopress or from our website www.archaeopress.com

Contents

Preface vii

Introduction

Chapter 1: The Meaning of Time Travel 1
Cornelius Holtorf

Part One
Emerging Possibilities in Virtual Time Travels

Chapter 2: Time Travel Using 3D Methodologies
Visualising the Medieval Context of a Baptismal Font 25
Nicoló Dell'Unto, Ing-Marie Nilsson† and Jes Wienberg

Chapter 3: The Kivik Grave, Virtual Bodies in Ritual Procession
Towards New Artistic Interactive Experiences for Time Travellers 47
Magali Ljungar-Chapelon

Commentary: Time Travel Paradoxes and Archaeology 79
Per Stenborg

Commentary: Taking Us to the Past and the Past to Us 83
Isto Huvila

Part Two
Time Travel as an Educational Method

Chapter 4: Use the Past, Create the Future
The Time Travel Method, a Tool for Learning, Social Cohesion and
Community Building 89
Ebbe Westergren

Chapter 5: To Make and to Experience Meaning
How Time Travels are Perceived amongst Participants 113
Niklas Ammert and Birgitta E. Gustafsson

Commentary: Forming Bridges Through Time Travel 129
Cecilia Trenter

Part Three
Living the Distant Past

Chapter 6: Performing the Past
Time Travels in Archaeological Open-air Museums 135
Stefanie Samida

Chapter 7: Being There
Time Travel, Experience and Experiment in Re-enactment and 'Living History' Performances 157
Mads Daugbjerg

Chapter 8: Face-to-Face with the Past
Pompeii to Lejre 175
Cornelius Holtorf

Commentary: The Power of Time Travel 191
Roeland Paardekooper

Commentary: Mediated and Embodied Pasts – A Comment 195
Carsten Tage Nielsen

Part Four
Time Travel on Screen

Chapter 9: Waterworld
Travels in Time between Past and Future Worlds 201
Bodil Petersson

Chapter 10: A Cup of Decaf Past
An Archaeology of Time Travel, Cinema and Consumption 213
Dawid Kobiałka

Commentary: On Time Travelling and Cinema 229
Laia Colomer

Commentary: A Cup of Decaf Past and Waterworld 233
Niklas Hillbom

Part Five
Time Travel and Contemporary Society

Chapter 11: History as an Adventure
Time Travel in Late Modernity from the Perspective of a European
Ethnologist 241
Michaela Fenske

Chapter 12: Time Travel to the Present
Interview with Erika Andersson Cederholm 257
Cornelius Holtorf and Bodil Petersson

Commentary: Time-Travelling Tourism
Reflections on the Past as a Place of Fascination as well as Refuge 271
Thomas Småberg

Commentary: Time Travels as Alternative Futures 277
Britta Timm Knudsen

Conclusion

Chapter 13: Anachronism and Time Travel 281
Bodil Petersson

About the Authors 299

Index 305

List of Figures

Introduction

Figure 1.1. Land of Legends, Lejre. A modern family temporarily living in the Iron Age, 2011 (Picture taken with my own camera, photographer unknown). 2

Figure 1.2. An overview of the three approaches to the past (from Holtorf 2007b). 7

Figure 1.3. The presence of futureness in a heritage context (Copyright: Citizen Skwith. Reproduced by permission) 10

Figure 1.4. The rebuilt past at Dresden Neumarkt: escapism or utopia? (Picture by X-Weinzar, 2011. Reproduced under Creative Commons Attribution-Share Alike 3.0 Unported license) 10

Figure 1.5. A framework for understanding contemporary time travel and its various dimensions (based on Holtorf 2012). 13

Figure 1.6. The popular annual munch-ball match, refereed by the Pope, during Medieval Week in Visby in 2003; genuine engagement with medieval heritage, good storytelling played out in a game, luring tourists to Gotland, or nonsense in bad taste? (Photograph: Cornelius Holtorf) 14

Time Travel Using 3D Methodologies

Figure 2.1. Dalby in Scania, Sweden (Photograph by Jes Wienberg 2010). 26

Figure 2.2. The crypt in the church of Dalby (Photograph Ing-Marie Nilsson 2010). 28

Figure 2.3. The baptismal font of Dalby (Photograph Ing-Marie Nilsson 2010). 31

Figure 2.4. A) Orthographic top view of the interior of the church; B) Top view of the cloud of points with the position of the scans (in green); C) Section of the virtual model of the church (Rendering and digital models Nicoló Dell'Unto 2013). 36

Figure 2.5. 3D models of the baptismal font of Dalby using image-based modelling techniques: A) Top view; B) Front view; C) View of the font with the colour projection; D) Decoration detail (Rendering and digital models Nicoló Dell'Unto 2013). 37

Figure 2.6. Virtual model of the interpretation of the crypt during the 12th century: A) Plan of the crypt – in red the modified area; B) Plan of the ceiling of the crypt – in red the modified area; C) Rendering of the virtual interpretation of the crypt with the font located in the centre (Rendering and digital models Nicoló Dell'Unto 2013). 39

Figure 2.7: Simulation of the space functionality using virtual characters: A) The distribution of the characters on the benches; B) The font on top of the podium from the point of view of a virtual character sitting on the reconstruct east bench; C) The font without podium from the point of view of a virtual character sitting on the reconstruct east bench; D) Rendering in perspective view of the Crypt during the hypothetical celebration of the baptism (Rendering and digital models Nicoló Dell'Unto 2013). 42

The Kivik Grave, Virtual Bodies in Ritual Procession

Figure 3.1. The 7th cist slab of the Kivik Grave (Swedish Rock Art Archives, photograph: Steffen Hoejager). 51

Figure 3.2. Bronze figure från Glasbacka in Halland (Kaul 1998, 26 after Montelius 1917). 55

Figure 3.3. The procession becomes alive. The white figure is led by the museum visitor's body gestures (Screen capture and 3D-modelling: Carolina Andersson 2012). 56

Figure 3.4. First drawing of the imaginary procession passing under a willow (Magali Ljungar-Chapelon 2013). 57

Figure 3.5. Ritual dance around a tree, an idea that we abandoned (Drawing: Magali Ljungar-Chapelon 2013). 58

Figure 3.6. Sunrays on an oak tree (First draft of 3D-modelling by Michael Orbing 2013). 58

Figure 3.7. Motion capture at the Humanities laboratory, Lund University (Photograph and 3D modelling: Carolina Larsson 2012). 63

Figure 3.8. Prototype test at the VR Lab, Lund University (Photograph: Stefan Lindgren 2012). 63

Figure 3.9. The virtual procession on a path in the surrealistic Scanian landscape, final version (Screenshot and interaction design: Sebastian Buks, 3D-modelling: Michael Orbing, Neues Interactive 2013). 64

Figure 3.10. Children as actor-participants in the VR arts play. 70

Use the Past, Create the Future

Figure 4.1. The old songs were sung again with lots of passion in the Time Travel event to 1968 in the mission church in Montague. 96

Figure 4.2. Reconciliation ceremony at the Isivivane, as part of the Time Travel event at Freedom Park. 97

Figure 4.3. Creative work in one of the groups at the Time Travel event to 1955 in W. W. Brown church in Kliptown. This group discussed the clause on how to share the land in the country and penned their ideas on placards, an illustration and a poem. 99

Figure 4.4. The public Time Travel event in Kliptown, Soweto. After the historical part, each participant chose one of the ten clauses from the Freedom Charter and interpreted it in today's society. What do equal rights, work and security, peace and friendship mean in South Africa today? 101

Figure 4.5. All the ten groups in the public Time Travel event in Kliptown presented their ideas of the Freedom Charter 2015, in a poem, speech, illustration, drama, song or a dance. 101

Figure 4.6. A group of hunter-gatherers meets a group of pastoralists at the water hole, the rapid start of a Time Travel event. Can we accept and respect the other? 102

Figure 4.7. Make a stone knife and discuss the key questions; work, talk and reflect at the same time. The Time Travel event creates learning areas where the key questions are discussed in smaller groups while working. Can we live together although we are different? Is it possible to use the same land and the same waterhole? How? 103

Figure 4.8. Everybody comes together at the end of the Time Travel event. What are the solutions? Can we make an agreement on the use of the land and the waterhole? How to make a sustainable living, together? The event often ends with a sign of togetherness: a ceremony, a small meal or a dance. 103

Figure 4.9. The announcement in the middle of the Belgrade Time Travel event to 1941: 'All Jews have to register'. In a moment the community of Jews, Romas and Serbs, that had been working closely together, became groups of 'we' and 'them'. 105

Figure 4.10. The commemoration event on the massacre of civilians in 1941 in Kragujevac, Serbia. The event were divided into three parts: remembering the past, seeking of forgiveness and manifest for the future. It included ceremonies, symbols, reflections and words of value. 106

To Make and to Experience Meaning

Figure 5.1. Time travel at an outdoor festival. 114

Figure 5.2. Casting: Kalmar County Museum. 120

Figure 5.3. The battle of Eketorp, July 2005 (Photograph by David Bergström, Barometern). 124

Performing the Past

Figure 6.1. Greek Festival in Berlin, 1886 (Illustrierte Zeitung, 10/7/1886, No. 2245). 139

Figure 6.2. Photography of the movie *Das Leben der Pfahlbauern* ([c. 1920] Institute of Pre- and Early History and Medieval Archaeology, University of Tübingen). 142

Being There

Figure 7.1. Cooking in the Confederate army's camp during the Annual Gettysburg Civil War Battle Reenactment, 2013. 163

Figure 7.2. Re-enactor's bivouac set up at Spangler's Spring, near Gettysburg, 2010. 163

Figure 7.3. Mounted Union officers taking in the scene prior to battle, at the Annual Gettysburg Civil War Battle Reenactment, 2010. 164

Face-to-Face with the Past

Figure 8.1: Transported into antiquity in the surprisingly well-preserved Roman town of Pompeii, Italy (http://commons.wikimedia.org/wiki/File:Pompeii-Street.jpg). 176

Figure 8.2: Face-to-face with Tollund man, a bog body from the pre-Roman Iron Age in central Jutland, Denmark (http://commons.wikimedia.org/wiki/File:Tollundmannen.jpg). 177

Figure 8.3: Unlocking the past; how wonderful things connect people, past and present. (Book cover of University Press of Florida, using an oil painting by Martin Pate, Newnan GA, courtesy of Southeastern Archeological Center, National Park Service, USA) 178

Figure 8.4: Face-to-face with the Iron Age in the full-size reconstructed village of Lethra at Lejre, Denmark (Photograph: Cornelius Holtorf 2011). 181

Figure 8.5: A modern time traveller's toolkit: gadgets bought on the internet (our knives), poorly executed home-made imitations (our dried shoes) and pure childhood fantasy ([my son's bow and arrows] Photograph: Cornelius Holtorf 2011) 184

Figure 8.6: At home in the Iron Age, Lejre, Denmark. Photograph: Cornelius Holtorf 2011. 187

Waterworld

Figure 9.1. Kevin Costner, the director of Waterworld, in the role as Mariner (© Everett Collection/ IBL Bildbyrå). 203

Figure 9.2. Dennis Hopper in the role as the villain Deacon (© Everett Collection/IBL Bildbyrå). 209

A Cup of Decaf Past

Figure 10.1a, 10.1b. Two versions of the same 'consumption' of the past (Grzybowo 2012, author Dawid Kobiałka). 219

Figure 10.2. Decaf past – a contemporary Viking (Photograph by Tomasz Marciniak). 221

History as an Adventure

Figure 11.1. Time travellers into the German Biedermeier, Werben, 2009 (Photograph by Michaela Fenske). 246

Figure 11.2. Time travellers into the German Biedermeier, Werben, 2009 (Photograph by Michaela Fenske). 246

Figure 11.3. Jadis flyer for time travelling (Reproduction in public domain obtained by Michaela Fenske 2008). 247

Anachronism and Time Travel

Figure 13.1. A local knight in the reconstructed medieval children's setting Salvestaden, close by Kalmar castle, Sweden. The image immediately caught a sense of balancing between past and present, and therefore I chose it as cover for my book (Petersson 2003) on reconstruction and re-enactment (Photograph by Jes Wienberg 2002). 282

Figure 13.2. A picture from the TV series Star Trek, 1966–1969, showing future technology and future dress codes (Photograph: Hollywood Pictures © IBL). 286

Figure 13.3. A church painting with people from a biblical story obviously dressed up in medieval clothing, here from the Old Testament about the prophet Jonah, soon to enter the stomach of the whale. Painting from Härkeberga church in Sweden (Photograph by Bodil Petersson 2010). 289

Figure 13.4. Example from folklore painting, here from a specific painting tradition in the Swedish landscape of Dalecarlia, where biblical stories were painted as if they actually took place in the year of the painting, which in this case is 1799. Dresses and houses are familiar to this region (Photograph: © Wikimedia Commons License). 290

Preface

The present book is the outcome of a project on *The Archaeology of Time Travel*, which we started back in 2007. At the time, we were both at Lund University in Sweden and had agreed that it would be interesting to explore in an interdisciplinary way how more and more people were experiencing the past with all their senses, whether virtually, in varieties of role play, or through other techniques of immersion. We were looking for the past that emerged in-between and indeed beyond archaeological sites and objects – not necessarily tangible, but all the same a very real, embodied, and living past. We decided back then that time travel was the future!

A decade later, we are looking back at the project. A major focus became explorations (led by Bodil Petersson) of how virtual and augmented realities can contribute to time travel experiences at archaeological open-air museums and reconstruction centres. The results were published in the book *Experimental Archaeology – Between Enlightenment and Experience* in 2011 (co-edited by B. Petersson and L. E. Narmo). We jointly organised a number of topical workshops and a seminar on "Archaeology as Adventure" in Lund (2007–2009). We also ran international conference sessions on Time Travel at the 14th Annual Meeting of the European Association of Archaeologists (EAA) in Malta (2008), the 11th Nordic TAG conference in Kalmar, Sweden (2011) and at the 8th conference of the National Network for Research in the Didactic of History at Kalmar, Sweden (2014).

Maybe the most rewarding result of our project is the creation of a network of more than 50 researchers and practitioners in Sweden, Scandinavia and across Europe interested in archaeological time travel from a range of disciplinary and professional perspectives. Although we cannot mention all by name, we wish to thank them for their valuable contributions to the project. The wide competence and broad intellectual horizons of this group is reflected in the contributions to the present book which almost became a *Handbook of Time Travel*.

Another outcome of the project was various other academic publications by either one or both of us (cited in the Introduction and Conclusion of this book), including a co-edited special section of *Lund Archaeological Review* (15–16, 2009-2010, 27–98) to which a number of other network members contributed as well.

As a parallel activity, Bodil Petersson created an academic course for international students on *Archaeology and Time Travel*, which was taught at advanced level at Lund University and subsequently further developed for Linnaeus University at ground level. In total, approximately 60 students learned about and engaged with our line of research in this way. We hope that the variety of critical perspectives in the chapters and comments that follow will render the present book into a useful one-stop shop for future students to learn more about the field of contemporary time travel.

Over the years we have been granted much support to investigate time travel as a means of understanding the role of the past in the present. We would like to thank the Carl Stadler Foundation, the Crafoord Foundation, the Hainska Foundation and the Krapperup Foundation for generous grants to research and publish on *The Archaeology of Time Travel*. We would also like to acknowledge our editor, Jerryll L. Moreno, who with much patience conducted substantive line editing of the present volume in exemplary fashion. All our authors deserve thanks for the labour they invested in their writing and revising. David Davison and Ben Heaney of Archaeopress ensured the smooth publication of the book both in print and in open access – thank you to you too!

We hope that archaeological explorations of time travel by the authors of the present book and many others will continue and that we will have many interesting meanings, either in the past or in the future . . .

We dedicate this book to the memory of our author and fellow time traveller Ing-Marie Nilsson, a colleague and friend who all too soon left this world.

Bodil Petersson and Cornelius Holtorf
Kalmar, April 2017

Chapter 1

Introduction
The Meaning of Time Travel

Cornelius Holtorf

Abstract

In this introductory paper I discuss the relevance of time travel as a characteristic contemporary way to approach the past. If reality is defined as the sum of human experiences and social practices, all reality is partly virtual, and all experienced and practiced time travel is real. In that sense, time travel experiences are not necessarily purely imaginary. Time travel experiences and associated social practices have become ubiquitous and popular, increasingly replacing more knowledge-orientated and critical approaches to the past. My discussion covers some of the implications and problems associated with the ubiquity and popularity of time travelling. I also discuss whether time travel is inherently conservative because of its escapist tendencies, or whether it might instead be considered as a fulfilment of the contemporary Experience or Dream Society. Whatever position one may take, time travel is a legitimate and timely object of study and critique because it represents a particularly significant way to bring the past back to life in the present.

Keywords: experiencing the past, pastness, popular culture, presence, reconstruction

For at least one afternoon we had all been transported back to the 19th Century. We had been at a Civil War battle site and had taken part in a real battle. . . . I felt that I had finally encountered a Civil War Moment. This made everything worth while. I later found out that most of the reenactors feel that way at various times and events, but this is an individual feeling and normally not everyone has this great experience. When this does happen a person swears up and down that he really was transported back into time and he knows exactly what was going on in the Civil War soldier's mind on that day when he was engaged in a certain battle. (Grunska 2003:60)

Bringing the past back to life in the present

Time travel can be defined as an embodied experience and social practice in the present that brings to life a past or future reality. What is most characteristic of time travel is therefore the possibility in contemporary society to experience the presence of another time period (Figure 1).

Figure 1.1. Land of Legends, Lejre. A modern family temporarily living in the Iron Age, 2011 (Picture taken with my own camera, photographer unknown).

Time travel to the past has become a widespread practice and desire amongst many age groups, with present society increasingly offering relevant opportunities. Prominent examples of popular forms of time travel in contemporary society and popular culture are living history, historical role play, re-enactment and first-person interpretation, often associated with cultural institutions of various kinds. But time travel also occurs, amongst others, in literary fiction, movies, TV docu-soaps, advertising, themed environments and, last but not least, in rapidly improving virtual realities and computer games. Time travel is thus linked to a wide range of contemporary phenomena. It occurs not only within and through people's minds and bodies but is equally the result of specific social practices that support, and indeed allow time travel experiences, especially a range of leisure activities, cultural tourism and the heritage industry as well as shopping, reading, watching movies and TV, playing games, and more and more the use of augmented and entirely virtual realities.

What the underlying proliferation of history and the past in popular culture signifies is, according to Jerome de Groot (2009:248), that the 'academy no longer has a monopoly on historical knowledge, and . . . that an entirely new way of thinking about history . . . might be necessary'. This assessment reaffirms Raphael Samuel's classic claim (1994:8) that the past in contemporary culture is not the prerogative of the historian but 'a social form of knowledge; the work, in any given instance, of a thousand different hands'. The emerging 'theatres of memory', Samuel argued in his book (1994: part II) are recovering and resurrecting the past in many different ways, sometimes including imaginary pasts and always attracting popular enthusiasm.

Over the past few decades, all these different forms of time travel have become increasingly significant in tourism, entertainment and education, especially museum and heritage pedagogy (see e.g. Gustafsson 2002; Hart 2007; Hjemdahl 2002; Hochbruck 2013; Holtorf 2012; Holtorf and Petersson 2010; Hunt 2004; Kalshoven 2012; Kruse and Warring 2015; McCalman and Pickering 2010; Samida 2013; Sénécheau and Samida 2015; Thompson 2004). Indeed, Kristian Kristiansen (2001) argued that the future of presenting archaeological heritage lies in recreated historical realities and visitor centres at particularly significant sites in the landscape where visitors can experience past realities directly 'where it happened'.

In Eugene Ch'ng's (2009:467) analysis of the prospects for virtual time travel for 'experiential archaeology' he suggests that

> it will not be long before the ancient past is brought back to life. Archaeological sites which are no longer in existence or are inaccessible due to time and space could now be accessed by anyone and anywhere, simultaneously... A scenario could be constructed where researchers could gather at a virtual site, taking on the role of a certain person in the past (virtual acting), or of an animal, carrying out their daily tasks while other researchers observe and interpret the scenario... The capabilities of these technologies and its implications for research and for educating the public are massive and are only limited by our imagination.

People have of course long been fascinated by imagining other periods and bringing them to life in some form, as reflected, for instance, in people taking part in historical processions, consuming historical novels, strolling through open-air museums or interpreting historic sites. Certainly there have been staged performances of historic events in the Roman period and during the Middle Ages (Samida this volume; Sénécheau and Samida 2015:35–38). Sites like Pompeij and finds like bog bodies and ice mummies, in particular, have long been seen as 'frozen in time', material objects in which 'the border between past and present becomes porous', and you can meet the past face-to-face as it were (Sanders 2009:224). For certain, a desire for time travelling, retrieving the past or envisioning the future is a cultural theme that goes back some two centuries at least and has occupied authors and scholars alike, amongst them H. G. Wells and Arthur C. Clarke who inspired many (see Chapter 2 in Lowenthal 2015).

The academic study of time travel goes back at least to the 1980s. Important starting points for the existing academic appreciation of the phenomenon of bringing the past back to life in the present are Jay Anderson's (1984) discussion of *Time Machines: The World of Living History*, the classic account of *The Past is a Foreign Country* by David Lowenthal (recently revised, 2015) and the first volume of Raphael Samuel's (1994) study of present-day *Theatres of Memory*. Since then a fair amount of relevant work has been published, as indicated not the least by the references given earlier. Concerning the history of historic open-air museums, Sten Rentzhog (2007) provided a comprehensive discussion from their beginnings with Skansen in 1891 up until the introduction of virtual time travels. Particularly interesting in this context is Bodil Petersson's (2003) research about archaeological reconstructions and their attempts at recreating different periods of the past. She found that in the reconstructed Stone Age, travellers find harmony with nature, simple technology and social equality; the reconstructed Bronze Age holds social hierarchies, fertility rituals and some ecological thinking; the reconstructed Iron Age appeals to some with homemade food, clothes and small-scale village life; the reconstructed Viking Age offers seafaring, long-distance trade and warfare, and even world peace; the reconstructed medieval period, finally, presents the time traveller from the present with markets and cultural festivals, clear social roles and knights' tournaments.

The significance of time travel

In our age, mainly thanks to new technologies and increased demand, time travel has acquired a new level of popularity and societal significance. Time travel does not only represent a new tool for research, as demonstrated by Dell'Untó, Nilsson and Wienberg's discussion (this volume) of the emerging possibilities of digital 3D-visualisations, but it also manifests the changed role of material culture in archaeology generally. As I argue (this volume), in experiences through which the past comes back to life we can observe that bodily sensations and evocative narratives substitute for the study and analysis of material evidence in understanding the past, so that archaeology may no longer be self-evident as the discipline par excellence of things. Now things may merely take the role of props facilitating larger stories and experiences (see also Petersson, this volume).

Time travel arguably represents an alternative way to approach the past in current society in general. Whereas the most common approaches to the past have been foregrounding either knowledge and insight or critique and politics, now credible experience and sensual immersion feature large. In all of this, references to past, present and future are often firmly interconnected – as argued especially by Bodil Petersson (2003 and this volume) – so that in the following, when I mostly discuss time travelling to the past, the future is often at least implied. Let me start by briefly discussing in more detail the differences between the three main approaches to the past I mentioned, so that the significance of time travel becomes clearer.

The approach we are probably most familiar with, not the least from school education and academic textbooks, is the evolutionary one. This perspective offers a long-term historical perspective that ultimately ranges from the beginning of the universe to the present day. As far as archaeologists are concerned, the periods studied stretch from the oldest distinctively human ancestors, living several million years ago, until the 21st century. Ninety-nine per cent or more of the entire human past falls within the archaeologists' remit, whereas historians and many other disciplines deal only with a very tiny proportion of human biological and cultural evolution at the very end of it. According to this approach, the past matters to the present because it explains its origins, where we all come from and how the present, in the long term, came to be the way it is. A special focus is on chronology and historical context. Without reliable dates for archaeological finds and sites it is impossible to contextualise them at the right point in the process of human evolution. Once fixed in time and space, archaeological evidence gains meaning and significance from putting it into a specific historical context that emerges from all the relevant, available information already known. This approach can demand of both archaeologists and their audiences' considerable knowledge about the course of human history, deriving from the accumulated insights of past research, which is why factual knowledge about past periods is so important here. In addition, a sound methodological expertise is required in order to be able to sort good scholarship, which produces valid insights, from bad scholarship which does not. The dynamic in this approach is one of historical causes and effects: 'why do humans walk upright?'; 'why did people become farmers?' and 'what lay behind the beginnings of 'civilisation?' Although not everything in the human past may be knowable, anything knowable is in principle relevant to this approach. The more we know about the human past, the better we are likely to understand the specific historical context and thus human evolution as a whole.

Another perspective has focussed on the politics of the past, investigating representations and alterations of past remains as phenomena of different presents. Every account of the past mirrors existing norms and expectations of the present in which it was constructed. This political perspective scrutinizes the specific circumstances in which a certain view of the past gains currency in a particular present-day context. Whose interests are served if the past is remembered in this way rather than another? Who controls the past in the present? In recent decades, this approach has become very popular amongst academics not only as part of a growing interest in critical theory but also as a consequence of an increasing interest in the history of research. Critical studies of the norms and rules that govern archaeological practice have led to insights about the politics of archaeology. If the past is defined and constructed differently in each present, the obvious starting point of attention for this approach is the emergence of this contemporary context. For example, it is pointless to ask about the meaning of prehistory or prehistoric finds for time periods before the 1830s when the concepts of *pré-historique*, or 'prehistoric', did not in fact exist. A key notion is critique. We need to ask why there was a need or desire to introduce the concept of prehistory in the mid-19th century and what function it has served ever since then, taking into account that the meaning of the concept may have changed. What this approach demands of both archaeologists and their audiences is the ability to ask critical questions and not take anything as self-evident. This kind of critical assessment demands a high degree of intellectual rigour. The underlying dynamic is one of political means and purposes. Pasts are promoted or adapted because they serve certain ends in the present. Nationalistic politicians aim to support their cause by choosing chauvinistic pasts. Visitors to amusement parks seek to maximise their enjoyment by preferring rides and attractions linked to historic themes that are easy to recognise, simple to grasp, and fun to join. According to this approach, the question is not how much can be known about the past, but what has been known about the past in which context, by whom and why. There is a politics of knowledge.

Time travelling, finally, differs from both these approaches insofar as it is directly linked to the lives and bodies of individuals in the present. It may begin at 8 p.m. on a particular TV channel. We are living in the present, but we are free to enter the past now! This perspective is neither about knowledge of human evolution nor about a critical analysis of our own age, but about our imagination and embodied experience. Key notions for the way in which the past becomes meaningful through time travel include credibility and engagement. The past does not have to be genuine in the sense that it once 'really' happened, but it needs to be credible as an authentic experience about a past that *could* have happened. Credible pasts are largely reliant on trust. We trust pasts either when they correspond closely to the past we already know, that is our expectations, or when they are vetted by experts whom we trust. Time travel does not demand a particular intellectual attitude towards either past or present but instead a readiness for an embodied engagement with different realities, involving both body and soul. Time travel is about getting immersed in another world, assuming the perspective of somebody actually living in that world, involving all the senses. A good example is provided by Magali Ljungar-Chapelon's interactive installation inviting the audience to join a Bronze Age ritual procession with their bodies and thus engaging with a past 'corporeality' (see her contribution to this volume).

The dynamic of time travel lies in a constant oscillation between life now and then. On the one hand, the time traveller never leaves the present and remains the person she is, with all the associated baggage in the form of world views, preconceptions and personal life histories. On the other hand, the time traveller is leaving that present and being transported to another reality governed by

	EVOLUTION	POLITICS	TIME TRAVEL
BEGINNING	First humans	Construction of the past	*Now!*
FOCUS	Chronology Historical context	Contemporary context Critique	Experience Credibility
DEMANDS	Knowledge about human history	Critical thinking	Embodied engagement
DYNAMIC	Historical causes and effects	Political means and purposes	Imagining life now and then
KNOWLEDGE	Anything is relevant	Questioning what is known and why	Importance of what cannot be known

Figure 1.2. An overview of the three approaches to the past (from Holtorf 2007b).

different norms and open to all sorts of fantasies and behaviours that may not be associated with our lived present. As Niklas Ammert and Birgitta Gustafsson discuss (this volume), the confrontation of 'now and then' in terms of 'similar and different' has a potential to assist pupils and other audiences in making sense of their own place in history. Ironically, many time travellers ultimately seek to find themselves in the past! However, some of the most significant aspects of time travel are based on knowledge that is next to impossible to ever be (re-)gained in a scientific way. Sensual perceptions, embodied experiences, habitual behaviour, emotions, dreams and not knowing what historically 'came next' have been crucial to life in any period, but archaeologists and others cannot easily reconstruct these dimensions from the evidence available today. It is hard to avoid imposing our own responses to these issues on other periods and thus constructing the past as an extension of the present. But arguably an extension of the present is precisely what is desired! Interestingly, each of the three ways in which the past is approached in the present can claim for itself to be the most important approach, subsuming the other two (Figure 1.2).

EVOLUTION puts all parts of our present into a long-term historical perspective. The very distinction between 'the present' and 'the past' as well as the notion of anachronism, deserve historical study and must be understood within the respective historical and cultural contexts in which they first emerged and later continued to flourish (Schiffman 2011). Even POLITICS and TIME TRAVEL are ultimately the outcome of a long evolutionary trajectory. A concern for the politics of the past cannot be appreciated fully without knowledge about critical theory's development in the 20th century, in particular as a response to fascist and nationalistic ideologies in Germany and elsewhere. Contemporary time travel is arguably a phenomenon arising in its present significance from a widespread fascination with heritage typical for postmodernity. The associated heritage industry is linked to the post-industrial society, first emerging during the final quarter of the 20th century and still developing today. By the same token, the evolutionary perspective itself can be contextualised. It emerged in its earliest forms during the 17th and 18th centuries within the intellectual frameworks of the Enlightenment, Romanticism and the beginnings of modern scientific thinking. Since the 19th century this perspective has remained fundamentally unchanged.

POLITICS applies as much to EVOLUTION and TIME TRAVEL as it does to any other way in which the past is given meaning today. Academic uses of the past are to be scrutinized in the same way as their purely commercial, ideological and other counter-parts. In each case, it is imperative to ask about the political agendas and interests behind particular phenomena. The most important question always has to be: who benefits? Time travel can be seen in the context of the heritage industry and often has certain commercial overtones (it *sells*). Although nothing may be wrong in supplying people with an experience they desire, surely we ought to be wary of anybody exploiting people's genuine dreams and desires in order to advance the financial and possibly ideological interests of a few. Simultaneously, we need to ask who wishes to travel in time and why? Time travel allows people to escape the present and access another world, thus helping them cope with the social reality in which they live. Similarly, the evolutionary perspective has always been a strong pillar in the secular and scientific world view of the modern world, at all times to a larger or lesser extent competing with religious world views. The political dimension of evolution recently came to the fore when a strong creationist lobby in America had some success in changing school curricula in certain states. Behind the debate on these changes lie fundamental political and ideological divisions in society. Finally, even the political perspective itself is political. It is no coincidence that many of its proponents are associated with the political Left. They are seeking to change not only our understanding of archaeology and other academic disciplines but ultimately society as a whole.

TIME TRAVEL is even at the heart of EVOLUTION and POLITICS. Arguably the past cannot be understood in any way if it was not for some kind of possibility to imagine what life was like in another age. The evolutionary perspective is based on the understanding that scientific knowledge about lived past realities can be gained – however limited and incomplete it might be. No matter how much scientists may emphasise the role of irrefutable facts and objective knowledge, they are at the same time likely to agree on the central role of the imagination in all sciences, including archaeology. Similarly, understandings of the past are politically and socially meaningless today if they do not invite and indeed provoke people to imagine what life was like then. The politics of the past is directly dependent on the power of reconstructions to bring the past to life and thus to engage and move people. It is precisely the suggested feeling that 'these people were like we are today' or that 'we are not at all like those people' that makes the past so powerful in society. Ebbe Westergren (this volume) pioneered an educational approach to time travelling which is now implemented in many countries through the organization *Bridging Ages*, which he founded. This method uses the power of bringing the past to life in order to address 'key questions' in contemporary society such as gender roles, democracy and social cohesion, illustrating the large potential for improving society by bodily representing the past in the present.

In sum, all three perspectives are able to give meaning and significance to the past in the present. Each can explain the other two, but to some extent they can also be combined with each other.

Is time travel actually possible?

But how can another period, whether past or future, become 'present' and a subject of embodied human 'experience'? Is time travel merely a clever metaphor, or can it be said to describe a social and cultural reality? Initially, it seems obvious that a discussion of time travel carried out while being firmly based in the present can only be either pure magic or a product of the imagination, thus being unreal and contra-factual. No one can *actually* travel either into the past or into the future. But let me unravel these issues in some more depth.

To start with, it is essential to ask what is actually meant by 'really' travelling in time. The statement that actual time travel, leaving present-day reality, is impossible employs a common-sense definition of reality: empirical, physical reality. According to this definition, *real* is everything physical, large or small, that we can empirically investigate, whether that may be an atom, a brain or an ancient sword. Within contemporary physics as we know it, there is no time travel allowing us to leave our own empirical reality – although there certainly are some other anomalies regarding time such as the fact that it slows down when travelling at high enough speed. Physical reality is however not the only way to understand reality, and it may not even be the one that is most significant to human beings. Reality might also be defined as the combination of human experiences and social practices. Reality, in this alternative view, is whatever humans experience during their lives and practices as social beings. This definition of reality is particularly pertinent here as it implies that all reality is partly virtual and all experienced and practiced time travel is real.

According to this view, past and future are not physical realities distinct in time from our own but themes that contribute to shaping specific human experiences and social practices in the present (Figure 1.3). Some contemporary experiences

Figure 1.3. The presence of futureness in a heritage context (Copyright: Citizen Skwith. Reproduced by permission).

Figure 1.4. The rebuilt past at Dresden Neumarkt: escapism or utopia? (Picture by X-Weinzar, 2011. Reproduced under Creative Commons Attribution-Share Alike 3.0 Unported license)

and social practices may be set at points in the past or the future. For example, the annual Medieval Week on the Swedish island of Gotland is a present event that allows participants to experience bodily aspects of the Middle Ages as a result not only of historical research and tourist management but also of pre-existing perceptions of the Middle Ages amongst the audience (Gustafsson 2002). By the same token, Jack McDevitt's (2001) science fiction novel *Deepsix* is set in the year AD 2223 and allows readers to experience aspects of the 23rd century as a result not only of the publishing industry but also of the author's writing style that is captivating and makes sense for an early twenty-first-century audience imagining the future. In either example, past or future are not being trivialized but brought to life through contemporary experiences and associated social practices and thus are able to make direct contributions to human lives and practices in the present.

Time travel has a lot to do with the presence of *pastness* (and indeed futureness – but my discussion will in the following be restricted to pastness). Pastness is the contemporary quality of an object to be 'of the past'. This quality comes with the perception of something to be of the past and is thus little to do with actual age (Holtorf 2010a, 2013). A case in point is the Neumarkt area in Dresden. Here, largely through a citizens' initiative in the form of a private foundation, an entire historic quarter of the city that was completely destroyed by Allied air raids in February 1945 is currently being rebuilt to match old views of the area (Figure 1.4).

The Frauenkirche at its centre and a large area around it have already been completed. The aim of this grand project has been clearly stated by the foundation behind it: 'We should not lose our unique chance to regain at the Neumarkt a piece of historical identity for our town, for the sake of our children and grandchildren. Let us give the new old Frauenkirche its old setting!' (cited after Holtorf 2007a:42). The terms 'regain', 'historical' and 'old setting' are not used here in a way compatible with linear, physical time. Indeed, most of the buildings referred to were not even built yet when the aim was formulated. Instead, the initiative is about creating a setting at the heart of contemporary Dresden that has the quality of being 'of the past'. In other words, the aim is to create buildings that are not old but manifest the presence of pastness.

But what does 'presence of pastness' mean: a vague perception that something might be old, a persuasive allusion that something actually is old when it is not or a seemingly complete immersion into the past? The concept of presence has in recent years attracted a considerable amount of research within a range of academic disciplines, including IT science, psychology, performance studies, communication science and media studies (Hofer 2016; Lombard *et al.* 2015). The defining notion of presence is a perception of non-mediation or immediacy, that is a perception of 'being there', even though the experience may actually be mediated to a considerable extent. For example, a sophisticated virtual environment provides a sense of presence when it convincingly suggests that you are visiting an actual place or meeting other people rather than looking at one or more digital screens, which is what you actually do. As with encountering such virtual places or people, whether or not pastness in time travel is perceived as non-mediated will depend on the extent to which

- the past reality presented is consistent and coherent,
- the audience is familiar with the medium and willing to suspend any disbelief,
- the audience's senses are persuaded through rich and vivid impressions, i.e. the underlying technical sophistication creating a sense of immersion,
- pre-understandings and expectations of the audience are matched and
- the audience is involved and engaged in a meaningful way (inspired by Lombard and Ditton 1997).

For children with their vivid imaginations it often takes far less to create believable realities set in the past or in the future (see Figure 1.6 below). Provided these conditions are satisfactorily met, even for adults a perceived presence of pastness and time travel that brings the past to life becomes entirely possible. At its best, the time traveller experiences what is known as 'period rush' or 'magic moments' of when another period suddenly comes to life (see Grunska cited at the very beginning and Daugbjerg, this volume). As I indicated earlier, time travel is a part of many people's lives already. Concerning virtual time travel, Wulf Kansteiner (2005:140) speculated more than a decade ago that 'memories of virtual worlds and virtual interactions will become our most cherished memories and therefore our most powerful and real memories', possibly changing our notions of memory and historical consciousness forever.

It is these emerging realities that now need to be taken seriously and investigated in a variety of social sciences and humanities, especially in the historical disciplines. The other chapters in this book offer examples of the kind of research needed in order to make sense of this popular and increasingly significant way of bringing other time periods to life.

Understanding time travel

Time travel can be conceptualised and different dimensions of time travel distinguished along the two axes representing degree of lived experience and degree of collectivity respectively (Figure 1.5; Holtorf 2012). The past may be played and performed or lived and experienced, collectively through group effort or separately in individual projects. Many forms of time travel combine playful and sincere aspects and have individual as well as collective, dimensions.

In some time travel, the past is a kind of game, a playful and sometimes superficial entertainment drawing on well-known imagery and behaviour commonly

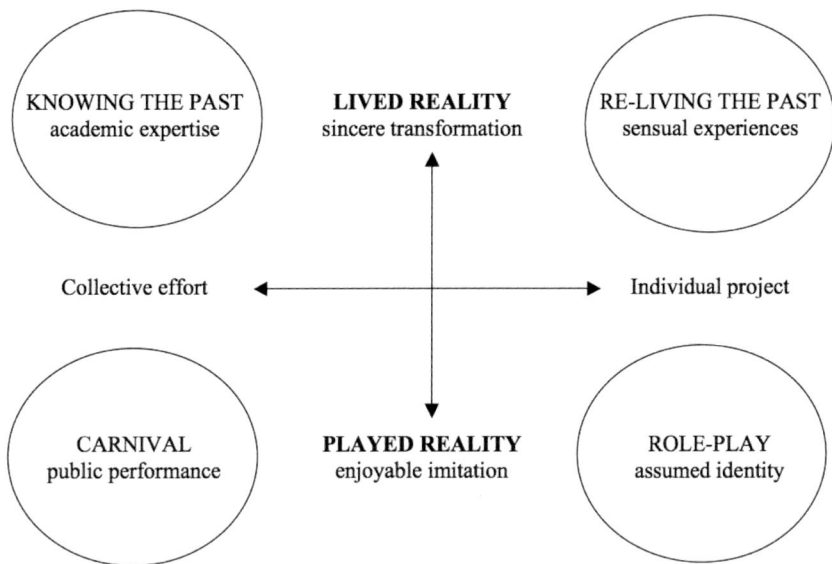

Figure 1.5. A framework for understanding contemporary time travel and its various dimensions (based on Holtorf 2012).

associated with the past. Playing the past can be as amusing and enjoyable for the individual participant assuming a historic role as for audiences of public performances that may be offered in a spirit reminding of carnival. Under the sign of "PLAY" the past is being staged somewhat tongue-in-cheek, and concessions to the present are willingly made for the sake of added fun.

In other time travel, the past is a lived reality, a heartfelt and sincere attempt at effectively representing the past in the present. Recreating past life may be achieved as a personal life project by effectively choosing to embody another person or collectively through the systematic acquisition of expertise and academic insight. Under the sign of "LIFE" the past is serious and given a new authenticity in lived experiences or accumulated knowledge of the present.

Discussing time travel

What many varieties of time travel share is that they bring to life stories set in the past or the future. Indeed, successful storytelling may be the most relevant factor affecting the success of creating immersion within a given space: 'Story is what holds a space together by linking elements, creating situations, establishing moods, and involving guests', writes Scott Lukas (2013:155) in his *Immersive Worlds* handbook. Stories that succeed in transporting audiences into a narrative world, for example in theme parks, may result in powerful effects in the real world, affecting attention, emotions, beliefs, attitudes and judgment (Green and Donahue 2009).

Figure 1.6. The popular annual munch-ball match, refereed by the Pope, during Medieval Week in Visby in 2003; genuine engagement with medieval heritage, good storytelling played out in a game, luring tourists to Gotland, or nonsense in bad taste? (Photograph: Cornelius Holtorf)

Similarly, it is the stories and meta-stories of archaeology that lie behind much of the potential and impact of archaeology in contemporary society. Powerful stories well told not only bring the past and archaeological finds to life but also touch people and benefit society so that, arguably, archaeology matters most when its meta-stories matter (Holtorf 2010c).

An important question about both storytelling and time travel in contemporary society is about the criteria that should be used to evaluate different stories and time travel experiences. The answer will in part depend on which specific example we are talking about, but are there certain qualities that are inherently more valuable than others (see Figure 1.6)? Are stories and time travels good or bad depending on the degree to which they are generally most persuasive? ... Academically true? ... Emotionally touching? ... Aesthetically pleasing? ... Commercially viable? ... Ethically acceptable? ... Or politically correct?

It is generally accepted that living history, historical re-enactment and virtual reality cannot bring the past back to life *as it really was*. The significance of this truism to present-day time travel is however a matter of some discussion (e.g. Hart 2007; Hochbruck 2013; Samida 2013), even amongst those participating (Jones 2010). Some commentators dispute that any time travel could ever be entirely genuine and authentic, however much attention is given to getting the historical facts right. Time travel, therefore, always remains flawed and problematic as anachronistic, to some extent misleading audiences about past realities, effectively representing stereotypes or fantasy and appropriating the past for some contemporary purposes (see also Samida this volume and Daugbjerg this volume). But others contend that all representations of the past originate in the present and are constructed for a specific purpose and in a particular context; historical research appropriates the past too and does not depict the past *as it really was* either. So why not use embodied experiences and the imagination to satisfy our historical curiosity?

The philosopher Kalle Pihlainen (2012:326) argued in an interesting thought experiment that even if we did have access to the past, could make our own observations in past worlds and thus check all the historical facts we wish, 'at the end of the day, it would still be our responsibility to make of the world what we will, both in terms of interpretation and in terms of actions and their consequences.' Similarly, Bodil Petersson discusses in the conclusion of this volume how plain anachronism, too, can be a very rewarding and illuminating tool helping us to understand the past in the present. The lessons possible to learn from actual time travel to the past would, therefore, not necessarily provide actual benefits to historical scholarship.

This will be especially true in cases where time travels lead to destinations that in any case are partly or entirely fictional and thus lack a solid factual basis. Should time travels to the lost worlds of Atlantis or Valhalla enjoy the same exposure in society as those to Classical Athens or Ancient Rome? Is it worrisome or encouraging when several thousands are visiting the Swedish region of Västergötland in the 'footsteps' of the fictitious historical character Arn derived from Jan Guillou's bestselling novels and subsequent movies (Mattsson and Praesto 2005)? Should the state provide public-service time travels to carefully vetted destinations with particularly desirable learning outcomes? Can time travel actually lead to inappropriate destinations? Fictional or semi-fictional pasts may be inappropriate destinations – but are not all pasts brought to life to some extent fictional and dependent on partly fictional assumptions? As Dawid Kobiałka argues (this volume), there cannot be any real archaeology without fictional elements.

Another important question is who determines, and on which grounds, which pasts are historically well grounded and appropriate to be used in education, and which are not. In 2011, Chinese authorities effectively prohibited TV dramas involving time travels for promoting fantasy and superstition in opposition to serious history and potentially challenging the Chinese regime (Kobiałka 2013:112–113). Such interference easily gives the impression of political censorship, and this may be a warning to any attempts at regulating time travelling.

There are different reasons why dark and troubled pasts may be inappropriate for time travel. For example, should people travel in time to experience Nazi extermination camps such as Auschwitz-Birkenau, and bring the early 1940s back to life there? Should such a trip be encouraged to remember the victims and keep the memory of the Holocaust alive? Or should it rather be discouraged or even prohibited out of respect for the victims' families and their legitimate expectation of respect? How realistic and educational could it be anyway and what sort of people would be attracted to embody the German perpetrators? In her study of Danish groups re-enacting World War II, Anne Brædder (2015) found that the Danish soldiers could not necessarily imagine to place their bodies inside a German uniform with a swastica on it. Even those representing German soldiers were not prepared to express Nazi ideology, perform the Nazi salute and enact murders, war crimes or deportations of Jews. They are content to embody the ordinary soldier's life in the army, but how content are the rest of us if that is what the Nazi period and World War II are being reduced to? How appropriate is time travel as a medium for bringing to life such dark periods? Arguably, even the negative sides of history have to be brought back to life. Indeed, many time periods are littered with mass murder and all sorts of terrible things that ought to be witnessed but at the same time must not be trivialized or left out. Perhaps we have a particular duty to travel to unpleasant destinations as we may in that way take important lessons and emotions back to present reality. The problem is what lines you have to draw, and how to enforce them, over and above the obvious need to prevent time travellers from committing actual crimes.

Another important issue is whether there are any risks or dangers in time travel, or in other words what a critical perspective on time travel may have to contribute. Time travel makes for embodied experiences that are potentially very persuasive and memorable as well as enjoyable and even delightful. Whereas these qualities may in many circumstances be celebrated, I have already indicated that these qualities may not necessarily be desirable when extreme ideologies or inhuman events of the past are brought back to life. When in 2013 on the 200th anniversary of the Battle of the Nations at Leipzig a particularly elaborate re-enactment of the battle was staged, the artist Bertram Haude responded to the widespread glorification of wartime and soldier life by creating an 'International Shattered Liberation Force (ISLF)'. This 'Force' consisted of a group of injured and demoralized soldiers and was supposed to disturb the picturesque image of the battle (Haude 2015). These defeated soldiers and their behaviour throughout the area of re-enactment reminded the audience of those events associated with the Battle of the Nations not otherwise remembered in re-enactments: illnesses and injuries, the forced quartering of troops, plundering, raping, widespread destruction and general misery amongst the population. Indeed, what is the message of playing war in battle re-enactments of various periods from antiquity to the 20th century when this occurs at the same time that many thousands of refugees seek asylum from the nightmares of currently ongoing wars and the resulting chaos and human suffering in Syria and elsewhere?

What is more, in the context of the popular American Civil War re-enactments, some critics see a proliferation of reactionary politics glorifying white American resistance and sacrifice while failing to express sufficient distance to racism and slavery: 'By virtue of their own appearance black participants become signs of themselves and their race. As such their appearance alone rehabilitates the narrative told at the event' (Hart 2007:114). And re-enactor Gordon Jones (2010:232) asks: 'Can you really favour racial equality while wearing a Confederate uniform?'

Another issue of concern is that many forms of re-enactment, especially those relating to conflicts and battles, are dominated by heterosexual men. Gordon Jones (2010:228–229) observed about gender roles in Civil War re-enactment that

> though many single men still resent any female presence as historically inaccurate, as long as women know 'their place' in 19th century, their acceptance by the majority of male reenactors is generally assured. It is only when women assert 'their place' as 20th century social equals and attempt to enter the male ranks dressed as soldiers that most men – and many women as well – draw the line on grounds of historical authenticity.

Much re-enactment therefore builds on traditional gender roles that contradict present-day ideals to achieve gender equality and ensure equal opportunities (Rambuscheck 2016). By the same token, for Jenny Thompson (2004:XXI–XXIII) on entering a decade of studying twentieth-century war re-enactors, there was no question that she was 'trespassing into a male-dominated territory', and on occasion the male-centred behaviour made her uncomfortable. In 2016, a theatre group performing in the well-known Viking village of Foteviken in Sweden was reported to the police for capturing and selling a woman on a staged slave-action without her consent. A group of archaeologists took the opportunity to point out that some modern Vikings exploited their hobby to live out sexist fantasies that lack any scientific basis (Ahlborn 2016).

An interesting and important question is also whether or not time travelling should in fact be seen as a form of escape from the present: dressing in period clothes, a changing of daily routines and adopting a different identity and value system while re-enacting historical scenes, or closely observing all of that, make participants and audiences temporarily suspend and forget their ordinary lives (Hunt 2004:399). According to Michaela Fenske's argument (this volume), time travels are spaces of sensual and embodied action and adventure where the alienated modern city dwellers can release some of their frustrations. Similarly, in our discussion with Erika Andersson Cederholm (this volume), she stresses that tourists travelling in time, or travelling in space, can lead to a heightened feeling of being present 'here and now' that many are longing for. In these ways, time travel may compensate for the deficiencies of present society rather than contribute to social improvements, thus rendering it inherently conservative in society. However, it could also be argued that time travel is not an escape from present society at all, but rather its fulfilment. If we really live in an Experience or Dream Society, as has been argued (Jensen 1999; Pine and Gilmore 2011; Schulze 1992), the proliferation of experiences and dreams, for example in the form of time travelling, corresponds to its true character. As Mads Daugbjerg argues (this volume) even scientific experiments may today take the form of embodied experiences. The critical task at hand would then lie in correcting any possible negative outcomes of time travels, not their abolishment. Indeed, time travel experiences of other realities may also popularize social utopias and instil in people very concrete models of alternatives to present society, so that their social impact might be rather revolutionary. All these issues warrant further discussion in the future.

Conclusions

In this introductory chapter I discussed the relevance of time travel as a characteristic contemporary way to approach the past. Time travel experiences and associated social practices have become ubiquitous and popular, in some cases replacing more academic ways of packaging the past for popular consumption. Knowledge-orientated and critical approaches to the past are still around but embodied engagements in time travel have gained a lot of ground in many contexts.

If reality is defined as the sum of human experiences and social practices, all reality is partly virtual and all experienced and practiced time travel is real. In that sense, time travel experiences are not necessarily purely imaginary. Time travel facilitates the presence of pastness (or futureness) in people's lives, emerging from contemporary human experiences and associated social practices and making a direct contribution to human lives and social practice in the present.

My discussion brought some of the implications and problems associated with the ubiquity and popularity of time travelling into view. They include the question by which criteria, and certainly by which institutions, time travels should be assessed and evaluated for the benefit of society. Are there time travel destinations that we should be warned of or prevented from reaching because of ethical concerns? Does time travel invariably promote the original dominant values (e.g. concerning race, sexuality and gender roles) of the periods of destination? And precisely what are we to make of the often-commercial overtones of some time travel opportunities? Finally, there is a continuing debate on whether time travel is inherently conservative because of its escapist tendencies, whether it might instead be considered as a fulfilment of the contemporary Experience or Dream Society or whether time travel might even popularize utopian visions that could make people want to work actively for a different society.

For all these reasons and ongoing considerations, time travel is a legitimate and timely object of study and critique involving scholars associated with any discipline investigating the past or with heritage studies, tourism studies, social anthropology, sociology, cultural economics, or film and media studies, amongst other fields. Many of these different perspectives are represented in the chapters of this book. All taken together, Bodil Petersson and I hope to place time travel into the larger societal context it deserves as a particularly significant way of bringing the past back to life in the present.

Acknowledgements

I am grateful to Bodil Petersson for inspiration and discussion about time travelling over a good number of years by now and for constructive criticism on a first draft of this chapter. I am also acknowledging that some sections of this introduction are reworked from texts originally published as Holtorf 2007b and Holtorf 2010b.

References

Ahlborn, Elinor 2016. Arkeologer ryter ifrån mot historielösa vikingar. *Swedish Television News*, 28 July 2016. Available at http://www.svt.se/kultur/vikingafantasin (accessed 21 August 2016).

Anderson, Jay 1984. *Time Machines. The World of Living History*. Nashville, The American Association of State and Living History.

Brædder, Anne 2015. Kroppen som medium til 2. verdenskrig. In T. Kruse and A. Warring (eds.), *Fortider tur/retur. Reenactment og historiebrug*: 67–89. Frederiksberg, Samfundslitteratur.

Ch'ng, Eugene 2009. Experiential archaeology: Is virtual time travel possible? *Journal of Cultural Heritage* 10:458–470.

De Groot, Jerome 2009. *Consuming History. Historians and Heritage in Contemporary Popular Culture*. London and New York, Routledge.

Green, Melanie C. and Donahue, John K. 2009. Simulated worlds: Transportation into narratives. In K. Markman, W. Klein, J. Suhr (eds,), *Handbook of Imagination and Mental Simulation*: 241–256. New York, Psychology.

Grunska, Kip M. 2003. *From Farb to Pard. A Story of Civil War Reenactment.* New York, Writers Club Press.

Gustafsson, Lotten 2002. *Den förtrollande zonen. Lekar med tid, rum och identitet under Medeltidsveckan på Gotland.* Nora, Nya Doxa.

Hart, Lain 2007. Authentic recreation: living history and leisure. *Museum and Society* 5(2):103–124.

Haude, Bertram 2015. Krieg als Hobby? Das Leipziger Völkerschlacht-Reenactment und der Versuch einer Entgegnung. *Forum Kritische Archäologie* 4:1–12. Available at http://www.kritischearchaeologie.de/repositorium/fka/2015_4_1_Haude.pdf (accessed 5 July 2016).

Hjemdahl, Kirsti M. 2002. History as a cultural playground. *Ethnologia Europaea* 32(2):105–124.

Hochbruck, Wolfgang 2013. *Geschichtstheater. Formen der »Living History«. Eine Typologie.* Bielefeld, Transcript.

Hofer, Matthias 2016. *Presence und Involvement.* Baden-Baden, Nomos.

Holtorf, Cornelius 2007a. What does not move any hearts – Why should it be saved? The *Denkmalpflegediskussion* in Germany. *International Journal of Cultural Property* 14(1):33–55.

Holtorf, Cornelius 2007b. Time travel: A new perspective on the distant past. In B. Hårdh, K. Jennbert and D. Olausson (eds.), *On the Road. Studies in Honour of Lars Larsson*: 127–132. Stockholm, Almqvist & Wiksell.

Holtorf, Cornelius 2010a. The presence of pastness: Themed environments and beyond. In Judith Schlehe, Michiko Uike-Bormann, Carolyn Oesterle and Wolfgang Hochbruck (eds.), *Staging the Past. Themed Environments in Transcultural Perspective*: 23–40. Bielefeld, Transcript.

Holtorf, Cornelius 2010b. On the possibility of time travel. *Lund Archaeological Review* 15–16, 2009–2010, 31–41.

Holtorf, Cornelius 2010c. Meta-stories of archaeology. *World Archaeology* 42(3):381–393.

Holtorf, Cornelius 2012. Review article: The past as carnival (Review of A. Dreschke, dir., *Die Stämme von Köln*, 2010), *Time and Mind* 5(2):195–202.

Holtorf, Cornelius 2013. On pastness: A reconsideration of materiality in archaeological object authenticity. *Anthropological Quarterly* 86:427–444.

Holtorf, Cornelius and Petersson, Bodil (eds.). 2010. The archaeology of time travel. Special section. *Lund Archaeological Review* 15–16, 2009–2010, 27–98.

Hunt, Stephen 2004. Acting the part: 'living history' as a serious leisure pursuit. *Leisure Studies* 23(4):387–403.

Jensen, Jörgen 1999. *The Dream Society. How the Coming Shift from Information to Imagination Will Transform Your Business.* New York, McGraw-Hill Education.

Jones, Gordon L. (2010) 'Little families': The social fabric of Civil War reenacting. In: J. Schlehe, M Uike-Bormann, C. Oesterle and W. Hochbruck (eds.), *Staging the Past. Themed Environments in Transcultural Perspectives*: 219–234. Bielefeld, Transcript.

Kalshoven, Petra T. 2012. *Crafting the Indian. Knowledge, Desire and Play in Indianist Reenactment*. New York and Oxford, Berghahn.

Kansteiner, Wulf 2005. Alternate worlds and invented communities. History and historical consciousness in the age of interactive media. In K. Jenkins, S. Morgan and A. Munslow (eds.), *Manifestos for History*: 131–148. London and New York, Routledge.

Kobiałka, Dawid 2013. Time travels in archaeology. Between Hollywood films and historical re-enactment? *AP: Online Journal in Public Archaeology* 3:110–130. Available at http://www.arqueologiapublica.es/descargas/1382781444.pdf (accessed 5 July 2016).

Kristiansen, Kristian 2001. Resor i tiden. In ETOUR (ed.) *På resande fot*: 144–153. Stockholm, Sellin.

Kruse, Tove and Warring, Anette (eds.) 2015. *Fortider tur/retur. Reenactment og historiebrug*. Frederiksberg, Samfundslitteratur.

Lombard, Matthew and Ditton, Theresa 1997. At the heart of it all. The concept of presence. *Journal of Computer-Mediated Communication* 3(2). Available at http://onlinelibrary.wiley.com/doi/10.1111/j.1083-6101.1997.tb00072.x/full (accessed 5 July 2016).

Lombard, Matthew, Biocca, Frank, Freeman, Jonathan, IJsselsteijn, Wijnand and Schaevitz, Rachel J. (eds.) 2015. *Immersed in Media: Telepresence Theory, Measurement & Technology*. Heidelberg, Springer.

Lowenthal, David 2015 [1985]. *The Past is a Foreign Country – Revisited*. Revised 2nd edition. Cambridge, Cambridge University Press.

Lukas, Scott A. 2013. *The Immersive Worlds Handbook. Designing Theme Parks and Consumer Spaces*. New York and London, Focal.

Mattsson, Jan and Praesto, Anja 2005. The creation of a Swedish heritage Destination: An insider's view of entrepreneurial marketing. *Scandinavian Journal of Hospitality and Tourism* 5(2):152–166.

McCalman, Iain and Pickering, Paul A. 2010. From realism to the affective turn: An agenda. In I. McCalman and P. A. Pickering (eds.) *Historical Reenactment from Realism to the Affective Turn*. Basingstoke and New York, Palgrave Macmillan.

McDevitt, Jack. 2001. *Deepsix. A Breathtaking Chronicle of Disaster and Discovery*. New York, Harper Voyager.

Petersson, Bodil 2003. *Föreställningar om det förflutna. Arkeologi och rekonstruktion*. Lund, Nordic Academic Press.

Pihlainen, Kalle 2012. What if the past were acceptable after all? *Rethinking History* 16(3):323–339.

Pine, B. Joseph, II and Gilmore, James H. 2011. *The Experience Economy*. Updated edition. Boston, Harvard Business Review Press.

Rambuscheck, Ulrike 2016. Lebendige Archäologie – stereotype Geschlechterbilder? Archäologisches Reenactment und Living History aus der Geschlechterperspektive. *Archäologische Informationen* 39, 193-194. Available at http://dx.doi.org/10.11588/ai.2016.1.33550 (accessed 6 Jan 2017)

Rentzhog, Sten (2007). *Open Air Museums: The History and Future of a Visionary Idea*. Stockholm, Carlsson.

Samida, Stefanie 2013. Aneignung von Vergangenheit durch körperliches Erleben. *Literatur in Wissenschaft und Unterricht* 46:105–121.

Samuel, Raphael 1994. *Theatres of Memory. Past and Present in Contemporary Culture*. London, Verso.

Sanders, Karin 2009. *Bodies in the Bog and the Archaeological Imagination*. Chicago and London, University of Chicago Press.

Schiffman, Zachary Sayre 2011. *The Birth of the Past*. Baltimore, Johns Hopkins University Press.

Schulze, Gerhard 1992. *Die Erlebnis-Gesellschaft. Kultursoziologie der Gegenwart*. Frankfurt and New York, Campus.

Sénécheau, Miriam and Samida, Stefanie 2015. *Living History als Gegenstand Historischen Lernens. Begriffe - Problemfelder - Materialien*. Stuttgart: Kohlhammer.

Thompson, Jenny 2004. *War Games. Inside the World of 20th Century War Reenactors*. Washington, DC, Smithsonian.

Part One

Emerging Possibilities in Virtual Time Travels

Chapter 2

Time Travel Using 3D Methodologies
Visualising the Medieval Context of a Baptismal Font

Nicoló Dell'Unto, Ing-Marie Nilsson† and Jes Wienberg

Abstract

Time travel is often associated with popular mediation. This article demonstrates how time travel using digital visualisation may also be a useful tool for research. The case study involves the medieval cathedral and monastery of Dalby in Sweden with a twelfth-century crypt and font. The crypt may have functioned as a baptismal chapel in the Middle Ages. Digital 3D techniques, including terrestrial laser scanner and image-based 3D modelling, are used to reconstruct the original architecture of the crypt and to conduct simulations of the use of the space during the liturgy.

Keywords: Middle Ages, digital time travel, 3D methodologies, baptismal font, crypt

Introduction

The metaphor of time travel may describe a wide range of techniques to explore the past and the present. One of these techniques is digital visualisation, which makes it possible to transgress both time and space and to investigate now-lost relations between architecture, sculpture and human actions. This case study from a medieval cathedral in Sweden focuses on the relationship between a font and a crypt. Three dimensional methodologies make it possible to unite what has been separated by centuries of modifications and by a thick stone wall as well as to move the font back into the crypt again. Furthermore, this methodology allows simulations of how the space may have been used during the liturgy.

Dalby – 'locus celebris'

In the first decades of the twelfth-century Dalby in Scania, Sweden (which was part of Denmark before 1658), the English chronicler Ailnoth described the cathedral as *locus celebris*, meaning the 'famous location'. The contemporary church in Dalby (Figure 2.1) is known for many reasons: as the oldest still-standing stone church in Scandinavia; as a bishopric for the German Bishop Egino in the 1060s; as a Benedictine monastery, which was transformed into an Augustinian monastery; for its relatively well-preserved monastic buildings from the Middle Ages; for the excavated remains of a royal palace for King Sven

Figure 2.1. Dalby in Scania, Sweden (Photograph by Jes Wienberg 2010).

Estridson and his sons in the 11th century; as a burial place for King Harold Hen in 1080; for its presumably nearby royal hunting park; for its estates at the reformation comprising roughly 450 farms; and finally for the so-called Dalby book and early Gospel book created in the monastery.

However, recent research on Dalby has revised and elaborated the history of the site (cf. Borgehammar and Wienberg 2012). For example, Dalby was the bishopric for Bishop Egino in the 1060s but then probably became the cathedral for the diocese of Lund from *c.* 1070 until the first decades of the 12th century. It then served as the cathedral of the archbishopric for a few years until the status was transferred to a new cathedral in the nearby city of Lund. This might explain the rather large size of the basilica in the 11th century. The so-called royal palace of Sven Estridson and his sons might rather have been the palace of the (arch)bishop or the monastery buildings. Contrary to previous thoughts, Dalby has never been the location for a Benedictine monastery. The convent of probably 12 canons took part in the gradual creation of the order of Augustinians. Historical analogies indicate that Harold Hen was probably buried in the nave in front of the Holy Cross and underneath a chandelier, from which a fragment was rediscovered among finds from earlier excavations. Because monasteries also used hunting parks, it is possible that the park was not associated with the royal palace. Arguments have also come to light that suggest that the Dalby Gospel book cannot have been written in Dalby, and probably derives from Hamburg-Bremen and possibly was brought by Bishop Egino. New research has also discovered a possible small medieval town at Dalby called 'Norrby'. Finally, the crypt may have functioned as a baptismal chapel with the font located at the centre of the room.

Time travelling with a font as luggage

Documentary evidence demonstrates that the baptismal font of Dalby has been located in the nave at least since the 19th century. However there are reasons to believe that the architectural context of the font from the beginning in the 12th century was in the western crypt of the church. Attempts have been made to envision in words and pictures how the font may have functioned both practically and symbolically in this context (Nilsson 2012). These theories will be expanded further in the following text since they function as the theoretical basis for the reconstruction. As the font is a heavy piece of carved stone and still in weekly ecclesiastical use, it cannot realistically be moved in order to answer research questions.

Could it be possible to travel back in time with the font? If so, what would the font then have looked like when placed in the crypt instead of the nave, and how would it have been perceived by people who used this space in the Middle Ages? One solution to this problem is to introduce a new 3D computer visualisation based on accurate 3D models acquired by means of 3D acquisition technology. The models processed in the frame of this work were generated to simulate a virtual environment where different scenarios could be assessed. For this reason, once processed, the 3D high-resolution models were optimized in order to be merged and visualized in the same virtual space. This operation allowed a 3D scene to be used to address a number of specific research questions. The creation of a very high-resolution model (due to the limited computational capacities of the machines) would have prevented the possibility of running the simulation; instead optimizing the models allowed us to merge several different models at a sufficient resolution.

The crypt

The crypt in Dalby, or anteroom as it is sometimes called, is a square room in the western part of the church (Figure 2.2). The floor of the crypt is now partly below ground level, just as it was in the Early Middle Ages (Anjou 1920:19). The church in Dalby has undergone many changes throughout its history, but the crypt is relatively intact. There are fairly few additions to the room that are

28 THE ARCHAEOLOGY OF TIME TRAVEL

Figure 2.2. The crypt in the church of Dalby (Photograph Ing-Marie Nilsson 2010).

later than the 12th century, and they are easily discerned. This makes the crypt well suited for a terrestrial laser scanner, an instrument capable of collecting 3D coordinates of an object's surface automatically and in real time (Böhler and Marbs 2002).

In the Early Middle Ages, there were no less than five entrances to the crypt. The portal facing west seems to have been the most prestigious one. This entrance originally lead to an adjacent building complex that may have been a royal palace, a bishop's palace or an Augustinian monastery. This is the only portal with figurative sculpture. A tympanum above the door shows a man with braided hair wrestling a lion; in all likelihood a representation of Samson, the great hero of the Old Testament. The crypt was also accessible through two entrances in the eastern part of the room. The southern portal is still open today, whereas the northern one was closed off, probably already in the Middle Ages. During this period the cloister was located north of the church, and the portal may have been sealed in order to restrict unauthorised access to the monastery. There are also two entrances from the nave located on either side of a central niche. Both these portals were closed off in the 19th century but were reopened in 1919 (Anjou 1930:60; Sjöborg 1830:pl. 45). With so many entrances, the crypt cannot be viewed as an enclosed space. On the contrary, it could be said that the layout of the room emphasises access and movement. It has been suggested that these portals may originally have been used for processions (Anderson 1926:15f).

The central niche in the eastern part of the room now contains an altar. This is not a medieval feature but a reconstruction from 1936. In the later part of the 19th century the original back wall of the niche was pulled down, and a new staircase connecting the nave with the crypt was installed (Rydbeck 1941:222f, 232f). The niche has from early on been interpreted as an altar niche (cf. Åkerman 1981:84), and this seems to be a likely explanation. If this interpretation holds, it means that the room would have had a distinctly liturgical character.

Another important element is the well that is situated in the north-eastern corner of the crypt. This feature seems oddly out of place, since it partly obstructs the northern (now blocked) external entrance. It is however an original item and may even be older than the present twelfth-century crypt. Wells and water reservoirs are sometimes found in important Romanesque churches and cathedrals and have not without reason been associated with baptism. In this respect Dalby may well be compared to the cathedral of Lund. This nearby and contemporary cathedral also has a crypt with a well in it, and the main altar of the crypt was consecrated to John the Baptist in the year 1123 (Rydén 1995:53). The argument has also been put forward that the crypt altar in Dalby may have been consecrated to John the Baptist (Cinthio and Mogensen 2010:107). Fresh water was an important element of the liturgy of the Mass. The well therefore seems to further underscore the ritual character of the space.

There is in this context one last architectural feature that is worth highlighting. In the western part of the crypt, the inner walls are provided with ledges, approximately 0.5m high and 0.25m wide. These ledges may possibly be viewed as seating places. Wall benches of stone are a feature that has been observed in several Scandinavian Romanesque parish churches. In these churches the benches occur mainly along the walls of the nave, but they are sometimes found in the chancel too. Ledges of almost the exact same type as in Dalby are also present in Lund cathedral, where they can be found along most of the free wall spaces in the crypt. If the ledges were used for seating purposes, this is a function that may not be primarily liturgical. In the Middle Ages people would have been expected to stand up and face the altar during the celebration of the Mass. It has, however, also been suggested that these wall benches may have been used in connection with religious or secular meetings (Holmberg 1990:29ff).

The closest architectural parallel to Dalby is the crypt in Lund cathedral. The two spaces share a close bond not only when it comes to the layout of the building, but also in regard to decorative sculpture and iconography. The two monuments were most probably constructed by people that belonged to the same building workshop. Functionally, however, the crypt in Dalby may also be compared to many ordinary South Scandinavian Romanesque parish churches. These buildings generally had two main entrances to the nave, which were located on the northern and southern sides. Sometimes there was also a western entrance, and if so, this portal was usually the most elaborate. As in all churches the main altar was located in the eastern part of the building, in the chancel. The main focus of the nave was the baptismal font. This item occupied a central position in the western part of the room, and along the walls of the nave there were sometimes stone benches. This outline recalls many of the basic features of the crypt in Dalby. In a sense, this space might be described as a church within a church.

There was probably a symbolic significance attached to the layout of the crypt. The crypt is a perfect square covered by nine cross vaults that rest on four central columns. The number four may in this context denote the four apostles. The symmetrical building may also be a reference to the idea of paradise in the shape of the Heavenly City, a theme explicated both by the prophet Ezekiel and the Book of Revelation (Ezek 40–48; Rev 21, 12ff).

The font

The baptismal font in Dalby is in many respects an exceptional piece of work (Figure 2.3). It is the product of a highly skilled stone carver with a good knowledge of the international Romanesque style (Liepe 2012). It is among the oldest stone baptismal fonts in Scania, and has been dated to the period 1140–1150 (Liepe 2012; Roosval 1916: 227f; 1918; Rydbeck 1936:94f). This is approximately a quarter-century older than the beginning of more widespread production of stone baptismal fonts intended for use in parish churches. Like the crypt, the font displays many similarities with Lund cathedral. It is probable that both crypt and font originated from the same Lund-based workshop (Roosval 1918:104f; Rydbeck 1936:94f).

The Dalby font stands out not only because of the quality of the craftsmanship but also for its sheer size. It is a very large item measuring 1.07m high. It is very unusual that fonts from the Early Middle Ages are this large. In Scania and Denmark the average baptismal font height is 80–90cm (Mackeprang 1941:37; Solhaug 2000:191; Tynell 1913-1921:147). The font consists of two parts: a cylindrical bowl with relief decorations and a circular base with four protruding corner sculptures. The bowl is large and cylindrical and quite deep (43cm). The baptismal water would originally have been let out through a central drain hole that would allow the sacred water to flow directly into the ground below. There is an extra square opening in the base of the font that is connected to the central drain hole. This may have been used as a drain for holy water (a piscina). The

Figure 2.3. The baptismal font of Dalby (Photograph Ing-Marie Nilsson 2010).

font would probably also have been painted in bright colours. Some traces of what seems to be an original reddish hue are still visible to the naked eye, but this aspect still has to be thoroughly analysed. Recent studies have however established that much of the now bare Scandinavian stone sculpture would have been covered with paint in the Middle Ages (Haastrup 1995, 2003).

The central image on the font, covering about a quarter of the bowl, is a large narrative scene that depicts the baptism of Christ. Jesus is shown naked with water welling up around him, with John the Baptist on his right side and an angel on his left. The importance of this motif is further underlined through a text in Latin around the brim of the bowl, which when translated to English reads: 'Here is the reality that once was foretold when on the cross a flow from Christ's side-wound welled'. The remaining three quarters of surface space is decorated with relief-carved medallions with figurative and non-figurative content. The two medallions next to the baptism scene show plant ornaments that seem to represent grapes and the tree of life, and thus relate to the theme of the blood of Christ as the redeemer of mankind.

Other medallions depict hybrid animal figures, griffins and horned lions. There are also two medallions that seem to be a rendering of a hunting motif. A man with a hunting horn, holding a dog on a leash, is seen to be in pursuit of a deer. This may be interpreted as a metaphor for the human quest for salvation, but deer hunting is also a recurring theme in several saints' legends, for example the legends of St Giles, St Eustace and St Hubert. In this context it is perhaps the St Giles legend that is the most relevant since one of the side altars in the crypt in Lund cathedral was consecrated to St Giles in 1131 (Rydén 1995:53). The hunting motif is also interesting since it may relate specifically to Dalby. It has been argued that Dalby hage, a woodland area close to Dalby, may have been used as a deer park in the Early Middle Ages (Andrén 1997).

The base of the font shows four figurative corner sculptures: two lion heads and two human heads, which are placed so that they diametrically oppose one another. The expressions of these figures are also diametrically opposed. One of the lions seems strong and dynamic and has an open mouth that shows off a set of menacing teeth. The other lion has a closed mouth and a much meeker look. One of the human heads has long, braided hair and a wide smiling mouth. The other has cropped hair and a much sadder appearance where the corners of the mouth points downward. In the Middle Ages, these figures would probably have had several layers of meanings attached to them; it has been argued that one of these layers may be referring to the story of Samson (Nilsson 2012:231). The vigorous-looking man with long hair then should represent the powerful Samson that is favoured by God, whereas the man with the shorter hair would represent the Samson that has sinned and thereby lost his strength. The font is at present arranged so that the 'powerful side' (with the roaring lion and smiling man) is placed directly underneath the central baptismal scene on the bowl. If this was the original placement, the two motifs can be seen as reinforcing one another. The interpretation would then be that the figures underneath the baptismal scene are strong because they have embraced the grace of God (the grace that is offered through baptism), but the figures on the opposing side are weak because they are still trapped in sin.

The crypt as a baptistery

There is little factual evidence to support the idea that the crypt was used for baptism in the Early Middle Ages, but there is quite a lot of circumstantial evidence. For example, it is possible that the well in the north-east corner of the crypt was not originally intended for the present crypt but is a remnant from an earlier structure. One important reason to have wells within or in close proximity to important churches in the 11th century was the possibility to perform baptism. In this period this would primarily have meant adult baptism in tubs or wells. If the well in Dalby was used for baptism in this time, as has been suggested by several scholars (Anjou 1930:69; Borgehammar 2012:82; Lindblom 1908:196; Lundberg 1940:214; Nilsson 2012:234), then the placing of the twelfth-century baptismal font in the crypt may represent a direct functional continuity. There is also archaeological evidence for a subterranean drain outside the crypt, the purpose of which may have been to divert water either from the well or the baptismal font. Further, the art historical material suggests that the font and the crypt were the result of the same building campaign. This may indicate that they were intended to function together. There are also some noteworthy iconographic connections between the font and the crypt. Lion representations are, for example, present both on the font and in the crypt. One of the central columns in the crypt has a base shaped as two lions, and the tympanum on the western portal depicts Samson wrestling a lion. As previously argued, the base of the baptismal font may also be a reference to the Samson legend. Finally, there is the comparative evidence from many Romanesque parish churches for the original placement of the font. Remains of elevated podiums for baptismal fonts have been found in Denmark, Sweden and Norway. In Denmark, the fonts generally seem to have been placed centrally in the western part of the nave (Hansen 1995; Olsen 1967:250ff; Solhaug 2000:68f). In Dalby the font may have occupied a similar position: in the middle of the room, between the four central columns. If so, the decoration on the font may give some further clues as to how the font may have been oriented. The decoration on the font has one main motif, the baptismal scene, covering one-fourth of the bowl's surface. Evenly spaced medallions cover the other sides. There is in this respect an interesting correspondence between the font and the crypt. This room also has three sides that are more or less uniform and a fourth side, the eastern side, which is distinctly different. We therefore propose that the font was placed so that the main scene faced east. There is a strong symbolism in that the most significant motif on the font faces in the most important direction, the direction of the Holy altar. There are however also practical arguments in favour of this placement. If the baptism scene faced east, it would have been clearly visible both to the priest at the altar in the crypt and to people passing through the many portals in the eastern part of the room.

Research questions for the 3D Model

This is as far as the theoretical argument regarding the relationship between the crypt and the font can be taken. The plausibility of the hypothesis of the original placement of the font has hitherto been difficult to gauge because the layout of the crypt has changed since the Early Middle Ages, and the font is difficult to move. Both these obstacles are however possible to overcome with the use of a 3D model. With a 3D model, we can explore and assess different possibilities relating to this proposed placement of the font, and different questions having to do with perception and movement in space can be considered. For the purpose of this experiment we have chosen a phenomenological perspective in that we focus on the basic properties and faculties of the human body (Tilley 1994). We want to examine the characteristics of the crypt via the human ability to physically occupy and through the senses experience a defined space (Paliou and Knight 2013).

In order to accomplish this, we have decided to focus on two principal themes: congregation size and visibility, and visual perspectives; and these themes can be broken down into three main questions:

How many people could have sat on the wall benches in the medieval crypt?

How many people could have attended a baptism in the crypt?

How would different font podium arrangements affect visibility and visual communication in the room?

It is however important to take into account that a virtual interpretation is the result of the combination of fragmented information, and for this reason it cannot represent an exact replica of the historical environment. It can however shed some light on whether a particular scenario is plausible or not (Baracchini *et al.* 2004; Forte *et al.* 2010).

Acquisition and 3D modelling

The reconstruction of the diachronic sequence characterising relations between different materials, shaping the actual aspect of historical structures, has always been considered of critical importance in historical archaeological studies. The contemporary remains of ancient buildings represent only the end of a transformation process, and the investigation of why and how this metamorphosis took place is often the result of different research approaches and methods.

In the last decade the exponential employment of visual technology has allowed the development of new research methodologies, which are able to describe and investigate with high precision and detailed accuracy the geometrical features characterising historical architecture. Specifically, tools such as a laser scanner or image-based modelling techniques allow the virtual simulation of historical interpretations of the past and open up new research questions and perspectives (Yastikli 2007).

Acquisition campaign

During a master course in digital archaeology organised by the Department of Archaeology and Ancient History at Lund University, the indoor environments of the church of Dalby were partially recorded in three dimensions combining different typologies of digital acquisition techniques. The digital acquisition was performed to teach the students how to execute a 3D acquisition campaign of an ancient building for the documentation, study and analysis of archaeological structures. Due to the complexity of the building, the documentation campaign was performed using different acquisition techniques. The environments of the church were acquired using laser scanner technology, while the architectonical features were documented using image-based modelling techniques. Once acquired, the data were processed to create a virtual simulation of the space with the aim of visualising an environment that does not exist any longer.

Laser scanner campaign

After an analysis of the building we started the acquisition from the crypt and then extended the campaign to the rest of the church. The campaign was performed using a Faro 3D scanner. This instrument is a high-speed terrestrial laser scanner that allows acquiring in few minutes detailed and accurate clouds of dense points. This technology measures 976,000 points per second and provides a 360-degree description of the surrounding environment in a range of 0.6m/120m.

In order to obtain a complete geometrical description of the spaces, the building and its geometrical features was studied with the aim to plan a sufficient number of scan positions for a full documentation of the environments. Because of the geometrical characteristics of the building we did not employ any markers for the automatic alignment of clouds of points, but instead we decided to postpone this operation during post-processing activities. Historical buildings are often characterised by complex geometrical features such as architectonical decorations or structural components, that in order to be studied need to be acquired to a sufficient resolution and then aligned into the same virtual space. Unfortunately, the management of high-resolution data is not an easy task, and often it is necessary to plan the acquisition campaign to acquire different geometries at different levels of detail.

To conduct such an operation it is important to have good archaeological and historical knowledge of the monument in order to establish which parts of the building require higher resolution and which elements can be represented with a lower number of points. Despite the possibility to use the instrument to its maximum capacity, for the acquisition of the crypt we decided to lower the resolution of every single scan to an average of 7.000.000 points (one-fourth of

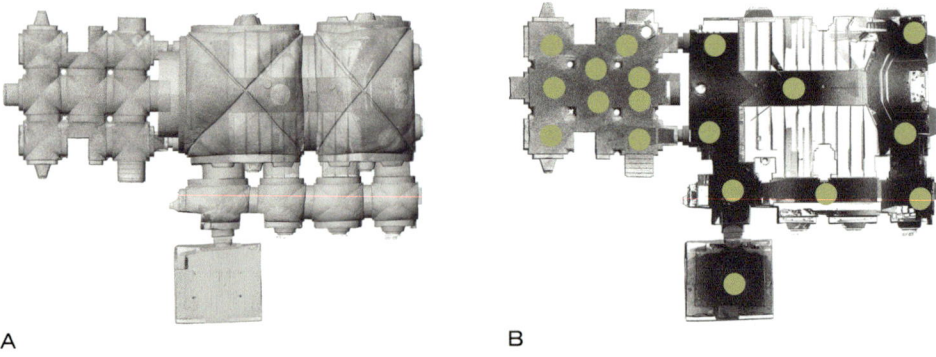

Figure 2.4. A) Orthographic top view of the interior of the church; B) Top view of the cloud of points with the position of the scans (in green); C) Section of the virtual model of the church (Rendering and digital models Nicoló Dell'Unto 2013).

the maximum resolution possible as declared by the company that produces the instrument).

By the end of the campaign we had acquired a total of 18 scans – 9 for the crypt and 9 for the main body of the church. Due to the fact that our main focus originally was the acquisition of the crypt, we used the same number of scan positions for two environments of different sizes (crypt and church body). When completed, we tried to get a sufficient number of scans from the main body of the church in order to create a model able to show and highlight the relations among the different parts of the building. Even though the scanner allows recording colours, we decided not to use this information to simulate the original aspect of the crypt since the lack of light inside the building did not allow us to record a sufficient quality of information to be employed in our simulation (Figure 2.4).

Image-based modelling techniques

We decided to use image-based modelling techniques for the acquisition of all the architectonical elements that would have been difficult or impossible to acquire with a laser scanner. The use of this method allows generating 3D models

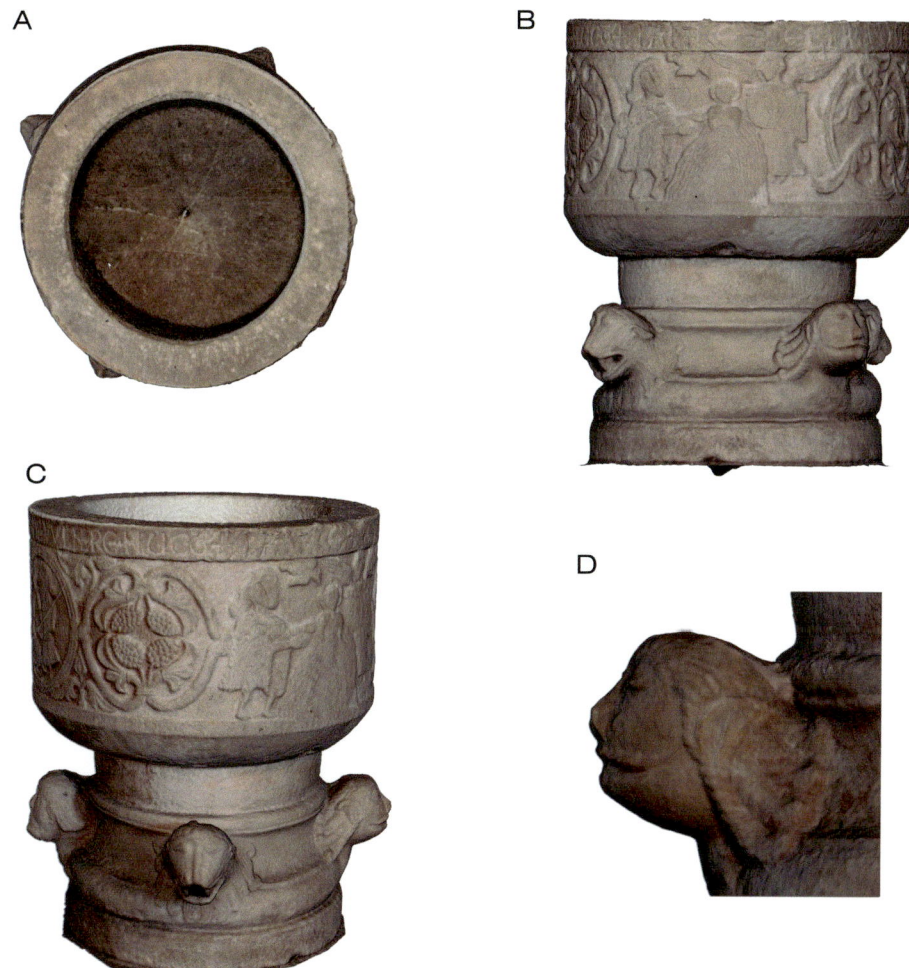

Figure 2.5. 3D models of the baptismal font of Dalby using image-based modelling techniques: A) Top view; B) Front view; C) View of the font with the colour projection; D) Decoration detail (Rendering and digital models Nicoló Dell'Unto 2013).

starting from a set of unordered images. This method is based on the combination of algorithms of *structure from motion* (SFM) and *multi-view stereo reconstruction* to build an accurate 3D model of a scene starting from an uncalibrated set of images. The software extracts and matches common features between each pair of images, estimating the camera parameters associated with each picture and calculating their corresponding positions and orientations in space. Then, using the pre-estimated camera parameters, a detailed model of the scene is created (Verhoeven 2011; Verhoeven *et al.* 2012).

This technique was used to acquire the medieval font of Dalby. Even if the scanner probably would have provided a more accurate description of the geometry, the use of such technology would have been extremely time consuming in this context; in fact, a large number of scanning positions would have been necessary to obtain a complete description of the font. Instead the use of digital images to produce the 3D model allowed recording of the object within a few minutes.

Post-processing and model construction

Once acquired, the data was elaborated following different workflows. The cloud of points recorded by the laser scanner was completely processed using MeshLab, which is an advanced 3D mesh processing software system oriented to the management and processing of unstructured large meshes. This software provides a set of tools for editing, cleaning, healing, inspecting, rendering and converting these kinds of meshes. Once acquired, the clouds of points were cleaned and aligned together in one project file in order to be processed as one single mesh. Despite the efficiency of the instrument in acquiring the data in a very short time, the post-processing was very time consuming, and the final result was the production of several models at different resolutions of the internal environments of the church. The post-processing of the images acquired for the generation of the 3D model of the medieval font was instead completely developed using Photoscan, Agisoft. The use of this product allowed us to easily and quickly process large sets of images in a very short time. Using this technique resulted in the creation of several virtual replicas of the font at different resolutions (Figure 2.5).

In order to build a new 3D model of the medieval crypt, we created a library of virtual architectonical elements to simulate the space as it could have been constructed originally. Although the crypt is a fairly well-preserved example of twelfth-century architecture, some alterations were done after this period. The northern portal is now closed off, and this was probably done at a fairly early stage. In the reconstruction (Figure 2.6), the portal has been reopened, and the stair arrangement from the south side has been copied. There are also two large rectangular supporting pillars in the middle of the northern and

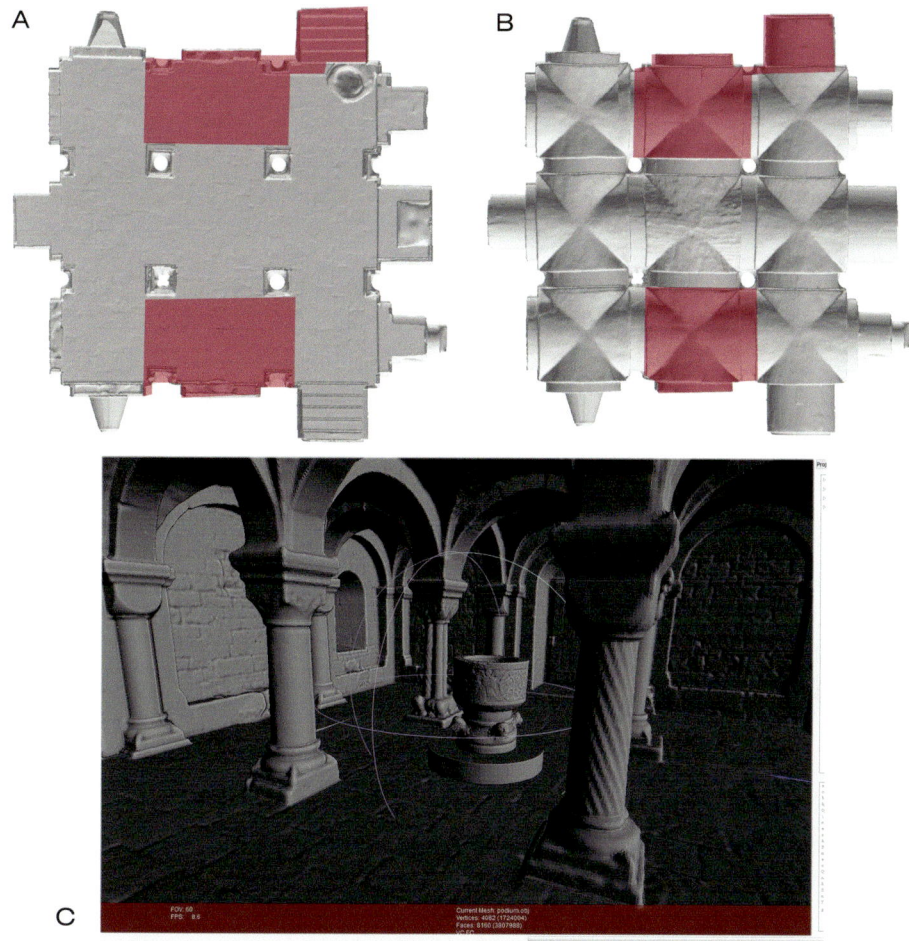

Figure 2.6. Virtual model of the interpretation of the crypt during the 12th century: A) Plan of the crypt – in red the modified area; B) Plan of the ceiling of the crypt – in red the modified area; C) Rendering of the virtual interpretation of the crypt with the font located in the centre (Rendering and digital models Nicoló Dell'Unto 2013).

southern walls. These pillars were added in the middle of the 13th century when the upper part of the tower was rebuilt (Cinthio 1992:7f). They have therefore also been digitally subtracted from the reconstruction.

Rebuilding the medieval crypt

Once the environment was reconstructed, we decided to virtually place the medieval font in the centre of the crypt. Performing such an operation in a virtual environment was easy by merging the two elements (crypt and font). The font is a large and heavy object that would have needed a firm surface to stand on, especially because about a hundred litres of water periodically would be emptied out into the floor below. Unfortunately, no proper archaeological excavations have been carried out inside the crypt, so we have no leads regarding the foundation beneath the font in Dalby. A reasonable supposition is, however, that the font would have stood on some kind of sturdy base, either a simple stone slab at floor level or an elevated podium.

Podiums for baptismal fonts have been documented archaeologically in a number of churches in Denmark, Norway and Sweden. On the Swedish island of Gotland several font podiums, plinths and stone slabs have been preserved. The podiums are generally circular and have one or two steps. The older podiums (from the first half of the 13th century) seem predominantly to have had one step, whereas the younger ones (from the middle of the 13th century) have two (Fåhraeus 1974:83, 172f). In England late medieval font podiums could have had up to five or six steps (Solhaug 2000:58). In many other parts of Sweden Romanesque font podiums with one or two steps have been discovered. At Götene in Västergötland, for example, a two-step podium from an early twelfth-century church has been uncovered (Dahlberg 1998:233f, 272). In Denmark several podiums from the 12th and early 13th centuries with either one or two steps are known. These podiums have been circular or semicircular, and in some cases there is even evidence for an elevated walkway between the font podium and the chancel (Hansen 1995; Olsen 1967:252ff).

In view of this we have chosen to reconstruct the font podium in Dalby as a circular structure with one step. Even if early two-step podiums are known, the unusual height of the Dalby font makes it less likely that such an arrangement would have been present here. The circular form is selected because it seems to have been the most prevalent, and it is also in accordance with the shape of the font itself. We have chosen a step height of 20–22cm, a height that has been confirmed in some Danish churches (Olsen 1967:253). The breadth of the podium is more difficult to assess, since the material gives only few and sometimes contradictory clues, and is of course ultimately dependent on the size of the font. Some podiums appear to have been designed with ample space around the font, while others seem be very narrow. In this reconstruction we have decided on a width of 1.4m. This would give the priest a reasonable amount of working space around the font.

The placement of the font is of central importance both regarding how the environment was perceived visually and in terms of functionality. We therefore wanted to test what implications the two possibilities would have had for the perception of the room: the baptismal font placed directly on the floor and the font placed on a podium.

An experiment of virtual time travel

Once rebuilt, the crypt was used as a platform where different historical events could be simulated. Specifically we wanted to gauge the approximate number of people in the crypt during different occasions such as a baptism or a community meeting. To run this experiment we imported the model of the crypt – complete with podium and font – inside 3DStudio Max. This instrument belongs to the family of 3D modelling software and allows building characters and animations. Since the goal of this experiment was an approximate estimation of how the crypt could have been used during the Middle Ages, we decided to use virtual characters (Paliou *et al.* 2014) with a height of 1.7m without any specific characterisation.

In the first scenario we simulated how many people could sit on the stone benches of the virtual crypt. To run this test we performed several recreations with the aim of having a general estimation of the functionality of the reconstructed space during specific events. Originally the crypt had 6 stone benches that – according to our simulation – had a maximum capacity to host 4 people each, giving a total of 24 seating places. However, without wooden furniture it is reasonable that each bench in the crypt was used only by two people in order to leave enough space for books and documents. This suggests an ideal situation of 12 seating places, one for each canon (Figure 2.7A).

Another simulation was run to achieve a general understanding of the visual perception of the rebuilt space during specific events. This second part of the modelling was performed by placing virtual cameras on top of the head of the characters sitting on the benches. This was done both with the font placed on a podium and placed directly on the floor. This allowed us to notice that if the font was placed on a podium in the centre of the room, it would have disturbed the visual connection between the opposing sides of benches and prevented any direct dialogue between the people sitting there (Figure 2.7B). However, if the font was placed directly on the floor, this problem was solved. This placement meant that top of the font was lowered, allowing a direct visual connection between the two sides (Figure 2.7C).

In the second scenario we tried to estimate the number of people able to follow a baptism in the crypt. Also in this case we conducted the procedure both with a font podium and without. In the first case the priest was placed on top of a podium, and the people were distributed in the spaces along the three sides of the central vault of the crypt. The eastern area of the crypt (the space between the altar and the font) was left empty. Virtual cameras were placed on top of the heads of several characters in order to understand what the limits were (in terms of the visibility) inside the crypt during the event. The simulation showed that in these specific conditions, an approximate number of 50–60 people would have had the possibility to visually follow the actions of the priest standing on top of the podium. In the

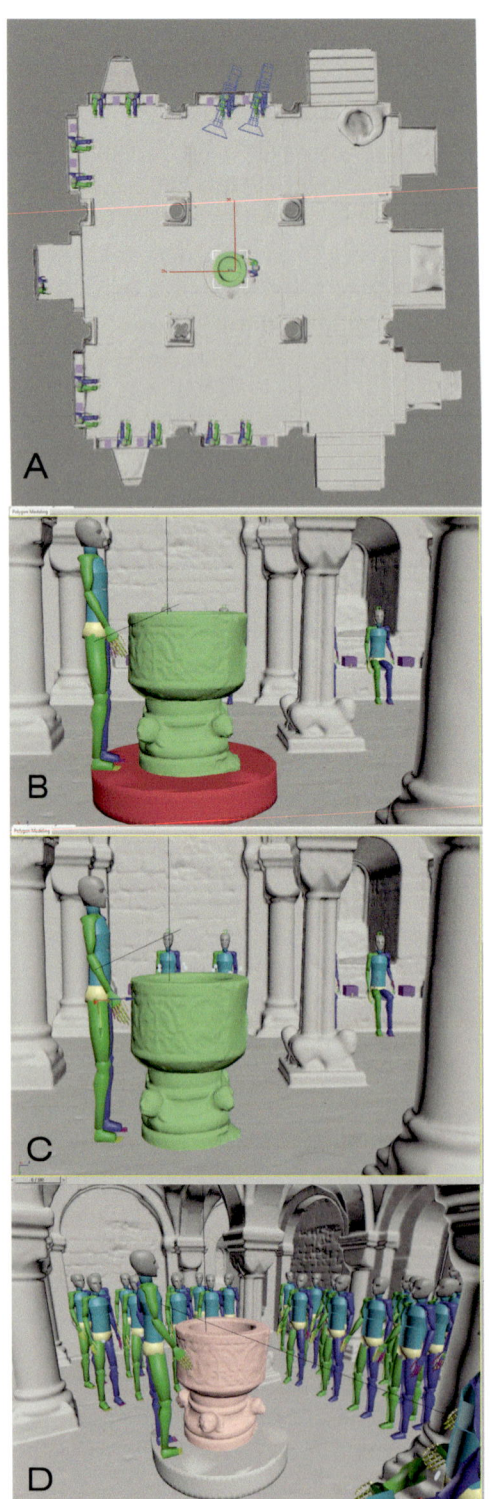

Figure 2.7: Simulation of the space functionality using virtual characters: A) The distribution of the characters on the benches; B) The font on top of the podium from the point of view of a virtual character sitting on the reconstruct east bench; C) The font without podium from the point of view of a virtual character sitting on the reconstruct east bench; D) Rendering in perspective view of the Crypt during the hypothetical celebration of the baptism (Rendering and digital models Nicoló Dell'Unto 2013).

second case the font and the priest were placed directly on the floor, which meant that both were approximately 20cm lower. It became obvious that this would have had a significant impact on the number of people having visual access to the event. Now only about 30–40 people would have had a good view of the priest performing the baptism (Figure 2.7D).

Conclusion

Time travel using digital visualisation is often perceived as a popular tool in mediating the past. In this case study we attempt to demonstrate that 3D methodologies may also be a useful instrument for addressing research questions. In the case study of Dalby, new technologies allowed us to recreate a medieval space, to edit out later changes, and to refurnish it with a baptismal font. The experiments hitherto conducted have explored questions regarding the placement of the font and how different people might have perceived the room.

It became evident that the use of a podium to elevate the font would have significantly changed the perception of the space inside the crypt. In the first scenario it was demonstrated that a podium would have represented an obstacle in terms of visual communication, and in the second scenario it was clear that the use of a podium would have increased the number of people that could have followed the baptism. This is an interesting result since it has further implications for the interpretation of the overall function of the room. And as the church of Dalby at present is planning to recreate the crypt as a baptismal chapel, these simulations may actually one day be transformed into reality.

References

Åkerman, J. 1981. *Försök till beskrifning öfwer Hellestads pastorat*. Dalby, St Nicolai Gille i Dalby. (1. ed. Lund 1828).

Anderson, W. 1926. *Skånes romanska landskyrkor med breda västtorn*, N. M. Mandelgren, Atlas till Sverige odlingshistoria, tilläggshäfte III. Lund.

Andrén, A. 1997. Paradise lost. Looking for deer parks in medieval Denmark and Sweden. In H. Andersson, P. Carelli and L. Ersgård (eds.), *Visions of the Past. Trends and Traditions in Swedish Medieval Archaeology*, 469–490. Lund Studies in Medieval Archaeology 19, Riksantikvarieämbetet, Arkeologiska undersökningar Skrifter 24, Stockholm, Riksantikvarieämbetet.

Anjou, S. 1920. *Redogörelse för undersökningsarbete vid Dalby kyrka*, Unpublished excavation report, Stockholm.

Anjou, S. G. A. 1930. *Heliga Korsets kyrka i Dalby samt de älsta kyrkorna i Lund, Roskilde och Odense. Undersökningar till 1000-talets arkitekturhistoria.* PhD thesis, Göteborg.

Baracchini, C., Brogi, A., Callieri, M., Capitani, L., Cignoni, P., Fasano, A., Montani, C., Nenci, C., Novello, R. P., Pingi, P. and Scopigno, R. 2004. Digital reconstruction of the Arrigo VII funerary complex. *VAST 2004: The 5th International Symposium on Virtual Reality, Archaeology and Intelligent Cultural Heritage*: 145–154. Aire-la-Ville, Eurographics Publications.

Böhler, W. and Marbs, A. 2002. 3D scanning instruments. *Proceedings of CIPA WG6 Scanning for Cultural Heritage Recording*, 1–2 September. Corfu, Greece.

Borgehammar, S. 2012. Symboler i Dalby. In S. Borgehammar and J. Wienberg (eds.), *Locus Celebris. Dalby kyrka, kloster och gård*: 55–87. Centrum för Danmarksstudier 28. Göteborg/Stockholm, Makadam.

Borgehammar, S. and Wienberg, J. (eds.) 2012. *Locus Celebris. Dalby kyrka, kloster och gård*. Centrum för Danmarksstudier 28. Göteborg/Stockholm, Makadam.

Cinthio, E. 1992. Dalby kyrkas stiftare och donatorer. En spekulativ bildtolkning. In M. Ullén (ed.), *Från romanik till nygotik. Studier i kyrklig konst och arkitektur tillägnade Evald Gustafsson*, 1–10. Stockholm, Riksantikvarieämbetet.

Cinthio, M. and Mogensen, L. 2010. Bondekyrkan och församlingen. In A. Larsson (ed.), *Dalby kyrka. Om en plats i historien*, 107. Lund, Historiska media.

Dahlberg, M. 1998. *Skaratraktens kyrkor under äldre medeltid*, Skrifter från Skaraborgs länsmuseum 28. PhD thesis, Skara, Skaraborg länsmuseum.

Forte, M., Dell'Untó, N., Di Giuseppeantonio Di Franco, P., Galeazzi, F., Liuzza, C. and Pescarin, S. 2010. The virtual museum of the Western Han Dynasty: 3D documentation and interpretation. In S. Campana, Forte, M. and Liuzza, C. (eds.), *Space, Time, Place, Third International Conference on Remote Sensing in Archaeology, 17th–21st August 2009*: 195–199. British Archaeological Reports International Series S2118. Oxford, Archaeopress.

Fåhraeus, F. 1974. *Dopfuntarna, deras tillbehör och placering på Gotland under medeltiden. En inventering*. PhD thesis, Stockholm universitet.

Haastrup, U. 1995. Bemalede romanske døbefonte i det middelalderlige Danmark. *Hikuin* 22:7–26.

Haastrup, U. 2003. Var al romansk stenskulptur i Danmark oprindelig bemalet? 'Materialets egen skønhed' kontra dansk middelalderlig stenbemaling'. *Romanske stenarbejder* 5:101–140.

Hansen, B. A. 1995. Arkæologiske spor efter døbefontenes placering i kirkerummet gennem middelalderen. *Hikuin* 22:27–40.

Holmberg, R. 1990. *Kyrkobyggnad, kult och samhälle. Landskyrkan i Lunds forna ärkestift genom tiderna*, Lund Studies in Medieval Archaeology 8. Stockholm, Almqvist and Wiksell International.

Liepe, L. 2012. Dalby kyrkas dopfunt. In S. Borgehammar and J. Wienberg (eds.), *Locus Celebris. Dalby kyrka, kloster och gård*: 437–446. Centrum för Danmarksstudier 28. Göteborg/Stockholm.

Lindblom, A. 1908. En gammalromansk torntyp från Östergötland. *Fornvännen* 1908, 178–200.

Lundberg, E. 1940. *Byggnadskonsten i Sverige under medeltiden, 1000-1400*. Stockholm, Nordisk rotogravyr.

Mackeprang, M. 1941. *Danmarks middelalderlige Døbefonte*, København, Selskabet til udgivelse af danske Mindesmærker.

Nilsson, I.-M. 2012. Trons visualisering. Dalby kyrkas västparti under äldre medeltid. In S. Borgehammar and J. Wienberg (eds.), *Locus Celebris. Dalby kyrka, kloster och gård*: 217–236. Centrum för Danmarksstudier 28. Göteborg/Stockholm, Makadam.

Olsen, O. 1967. Rumindretningen i romanske landsbykirker. *Kirkehistoriske Samlinger* 1967: 235–257.

Paliou, E. and Knight, D. J. 2013. Mapping the senses: Perceptual and social aspects of late antique liturgy in San Vitale, Ravenna. In F. Contreras, M. Farjas and F. J. Melero (eds.), *Proceedings of CAA 2010, Computer Applications and Quantitative Methods in Archaeology, International Conference, Granada 6-9 April, 2010*: 229–236.

Paliou, E., Lieberwirth, U. and Polla, S. (eds.) 2014. *Spatial Analysis and Social Spaces: Interdisciplinary Approaches to the Interpretation of Prehistoric and Historic Built Environments*. Topoi – Berlin Studies of the Ancient World, Berliner Studien der Alten Welt 18. Berlin, De Gruyter

Roosval, J. 1916. Byzantios eller en gotländsk stenmästare på 1100-talet. *Fornvännen* 1916:220–237.

Roosval, J. 1918. *Die Steinmeister Gottlands. Eine Geschichte der führenden Taufsteinwerkstätte des schwedischen Mittelalters, ihrer Voraussetzungen und Begleit-Erscheinungen*, Kungl. Vitterhets-, historie- och antikvitetsakademien 11. PhD thesis, Stockholm, Fritze.

Rydbeck, M. 1936. *Skånes stenmästare före 1200*, Arkiv för dekorativ konst 1. PhD thesis, Lund, C. W. K. Gleerups.

Rydbeck, O. 1941. Dalby heligkorskyrkas förhall och dess restaurering. *Meddelanden från Lunds universitets historiska museum* 1941: 212–233.

Rydén, T. 1995. *Domkyrkan i Lund*. Malmö, Corona.

Sjöborg, N. H. 1830. *Samlinger för Nordens fornälskare*, III. Stockholm, J. Hörberg.

Solhaug, M. B. 2000. *Middelalderens døpefonter i Norge, 1*. Acta humaniora 89. Oslo, UniPub.

Tilley, C. 1994. *A Phenomenology of Landscape: Places, Paths and Monuments*. Oxford: Berg.

Tynell, L. 1913–1921. *Skånes medeltida dopfuntar*, 1–4. Stockholm, Kungl Vitterhets Historie och Antikvitets Akademien.

Verhoeven, G. 2011. Taking computer vision aloft archaeological three-dimensional reconstruction from aerial photographs with photoscan. *Archaeological Prospection* 18(1):67–73.

Verhoeven, G. J., Doneus, M., Briese, C. and Vermeulen, F. 2012. Mapping by matching: a computer vision-based approach to fast and accurate georeferencing of archaeological aerial photographs. *Journal of Archaeological Science* 39(7):2060–2070.

Yastikli, N. 2007. Documentation of cultural heritage using digital photogrammetry and laser scanning. *Journal of Cultural Heritage* 8:423–427.

Chapter 3

The Kivik Grave, Virtual Bodies in Ritual Procession
Towards New Artistic Interactive Experiences for Time Travellers

Magali Ljungar-Chapelon

Abstract

This paper explores how to link and combine artistic, archaeological and technological skills and research findings in order to explore new ways to engage audiences in a time travel experience. It departs from a case study related to the shaping process of an installation based on natural interaction and is inspired by a ritual procession depicted on a cist slab from Sweden's most famous Bronze Age grave. In this interactive experiment, defined as virtual reality arts play, the user and museum visitor – in the shape of a wondrous rock art figure and by means of body gestures – was given the opportunity to become an interpreter of the procession. The questioning process of rock art imagery as part of an overall existential human wondering without definite answers is at the core of this multi-disciplinary project. It is apprehended from a hermeneutical perspective from the shaping phase of the virtual reality arts play to its meeting with the audience in various exhibition contexts. The main argument developed here is that interactive artistic representations and installations that physically and emotionally involve an audience might open new ways to engage the audience as actor-spectator in time and space and interpreter of the past. This kind of interdisciplinary process may also generate new cognitive maps at the crossover between archaeology, visual and performing arts and digital technology

Keywords: Archaeology, interactive audience experience, actor-participant, virtual reality, corpo-reality, intersensoriality

Introduction: what, why and how?

Departing from a case study related to an artistic and interactive installation inspired by cist slab images from Sweden's most famous Bronze Age grave, this chapter's purpose is to discuss how to link and combine artistic, archaeological and technological skills with research results in order to explore new ways to engage audiences in a time travel experience.

The shaping process of the prototype towards the final installation is apprehended as a hermeneutical questioning about what might happen when an artistic researcher departs from cist slab images, archaeological research results and interpretations made by museum officials in an endeavour to interpret body gestures so as to visualise and restage them in a virtual reality-based setting. In an attempt to figure out body gestures performed in a ritual context more than 3000 years ago and restage them in various contexts such as the high technological environment of a virtual reality laboratory, an art museum or a culture historical museum, the central aspect is the questioning process itself and not the unravelling of an ever-evanescent truth. It is most likely this timeless existential questioning without any simple answer that makes these cist slab images of a ritual procession so fascinating to both professionals and an overall audience. Finding ways to figure out where human beings may come from, what they are and where they are going by using the human body as key to the time travel experience is here a central issue, what I later introduce as *corpo-reality*. Hence in this experiment the question of how to open the interpretative process to the audience is central and has been addressed by drawing the user's body into an interactive gestural, visual and musical sensory experience.

I would argue that artistic representations and installations that physically and emotionally involve an audience might open new ways to engage the audience as actor-spectator in time and space and interpreter of the past. In this specific case study and as regard to the audience reactions, the interactive time travel experience is defined as *virtual reality arts play* (later referred to as VR arts play). Furthermore, I would claim that digital, visual and performing arts can be critically used as hermeneutical tools and challengers in a multi-disciplinary research context in order to experiment with and question symbolic and cosmological interpretations of archaeological imagery with body gestures. In this sense, this paper represents a contribution from the lens of artistic research to new scientific experimental approaches at the crossovers amongst archaeology, arts and technology.

This article is structured in the following manner. In the first section, the questioning process of the cist slab imagery at the origin of the artistic ideas is enlightened from a hermeneutical perspective and set in the broader context of the relationship between artistic and archaeological research. In the second section, the figuring out of the virtual procession is exemplified by exposing which archaeological interpretations were to be integrated and melted into the interpretative artistic process and how the dramaturgy of the VR arts play was conceived.

In the third section I propose and introduce the term *corpo-reality* as reality of the body expressed through its representations in time and space and seen from various horizons of knowledge in the history of mankind. Doing so, I discuss the idea of getting away from entrenched notions of separate senses by looking at the whole bodily experience, this embodiment allowing 'the touching of time through space'. In the section entitled 'Ritual Reality Meets Virtual Reality', I explain how corpo-reality has been handled in this particular VR-based technological context. In the next section I propose the idea that in this artistic experiment ritual reality and virtual reality meets beyond the time gap and that corpo-reality is central to the representation and perception of the ritual.

In 'Virtual Reality Arts Play for Time Travellers' I define this artistic experiment and interactive installation as Virtual Reality Arts Play, referring to previous research and audience experiences. Afterwards I comment on how various visualisation contexts triggered various expectations from the audience when the prototype was tested. Then preliminary results concerning audience reactions at the exhibition *Petroglyfiskt – Virtuella Upplevelser Kring Hällristningar* (Petroglyphic – Virtual Rock Carvings Experiences, May 2013–December 2014) at the culture historical museum of Österlen (Southern Scania) are exposed referring to the ongoing research project.

In the final section, in order to contextualise the VR arts play, I briefly present three innovative virtual reality-based archaeological reconstructions and ongoing discussions in the cultural heritage field concerning the dramaturgical and narrative challenge not to produce dead models of the past. Finally I discuss the kind of knowledge this type of interdisciplinary work may nurture and who will benefit, concluding that the knowledge achieved proceeds principally from emotional intelligence through an intimate or collective sensory experience for a museum visitor engaging body and mind.

Since the first version of this article had to be written in the spring of 2013 before the production process of VR arts play was achieved for the petroglyphic exhibition, the main phase of the writing proceeded parallel to this hectic, intense and complex artistic, technical and archaeological process so that it at times mirrored and at times collided. Even though the publication process took time, at the end of it the interactive installation had been achieved, set up in its exhibitional context and had met its audience for more than one year that included an audience survey, observations and group discussions with school children conducted within the frame of a research project about audience reactions in this particular digital heritage exhibitional context. Before the project was achieved, some results were already available. For this reason, in agreement with the publishers it was decided to make a slight shift of perspective taking into account the final exhibition in its meeting with the audience. Nevertheless, actualising the first version and broadening the time gap, I found it essential not to lose focus on the dynamics of the artistic shaping process at its early stage. Thus I kept comments on contradictory ideas as they popped up during this creative phase without rewriting them with hindsight of the VR arts play in its final exhibition shape. The main focus of this article, therefore, still lies in the exploring phase of an artistic research process raising more questions than it may present results. Even though, it includes preliminary results and reflections about the final installation in its meeting with the audience at the culture historical museum.

Artistic and archaeological research

The artistic idea behind this project is born from my fascination for an image on a stone cist with elaborated rock art representing a human procession carved in stone more than 3300 years ago. It is part of the famous monumental Bronze Age cairn Bredarör in Kivik, acknowledged by archaeologist and professor Joakim Goldhahn (2009) as one of the largest burial monuments in northern Europe with its decorated stone coffin or cist, which has been described as a 'pyramid of the north'. The tomb – long regarded by scholars as a king's grave – actually contained remains from at least five human beings deposited during several phases over a period of time of about 600 years, which opens for a number of interpretations (Goldhahn 2009:359).

On the cist slabs there are images of people, animals, ships, lures, symbolic signs and a two-wheeled cart pulled by horses (Figure 3.1). The particular image, at the lowest part of the seventh cist slab that directly caught my attention and became the object of this artistic research project stages nine human figures in what looks like a procession and in a specific context, that of the representation of significant rituals and offerings related to life and death (Coles 2003; Goldhahn 2013; Kaul 1998; Oestigaard and Goldhahn 2006). Why this particular image is mind bending and struck my attention when I first visited the cairn many years ago is due to the mysterious character of this procession engaging figures – human or not (?) – in strange body moves.

What are those eight robed and hooded figures? Are they real persons with a ritual garment with a bird-like head bearing a kind of mask with beak-foreheads? Are they moving slowly forwards following the human figure with upraised hand on the left? At the same time something in the curved inclination of the figures reminded me of the smooth and flexible movement of snakes. Those thoughts popped into my mind.

From this single image, an excerpt from a complex burial ceremonial context thousands of years ago, I wanted to figure out a gestural interpretation. I could have chosen to shape an artistic work inspired by this single cist slab image without any connection to the burial context as a whole and without any references to archaeological research. Nevertheless that was not really my intention: what fascinated me was to try to formulate an artistic hypothesis through a gestural, interactive and visual interpretation that might be perceived as a time travel experience. The idea of time travel implies the endeavour to try to shape some kind

The Kivik Grave, Virtual Bodies in Ritual Procession 51

Figure 3.1. The 7th cist slab of the Kivik Grave (Swedish Rock Art Archives, photograph: Steffen Hoejager).

of connection between our contemporary life world and this of the Bronze Age. To immerse oneself back into the Bronze Age ought to be an impossible task, at least from a positivistic scientific perspective. It is indeed impossible to interview Bronze Age people about rock carvings and their meaning. Nonetheless my perspective is not positivistic but hermeneutical. Following philosopher Hans Georg Gadamer (1990 [1869]; 2004) in *Truth and Method* I defend myself against the idea that there is an objective truth to reach through empiricism that would, moreover, be an absolute truth within a whole coherent knowledge system (Ljungar-Chapelon 2008:98). To nurture a hermeneutical process what could be done was to try to get an overview of what archaeological research had discovered concerning rock art imagery of human figures in general and the Kivik Grave in particular.

That is what I did in the middle of the artistic process and not at the beginning prior to figure out an artistic interpretation. I guess that this back-and-forth movement from artistic intuition to scientific analysis would have been impeded had I sought to get a too-complete picture of the archaeological knowledge and interpretations concerning the Kivik Grave and this cist slab prior to beginning to figure out body gestures. Consequently using a hermeneutical lens meant interweaving artistic and scientific approaches in order to interpret archaeological results and material and reshape them into an experience of art inviting the spectator to participate into this questioning and interpretative process. Finally, in relation to the writing process of this paper, following a hermeneutical approach has meant finding ways to express and clarify the very act of artistic representation through a mirror of concepts.

On the way this has also meant studying thoughts expressed by archaeologists about how far they are able to reach in their interpretative processes. Professor and archaeologist Flemming Kaul (1998) examines the question in relation to archaeological material connected to Bronze Age religion and rituals. He means that there is an important distinction to be done between rituals and beliefs: 'our archaeological material suffers thus to some degree from the limitation that it does not necessarily directly reflect the beliefs but rather the rituals that served to encourage people to adhere to these beliefs' (Kaul 1998:11). Applied to rock carvings this means that cist slab images show traces of rituals that might have been performed, but they cannot give us direct access to the conceptual content of the religious beliefs at stake. It is precisely this very limitation acknowledged by Kaul that triggered my curiosity and fascinated me, the fact that there is no definite all-comprehensive answer to be found concerning beliefs at the origin of the rock carving imagery from the Kivik Grave. In other words, the impossibility to exactly know which body gestures and rituals the processional image I focussed on is representing is a limitation that at the same time becomes an opening for an artistic hermeneutical questioning.

Accordingly the quest for all available interpretations concerning the Kivik Grave imagery, a task perpetrated by several generations of eminent archaeologists since the grave's discovery in 1748, is not a condition sine qua non for this project. Its incitement is the questioning process itself inspired by some of the major archaeological results and focussed on a specific processional image from the perspective of artistic research. More specifically this is the questioning process of an artistic researcher in the field of digital representation with a background within dance and theatre, a particular interest in performing and digital arts related to the human body. Collaborative projects involving archaeologists and artists opens for new interpretative paths. One former Scandinavian example based on the finding of the burial remains of a young woman from the Bronze Age period is the performance of a ritual fertility dance called 'Egtvedpigens Dans' imagined and performed by Danish dancer Anni Brøgger in collaboration with the Danish National Museum in Copenhagen (Brøgger 2003). This explorative experiment permitted among others to figure out movements and activities that might or might not have been possible to perform considering the clothes the young woman was wearing as she was buried. In this particular case the performance at the archaeological site was not based on new technology and digital arts and was documented by a video and a book written by the performer. In the case of the Kivik Grave the type of garment the eight robed figures wear – which does not seem to enable ample movements of the legs – was also an aspect taken into account in order to imagine the procession in movement.

Archaeologist Colin Renfrew (2003) considers that archaeologists and artists share parallel visions grounded on a common existential questioning, a need to figure out what we human beings are and where we come from. Michael Shanks, archaeologist and Director of Stanford Archaeology Center's Metamedia Lab, is a front figure working at the borderlines between archaeology, arts and new technology. He was a principal investigator for 'Performing Presence: Between the Live and the Simulated', a large-scale research project, which he led in collaboration with Gabriella Giannachi and Nick Kaye, both researchers in performance and new media (Giannachi and Kaye 2011). With many renowned performance artists such as Lynn Hershman Leeson, one of the most influential new media and performance experts, they explored what creates a sense of presence in, for instance, ruined remains, a life stage performance or in a virtual environment. On his website, Shanks expresses an existential quest similar to Renfrew's: 'the Arts and Humanities can be a fascinating research laboratory, helping us think freshly about how we have got to be where we are – and what we might do about it' (Shanks 2013). That is precisely this existential questioning, its very expression preserved on the stone and performed by human beings thousands of years ago and what this can mean for us in the present time that is at the core of my questioning.

Is the parallel vision between artists and archaeologists acknowledged by Renfrew and explored by Shanks to be extended to artistic research too? It is an underlying question for this chapter that I will come back to and comment on further later. So far I just want to briefly explain my position as an artistic researcher. Artistic researchers are supposed to handle and combine two challenging and at times contradictory and colliding roles and identities as both artists and researchers, creating works of art while reflecting, discussing and writing about their own artistic processes. Artistic research in this particular form is still considered a newcomer that relatively recently has made its entrance as a discipline in an academic context (since the beginning of the 21st century in Sweden). There are many opinions concerning the goals and challenges for artistic research. They bear the stamp of various artistic disciplines, individuals and institutions, and it would probably be a hard and intricate task to gather and summarize all those opinions. Personally, relating to my experience within the field of digital representation and performing arts, I consider that the challenge for artistic research is to produce knowledge and share results – works of art and science – that do not necessarily fit into an academic system but that contribute to the debate within the academic and artistic communities and eventually benefit the cultural sector and/or other scientific and societal fields. In my doctoral thesis I described this process as *artistic knowledge shaping*: 'it is the shaping of knowledge and creation of meaning through artistic means that includes the shaping process of new artistic worlds and artworks, which, in combination with conceptual constructs, reflect the world we are living in' (Ljungar-Chapelon 2008:10).

Figuring out a virtual procession

Explaining in a thoroughly detailed manner the production process involving a multi-disciplinary production group with an artistic researcher, archaeologists, research engineers, students and experts within digital representation, interaction design, virtual reality, 3D-art and music from a pilot study to the launching of a prototype in a virtual reality laboratory and towards its further development for the rock carvings exhibition at the culture historical museum of Österlen, is beyond the scope of this article. It is above all the way by which archaeological interpretations melted into the artistic shaping process that is exposed in the present section with comments on some of the archaeological results that have inspired both the launching of the prototype and its further development for the exposition at the culture historical museum of Österlen.

The conception shared by scholars that this ritual ceremony may have been performed live and witnessed by many attendants denotes its societal importance (Coles 2003; Goldhahn 2013; Kaul 1998; Oestigaard and Goldhahn 2006). This strengthened my idea to figure out a way for a contemporary audience to witness part of it. Considering my interest for bird-like masks and previous work as artistic leader of dance and outdoor theatre performances in festival contexts with actors bearing Venetian-inspired masks, the fact that the eight mystical figures on cist slab No. 7 (Figure 3.1) were interpreted as disguised human beings probably wearing a ritual garment with 'beak'-foreheads (Kaul 1998:26) caught my interest at once. Bird-like masks are still created for and used in ritual, religious, performing artistic and festive contexts nowadays where disguise and processions fill important societal functions (as for instance during the festivals of Venice or Rio de Janeiro). Hence from a time travel perspective bird-like masks may possibly be viewed as vectors of human expressions transcending time and space. The parallel drawn by Randsborg (Randsborg 1993:103–104), between the beak-forehead and what Kaul describes as 'the peculiar figure from Glasbacka in Halland, intended to be fitted on a poke or the like' ([Figure 3.2] Kaul 1998:26) and whose eyes, according to Åsa

Figure 3.2. Bronze figure från Glasbacka in Halland (Kaul 1998, 26 after Montelius 1917).

Fredell probably represent the sun and the moon (Fredell 2003:238), appeared as a captivating thought.

On the whole, mythological cosmological aspects regarding the importance of the sun and related to the cycle of life and death were sources of inspiration. According to Kaul 'there is hardly any doubt that opinions about the sun and its course across the heavens were one of the most important elements in Bronze Age religion and that the sun cult was a significant "ingredient"' (Kaul 1998:52). Goldhahn interprets motifs of the sun, horses and ships – all of them depicted in the Kivik Grave – as a mythological triad that on a metaphorical level unites the Bronze Age landscape to a cosmological world order (Goldhahn 2005:48). He proposes the idea that the sun is with the deceased in the Deads Kingdom waiting for the sun horses and ships to bring him (archaeological evidences show that the grave was built for a man/men) back to the east (Goldhahn 2005:107). In that meaning the cosmological triad seems to correspond to the human cycle of life and death and to the idea that some human beings can be reborn.

The evocation of the deceased joining the sun was particularly inspiring from a dramaturgical point of view and strengthened my own artistic idea of processional figures as kinds of spiritual guides helping the deceased and all the attendants (relatives and other witnesses of the ritual) through rites of passage between several environments and levels of awareness. I thought of the deceased as being present but invisible among the mysterious figures and/or unified into one of them in those rites of passage. I imagined how those wondrous creatures may accompany him out of the cist – out of the grave mound.

Then without transition, like in a dream they would suddenly appear slowly stepping forward with incantatory gestures on a peaceful scenic path in a green but autumnal countryside scenery (alike the south-eastern Scanian landscape where the procession may have been performed live) towards majestic trees bathed in sunshine. With their root systems and branches those oak-like, bronze-coloured trees may be perceived as symbolic links and intermediary between the earth and the sky. Reaching the bronze-coloured trees the procession's participants would intensify their incantatory ritual dance raising their arms to the sun and possibly fade out and metamorphose into kaleidoscopically flowing light particles melting with the sun rays. Then, without logic, like evanescent dream pictures, the gravestone would reappear in the sunlight and the procession figures reintegrate their former shape and place on the cist slab. They would stop moving and breathing, going back to their thousands-year-old recumbency in the rock. The dream would be over. It is this intimate experience that I wanted

Figure 3.3. The procession becomes alive. The white figure is led by the museum visitor's body gestures (Screen capture and 3D-modelling: Carolina Andersson 2012).

Figure 3.4. First drawing of the imaginary procession passing under a willow (Magali Ljungar-Chapelon 2013).

spectators (one at the time) to identify with by leading and embodying one of those figures during this imaginary ritual. The museum visitor would become all at once spectator of the ritual like an attendant witnessing the procession and participant into it by embodying and leading one of those amazing creatures (Figure 3.3).

Those are artistic ideas that the production group discussed and figured out. This means that the production process was a collective creative process with ideas being tested and submitted by several team members through, for instance, drawings, photographs, 3D models, motion capture and video recordings (Figure 3.4). Those proposals were apprehended from an artistic, technical and archaeological perspective within the group in an endeavour to reach a compromise upwards. Several ideas were left behind like the shape of a magnificent willow tree, more common in the western part of Scania than in the Kivik Grave's environment.

The idea of a ritual dance performed around a symbolic tree bathed in sunshine (Figure 3.5) was also abandoned since there are, according to archaeologist Lena Alebo, chief of the museum of Österlen, no archaeological evidence of dances performed around trees during the Bronze Age.

Figure 3.5. Ritual dance around a tree, an idea that we abandoned (Drawing: Magali Ljungar-Chapelon 2013).

Figure 3.6. Sunrays on an oak tree (First draft of 3D-modelling by Michael Orbing 2013).

Strangely enough it was shortly after having imagined a symbolic tree linked to the renewal cycle of life and death and bathed in sunshine that I read 'The divine appearance of Härn. Determining the identity of a Bronze Age metal hoard' by Margareta Forsgren (2010) and found out that 'the tree of the sun' actually existed albeit in more recent Baltic mythology and was considered to be the centre of the world and the tree of life. Furthermore the author points out that Yggdrasil, a comparable conception of the World Tree in Norse tradition, possibly goes back to the Bronze Age (Forsgren 2010:112). Hence this archaeological suggestion makes an artistic vision of a symbolic sunbathed tree possibly less anachronical than I first thought it was. From both an archaeological and artistic perspective we decided not to design something too specific that directly induced the idea of tree or life and/or a sun tree – a too-hazardous if not fallacious interpretation in such a rock art exhibition context. At the same time we decided to keep the main idea of sunrays on autumnal oak trees leaving all possible interpretations open for the museum visitor (Figure 3.6).

Other suggestions, like a background perspective reminiscent of the magnificent shape and natural area of Stenshuvud close to the Kivik Grave is an example of a consensual proposal made by the museum chief that we concretised and figured out. As previously mentioned, even though I was intrigued by the beak-like forehead of the procession figures, I perceived the inclination of their body curves as smooth and somewhat snake-like. Considering the importance of snakes in Bronze Age eschatology and cyclic renewal imagery – according to Kaul's explanatory cosmological model, alike and after the sun horses – the snakes might have picked up the sun from a ship and led it across the sky and under the horizon (1998:259–265). It was quite natural to imagine those procession figures considered by archaeologists as dancing mourners (Goldhahn 2006:178) performing burial rituals and offerings through snake-like undulating movements. In Baltic mythology too snakes were regarded as bearers of cosmic energy. Furthermore, they were considered as able to resurrect after death and to revive others (Forsgren 2010:111). Despite the time gap I found it an inspiring thought to imagine this procession as strong snake-like creatures, somehow ambivalent beings capable of prompting and mastering death, invocating the sun with smooth repetitive and incantatory ritual gestures and possibly reviving some of the deceased. But at the same time it is the ambivalence of those wondrous beings, all in one animal and humanlike, greater than a more specific interpretation and resemblance to snakes or birds that I sought to comprehend and figure out. Group discussions conducted afterwards with more than 60 children experiencing the exhibition showed that children also apprehended the cist slab figures as ambivalent animal-like creatures mostly looking like penguins, dolphins, snakes, worms, horses or moose, and viewed as males (often little scurrying 'läskiga gubbar') or females. What was interesting was that even if the responses related to gender or animal species varied, each child was very determinate in his/her interpretation referring to one animal only and to either male or female figures, which in its turn had an impact on how the virtual experience was apprehended and understood as a whole.

From a gestural point of view I found the interpretation advocated by many scholars (Randsborg 1993:108) about the first human figure with upraised hands as a male procession leader and worshipper in a so-called 'adorant position' most truthful. Nevertheless, in the first gestural interpretation of the prototype, I deliberately chose to make an experiment with quite an opposite option, since I found it challenging. It was submitted to me by Alebo, who imagined the first person as participating in an offering ceremony as the one to be sacrificed and therefore scared – the upraised hands expressing fear. Therefore in the prototype version the first figure does not have a martial attitude. On the contrary he seems somehow reluctant stumbling forward and pushed by the following figures. Maybe this one was not to be revived? Meanwhile, in the final version for the petroglyphic exhibition, I chose to propose both gestural interpretations choreographing at the beginning the first figure as a scared person in the grave environment and later on more as a leader moving forward with firm steps in the surrealistic countryside environment so as to open up several interpretative paths for the audience.

All those interpretative questionings were at the end concentrated into one dramaturgical sequence in the form of a short and intimate gestural, visual and musical sensory experience engaging the museum visitor as time traveller and interpreter of the cist slab imagery. The musical landscape was built upon a sound collage comprising – among other sounds – interpretative sequences performed on original Bronze Age instruments such as two so-called Danish bronze lurs, and produced by music archaeologist Cajsa S. Lund (1991). In this time travel experiment the spectator's body image, transformed through technology, was thought to be *the* mediator and vehicle (http://projekt.ht.lu.se/digital-heritage/projects/petroglyphics-virtual-rock-arts-experiences/).

We live, indeed, in a technological world, a world where also body image plays an important role. Therefore, the idea was to apply technology to the physical body of a spectator as well as to a projection of its image metamorphosed into a wondrous creature on a screen, in order to accomplish a travel back in time to the world of Bronze Age humans so as to imagine and share the timeless existential questions: where do we come from? What are we?

Corporeality in time and space

The human body, physical appearance and body image take a central place in Western culture and media debate today *Corporeality*, 'the reality of the body', is from Latin *realitas* and *res*, which mean 'thing' or 'matter', and from *corpus, corpor* – body. The quality of having a physical body or existence is a concept from the 17th century (1651) related to the materiality and carnality of the history of humankind as regards to its representations and beliefs. Since time immemorial and by representing and picturing the human body and people in action, human beings have left tracks about their bodily and spiritual condition and their views on the powers and creative principles of the whole universe. Rather than the seventeenth-century concept of *corporeality* with its loaded connotations to Christianity and religious, historical and philosophical debates concerning the unity or discrepancy between body and soul and the essence of mankind as divine incarnation or not, I prefer here to launch and propose the term *corpo-reality*. By *corpo-reality* I think about a more encompassing concept neither tied to a specific time frame nor to particular religious beliefs but to the reality of the body expressed through its representations in time and space and seen from various horizons of knowledge in the history of mankind.

In this meaning rock carvings representing human figures in a procession-like formation is an example of corpo-reality carved in the rock for and by Bronze Age people and expressing their rituals, beliefs and thoughts. Meanwhile a digital visualisation of human figures in movement inspired by a Bronze Age image becomes in its turn another example and interpretation of corpo-reality from another age apprehended from the standpoint of an artistic researcher and production group looking back in time through the lens of the second millennium. So what we have sought to do is a 're-presentation', i.e. another way to present this particular image and reach a contemporary audience by using new technological means in an attempt to bridge and question a time gap of over 3000 years.

Another reason for proposing the term corpo-reality is that it allows a look at presentations and 're-presentations' of human figures in movement by considering the whole body experience beyond too-entrenched notions of five separate senses. According to Corine Schleif, professor of art history and participant in the forum The Senses, (quoted in Gregor and Heal 2014:261), 'embodiment is key to our understanding of almost everything' and 'perception is never limited to information received by only one sense organ'. Furthermore she ascertains that under certain circumstances the perception of the accumulation of various sensory stimuli is 'superadditive', i.e. more important than the sum of the respective stimuli. One might actually wonder how intersensoriality worked and which senses were most stimulated during the procession as it was performed during the Bronze Age: sight and hearing of course but even touch and smell and perhaps even taste for the performers or the attendees. In the virtual procession sight and hearing were obvious stimulated senses. But, not only sight and hearing were involved: there were body movements performed in space too. The audience survey confirmed that their effect was superadditive, what I already observed in a former research project about an interactive surrealistic virtual journey (Ljungar-Chapelon 2008).

So, like Schleif I think that embodiment is a key to our understanding of cultural heritage, and I suggest that when it functions properly and through intersensoriality, this key is able to open a feeling of identification perceived as the reality of the whole body. The fact that the majority of the audience underlined a feeling of belonging as 'being a participant in the procession' seems to confirm this idea and might be interpreted as what I would call 'the touching of time through space', i.e. a full body experience in space opening for a mental travel in time.

All in all, confronting, questioning and melting corpo-realities from several millennia by using technology so as to physically involve an audience in a time travel experience was the very challenge of this artistic and multi-disciplinary experiment and case study. This meant using virtual reality and interaction technology as a medium in order to imagine and stage human bodies in movement so as to express corpo-reality in time and space. Corpo-reality is intended to be at the heart of the experience, and the type of human-computer interface chosen for this purpose was based on 'natural interaction'. This means that in order for the interaction within the virtual environment to be conceived as naturally as possible, it is being triggered by the user's arms and body movements only and not by the use of any joystick or other devices that could be perceived as a technical filter impeding the experience.

Ritual reality meets virtual reality

Virtual reality is a broad term that comprises a large range of digital media from simulated environments to fully representational spaces. It refers to the experience of immersion in an environment constructed with computer graphics with which the 'user' has some degree of interaction (Lister *et al.* 2003:35). In *The Metaphysics of Virtual Reality* Michael Heim defines virtual reality as 'an event that is real in effect but not in fact' (1993:108). Thus it implies the idea of illusions made real, perceived as real, in the sense of truthful.

In this project the idea was to merge corpo-reality and virtual reality – capturing body movements from a single person so as to transform and duplicate them – thanks to computer graphics and animation into a procession of nine fabulous beings in a 3D-based environment (Figure 3.7). Then, thanks to interaction and motion-capture technology the spectator witnessed the ritual procession projected on a large screen and was given the opportunity to act as a participant leading one of those fabulous beings in real time through their own body gestures (Figure 3.8).

In the final version, the experience starts with the spectator entering a dark room and stepping on foot prints on the floor. The stone slab is projected on the wall in front of the user. The wondrous beings emerge from the stone. They are led by the person raising his/her arms in an adorant posture (Figure 3.9). Bronze lurs begin to sound, whereupon the red, robed figures begin to move forwards with their smooth snake-like body gestures. The application uses a Microsoft Kinect to track and connect the user's movements to the white figure in the procession. The user can now experiment with body gestures that differ from those of the robed figures

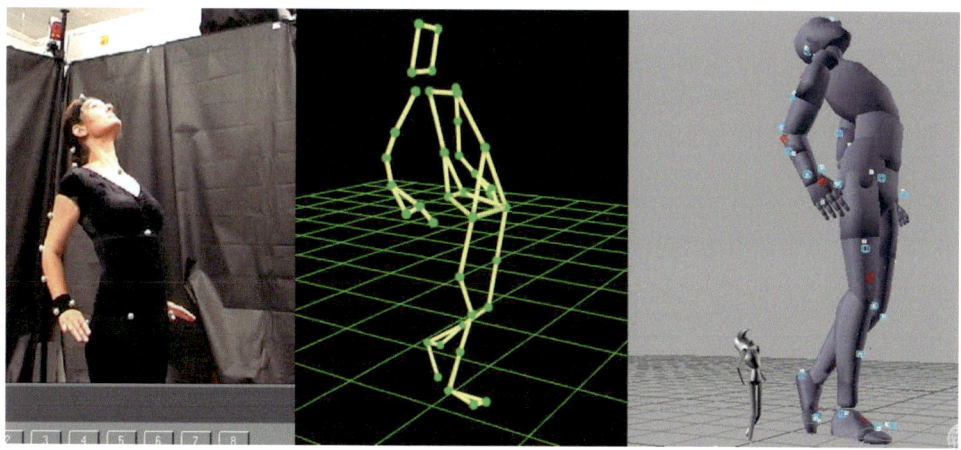

Figure 3.7. Motion capture at the Humanities laboratory, Lund University (Photograph and 3D modelling: Carolina Larsson 2012).

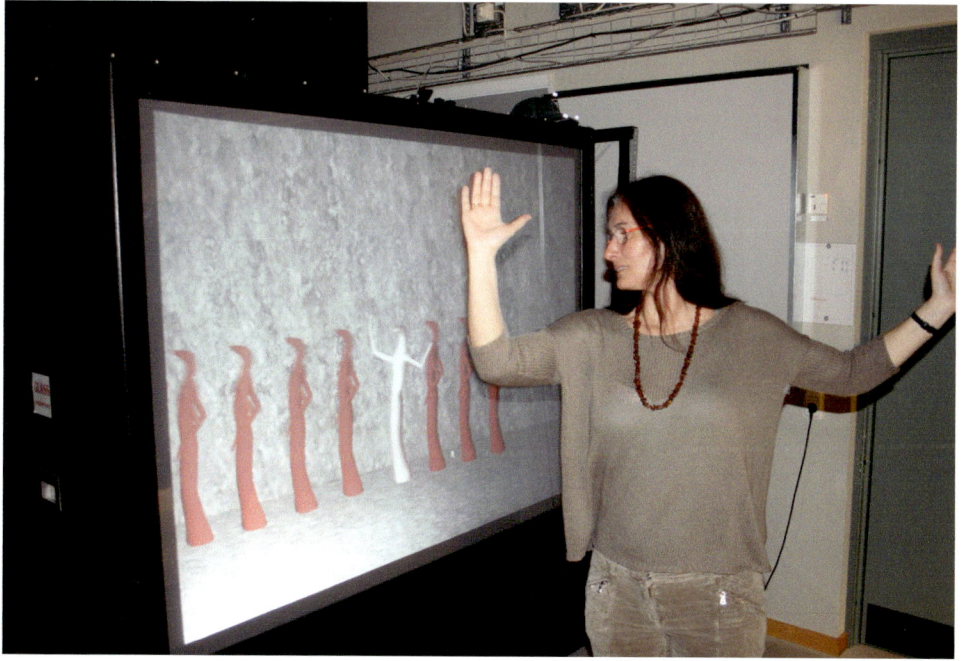

Figure 3.8. Prototype test at the VR Lab, Lund University (Photograph: Stefan Lindgren 2012).

or try to mimic the movements of the others in order to melt into the procession becoming red like the others and/or just enjoy the experience in the way he/she finds fit.

Figure 3.9. The virtual procession on a path in the surrealistic Scanian landscape, final version (Screenshot and interaction design: Sebastian Buks, 3D-modelling: Michael Orbing, Neues Interactive 2013).

In his study on Bronze Age religion and iconography, Kaul writes 'what looks like a fabulous being can often be something real – but, it must be noted, in a reality that was being manipulated by human beings – a reality that can be described as a *ritual reality*' (Kaul 1998:30). Reflecting on the time travel phenomena and the medium used in order to perform and express an important ritual thousands of years ago and one artistic representation of this ritual today, one thought struck me. Virtual reality is a reality 'manipulated by human beings' too, and – in this artistic experiment – virtual reality proceeds from something real: a real human body. Furthermore, we represent this ritual through visual and performing arts with both body gestures and sounds performed on Bronze Age instruments: meanwhile Bronze Age people left traces of their ritual ceremony through rock carving, a visual medium too. Besides they most likely performed this ritual live through ceremonies and processions using body gestures and musical instruments as depicted on the cist slabs. All in all I suggest that in this artistic experiment ritual reality, as above described by Kaul, meets virtual reality in the idea that illusions are made real, perceived as real in the sense of truthful and that in both cases corpo-reality is central to the representation and perception of this rite of passage.

Virtual reality arts play for time travellers

In a thesis about artistic experiences in immersive virtual environments I refer to Gadamer's concept of play (*spiel* in German, also game and drama) in reference to the experience of art in order to define VR arts play as a type of experience where several art forms interweave and in which a spectator is given the opportunity to become physically part of the play and interact with the virtual environment (Ljungar-Chapelon 2008:13, 100–103).

Originally the word *spiel* meant 'dance'. Play is a concept that has had a major role in aesthetics. Gadamer concentrates on its metaphorical senses, giving examples like 'the play of light' or "the play of waves", i.e. a to-and-fro movement, not tied to any goal that would bring it to an end' (Gadamer 2004:104). In an experience of art, the philosopher explains that the medial sense of play is central to the mode of being of the work of art, i.e. that the work of art is not an object that stands against a subject (spectator or actor) for itself. Play is the whole, comprising actors/players and spectators, artistic material and the medial process in between (Ljungar-Chapelon 2008:100–103).

Being drawn as participant in the play entails taking an active role. In Gadamer's words: 'The being of the spectator is determined by his "being here present" (Dabeisein). Being present does not simply mean being there along with something else that is there at the same time. To be present is to participate' (Gadamer 2004:121).

Accordingly, Gadamer's concept of play mirrors at a theoretical level our artistic goal to address an audience as not merely spectator but even as actor/participant in an artistic and archaeological surrounding and in a medial process about time travel. The original meaning of the word *spiel* as dance espouses particularly well the idea of becoming actor-participant in a ritual ceremony with dancing figures. At an empirical level this idea was confirmed by the audience survey as far as the majority of the audience viewed themselves as participants in the ritual procession: whereas fewer apprehended themselves as spectators. Asked to qualify their state of mood during the experience, the museum visitors most often chose the qualitative curious, playful and peaceful – three words underlining the concept of play.

In this interactive play several artistic forms interweave in a virtual reality context and in the form of visualisations based on body gestures, 3D-art and modelling as well as on sound and musical components. Therefore, even though the experience this time did not evolve within a fully immersive environment and virtual reality theatre like a virtual reality cube (see Ljungar-Chapelon 2008:3), I define this time travel experience as a VR arts play.

Prototype testing, visualisation contexts and audience expectations

Generally speaking, the context in which a visualisation is developed and presented to an audience and the type of audience involved have an impact on the audience expectation and its understanding, and it may influence the experience as a whole. In this specific case the prototype was shown in two very different contexts for various audience groups: first in the virtual reality laboratory at the Institution of Design Sciences from Lund University, i.e. an educational, academic and highly technological context, then as 'work of art and science' at the Museum of Sketches in Lund, a museum of art. The final version was shown at the culture historical museum of Österlen in Simrishamn, Southern Scania. This section concerns the prototype testing in the first two contexts. Even if the academic audience might have been partly similar in both cases given the fact that the presentation at the Museum of Sketches occurred during and was part of the international conference *Innovation in Mind 2012*, the radically different surrounding environments – a high-tech surrounding in the VR lab and an artistic and experimental one at the Museum of Sketches reinforced by the label 'work of art and science' – might have triggered slightly different expectations towards the prototype's content as regards its technological, artistic and archaeological content.

One might, for instance, expect that a museum art's audience might have higher expectations concerning the artistic content of the experience as a whole than a VR lab audience. No audience surveys or interviews were done at those first occasions that would have enabled us to confirm or contradict this hypothesis. Hence, what I can comment on is merely based on general observations that I as an artistic researcher made when I looked at spectators trying the prototype or watching others using it as well as on what I recalled of reflections and questions by a few audience groups: most of whom were academics. Among them was a group of archaeologists and humanists as well as an general audience during a cultural, annual event called *Kulturnatten* [The Cultural Night] organised by the municipality of Lund.

Archaeologists living in Scandinavia understood at once which archaeological context this gestural interpretation was inspired by. Most of them seemed to apprehend the idea of experiencing a gestural interpretation while testing body gestures on their own as an interesting way of questioning archaeological material; several among them expressed the idea that figuring out body gestures might trigger new thoughts and interpretations regarding rock carvings' meaning and manifoldness, something that could be used for discussions within archaeological contexts. One archaeologist interpreted, for instance, the gestures of the procession figures as rowing gestures performed by a ship crew in ritual travel in the underworld. One humanist drew a parallel between the hermeneutical process related to text analysis and the artistic and hermeneutical process at work through the gestural interpretation of rock carving figures.

One trait that at first surprised me a little was that users of the prototype, generally speaking, often seemed more eager to imitate the gestures of other figures of the procession than trying to figure out their own gestures. Thus, the majority of the users seemed to intuitively understand the goal of the experience as this of becoming a fully integrated member of the ritual procession, which was definitely an option but not the only one. One of the possible explanations could be that entertaining experiences based on interaction and visualisation technologies often are based on competitive elements towards a well-defined goal. For audiences familiar with video games such as Wii games or more specifically Kinect-based dancing games, where a good player has to imitate a dancer's body moves as well as he/she can in order to be successful, it might have been most natural to try to imitate the other moving figures of the procession as well as they could. The fact that a single user was watched by other spectators during their performance – which would not automatically be the case in the subsequent exhibition –could have reinforced this behaviour.

Professionals and decision makers within the cultural heritage sector, cultural tourism and the museum world were particularly interested in the idea of using new technology to create experiences that could physically involve and immerse a museum visitor as participant into an archaeological setting somewhere at the borderline between art, entertainment and knowledge production. Several children, even very small ones, the youngest being five years old, were also eager to participate when the prototype version was shown.

Audience experiences at the petroglyphic exhibition

At the culture historical museum in Simrishamn I conducted a research project in 2014 for the Region Council and the Board of Cultural affairs in order to analyse how museum visitors reacted to the virtual procession and other digital experiences within the frame of this exhibition. The working title of the rapport was *Virtuella hällar genom åskådarens kropp och ögon* (Virtual Petroglyphs through the Audience Body and Eyes). Later on the final title would be *Digital teknik och konst mot nya kunskapsupplevelser* (Digital technology and Art towards new knowledge-experiences) in order to better highlight the research results (Ljungar-Chapelon 2015). An audience survey was distributed to museum visitors by a museum host under a shorter period of time and was answered by 174 visitors: it had an unexpected high response rate of 96 per cent for this type of survey. A targeted group of museum experts answered the same survey later on, and observations, children surveys and group discussions were conducted with over 60 school children 9–15 years old – all in all about 250 persons. The research project was not achieved at the time I wrote this chapter, but below there are some preliminary results and reflections concerning the reactions of the overall audience.

A central issue in the audience survey as regard to the artistic goal was to try to understand the character of the museum visitor's experience and appreciate his/her level of interest and involvement. Seventy-five per cent of the audience tested the procession. Those who didn't preferred to look at somebody else performing. One question aimed to ascertain if the museum visitors viewed themselves mostly as spectators or rather as actors/participants in the VR arts play. It was formulated as follows: which was your role as regards to the Bronze Age procession? The visitor could choose more than one of the multiple choice alternatives. Seventy-two per cent of those who actually performed felt as participants. Considering the whole audience, i.e. those who performed by themselves and those who did not, the available alternatives and respective percentages of answers looked as follows: participant, 58 per cent; spectator, 45 per cent; neither spectator nor participant, 5 per cent; somebody/something else, 1 per cent. Hence, as acknowledged earlier, the majority of the audience viewed themselves as participants. I had hoped this but doubted it because the virtual procession only lasted about four minutes, which I feared could be too short to get people gesturally and mentally involved. But that was not the case, as is expressed in written comments like 'I felt like coming nearer to the roots of time', 'mysteriously belonging' or 'being in communion with the universe'.

What I wondered about is the fact that only a few visitors happened to apprehend themselves as both participants and spectators at the same time (12 per cent). On closer reflection I think that 'participating in' and 'looking at' are attitudes that are natural to combine for me as an artistic researcher or for others with a similar horizon of knowledge but that are most likely apprehended as opposites by an overall audience. Nevertheless, an interesting result points towards another explanation for four persons among those who perceived themselves as both participants and spectators and who did not in fact test the VR arts play on their own. This means that their feelings of participation was only grounded on looking at other museum visitors performing and not on their own physical involvement. Thus the concept of 'participation' in regard to an interactive experience engaging the user's body uncovers multi-faceted interpretations and the feeling of being a participant in a physical interactive experience, which is not automatically related to an active physical involvement. For the nine visitors who felt as neither actor nor spectator, I noticed while looking at the correlative results that this did not necessarily mean that all of them considered the VR arts play uninteresting. Although three of them did, the others were rather positive: three persons gave the next best appreciation for the experience as a whole.

This leads us to other results concerning how the experience was perceived as a whole and how various aspects of the experience among them (visual, physical, interactive and musical) were perceived separately or in combination with each other. The museum visitors were asked to rate various alternatives on a scale of 1 to 5 in which 1 meant uninteresting, and 5 meant very interesting. Those alternatives were to:

See an example of how a Bronze Age procession might have looked like,

See oneself in the shape of a rock carving figure,

Influence what happens with body movements,

Follow the procession in a virtual landscape inspired by Österlen,

Listen to sound/music with original Bronze Age instruments,

Experience the visual representation, music/sound and movements as a whole.

The detailed analysis is beyond the scope of this paper, but what can be said is that the opportunity to interact with the body was appreciated by the majority of the audience even if it was not necessarily considered as an easy task. Additionally, the experience as a whole was considered as interesting or very interesting by 84 per cent of the audience. As briefly mentioned before, the effect of the combination of various sensory components was superadditive, so that the experience as a whole (F) was more rewarding than the sum of its visual, musical, interactive and physical components (A, B, C, D and E). Almost 50 per cent of the audience rated their experience as a whole with the highest mark, F5 (very interesting). Meanwhile the average percentage corresponding to the audience appreciation of the respective components (A5, B5, C5, D5 and E5) was lower, i.e. 42 per cent. The next highest mark, F4, was given by 34 per cent of the audience: meanwhile the corresponding percentage relative to the added components (A4, B4, C4, D4 and E4) was lower too: 24 percent. Concerning the lowest marks of uninteresting and rather not interesting (F1 and F2), they were attributed to two persons only (1 per cent of the audience). At the same time 8 per cent of the overall audience opted for the average appreciation, F3. The effect of the three lowest marks related to each question (from A to E) was superadditive too, towards a more positive appreciation of the experience as a whole.

Another important result is that the VR arts play proved to open various interpretative paths, which was in line with the production team's intention and artistic aims. Generally speaking, one might say that the overall audience most often interpreted the figures in the procession, their gender and roles with the same variations and in a rather similar way as archaeologists, whereas children came up with more individual interpretations and explanations concerning, for instance, comparisons with animals (Figure 3.10).

Figure 3.10. Children as actor-participants in the VR arts play.

A central aspect that will be developed in the ongoing research study is the collective and individual impacts of the experience on school children who attend with a group in relation to group dynamics, gender and age. Those three combined factors proved to be able to enhance or impede the experience as a whole.

In an answer to the following question, 'do you think that new technology combined with art that engages the viewer's body opens for new forms of knowledge and audience experiences?', the results showed that 94 per cent of the overall audience and children answered 'yes'. One of the major explanations for this massive affirmative answer given in the overall survey and during group discussions with children was that interactive experiences were joyful/playful ('It is much more fun!'), making things easier to understand, easier to learn and remember as far as it is possible to actively participate with the body. The audience meant that this enabled them to look at archaeological finds and events differently, and it facilitated a stronger connection to cultural heritage through a form of identification to the past. ('Because then you become a little bit more like a part of the exhibition. It is also good when you can test and do what was done in the past' – a 12-year old child).

One might then perhaps wonder if digital experiences may impede the need to look at real finds and treasures of the past. The survey results as well as group discussions with schoolchildren, pointed towards the opposite. That is, 94 per cent of the overall audience, who had not visited the real monument of the Kivik Grave, acknowledged that they would like to do so after having experienced the virtual procession and the showcases with, for instance, grave urns containing human bones presented by a skilled museum pedagog and archaeologist. So archaeological finds introduced by skilful guides remains a clear must even if interactive artistic experiences engaging the user's body can be effective and highly appreciated by an audience when they contribute to open for new ways of learning and interpreting the past through emotional involvement and a feeling of 'being there' as actor/participant, spectator or actor-spectator.

Virtual reality-based archaeological reconstructions

There are many virtual reality reconstructions of archaeological sites, CAD (Computer aided- design) architectural models visualized in 3D that are based on scientifically approved acquisition, digital restoration and 3D-reconstruction methods. Some of those models represent tremendous technical and visual achievements. They provide a feeling of the space, and the user can walk through them on a computer screen, by means of a device, and discover details such as furniture, ceramics, sculptures or other objects of the past. Giza3D, a project about the pyramids of Giza (Guilbert 2013) is in my view such an amazing example. Those reconstructions are considered by many scholars to be of great value for archaeological research, as they at times enable them to figure out other theories and reach results other than those obtained by traditional documentation practices.

Though in an article entitled 'Here and Now' in which Shanks transcribes a discussion with Hershman Leeson (HL), the archaeologist expresses a concern about virtual reality-based reconstructions of ancient sites and gives examples such as the Roman forum, and says 'it's meant to be a very engaging experience of the past – history reconstructed in some kind of photographic verisimilitude – so that it's present to you now. But I find them utterly, utterly empty and dead'. Asked by HL why he replies that even if those models can be flashy and highly naturalistic 'what generates a sense of being there is not this kind of authenticity, but the fidelity of narrative' (Giannachi, Kaye and Shanks 2012:227). In my view, Shanks raises here a central issue, the issue of how to engage an audience that is dependent on a powerful narrative beyond the external appearance of things – what I myself in this particular case study call the dramaturgy of play.

To use natural interaction, as we have done in the Kivik Grave project, is one possible way and an attempt to work towards audience engagement beyond the external appearance of things. Yet there are, to my knowledge, still relatively few ongoing or achieved archaeological research projects seeking to improve the user experience through natural interaction. Three reviewed and/or awarded examples are:

The Etruscanning Project: This is a European Union-funded project on the virtual reconstruction of the Regolini-Galassi Tomb at Ceveteri, one of the richest and most famous Etruscan tombs of the Orientalising period, in which a visitor easily can visit and look at specific funerary goods inside the tomb by moving in the space in front of the projection. To do so, the user has to apply a specific gesture-grammar connecting arm gestures to various directions in space where he/she intends to go (Pietroni, Pagano and Rufa 2013).

Imago Bononiae: This is a 3D real-time application focussed on the VR reconstruction of the city of Bologna during the Roman age in which the user can move through ancient roads, meet a virtual crowd made by moving human avatars and discover Roman theatres and Fora as well as the future urbanisation of the city (Fanini 2013).

Livia's Villa Natural Interaction: This is a VR application based on the 3D-reconstruction of a very important suburban Roman villa connected to the imperial history and Emperor Augustus's wife. The application is intended to be placed in the Roman national museum (Pietroni 2013).

All three examples above are single-user applications based on thoroughgoing reconstructions of archaeological sites seeking the enhancement of the user experience. All are innovative in various ways. Generally speaking, I think that there is still a lot to explore and achieve in order to deepen the user engagement in gesture-based applications through improved narratives and a dramaturgy of play in the sense meant by Shanks. That could be achieved by enabling freer types of movements and interactions and enhancing the narrative through a dramaturgy of play depending on the user's choices, the rhythm of the narrative and rich musical compositions. In order to situate the Kivik Grave experiment in relation to the above examples and discussion, I would say that the realistic reconstruction of the archaeological site and its environments was not the scope of the VR arts play. Even if the 3D model of the grave stones in the first and last sequences were naturalistic, the focus relied instead on the dramaturgy of play and was built upon the suggestion of a surrealistic journey through a dreamlike landscape.

What kind of knowledge?

Rock-art research must contribute directly to archaeology if it is to achieve anything of value.
—Bradley (1997) quoted in Goldhahn (2008 [2006]:130)

The quotation above, made by Goldhahn, shares the point of view of a fellow archaeologist in a concluding part to a book about trends and traditions for rock art studies. It is interesting to consider for an artistic researcher working with a project inspired by rock carving imagery. Considering this particular artistic work and paper in relation to this statement, one may ask what is happening when rock art, a working field within archaeology, is reconsidered within the lens of artistic research. Is it so that a contribution within the field of artistic research has to directly contribute to rock art research and archaeology too in order to achieve anything of value? Given the fact that the VR arts play was developed for a culture historical museum as an integrated part of a rock carving exhibition, i.e. in a cultural, archaeological and educational context, it is indeed legitimate to ask if the artistic aim of such an audience experience is or is not to strive to coincide with the aim of rock art research as a contribution to archaeology.

Hence positioning the kind of knowledge that such an experimental and artistic-based entrance to a hermeneutical research process staging the past may convey is an important issue. This positioning has to be addressed in order to avoid misunderstandings and in an endeavour to convey to the reader the status of knowledge that such a project may represent. At first sight this positioning may seem a rather simple task. Questioning the past from the lens of artistic research and through a virtual reality-based visualisation by figuring out a choreographic sequence of body gestures departing from a single image of a ritual procession on a cist slab ought to fit into the domain of the utmost hypothetical as opposed to an evidence-based type of knowledge. Isn't it so?

The London Charter (Denard 2009), launched by a group of scholars in archaeology, new media and computer sciences, aims to define broad principles in order to enhance the rigour with which computer-based visualisation methods and outcomes are used and evaluated in heritage contexts. In the charter a distinction is made between the reconstruction and evocation of cultural heritage for scientific proposes and, for example, contemporary art. The idea advocated is that the charter's principles only have relevance for the reconstruction and evocation of cultural heritage and do not apply for works considered as works of arts. 'It has relevance, therefore, for those aspects of the entertainment industry involving the reconstruction or evocation of cultural heritage, but not for the use of computer-based visualisation in, for example, contemporary art, fashion or design' (Denard 2009:3).

As we see the text considers 'contemporary art, fashion or design' but does not mention works of art and science as results of artistic research in those fields. Additionally, in regards to its implementation (principle one) the charter 'signals the importance of devising detailed guidelines appropriate to each community of practice' (Denard 2009:3). In this particular case study I would argue that there was not one homogenous but several communities of practice involved. As previously said the production process and presentation of the prototype was generated from an existential and artistic questioning inspired by archaeological research results that took shape in a VR laboratory and a humanities laboratory (two different research environments and faculties within the humanities and technology fields) and a museum of public art. Meanwhile the VR arts play took shape in a culture historical museum. All those institutions represent various domains: academic, artistic educational as well as curatorial domains with various priorities and audience focus. Furthermore within the academic community there are several disciplines involved: artistic research, archaeology and engineering being the principal ones. Thus, I will claim that the type of knowledge achieved in this case study cannot be referred to as something that stems from a single 'community of practice'.

The question then is whether works of art and science concerning cultural heritage from the perspective of artistic research should or should not follow the charter's principles. In my view, there is no simple and univocal answer to this question. It depends on the visualisation and/or performing project. In this particular case study it was fruitful to be aware of those principles for the writing of this chapter. But for the artistic part of the work, striving to follow methodological principles towards well-defined aims could have impeded an artistic process based on intuition, trial-and-error method and metaphorical thinking. As a matter of fact my artistic intention implied that 'the aims' should not be that obvious and well defined but on the contrary left to the interpretation and definition of an audience associated with the creative process through play. So, in my opinion, this contribution as artistic research (first the prototype, then this chapter at the beginning of the production process of the VR arts play and after its meeting with the audience) ranges in between artistic intuition and scientific analysis but was at the beginning much closer to a free hypothetical artistic questioning than a more evidence-based type of knowledge. During the following phase, when the VR arts play was integrated into the exhibitional context of *Petroglyfics*, the research study focussed on audience reactions was conducted. The empirical methods chosen during this second phase based on my audience surveys at the museum and interviews with experts in the field ranged within the realm of a more evidence-based type of knowledge. Consequently, regarding the project as a whole, the research process can be described the same way as in my former thesis work as the interweaving of empirical and theoretical functions, i.e.' two functions that are not hermetically separated from each other but that proceed on parallel tracks crossing each other, joining each other and affecting each other's courses' (Ljungar-Chapelon 2008:12).Without anticipating future results I would argue that the evocation of cultural heritage related to body gestures through artistic research in a multi-disciplinary context opens for new scientific experimental approaches at the crossover between archaeology, arts and technology.

As emphasised before one of the underlying questions behind the project is what kind of shared cognitive maps this type of multi-disciplinary-based project may or may not establish between artistic researchers, archaeologists and experts within high technology. Will their vision be parallel, converging or colliding concerning an artistic process of re-interpretation of a rock carving image? There is at first sight a huge difference between thoroughgoing contributions made by archaeologists to a body of knowledge concerning human gestures and processions within rock art in general and the Kivik Grave imagery in particular – explicated through photos, evidence-based restorations, drawings and reconstructions – and an artistic interpretation brought up by an artistic researcher within a multi-disciplinary production team. Nevertheless I would argue that the questioning processes of archaeologists and artistic researchers have more in common than it may seem, and I would claim that digital, visual and performing arts can be critically used as hermeneutical tools and challengers in a multi-disciplinary research context in order to experiment with and question symbolic and cosmological interpretations of rock art imagery with and through body language. All in all this artistic multi-disciplinary time travel project, although never intended as a direct contribution to rock art research and archaeology, may possibly and eventually appear as an indirect contribution depending on the way archaeologists and other scholars apprehend it in sharp contrast *or not* to their own research processes and results.

But most important of all, this project was grounded on an endeavour to emotionally and physically engage a broad audience, adults as well as children, as participants in a time travel experience and VR arts play. To depart from the artist's and spectator's bodies in order to question, interpret, imagine and explore corpo-reality in time and space is in my view a way to appeal to the notion of *emotional intelligence* as developed during the last decade by psychologists or neurologists like Antonio Damasio, bridging the gap of dichotomous thinking between emotion/feelings and rational/logical abilities (Ljungar-Chapelon 2008:11). Damasio shows how our consciousness, our sense of being, arose out of the development of emotions and suggests that 'certain levels of emotion processing probably point us to the sector of the decision-making space where our reason can operate most efficiently' (Damasio 1999:42). So following Damasio I would suggest that the essence of knowledge achieved through artistic research in this project proceeds principally from emotional intelligence and embodiment, first within the production team during the creative process and second through play in Gadamer's meaning with the audience in what is conceived to be an intimate interactive sensory experience for a museum visitor engaging body and mind. The final results of the research study, tracing audience reactions in the exhibition context at the museum, will show more completely if and how this goal has been achieved. So far some of the most rewarding feedback for me is the image of a twelve-year-old girl joyfully skipping on her feet after having tested the prototype, raising her arms above the head and exclaiming several times, 'when I grow up, I want to be an archaeologist!' Then she looked attentively at a photography of the seventh cist slab on a stand and gave me her interpretation of the first figure in the procession: 'this is a man because you see his legs' . . . and about the eight following figures: 'those are women because they wear dresses'.

References

Brøgger, A. 2003. *Egtvedpigens Dans. Historien om en drøm, der blev til vikelighed,* Braedtrup: Förlaget Mammut. http://www.youtube.com/watch?v=qY6Lz7RdAMY, video (accessed 2 January 2014).

Coles, J. 2003. And on they went... processions in Scandinavian Bronze Age rock carvings. *Acta Archaeologica* 74:211–250.

Damasio, Antonio R. 1999. *The Feeling of What Happens: Body and Emotion in the Making of Consciousness.* New York, Harcourt Brace.

Denard, H. (ed.) 2009. *The London Charter for the computer-based visualisation of cultural heritage.* Version 2.1 (February 2009). http://www.londoncharter.org/downloads.html (accessed 1 January 2014).

Fanini, B. 2013. Imago Bononiae. Proceedings of the 2013 Digital Heritage International Congress 28 Oct–1 Nov, Marseille, E-catalogue of the Congress Expo (Digital Heritage 2013 Expo) *Federating the 7th ArcheoVirtual Exhibition, 7th Digital Art Week* 3:75–76.

Forsgren, M. 2010. The divine appearance of Härn. Determining the identity of a Bronze Age metal hoard. *Current Swedish Archaeology* 18:105–126. Nordic Academic Press.

Fredell, Å. 2003. *Bildbroar. Figurativ bildkommunikation av ideologi och kosmologi under sydskandinavisk bronsålder och förromersk järnålder.* Gotarc Serie B. Gothenburg Archaeological Thesis n 25. Göteborg 2003, ISBN 91-85952-85-0.

Gadamer, Hans Georg 1990 [1969]. *Hermeneutik I, Wahrheit und Methode, Grundzüge einer philosophischen Hermeneutik.* Tübingen, Mohr.

Gadamer, Hans Georg 2004. *Truth and Method,* second revised translation of *Wahrheit und Methode* by Joel Weinsheimer and Donald G. Marshall. New York and London, Continuum.

Giannachi, G. and Kaye, N. 2011. *Performing Presence: Between the Live and the Simulated.* Manchester, Manchester University Press.

Giannachi, G., Kaye, N. and Shanks, M. 2012. *Archaeologies of Presence: Art, Performance and the Persistence of Being.* London, Routledge.

Goldhahn, J. 2005. *Från Sagaholm till Bredarör – hällbildsstudier 2000-2004.* Gotarc Serie C. Arkeologiska Skrifter No 62. Göteborg.

Goldhahn, J. 2006. Från landskapens monument till monumentens landskap - om döda och efterlevande med exempel från äldre bronsålder, 1700–1100 cal BC. *Lik og ulik : tilnærminger til variasjon i gravskikk*: 171–202.

Goldhahn, J. 2008 [2006]. *Hällbildsstudier i norra Europa: trender och tradition under det nya millenniet.* Göteborg, Institutionen för arkeologi, Göteborg universitet.

Goldhahn, J. 2009. Bredarör on Kivik: A monument cairn and the history of its interpretation. *Antiquity* 83:359–371.

Goldhahn, J. 2013. *Bredarör på Kivik - en arkeologisk odyssé*. Simrishamn: Artes liberales.

Gregor, N. and Heal, B. (eds.) 2014. Forum: 'The senses'. *German History* 32(2):256–273. doi:10.1093/gerhis/ghu034, http://gh.oxfordjournals.org/ (accessed 20 July 2014).

Guilbert, K. 2013. Giza3D. Proceedings of the 2013 Digital Heritage International Congress. 28 Oct–1 Nov, Marseille, E-catalogue of the Congress Expo (Digital Heritage 2013 Expo) *Federating the 7th ArcheoVirtual Exhibition, 7th Digital Art Week*, 3:23–24. http://www.3ds.com/giza3D (accessed 3 September 2014).

Heim, M. 1993. *The Metaphysics of Virtual Reality*. New York, Oxford University Press.

Kaul, F. 1998. *Ships on Bronzes: A study in Bronze Age Religion and Iconography. 2, Catalogue of Danish Finds*. Copenhagen, National Museum.

Lister, M., Dovey, J., Giddings, S., Grant, I. and Kelly, Ki 2003. *New Media: A Critical Introduction*. New York, Routledge.

Ljungar-Chapelon, M. 2008. *Actor-Spectator in a Virtual Reality Arts Play. Towards New Artistic Experiences in Between Illusion and Reality in Immersive Virtual Environments*, ArtMonitor, diss. Göteborg, ISBN: 978-91-977757-1-7. http://gupea.ub.gu.se/dspace/handle/2077/18849.

Ljungar-Chapelon, M. 2013. Kiviksgraven, Virtuella kroppar i rituell procession/ *The Kivik Grave, Virtual Bodies in Ritual Procession*, Virtual Reality Arts Play by PhD Magali Ljungar-Chapelon, concept and artistic director in collaboration with Lund University Humanities Lab, the Department of Design Sciences, Lund University, Neues Interactive, Craze Music productions and the museum of Österlen within the exhibition *Petroglyfiskt-virtuella upplevelser kring hällristningar/ Petroglyphic – Virtual Rock Arts Experiences (May 2013-Dec.2014)* http://projekt.ht.lu.se/digital-heritage/projects/petroglyphics-virtual-rock-arts-experiences/).

Ljungar-Chapelon, M. 2015. *Digital teknik och konst mot nya kunskapsupplevelser – Publikstudie om virtuella interaktiva upplevelser vid utställningen Petroglyfiskt på ÖsterlensMuseum*, Rapport. Institution för designvetenskaper, LUP, Lund University Publications, ISBN 978-91-7623-310-8 (PDF): http://lup.lub.lu.se/record/5257240.

Lund, C. S. 1991. *Fornnordiska klanger/The Sounds of Prehistoric Scandinavia*. CD including a booklet. Stockholm. Musica Sveciae, MSCD101.

Montelius, O. 1917. *Minnen från vår forntid*. Stockholm, Nordstedt.

Oestigaard, T. and Goldhahn, J. 2006. From the dead to the living: Death as transactions and re-negotiations. *Norwegian Archaeological Review*. 39(1):27–48. http://goldhahn.se/Publicerat_files/Oestigaard_Goldhahn.pdf (accessed 21 January 2013).

Pietroni, E. 2013. Livia's villa natural interaction. Proceedings of the 2013 Digital Heritage International Congress 28 Oct–1 Nov, Marseille, E-catalogue of the

Congress Expo (Digital Heritage 2013 Expo) *Federating the 7th ArcheoVirtual Exhibition 7th Digital Art* Week 3:47–50.

Pietroni, E., Pagano, A. and Rufa, C. 2013. The Etruscanning project: Gesture-based interaction and user experience in the virtual reconstruction of the Regolini-Galassi tomb. Proceedings of the 2013 Digital Heritage International Congress 28 Oct–1 Nov, Marseille, *Visualization and Interaction*, Vol.1, Track 2:653–660.

Randsborg, K. 1993. Kivik. Archaeology and Iconography. *Acta Archaeologica* 64 (I). Munksgaard.

Renfrew, C. 2003. *Figuring It Out. What Are We? Where Do We Come From? The Parallel Visions of Artists and Archaeologists*. London, Thames and Hudson.

Shanks, M. 2013. Nov 14. Understanding creativity and innovation. *Academic website. Home.* http://chorography.stanford.edu/MichaelShanks/11 (accessed 3 January 2014).

Commentary

Time Travel Paradoxes and Archaeology

Per Stenborg

The chapter by Dell'Unto, Nilsson and Wienberg presents a good example of the use of 3D models as an instrument for evaluating different possible interpretations of past conditions. Although referred to as phenomenological, the approach also has traits of functionalism and focuses on evaluating possible spatial arrangements inside a crypt of a medieval cathedral.

The time travel takes place inside the western crypt of the medieval cathedral and monastery of Dalby in South Sweden. A large baptismal font is currently located in the nave of the cathedral. The text argues that, based on architectural traits, the original place of the font was in the eastern crypt of the church, rather than in the nave. This raises the question of how the font was placed in the crypt. Devoid of direct traces of how that placing, the paper sets out to evaluate the different hypothetical positions of the font from a functionalist perspective as regards the spatial arrangement of the crypt.

A digital model of the interior of crypt as it may have have been shaped back in the 12th century was created based on precise measurements on the building as it stands today and data on known renovations, thereby creating a reconstruction of what the medieval crypt may have looked like. Estimates of the number of people able to sit, respectively stand, inside the crypt in connection with two different kinds of activities (scenarios) were undertaken to provide a base for visibility analyses. The activities that are considered are community meetings and baptism.

The model was imported into a 3D software and the visibility analyses are carried out using the software as a test-chamber. More specifically the analyses deals with the effects of the presence or absence of a particular element (a podium) on visibility as well as intervisibility – the latter term describes the situation when two places are in positions that allows an observer at either one of them to observe the other place (which also means that two individuals with their eyes positioned at these points will be able to maintain eye contact with one another). The visibility analysis could hypothetically have been undertaken in the real physical room, with real people taking the places of medieval crypt. An impediment to this was however the weight of the font; which for the analysis was to be moved up on a podium. Hence, the choice to undertake the lifting of the font inside a 3D model of the crypt may therefore have been a way to save peoples backs as well as to avoid exposing the font to unnecessary risks.

For the case of the 'meeting room scenario' the result indicates that a placement of the font on a podium would have had a negative impact on the crypt's suitability as a meeting room as it would prevent people sitting on opposite sides of it from maintaining eye contact. This result seems to suggest that the font was placed directly on the floor, rather than on a podium. However, in case baptism was undertaken in front of a standing audience (the second scenario), almost twice as many in the audience would have been able to see the activities of the priest in case he was standing on a podium, rather than on the floor. If a podium was used it is thus more likely to have been used as a rostrum to place a baptizer in an elevated position, than as a fundament for the font.

Visibility analyses are quite commonplace in GIS (geographical information systems), usually performed on terrain-models. In many cases, analyses of historical and prehistorical settings are difficult due limited knowledge about vegetation conditions at the time to be analyst, as presence or absence of trees can have great influence on the view seen from a certain position. By comparison, this paper undertakes a visibility analysis at a micro-scale. As in terrain analysis there is uncertainty regarding some preconditions, and certain assumptions must be made to allow for an analysis. Analyses of past conditions of visibility are therefore, as a rule, of hypothetical character. The article systematically pursues the analyses based on the necessary assumptions. It shows in a fascinating way the potentials of combining logical reasoning with 3D analysis.

In terms of time-traveling; the font has already made a journey from the 12th century to the present. By means of digital 3D techniques it is allowed to enter an exciting return trip to the Middle Ages.

The chapter by Ljungar-Chapelon presents a study oriented towards methodology research. The interpretation of a rock carving was the basis for an installation in which the museum visitors were given the opportunity to take the place of one of the figures from the carving. The participant's body movements were registered and reproduced as were they those of a figure interpreted as walking in a ritual procession.

While game-like exhibitions generally aims at activating its audience; the 'participating through corporal motion' approach applied here, nevertheless differs from the mainstream of such exhibitions. Traditionally exhibitions are experienced through vision and hearing, rather than through touch or body movement – why the involvement of other senses in the experience in itself often can be regarded as a renewal of exhibition techniques.

The museum visitor's participation in the activity interpreted and presented as a procession appears to imply the participation in a performance –a Bronze Age staging of a mythological 'play' (i.e. the participant takes the place of one of the performers). This may be the only reasonable way to clarify the destination of the activity in terms of a time travel. In that respect it would have been easier, but also less innovative, to let the museum visitor take the place of the rock carver – or that of a Bronze Age observer of the carving.

An experimental study of exhibit methodology would be of limited value without an examination of the visitor / user experience. Hence, a survey was undertaken in order to find out how the visitors experienced the exhibition, and part of the results are presented under the heading 'Audience Experiences at the Petroglyphic Exhibition'. Although no complete account of the survey's results is included in the paper (for reasons of limited space), it is nevertheless evident that the majority of the visitors / users felt that their visit had been a rewarding one. No less than 94 percent of those of the respondents that had never been to the Kivik Grave (where the rock carving on which the installation was based is found) felt motivated to visit the ancient monument after having experienced the exhibition. It would of course also be interesting to compare the views of such visitors to the Kivik Grave, to those of other first-time visitors who have not been at the exhibition – maybe this could form part of a complementary study.

Although not particularly emphasised in the article, the study also constitutes a good example of contemporary reuse of cultural heritage and of computer aided reenactment. I think that the reuse, recycling and renewal of the assets of history has the potential to make history more relevant and important for the present, something to which I will return below.

The user's ability to alter the installation through body movements (interaction) seems to have been quite restricted in this case. It may still be worth noting that the notion of influencing past events through time traveling constitutes one of the main themes in fictional depictions of time travels. The time-traveling paradoxes explored by science fiction (sometimes entailing that the time traveller intentionally or unintentionally alters the past and thereby removes the preconditions of his/her own existence – which, in turn, implies that history cannot have been changed as the time traveller doesn't exist in the new present, let alone have been able to travel back in time) are not entirely transferable to the metaphorical application of the time traveling act, but even so some reflections based on the lines of thought developed by the likes of Isaac Asimov, Robert Silverberg, Harry Harrison and Philip K. Dick can be made. Another version of the time travel paradox turns the problem of interventions by time travellers from the future upside down: in case time travel eventually becomes possible, then the history, present and future are the products of any impact that time travels may have led to. Thus, instead of undermining their own existence, time travellers are bound to affect history and thereby create conditions for the historical development leading up to their coming into existence (as chronologically these interventions must have occurred long before the time-travellers were born). Regardless of whether one considers this or some other variation on the theme of time travel paradoxes – time traveling appears to be a tricky business. While the consequences of time traveling in a figurative sense to a digitally reconstructed (or 'virtual' as it is often called) past may be far less dramatic, it offers us the opportunity to influence a version of the past, and the temptation to correct or improve the (hi)story may crop up also in that case. Therefore, I particularly notice that, to my understanding, this study situates the audience's encounter with prehistory in the present, rather than in the past – it is more of a question of moving the past to the audience (and therefore to the present) than of sending the audience as time travellers back through history.

Commentary

Taking Us to the Past and the Past to Us

Isto Huvila

There is an apparent contradiction between the regularly outspoken capability of virtual technologies used to take us back in time and the comprehensive studies of how these possibilities can be realised in practice, and it is nothing but fascinating. The two, in many ways are different. But at the same time related texts by Nicolo Dell'Unto, Ing-Marie Nilsson and Jes Wienberg, and Magali Ljungar-Chapelon take important steps towards a more explicit understanding of what the possibilities are (or rather, what kinds of possibilities might exist) and how (and where) they are emerging. My reading of the two texts substantiates my earlier ponderings that there are indeed possibilities and not a possibility that pertains to the very core of how digital technologies (re)organise our relation to things we are pursuing to know about (Huvila 2013). At the same time, they similarly (re)organise us in relation to, for instance, geographically and temporally distant milieus.

A central underpinning of both chapters is the claim that a certain approach helps us to go beyond conventional methods of travelling back in time. Their take on the principal method of how this is done differs from each other. Dell'Unto *et al.* pursue a rather technical path of travelling in time and take us back to observe the interior and spatial arrangements in the medieval church of Dalby. This reminds us of the classical stories of travelling in time with a central theme of suddenly taking a modern-day observer to witness a chain of events in the past. The virtual is a measurement device that gives us a chance to analyse a space that does not exist (as such) and juxtapose contradictory scenarios of how things might have been. By scanning and modelling, Dell'Unto *et al.* give researchers an opportunity to travel in time and space in an analogous manner reading a textual account of the past gives a possibility to travel in time in a narrative.

Ljungar-Chapelon's take on time travelling is different, as her focus is not to take a modern-day observer back in time as a modern-day observer but to take us there and (to a degree) go native. Instead of focussing on what happened, she is interested in travelling back to personally sense how it felt. It is tempting to dichotomise the two approaches, to see Dell'Unto and colleagues as distant observers, nineteenth-century ethnographers making notes of the people of the past, and Ljungar-Chapelon as an intimate participant who dives into the lives and experiences of the past individuals. But instead of portraying them as contradictory, it could be more fruitful to see them as complementary to each other and even more so, as illustrative of the twofold possibilities and consequences, of digital (or virtual) technologies (or approaches).

A virtual environment, whether it is three-dimensional or not, and whether its premises are in fiction or in fact (as far as they are known to us), is a system that (re)organises things it contains and refers to, and makes them understandable and knowable to us (Huvila 2013). It is a knowledge organisation system that (re)creates a perceivable structure of how things are related to each other in a specific context of the past and as a time travelling device, an arrangement that attempts to bring us closer to how things were arranged at the time. The key is that the two approaches in the two texts lead to very different types of arrangements. They both can be understood from the perspective of hermeneutics as processes of meaning-making and the bringing together of the past and the present individuals (Gadamer 2004). Both approaches are guided by their associated pre-understanding of the significant aspects of the past and lead to a particular kind of understanding of the past, knowledge that is supported and arranged by the time travelling device.

The principal difference of the two approaches, and in broader terms, of the use of digital technologies and 'the virtual' as instruments of knowing about the past, is what they see as a premise and as an outcome of the process. In time travelling there is a difference between travelling from the present to the past or from the past to the present. Similarly, there is a difference between using virtual technologies to (re)make the past for the present (us) or to take us to the past – to attempt to organise the past for us to understand, or to make us to understand the arrangements of the past. In the essence, I see that Dell'Unto *et al.* are engaged in the first-mentioned approach whereas Ljungar-Chapelon has chosen the second one. The church of Dalby comes to us, whereas we are supposed to go to the Kivik grave.

It would be undoubtedly useful to discuss further which of the approaches would be more useful in specific contexts and how they would complement each other in different cases. Ljungar-Chapelon's arts-based approach could help us to understand the crypt of the church in Dalby, what it was like to participate in a baptism in the crypt and how virtual reality could bring us to the ritual reality of the medieval Scanians. Similarly, there are endless possibilities to model and analyse different aspects of Bronze Age graves using the approach by Dell'Unto *et al.* and to bring it to us. However, putting on my hat of an information scholar, my concern is (and is probably supposed to be) how this all influences our knowing of the past. The difference between attempting to structure the past for us and structuring us for the past is not insignificant. Both can be useful, but what is important is to be reflective of the consequences of choosing one of the two alternatives. Without disputing their significance, archaeological 3D models tend to put very considerable emphasis on features like the line of sight, size of spaces and access from one location to another. Similarly and in contrast, arts-inspired research tends to emphasise such aspects as making, personal exposure and corporeal experience. The strengths of the respective approaches can be paralleled to the recognised difference of material and textual research. Our understanding of the medieval times would be very different if only historians or archaeologists would be in charge of creating knowledge of the past. Similarly in the future, our understanding of the past would be very different if we would try to travel in time only to one of the two possible directions and tried to structure, organise and systematise knowledge into arrangements that would fail to acknowledge the difference of organising the past for us and helping us to understand the organisation of the past.

References

Gadamer, H.-G. (2004). *Truth and method.* New York, NY: Continuum, 2 ed.

Huvila, I. (2013). Sorting the metaverse out and how metaverse is sorting us out. In D. Power, & R. Teigland (Eds.) *The Immersive Internet: Reflections on the Entangling of the Virtual with Society, Politics and the Economy*, (pp. 192–203). Basingstoke: Palgrave MacMillan.

Part Two

Time Travel as an Educational Method

Chapter 4

Use the Past, Create the Future
The Time Travel Method, a Tool for Learning, Social Cohesion and Community Building

Ebbe Westergren

Abstract

Kalmar County Museum and the international organization Bridging Ages have developed a Time Travel concept, an educational method that uses local heritage to create reflection on contemporary issues, aiming at social cohesion, learning and community building. The Time Travel method is seen both as a process, where people meet, research, discuss and prepare an event, and a role play based on a fictional story at a local site. The event is centred on key questions for reflection and discussion, practical activities, learning areas and problems to solve. Six examples of the Time Travel method are described and discussed, four from South Africa and two from Serbia with focusses on social and environmental sustainability, reconciliation and tolerance. The start, development and the basis of the Time Travel method in Kalmar is explained, also the methodology and principles as well as benefits and challenges of the concept.

Keywords: Time Travel method, Bridging Ages, Kalmar County Museum, key questions, applied heritage

Introduction

Time Travel is a word with multiple meanings. Kalmar County Museum and Bridging Ages, International Organisation in Applied Heritage and Time Travels have developed a concept that engages people in their local history, but the focus is on issues of today. The Time Travel concept is an educational method, to create reflection on contemporary issues, using local sites and stories. Local heritage is applied to today's issues in the community. The aim is to contribute to community building and social cohesion using heritage and education. This is *applied heritage*, and the method is sometimes called *historic environment education*, but more often it is referred to as the *Time Travel method*.

This chapter describes and discusses the Time Travel method and applied heritage as used by Kalmar County museum and its collaborative partners. A special interest is given to an international context. The chapter consists of a short background followed by a discussion of how the method has developed since the beginning of the 1980s, the main features of the method, and finally several examples from South Africa and two from Serbia will be described and discussed.

Background

Kalmar County Museum 30 Years Ago to Today

The Swedish primary schools (grades 1–9) got a new curriculum in 1980 that emphasised the experience of the pupils and their own 'research', which opened space for more use of local history and life experiences in education. The new curriculum marked the beginning of a pilot project between Kalmar County Museum, Regional Department of Education in Kalmar County, and three schools on local sites and stories that connected nearby history with pupils' life realities. The three schools worked with different historic time periods, according to what was mentioned in the curriculum. One of the schools chose the Stone Age for their grade three classes. Instead of teaching about the Stone Age as a distant land with remains far away from the school, they focussed on a Stone Age site close to the school and used the pupils own questions to research the life of the Stone Age people. The idea was to connect the pupils' lives with Stone Age people who lived in their own surroundings several thousand years earlier. The Kalmar County Museum supported the activity with historical facts and training days for teachers and in this way helped the school to implement the curriculum.

The curriculum encouraged students to do their own research and to raise their own questions about the Stone Age or other chosen time periods, which motivated them to do research and find the answers. In this pilot school the students were given a short background at the actual Stone Age site before they could raise any questions about the Stone Age people. The questions were divided into categories that gave the basis for the students own research: environment, humans/family, building/settlement, economic conditions/food, social life, religion, society/tribe and diseases/death. The museum and the Regional Department of Education supported the project with books, articles, films and radio programs to find the answers. The museum also wrote fact sheets on the topics that the students raised. Several subjects in school were involved: social sciences, natural sciences, craft, art, Swedish.

The Time Travel method is a good learning method because it uses all senses. The project team decided that for one day the pupils together with teachers and museum staff would experience life at a local Stone Age site that is close to the school. The pupils became the persons who lived 5000 years ago – those they had researched and studied. The students chose topics and issues to focus on. This very first Time Travel event was organised in 1986 after more than a year of preparation.

After three pilot years the Time Travel method was opened to all schools in the Kalmar region. And in the first year, 1990, more than 50 schools were already involved. Kalmar county museum organised many training days with the teachers about local history and useful sources for the students' research. Up to 100 Time Travel events per year were held for school classes with a lot of hands-on activities based on ancient techniques. The local sites, from time periods spanning the Stone Age to the 20th century were always close to the schools and in walking or biking distances. In the 1990s, this learning concept opened up for adults, local historical societies and study circles. The local study groups and the museum also arranged big public historical events at local sites.

In 1997 Kalmar celebrated the 600-year anniversary of the Kalmar union in 1397. Research resulted in teaching material, books and fact compilations on the web. Many hundreds of historical events were organised by Kalmar county Museum in the Kalmar region, and a national TV series was made. The work of the museum was noticed all over the country, and in the year 2000 the museum got a three-year National Commission from the Department of Culture and the Swedish government to inspire others throughout Sweden to do something similar.

In 1999 a local 'Folkhigh School' in Vasa, Finland, and American Swedish Institute in Minnesota, USA, invited Kalmar County Museum to go abroad with the Time Travel method. In the years to come the museum was invited to other countries. In 2004, 40 persons from 8 countries gathered in Vimmerby, Sweden, for a seminar on Historic Environment Education and Time Travels. The participants decided to form Bridging Ages, international organization in Applied Heritage and Time Travels. Kalmar County Museum became the coordinating institution. In 2007 Bridging Ages was transformed into a formal organisation with its head office at Kalmar County Museum.

Since then Bridging Ages has grown. As of 2016 its members reside in 25 countries on 4 continents; about 20,000 people take part in Time Travel events every year and more than 200,000 people since the start in 2004. National branches of Bridging Ages have been launched in many countries. Kalmar County Museum has had projects in most of these countries. The most active countries are Finland, Estonia, Latvia, Lithuania, Serbia, Italy, Ireland, Turkey, the United States, Kenya, Uganda, South Africa and Sweden. Institutions from one or two new countries join every year. Training courses and workshops are an integrated part of the work. University courses exist in New Mexico, United States, and Sweden and are planned in other countries.

The Time Travel method
Applied heritage, methodology and principles
Much of the ideas from the early 1980s are still part of the Time Travel concept: the use of local sites and stories; start from one's own point of view and interest to motivate research and studies; using all senses and emotions. Any historical time period can be chosen with a wide range of sites. At the same time the concept is continuously developing and changing according to various conditions in different countries and societies as well as the interests of the participants.

Over the last ten years the concept of the Time Travel method has been more and more focussed on contemporary issues by using the past. 'Using the past, creating the future', is an expression of the Time Travel method from the cooperation with Department of Arts and Culture in South Africa. The definition of the Time Travel method often used in presentations today is 'an educational method using local heritage in a learning process, to create reflection on contemporary issues and provide tools for community building.' 'The goal is to promote learning, social cohesion and contribute to community building.' This can be done in several ways adapted to the local situation and conditions, but there are some main features that are summarised in the five principles of the Time Travel process and event below.

Five principles

In 2008 in Worcester, South Africa, a group of about 30 people participating in the Bridging Ages activities in various parts of the country came together with the Swedish partners and discussed what the Time Travel method is and what it is not. The participants at this meeting identified the five following principles in the Time Travel method confirmed at a Bridging Ageas seminar in Pretoria in 2015, which extend to all of its member countries:

It focusses on local sites and the stories of the sites.

It uses several perspectives, generally bottom up or 'history from below'.

In the key questions today's issues are expressed and reflected on in a historical context.

There is an interaction with several partners, the community and the schools in research, education/studies and Time Travel events.

A Time Travel event always has a reflective dialogue: learning by doing, reflecting and challenging.

The Time Travel process and event

The Time Travel method is not only an *event*; it is a *process* of several components. The process can take a month or two or even more and is just as essential as the event. In the process partners from different groups in the community come together to meet, discuss, research, plan and implement with support from museums and universities.

The process consists of several components that could be used in sequence, combined or separate. The partners agree on what to achieve and what contemporary issues/

topic to focus on. They choose a historical site and a narrative. The contemporary issue/topic, the site and its story should be well connected. After topic and site is decided, it's time to do research, interview people, review documents or study artefacts. Research can be done at all levels – community, university and students.

Another component is the interpretation of the landscape and how the site is connected to its surroundings. The process often includes trainings with all partners, teachers and community groups. If it is a school group the Time Travel should be in line with the curriculum. Any subject in school could be included. The students study the chosen time period and the topic and write their own character in the scenario.

The Time Travel event is most often the highlight of the process, even though the overall process itself can be just as important. Before the event the scenario is written, most often by the museum and the community group/teachers together. A historical scenario is a more or less fictional story based on the facts known from the site. It is always about one site, one topic, a certain story/event or a special day or year. Some examples include: Kronobäck monastery ruin dating to 1482, preparing for the opening of the church, topic on values of life (seven virtues); Funkabo suburb in Kalmar 1958, a spring feast for the residents, topic on creating the good society (welfare state); Freedom Tree, Entebbe, Uganda 1954, a public/political rally, topic on independence and democracy; Knjazevac, Serbia 370 AD, the god of Mars festival; topic on war or peace.

From a critical point of view, one can analyse the stories chosen. Why these stories? To whom is it important? Who is the target group? The basic idea is that the scenario of the site should be connected to today's life in the community. And also give space for reflection on various perspectives. But of course there is no 'objective' story from a site. The scenario is focussed on what the community group or school group feels is important today and is grounded on historical facts of the site. In the future there might be other stories and perspectives.

When the students embark on the Time Travel event at the historical site close to their school, they have prepared for several weeks in school, maybe written their own character and have an opinion on the key questions. On that very day they become another person in another time, but at the same time they are themselves, keeping their age and sex. During the event they do activities in line with the story; for example, they prepare for a feast or the opening of a church at the same time that they discuss and argue on the key questions. Often they have a problem to solve or are given tasks to present at the end of the Time Travel event. Every Time Travel event is unique: a local place, a specific year and a specific event. An evaluation is done immediately after the event to obtain the first impressions. It is important also to evaluate one or two days later, in school or in the community group, after participants have had the time to rethink a little bit. But the most important part is to compare the past to today. What are the similarities and lessons for today?

Reflection, learning areas and key questions in the Time Travel event

Reflection and learning are the main areas of a Time Travel event. You have the chance to reflect on important issues of today as expressed in the topic of the Time Travel. As indicated above, it could be any social, spiritual or economic issue: democracy, gender, violence, religion, education, human rights, environment, diversity, migration, employment or reconciliation. In the Time Travel event participants compare the issue of today with a similar issue of the past. How did they address these problems in the setting of the Time Travel? Participants formulate key questions around the topic that were also relevant in the past, normally with no definitive answer. These key questions are the centre of the whole event. How do we create a good society for everybody (Funkabo 1958)? What is the right way to live (Kronobäck 1482)? What are the needs and dreams of my town and our country (Entebbe 1954)? What is my/our responsibility for war or peace in the future (Knjazevac 370 AD)?

In the Time Travel event the participants are divided into smaller groups and learning areas with a certain task/activity to fulfil. Participants do practical activities as indicated in the scenario: prepare for a rally or the arrival of somebody, or they do the final work of a construction. Participants work with their hands in the group while they talk about the key questions. The whole brain is activated. These learning areas are an essential pedagogical part of the Time Travel event. Group members have an opinion that other people will question, argue against or reflect upon. It is often a good idea to bring in a new person in the middle of the event to give more fuel to the discussions and arguments. At the end of the Time Travel event all the participants come together for a meal, a small feast, start of a political rally or welcoming of a guest. The key questions are discussed, and the reflections from the smaller groups are taken to all. From this, participants come to an agreement, a plan of action and a conclusion.

The learning process in a Time Travel is relational, that is you learn together with others. Learning is not repeating what somebody is saying or what you read in a book. Learning is seen as a more creative process, where you reflect and discuss different opinions together with others. At the end you might come up with new ideas, new learning. The event also includes experiential learning, through first-hand experiences.

While reflecting, discussing and doing practical activities, participants not only learn a lot about the historical time period but also about themselves and today's society; they learn through history. The Time Travel method gives a chance to reflect on dark sides and sensitive issues. It is a lot easier to discuss a sensitive issue in a Time Travel event than around a table. It can help to achieve reconciliation and healing. One of the strengths with the Time Travel method is that participants release emotions. You learn with all your body, brain, heart, soul and all your senses. This gives a deeper knowledge and understanding than reading or listening.

Rebuilding a diverse society in South Africa

Kalmar County Museum and Bridging Ages have worked in South Africa with applied heritage and Time Travels since 2006. Through their work in South Africa, the museum gradually changed the focus of the Time Travel method from reliving the past to reflecting on contemporary issues using the past. The museum started their work in the Western Cape and then continued in several other provinces: KwaZulu-Natal, North West, Mpumalanga, Gauteng and Northern Cape. In 2008 Bridging Ages, South Africa, was launched, after which they branched out to the provinces.

A few examples of the Time Travel method in South Africa follow below. The work is strongly focussed on rebuilding a diverse society and reaching social cohesion. This approach focusses on contemporary issues and key questions, and it has in the last few years influenced the Time Travel work in several other countries as well as in Sweden.

Social cohesion and reconciliation in Montague

The small town of Montague, Cape Winelands, three hours north of Cape Town, is like many towns in South Africa. The legacy of apartheid is clearly seen in the segregation of people in residential areas, schools, elderly homes, churches and so on. Elderly homes in Montague were, in 2012–2014, part of the project More Living – Active Age, together with several other elderly centres in Cape Winelands and the Kalmar region of Sweden; the project focussed on the needs of the elderly, their life experiences and local heritage. In Montague, one white and one 'coloured' elderly centre decided to work together and use the Time Travel method as a way towards reconciliation and cohesion.[1] The elderly and staff of the centres met in a working group almost every week for many months to find common topics and interests. They wanted to address segregation in society. Finally they decided to develop a Time Travel event to 1968 at a church that the 'coloured' community was forced to leave that year. The centre of the event was the last church bazaar before they left.

---

[1] The apartheid regime in South Africa divided the people in South Africa in various races: blacks, coloureds, whites, Indians and so on. The names of the races are still used in the country.

The development process was quite long, almost a year. The community members held discussions, conducted interviews and did a lot of practical preparations before they agreed on a detailed scenario. In the Time Travel event and in the activities they reclaimed the church, sang the old songs and for the first time did it together, the 'coloureds' and the whites (Figure 4.1). Two hundred and fifty persons gathered and celebrated this Time Travel event. The elderly took the initiative to implement the Time Travel concept as an obvious act of reconciliation in the town. Though the Time Travel event was about 1968, it was clear for everyone that it was also about today.

So, what were the results? The main objective of the Time Travel work in Montague was to bring people together, 'coloureds' and whites, in a reconciliation process. As mentioned, South Africa is still a divided society, and in many ways it is easier to do a Time Travel instead of some other possible reconciliation activities. The meetings and preparations among the elderly before the event were essential. Working together for a common goal was a chance to get to know each other and also understand the life situation of the other. When you work closely for a large event you have to trust and rely on 'the other', and you have to do quite a lot together. The Time Travel process, all these preparations and meetings, were actually more important than the event itself, but without the event it wouldn't have happened. One of the leaders

Figure 4.1. The old songs were sung again with lots of passion in the Time Travel event to 1968 in the mission church in Montague.

of the 'coloured' elderly centre said afterwards that it was so important to tell this story, to work the whole problem through and to make the others understand in order to leave it behind and to reach a peace of mind.

The critical question is, of course, whether this work is sustainable or whether it was a one-time project and event. And have other groups followed? It is still too early to give reliable answers. But there are promising signs, as the Montague event inspired other reconciliation initiatives in the town. And two years after the Time Travel, the two elderly centres are still working together and have even increased their collaboration. However, there is a long way to go to reach an inclusive society.

Freedom Park

Freedom Park in Pretoria is an iconic heritage place in the new South Africa, a result of the Truth and Reconciliation process after democracy in 1994. It is the second example how the Time Travel method has been adapted to the South African conditions. This program is developed together by Freedom Park, Department of Arts and Culture in South Africa, Kalmar County Museum and Bridging Ages. When a group of students and community members are coming to Freedom Park for the program they bring a problematic issue from their own community related to their struggle for freedom, something that needs to be reconciled. It could be a very difficult issue such as a massacre or xenophobia attacks, or more common problems like poor housing, unemployment or corruption. The issues are addressed and given cultural expressions in a Time Travel event. After that,

Figure 4.2. Reconciliation ceremony at the Isivivane, as part of the Time Travel event at Freedom Park.

the participants go to a ceremonial place for reconciliation with the past. At this sacred place, the Isivivane, the problems are lifted up to the spirits and ancestors as part of traditional ceremonies and African spirituality. When participants have reconciled with the past at the Isivivane the group walks to the Lekgotla, a place for shaping the future and the way forward. This Time Travel event has three components: expressing the problems, reconciliation and the participants' responsibility for the future.

To make this Time Travel successful, much depends on the interaction and trust between the leaders and the group. And this regards both the preparations and the event itself. The leaders need to be very sensitive to the participating group, the problems they bring and the use of traditional ceremonies (Figure 4.2). The ceremony at the sacred place lifts the problem to an existential level, and the whole body and mind is involved with all senses and emotions. One of the difficulties is to get both sides, the perpetrators and the victims, in the same program. It will take more time before this is achieved. And we still do not know what happens when the Time Travel participants come back to their community; the program is new. Will there be a change, and will the program contribute to deeper reconciliation?

Participation and community building

Kliptown, Soweto

Kliptown, Soweto is a quite large community in the outskirts of Johannesburg with many challenges in terms of housing, employment, education, infrastructure, crime, electricity and so on. Kliptown is well known for the Freedom Charter, one of the most important documents in South African history, which was adopted here in 1955. At that time, people from all over South Africa gathered at illegal and secret meetings to develop a set of demands. A committee in Kliptown categorised the demands in 10 clauses, and at the end they were adopted by 3000 people, from all over the country, at a big meeting in Kliptown in June 1955 before the police dispersed the crowd. These 10 clauses are today the basis for the constitution in South Africa, and they reflect a democratic and free country.

In 2010 Kalmar County Museum was invited to Hector Pieterson Museum and Memorial and Kliptown Museum in Soweto, Johannesburg, to introduce the Time Travel method. At a workshop in Kliptown a year later, representatives from the community, youth groups, museums and schools discussed the challenges in Kliptown and the opportunities of the Time Travel method for both the community and the local schools. The participants elected a working group with people from all the stakeholders. Several heritage sites in the township were identified and they agreed to focus on the Freedom Charter. In a follow-up workshop in 2012 community members presented life in Kliptown, today and in the past. Eventually, a Time Travel event was carried out to the year 1955, just before the Freedom Charter congress in June the same year. The demands from the country were discussed at that time. The Time Travel working group chose four of the ten clauses to be the focus of the event: land ownership, mineral wealth, education and human rights. In the Time Travel event the 60 participants relived a meeting in the W. W Brown Baptist Church, where these categories were originally discussed. The participants were divided into four groups for the four clauses, and each participant chose one of the groups/one clause (Figure 4.3). The clauses were vividly discussed in the groups, and each one decided how to express the clause: in words, a poem, a song, a slogan, an illustration or a placard. The groups were exceptionally creative; many ideas, demands and solutions came up to the surface and were expressed in different ways. At the end everyone came together in the church, and each group presented their ideas. It was not difficult to make the other participants want to join in a song, a dance or a slogan. Everybody realised that although it was a Time Travel to 1955, the problems and demands discussed and expressed were those of Kliptown and South Africa of today. The Time Travel event gave space for reflection, expressions and learning.

Figure 4.3. Creative work in one of the groups at the Time Travel event to 1955 in W. W. Brown church in Kliptown. This group discussed the clause on how to share the land in the country and penned their ideas on placards, an illustration and a poem.

What is the result of the Time Travel work in Kliptown, and the process from the first meetings to the actual Time Travel event and later? The Time Travel method is a process that opens for creativity and initiative. Since the start of the Time Travel process, there has been a lot of engagement in the study group. It was not difficult to get the group together and inspire them. Many persons spent a lot of time planning, researching, recording historical buildings and interviewing people. The Time Travel work sparked various ways to continue learning for some of the participants. For example, leaders and youngsters from a youth centre in Kliptown that took part were very inspired to find out more about the local history of Kliptown. They interviewed people, reviewed documents, recorded buildings and so on. The Time Travel made the local history important; their own neighbourhood became 'historical'. In 2015 the group had grown extensively and decided to start a non-profit organization called the Kings (Kliptown Innovative Native Group of Services), whose purpose is to use local heritage, education and the Time Travel method to improve conditions in Kliptown by addressing social conflicts and unemployment.

It is obvious that it was the participation in the Time Travel process and in the actual event that inspired a reaction and a continuation for the Kings youth group and for the staff of the Hector Pieterson Museum. People who joined the study group, were involved in the preparations and finally exposed at the emotional level in the Time Travel event were affected and inspired. But it was difficult to tell in the beginning who would be the most engaged. If there is a driving person in the group it is also easier for others to join. The Kings now have an interest to continue to support and promote Time Travels. Another result that became clear is that difficult and sensitive issues like land use and ownership related to mining could be approached outside of the political sphere within a Time Travel context, which changes the whole mental environment. The problem is transformed and, even though it is the same issue, is not so dangerous to discuss. The transformation makes it easier to throw up ideas for solutions.

June 2015 was the 60th anniversary of the adoption of the Freedom Charter. Because the success of the first Time Travel events, the project team (Hector Pieterson Museum, Department of Arts and Culture, Kalmar County Museum and Bridging Ages South Africa) decided to make a public Time Travel event at the Freedom Square in the middle of Kliptown/Soweto. After half a year of preparations in Time Travel groups all over South Africa and in the coordinating team, 400 participants, half from various parts of the country and half community members celebrated the historical event in Kliptown. Most importantly they expressed what the ten clauses of the Freedom Charter mean today in words, poems, songs, plays and illustrations (Figures 4.4 and 4.5).

Figure 4.4. The public Time Travel event in Kliptown, Soweto. After the historical part, each participant chose one of the ten clauses from the Freedom Charter and interpreted it in today's society. What do equal rights, work and security, peace and friendship mean in South Africa today?

Figure 4.5. All the ten groups in the public Time Travel event in Kliptown presented their ideas of the Freedom Charter 2015, in a poem, speech, illustration, drama, song or a dance.

Environmental sustainability

One topic that is essential in sustainability issues and for our shared future is the environment, and it is a common theme in Time Travels. Cape Nature in Western Cape, South Africa, together with Kalmar County Museum, is developing landscape education programs in several nature reserves and world heritage sites in the Western Cape as a way to encourage people to reflect on sustainability and the use of resources. Ratelgat, a nature preserve, is a semi-arid region in Western Cape that is very sensitive to over-exploitation. The Ratelgat region also has similar problems as many parts of South Africa: segregation and tension between different ethnic groups.

Staff from Cape Nature, educators and the local community established a working group in Ratelgat. They developed a Time Travel process that made people reflect on sustainable land use. Today sheep farmers, tourists, mining companies, development advocates and conservationists are the main actors in the region.

The Time Travel event focussed on an interaction between a hunter-gatherer group and a pastoralist group 1800 years ago that took place close to an archaeological site with remains of worked stone and rock art from that time period. Half of the participants in the Time Travel event played the role of hunter-gatherers and half pastoralists. The groups are different; they speak different languages, have different traditions and use the resources in different ways. Can they still live

Figure 4.6. A group of hunter-gatherers meets a group of pastoralists at the water hole, the rapid start of a Time Travel event. Can we accept and respect the other?

Figure 4.7. Make a stone knife and discuss the key questions; work, talk and reflect at the same time. The Time Travel event creates learning areas where the key questions are discussed in smaller groups while working. Can we live together although we are different? Is it possible to use the same land and the same waterhole? How?

Figure 4.8. Everybody comes together at the end of the Time Travel event. What are the solutions? Can we make an agreement on the use of the land and the waterhole? How to make a sustainable living, together? The event often ends with a sign of togetherness: a ceremony, a small meal or a dance.

together? In the scenario both groups have an interest in a waterhole that is full of water at a certain time of the year. The question is how to use the water and land together so it is not damaged for the future or for the other group. While settling 200 metres from the waterhole, the groups negotiated. Learning areas were created for each activity, and participants worked and talked in smaller groups. While making rock paintings, preparing food or collecting plants, they argued and discussed the issues, and they tried to be creative to find solutions (Figures 4.6, 4.7 and 4.8). At the end of the event, the two communities shared a meal, and the ideas in the smaller groups were negotiated with all. There were many arguments and several suggestions, so the ending was not certain.

In this Time Travel event in Ratelgat the difficult issue of land use, with lots of economical and emotional interest, was transformed and brought into a safe space. This opened up the locks between the groups. It made the participants listen to the ideas from the other group, to find new creative solutions and to negotiate. It was so obvious in the Time Travel event that if you did not try to understand the other group's point of view, it was impossible to find an agreement. How much can the environment stand? How do we find sustainability?

It's easier to discuss those issues if there is no audience. Everybody is in the same situation in a Time Travel event; you are in a safe environment. The Time Travel does not solve this issue, but it makes people listen, show respect and reflect in a new situation. But there has to be a follow-up to the Time Travel work to go farther. Otherwise there is a risk that it is not leading to the change you want. At the same time the participants discussed and worked in the Time Travel event, they not only reflected on an important issue but, without almost realising, they also learned a lot about the local history and the site, and about the life of the hunter-gatherers and pastoralists almost 2000 years ago.

Tolerance, discrimination and the effects of war in Serbia

Several Time Travel programs have been developed in Serbia since 2008 on the effects of war as part of a partnership between two cultural organizations in Serbia, the Swedish embassy and Kalmar County Museum. Serbia is a country that has been badly affected by war over the centuries, and most people today have experiences of war. How do you build up hope and tolerance for the future in this setting when it is often sensitive to speak about recent atrocities that people still have fresh in their minds and when the combatants sometimes even know each other? When the Time Travel method was introduced in Serbia in 2008, project leaders decided to go back to World War II to create distance from the Yugoslav Wars in the 1990s. It was also hoped that this would make it easier to discuss issues of tolerance, ethnic cleansing and discrimination and to reflect on whether a change could really be made.

Figure 4.9. The announcement in the middle of the Belgrade Time Travel event to 1941: 'All Jews have to register'. In a moment the community of Jews, Romas and Serbs, that had been working closely together, became groups of 'we' and 'them'.

A children's rights organisation, C31, and Fund B 92 media-company, with support from Kalmar County Museum, developed a program at the former Jewish cultural centre in Belgrade. They held several workshops for pupils; the last workshop included a short, one-hour, Time Travel event to 16 April 1941 followed by a discussion/reflection of today on discrimination, tolerance and solidarity. The participants in the Time Travel event were divided into Jews, Romas and Serbs. In the beginning of the event everybody worked together to help wounded and homeless people in Belgrade – recently occupied by the Germans (Insert Figure 4.9). Suddenly it was announced that all Jews had to register within three days, otherwise they would be shot. Immediately Serbs and Romas asked themselves 'do I support the Jews'? And the Jews asked themselves 'do I go underground or do I register'? There was a vivid discussion with many ideas.

It was interesting to see the change of atmosphere after the announcement. Though the groups that worked to help the needy were united in the beginning, they became a disoriented and puzzled group of hesitant people, many thinking about themselves and their own group. The 'we' changed, and some of the persons in the 'we' in only a few minutes became 'them'.

During the workshop after the Time Travel event there was an immediate connection to today and to the war in the 1990s. Participants asked 'who are 'we'? 'Who are 'they'? Can even 'they be included in 'we'? The Time Travel event opened up space for reflections and discussions.

The organisation C31 also developed a program in the city of Kragujevac to address the massacre of more than 2700 civilians on 21 October 1941. This massacre has affected the city ever since. Several monuments and a museum building have been built recently and the massacre is commemorated every year. The goal of this project was to look more into the future than into the past, to create hopes and visions by young people. About 100 students from ten schools took part in several workshops to prepare for the event. The final commemoration event included a remembrance of what happened in 1941, then an act of forgiveness to humanity to make it possible to leave the horrible past and finally the way forward, where the students wrote short manifests for the future.

Figure 4.10. The commemoration event on the massacre of civilians in 1941 in Kragujevac, Serbia. The event were divided into three parts: remembering the past, seeking of forgiveness and manifest for the future. It included ceremonies, symbols, reflections and words of value.

So, what is the conclusion from the programs in Serbia? One insight is that it is highly sensitive to deal with recent conflicts. The Time Travel outcomes suggest that it is sometimes better to take up sensitive issues in a past setting, like World War II. This makes it easier for people to speak openly. Program results also indicate the importance of the process: meetings, workshops and finally the event. It would have been a lot more difficult to find an understanding and engagement without this multi-level approach. In the process participants meet in mutual learning and commitment. Another experience is that ceremonies mean a lot to people, when hard facts are connected to emotions, the mind and the soul, in ceremonials and visualization (Figure 4.10). The event in Kragujevac, though keeping the terrible massacre in mind, focussed on the future. The act of forgiveness in the event, between the past and the future, worked as a way to leave behind mistrust and find strength for the future. The evaluations show that the programs have allowed the students to learn critical thinking on the use and misuse of history, causes and results of discrimination, and have promoted tolerance and diversity. The next step would be to involve the youth to effect change in the local community.

Applied history

The Time Travel method, in the way it has been developed by Kalmar County Museum and Bridging Ages, is a pedagogical tool to address contemporary issues by using the local past. Sometimes a Time Travel event looks like a re-enactment of the past, but that is not the main idea. The Time Travel method is a process based on the use of history today – applied history. It is about today but uses local historical experiences and modern pedagogical tools. In the Time Travel concept history becomes relevant and meaningful for people of today. The matter is not to convince people of the importance of history or local historical sites. The point of departure is instead today's issues and today's people in a historical perspective; that is to find the benefits of heritage in our lives and society to make a difference.

An important idea in Time Travel is *reflection* – to give a chance to reflect on today's issues by using similar events from the past. Key questions are formulated in the Time Travel event, questions of today and the past. 'Learning areas' are created where the chosen issues are discussed. The historical setting makes it easier to relax and open up for reflections and discussions. The Time Travel event gives a historical comparison of how a similar issue was solved in the past; it transforms the issue, opens up for reflection in a 'safe space' where sensitive issues can be discussed while doing something with the hands at the same time.

A Time Travel does not solve the problem addressed; it provides the opportunity for problem solving. As a person expressed after a Time Travel event, 'reflection starts reaction'. It needs to be put into a bigger context to be effective. The preparation before the event and the evaluation afterwards is an essential part of the concept. The Time Travel method is a process that often takes quite a lot of time. If it becomes a one-day event, the impact is more shallow. Maybe the most important advantage is bringing people together, often people of different ideas and traditions, to meet, discuss in a mutual respect and have a common goal to organise a historical Time Travel or a similar event. The Time Travel method is a way to use 'soft power', the ability to attract, cooperate and find common solutions instead of using force, commands and hard power.

The Time Travel method has grown into new countries and organisations and engages a lot of people. The concept is developing all the time in different contexts. The concept was not the same ten years ago as it is now, and probably it's going to be similar but different ten years from now. The goals, content, methods and target groups always need to be up for discussion and adapted to new demands in an ever-changing society.

There are many pitfalls. It requires quite a lot of effort to be successful. The Time Travel process takes time, and it is quite an amount of effort to use several of the components. Not everybody is prepared or has the time to do that. The extensive work is probably the main reason why more organisations have not followed. And the process needs a driving person and a committed team. The skills of the leaders in the event itself are essential to reach a positive outcome. If the leader in an activity cannot raise the key questions in an inclusive way, the discussion might fail. And if the participating group is not prepared for the content of the Time Travel event, it is difficult to have the interaction that is needed. Also it is not always easy to evaluate after the Time Travel process if you have achieved your goals, in what way the project has contributed to cohesion and understanding?

Returning to Sweden, the Time Travel programs have continued in the Kalmar region all the time with many trainings and events. The change to focus more on contemporary issues, not the history itself but how it is used today and the usage of key questions, started abroad, especially through the Time Travel programs in South Africa. The Time Travels in the Kalmar region have also started to shift focus from learning about history to learning through history by focussing more on social inclusion. Integration and social cohesion has become more and more emphasised in the work. It was an advantage for the Time Travel method to go abroad, to be challenged and to modify the focus. And the shift is supported by recent trends in the society and in museum education.

Conclusion

The Time Travel method as developed by Kalmar County Museum has a focus on contemporary issues in a learning process, using the local past. In the examples the contemporary issues have been segregation, cohesion, democratic development, sustainable land use and effects of war, but any issue can be used. Emphasis in the pedagogical method is on the Time Travel process, where people meet, discuss and research in informal education as in study groups or in formal education for students at school. Emphasis is also on the Time Travel event, a fictional role play at a local historical site. The key questions give the focus in the event, where the learning takes place in small groups when participants discuss and do practical work with the common decisions at the end.

As the Time Travel concept has grown, there has been a need to define the method, both to keep the Bridging Ages group together and to delimit other groups who might be doing Time Travels in other ways. According to the five principles local sites and stories are important, and connection to today in the key questions are essential as well as several partners and several perspectives and dialogue. The Time Travel process is underlined and the event is part of this process. Of course it is inevitable that when so many countries and institutions are involved, the Time Travel method is also adapted to the local situation and the local interest. The examples in this chapter are taken from developing programs where the Time Travel clearly has met the needs in society: the need for reconciliation in Montague and Freedom Park; the need for sustainable land use in a semi-arid region (Ratelgat); the need for a local democratic engagement (Kliptown) and to develop hopes and tolerance in Serbia. The Time Travel method has been a way to make people meet, reflect and contribute to the building of the community.

There are many challenges. It is easy to inspire and start but more difficult to sustain. It would be interesting to come back to the communities mentioned in five or ten years. What is left? Did the projects give a push for change?

In the Time Travel method the role of cultural historians and museums has extended to contribute to any issue in society, for cohesion and community building. According to the ICOM statues, 'A museums is an institution in the service of society and its development' (ICOM Statues 2007). This is what the Time Travel method tries to do.

Acknowledgements

I thank my colleagues at Kalmar County Museum, Sweden, for the many years of cooperation. I also thank my partners in the Bridging Ages organization, in all the 20 countries where I have been working; for this article a special thanks to friends and colleagues in South Africa and Serbia.

References

Hunner, Jon and Westergren, Ebbe. 2011. Engaging the Present through the Past. *Museum International* Vol. 249–250.
  This Unesco museum magazine used a double issue to publish several of the presentations from the Bridging Ages conference in Kalmar, Sweden 2010.

Ozola, Agrita. (ed.) 2006. *Time Travels. Innovative and Creative Methods of Historic Environment Education in Modern Museums.* Tukums museum, Latvia.
  Various authors describe creative methods of Historic Environment Education and Time Travels from the museum perspective. The book was launched at the Bridging Ages conference in Tukums, Latvia 2007.

Westergren, Eklund, Aldestam, Marais, Weldon, Jordan, Randle, Laubscher, Mangiagalli, Parkington, Khan, Fatyela, van Rensburg 2012. This Place has Meaning. Case Studies of Time Travels and Historic Environment Education, South Africa 2006–2010. 3rd edition.
  This booklet presents the start of the Time Travel method in South Africa, background, learning and seven examples of Time Travel events in Western Cape, KwaZulu-Natal and North West Province. The title is a quotation from a teacher after a Time Travel at a site that is now used for camping.

Westergren, Ebbe. 2006. Seven Steps towards In-depth Teaching in Historic Environments. Time Traveling as an Educational Method. Kalmar läns museum, Sweden.
  The English version of the SEVEN steps describes short the steps in the Time Travel process. It is a short summary of the manual in Swedish.

Westergren, Ebbe. (ed.) 2006. Holy Cow – This is great! Report from a Symposium on Historic Environment Education and Time Travels in Vimmerby, Sweden, November 2004.
  Here are all the 13 presentations from the first Bridging Ages meeting, in Vimmerby, Sweden.

Westergren, Ebbe. (ed.) 2004. 'Jag trodde det skulle bli tråkigt, men...'. Kulturmiljöpedagogik och historiska tidsresor under 20 år. Årsboken Kalmar län.
  In this annual book from Kalmar County Museum in 2004, many perspectives of the Time Travel method are described: museum, school, community. The focus is on Kalmar County, but there are also several international contributions, in Swedish.

Use the past, Create the Future, The Freedom Charter 1955–2015, Public Time Travel event in Kliptown, South Africa, in print.
  This is a presentation of the public Time Travel event in Kliptown, Soweto, June 2015. Half the book gives a presentation of the historical scenario and event, half the book includes how the participant interpreted the ten clauses of the Freedom Charter in today's South Africa, 2015.

Sites and Stories. The Time Travel method in Entebbe, Uganda. December 2015.
  A magazine that presents the introduction of the Time Travel method in Uganda 2013–2014.

Webpage. www.bridgingages.com
The homepage of Bridging Ages organisation with goals, missions, definitions, newsletters and examples of Time Travels throughout the world.

You Tube. www.youtube.com/watch?v=0kPV14QSlV0&t=641s
A Legacy of Wisdom - a Time Travel to 1986 in Ikageng, Potchefstroom.
A 15-minute video on a Time Travel event in the township of Ikageng, Potchefstroom, South Africa, including explanations of the Time Travel method

Chapter 5

To Make and to Experience Meaning
How Time Travels are Perceived amongst Participants

Niklas Ammert and Birgitta E. Gustafsson

Abstract

Time travels provide the opportunity for participants to make an imaginary trip back in time to learn about places, times and events, and to learn about themselves. To travel in time can be described as an encounter between the past and the present. Such an experience encourages participants to relate the present to the past and to reflect upon their own lives as they interact with another time. In that way one can replace an 'us and them' attitude with an approach that unites people and highlights what they have in common. This type of encounter carries the potential for meaning-making. Merging the 'now and then' with 'similar and different' can make it possible to understand one's own place in – and relation to – history. But how do participants perceive time travels, what do they learn, what is their view of the past, the present, the future, themselves and the other? In the participator's reflections we have identified how they perceive different narratives with potential for meaning-making.

Keywords: Time travels, participants, narratives, meaning, pupils

Introduction

Time travelling, professionally arranged by museums at historical sites, provides the opportunity for participants to make an imaginary trip back in time to learn about significant places, times and events, and to learn about themselves. To travel in time can be described as an encounter between now and then. Such an interlude encourages participants to relate the present to the past and to reflect upon their own lives as they interact with the unfamiliar time. In that way one can replace an 'us and them' attitude with an approach that unites people and highlights what they have in common. This type of encounter carries the potential for meaning-making. Merging the 'now and then' with 'similar and different' can make it possible to understand one's own place in – and relation to – history. 'Dealing with the past is not an escape; escape is when you focus on the present and future with dogged concentration that is blind to the heritage of the past that influences us and that we must live with' (Schlink 1999).

In this chapter, from a didactic position, we first discuss time travels as meaning-making processes. Second, we present a model to analyse how participants interpret time travelling and in what way the participants express meaning when talking about time travels and their historical experiences. The participants are pupils in secondary school and visitors – mainly tourists – at historical sites in southern Sweden. Our goal is to provide a useful tool for teachers and organizers of time travels when staging and evaluating time travels as a meaning-making event.

Learning in terms of meaning-making

Meaning-making is a crucial concept in this chapter. The term *meaning-making* refers here to an educational approach in which learning occurs during interactions between people or between people and a narrative. It cannot be seen, therefore, as something that is isolated and occurs within the individual's own head. Learning is, from this perspective, a process in which individuals in a social context challenge

Figure 5.1. Time travel at an outdoor festival.

themselves and their existing thought patterns through cultural and temporal encounters. Time travels provide for such cultural encounters, which can occur amongst individuals, groups, ideas and conceptual worlds.

Meaning-making entails being able to relate oneself to the events of the time travel. The participants understand the world if they are involved in the events that are enacted. Time travelling can be seen as an arena in which one can understand oneself in relation to one's surroundings. In this approach meaning-making can be seen as a confrontation that sets one's own experience in motion. It hereby creates the possibility of catching a glimpse of what are hidden as prejudices and that which is often taken for granted. When experiences from time travelling are subjected to discussion and a common reflection, new meaning can be created. This can be viewed as a creative act, and something new emerges from these conversations that is greater than what each individual can envision on his/her own (Fritzén and Gustafsson 2007).

Time travels thus bring along didactic questions: how do the participants express meaning when talking about the time travel experience or experiences from historic role playing (Figure 5.1)? What relation between the past and the present is created through encountering the time travel narratives (see also van Boxtel *et al.* 2011)

Meaning and narratives

What is the background for the discussion about learning as a meaning-making process? The theoretical starting point of our argument has drawn inspiration from the philosopher Charles Taylor (1991) and his discourse and analysis of modern Western society. Taylor sees societal phenomena as a series of life dilemmas. Western society today is coloured by individualism, argues Taylor. When the external and uniting 'order' (context of meaning) collapsed in the mid-20th century, the context of meaning changed. Uniting orders were no longer comprehensive and shifted towards an emphasis on individual well-being. This relocation of meaning was the source of the modern freedom to choose one's own lifestyle from a myriad of possibilities. When contexts of meaning collapse, instrumental explanations are given more room in people's lives. Taylor (1991) also argues that people are increasingly captured by instrumental and common-sense reasoning – rational thinking that has nothing to do with overarching value systems. If a value system is unclear, then it is difficult to ensure normative functions in everyday life. What is considered right and true are the ideas that correspond to one's own values. When a common value system is lacking, there is a risk that such a society – according to Richard Harvey Brown (1987) – can create a sense of lack of belonging, social isolation and mindless conformism. In such a society, the route to self-understanding becomes each individual's responsibility to find. And only in a genuine interaction with others can I, according to Taylor (1991), find my self-understanding.

This interpretation of Taylor and Brown, theories that are written in a context other than the educational lead, in our perspective, to challenges for schools, museums and other potential organisers of time travels who are responsible for staging conditions for learning. In an individualized society we argue that education needs to engage more than concepts, dates and facts. Education also needs to take responsibility in challenging the learning individual´s values, attitudes and moral standpoints to confront each one's meaning-making. If education is to prepare for life, then the future school, and education in general, needs to be involved in the discourse about learners' meaning-making (Gustafsson 2008). The challenge we discuss in this chapter is a question of how to stage the time travel or historical role play as a meaning-making arena that creates opportunity for the participants' self-understanding and understanding of the world.

There is an applicable approach to meaning-making in our argumentation. History creates conditions for meaning as people interact in context and are able to understand, interpret and relate to the content. However, meaning-making here is considered a bidirectional process, and a pre-understanding is of importance for the interpretation of narratives. In this way and at the same time, the encounters with history offer and create meaning. History is narratives about people, societies, events, change and continuity in complex contexts that create meaning (Almqvist *et al.* 2008).

The German historian Jörn Rüsen stresses the importance of meaning to understand the content of history and how history is effective over time as a historical culture. Rüsen argues that history is when the past – and the story of the past – creates meaning; 'history is time transformed into sense' (Rüsen 2000:61). When we interpret the narratives, and when they encounter our experiences, new pieces of knowledge can fit into a wider context. History is not only an object to study. It becomes a part of our lives as we use history to interpret and understand our present time and future. The central function of the narrative is therefore to stimulate and develop historical consciousness amongst individuals as well as groups. The philosopher Paul Ricœur (1984) describes people's ability to experience reality as narratives, which are necessary for the historical consciousness. To develop knowledge and to experience meaning, individuals interact with the content through their questions. This is a process that is built on experiences, knowledge and references but also prejudices and common assumptions. This meaning-making process is, as we mentioned initially, a sociocultural activity where individuals interact (Öhman 2008; Rogoff 1995). In a time travel context, this perspective is highly relevant.

Time travels create a common experience that can become a new interpretative horizon. It is in the encounter with a new horizon, with the unfamiliar, that one's own limits of understanding might expand (Biesta and Burbules 2003; Gadamer 1989). Learning is here described as a situational process, which means that everything must be understood in relation to the system of which that learning is a part (Säljö 2000). A travel through time creates this kind of situational context of meaning. Through time travels and emersion in historical role playing, the participant encounters a narrative that contains characters and events that bring the past to life. A way to achieve this is to allow the framework story to be the common thread that weaves together all of the subplots into a cohesive work of realistic fiction. Short stories and the basic elements of drama can be useful here for establishing time, place, character and dramatic events. The plot can be based on a work of literature, a letter, a piece of music or a work of art to place the participants into a certain context. The time travellers interact with the plot; therefore, it must offer a context that creates meaning. In what way the narrative comes alive for the participant depends also on the staging of the narrative and the participant's own personal narrative. If time travel is staged as somewhat ambiguous, intimate and complex with a dramatic plot that has intrigue, subplots and tension, then it will result in a greater effect on the participants and a higher chance for their involvement. The more complex the plot is, the greater the participants' freedom is to construe their own interpretations of the narrative that are challenging and unfamiliar (Fritzén and Gustafsson 2007).

Analytical concepts

Jörn Rüsen's categories of narratives give us analytical tools for the interpretation of how time travels are perceived amongst participants (2005). Rüsen's categories describe how different kinds of narrative send diverse types of messages from the past and how the past is related to the present and future. The narratives have variant basic structures that are interpreted by the participants who use their narrative competence and their historical consciousness. The categories express different types of narratives that become useful in our interpretation of the participants' meaning-making when encountering the past. In this chapter we do not analyse the time travel narratives themselves; we change perspective and analyse how participants describe, experience and interpret the narratives offered in time travels or historical role plays and, in particular, how the participants express meaning. The categories of narratives must not be considered as stages in a hierarchical system, rather as a non-linear framework.

According to Rüsen's (2005) categorizing, there are four different types of historical narratives with ambition to tell about the past. First, the *traditional narrative* describes the past as eternal, permanent and evident. Nothing changes, and the past may be repeated as sameness over time. In this category we place messages that say 'that is how it was at that time; sometimes it is the same today'. History is just waiting to be unveiled by historians and archaeologists looking for 'the truth'. It is possible to make the past come alive, but it happened in the past and belongs to the past. The second category is the *exemplary narrative*, which stresses rules, patterns of life and codes of conduct as guiding principles for society and for people. A picture/view of affinity and proximity from people in the past are given. It is *historia magistra vitae* (Cicero 1862), on a macro as well as on a micro level. The third category Rüsen describes is the *critical narrative*. This narrative takes its starting point in present time, and the historical events are related to the present. The past is no longer particularly valuable from our point of view. This category indicates the fact that time changes, and it is important to formulate a critical history. This critical and alternative narrative offers relief or distance. In this category, the past is considered as a more or less isolated time dimension. The fourth category is the *genetic narrative*, where the past is changeable and necessarily embedded in the always-vanishing present time. The narrative expresses the idea of change as natural when regarding the past. Genetic narratives show that every epoch reflects what is unique for that period and that different narratives are told at different times. We are a result of the past, and at the same time the path to the future. The present is a stage of change between the past and the future.

The participants' encounter with the past

We now turn to the empirical material for a discussion about how participants in time travel and historical role play relate the past to the present. Moreover, in what way do they reflect upon their own life when talking about the unfamiliar time they encountered in the time travel or role play?

The analysis in this chapter builds on the following earlier studies, and we emphasize that it is not primary data that are used. Our study derives data from: Lund (2000), Sundberg (2000), Fritzén and Gustafsson (2007), Gustafsson (2002), Ammert (2009) and Gustafsson and Pros (2013).[1] Lund (2000) and Sundberg (2000) have evaluated time travels at Kronobäck and Södra bruket. Kronobäck, 40km north of Kalmar in southern Sweden, is a thirteenth-century hospital and later a monastery for the Order of St John. Södra bruket is an industrial environment on the island of Öland. A century ago alum was produced there. Lund´s and Sundberg´s studies focus on how primary and secondary school pupils experience time travels. In Lund´s study the pupils travelled back in time to 1899, and in Sundberg´s study to 1490. The result shows that the pupils appreciate the community and friendship. They enjoyed 'acting', and they found it natural to discuss different ways of living. Amongst the primary school pupils there is a risk that the activities and the 'doing' is more important than the issues about how people lived in the past and how

---

[1] The authors have given their oral consent for their use of empirical data from their reports.

people live today. The results of Lund´s (2000) and Sundberg´s (2000) studies are relevant for the present study because of the pupils' answers and discussions about how they experienced and interpreted the past during a time travel.

Fritzén and Gustafsson (2007) have observed time travels arranged for pupils 10–11 years old in primary school and a time travel program for tourists at Eketorp castle on Öland in southern Sweden. On Öland there are several castles from previous ages. Eketorp was used in the Bronze Age, in the Iron Age and even later in medieval time. Today it is restored and used as a living museum for guided tours, role plays, historical events and concerts. The observations were conducted on behalf of the Kalmar County Museum in order to provide a basis for the development work of the museum's educational program and particularly the time travels. The result from Fritzén and Gustafsson's study showed that for the organizer of educational events such as time travels, there is a need to keep up an open discussion of which perspective(s) the museum wishes to stage in the time travel. In what way do the narratives that are staged in a time travel contain harmony, threat, fear or protection? The time travel can challenge boundaries and become a starting point for reflection and critical discussion (Fritzén and Gustafsson 2007).

Gustafsson's (2002) study focuses on how two primary school classes, with pupils, 11–12 years old, together with classmates and their teachers, experienced a time travel. The time travels were arranged by and took place at a museum in a reconstructed historic environment. The study discusses the conditions for the pupils' experiences of being moved in time through the time travel and to what extent the historical experience created the opportunity for the pupils' self-understanding by relating to the past.

Ammert (2009) studied how 12-year old pupils in primary school and tourists encountered the uses of history, the historic narratives and the historic environment at Eketorp castle. The results show that scientific, political-pedagogical and commercial uses of history are most common. The scientific use of history means that the exhibitions and the time travels mainly convey facts. At the same time there is a political-pedagogical message about openness to strangers and the importance of democracy. For Eketorp it is necessary to purchase merchandise and to arrange concerts and events. In that way they perform a commercial use of history.

In Gustafsson and Pros' 2013 study 115 pupils, 14 years old in secondary school, answered a questionnaire about their experiences in encountering the past staged as a time travel at Kalmar castle. Kalmar castle is a well-restored renaissance castle in the city of Kalmar. Gustafsson and Pros present how eighth-grade pupils reflect on a time travel focussing on crimes and punishments. The pupils were fascinated by the 'living history', and they found it interesting and effective for learning. They also reflected on similarities and differences regarding crimes and punishments in the past and the present.

In the following section we analyse the statements drawn from these previous studies. We will identify in what way the statements express the relation between the present and the past. We discuss how the participants talk about their interpretations of time travels and how the participants express meaning. For example, a participant in Lund (2000:90) stated: 'I don't think I have learnt how it was and how they lived, I have experienced it' (Figure 5.2).

Figure 5.2. Casting: Kalmar County Museum.

Sameness over time – traditional narrative

'Yes, a lot of history we study explains why it is like it is nowadays.'

'You can see the obvious patterns and mistakes in the past repeated in present time.'

'You learn to reflect on the past and the present'
(Gustafsson and Pros 2013, 18).

The pupils' experiences from the time travel at Kalmar castle, expressed in the quotations above, show how the participants relate the past to the present. The past appears as an explanation for how society looks today. They perceived similarities and patterns between the past and the present. The likenesses seem to serve as a way to understand the past in light of the present, and in that way the narratives about the past create meaning. At the same time patterns from the past help pupils understand the present. In Sundberg (2000:69) a pupil points at resemblances over time in a very concrete way when stating the following about the principles for agricultural implements: 'the plough, there are certain similarities. . . . There are not many differences'.

When the pupils talk about the parallels to today's society, these statements fall within the traditional narrative category as sameness over time (Rüsen 2005). This is not surprising since time travel organisers often point out in their explanations for tourists and pupils 'that's how it was at that time'(Ammert 2009). It is not clear whether this means that people in the present should regard the past as a contrast or if it is meant to be the key to helping us to understand the past and to see it as natural, conceivable and valid for the conditions at that time. Such ambiguity arises when the past is brought to life as a narrative that offers us glimpses of a different life

A message from the past – exemplary narrative

After spending a day at Kalmar castle with time travel experiences and activities on the theme 'crimes and punishments', the pupils expressed their experiences: 'the punishments were more brutal in the past. I miss that a little today. They [the punishments] are more humane now, but it was right in the past' (Gustafsson and Pros 2013: 19). In this quotation the pupil does not dismiss the punishments in the past. This statement can be based on the view that today's punishments can be seen too 'humane'. Such a statement expresses that the pupil has internalised the issue and collated it to a personal opinion. The expression can be seen as an example of how the pupil experiences both affinity and proximity from people in the past, which can be understood according to Rüsen (2005) as an exemplary narrative category.

At another cultural environment, Eketorp fortress on the island Öland, the following incident unfolds.

Suddenly, an unfamiliar man appears in the fortress. There is something mysterious about him. Hulda and Frödis tell the children to follow him and see what he's doing. In these troubled times one cannot always trust a stranger who enters the fortress. Some children are sent to fetch the chief of the fortress. The stranger claims to be a fishmonger, and he starts to ask the children about life in the fortress. The children are quiet and suspicious in response. Chief Edmund senses danger and becomes involved. He orders everyone to imprison the fishmonger. The children react immediately, taking the man prisoner, locking him up, and then carefully examining his basket. The drama escalates. (Fritzén and Gustafsson 2009:40)

In this time travel at Eketorp the pupils encounter how strangers were treated at that time. People in a small society like the castle were dependent on each other, not least in times of threat and trouble. Eketorp is a castle for defence where people moved in times of trouble and war. There is a message of affinity in the time travel narrative in relation to strangers and foreigners. This message is drawn from the past as something for the pupils to consider in the context of their own time. The narrative carries a possibility for the time traveller to reflect upon how to treat and encounter strangers. The incident ends up as a moral message of openness to strangers, the value of plurality and how we in present times should treat strangers. The challenge for organisers of the time travel is to stage these exemplary narratives where human and societal needs are used in the narrative to illustrate phenomena that take place in the past as well as in the present. To achieve this it is important to let values and ideals from the present encounter values and ideals from the past. And in this way they challenge the participants' beliefs about the norms and values of our time. Our values serve as a framework for the meaning-making and for the interpretation of the past.

It is a better life today – critical narrative

The time travel at Kalmar castle with pupils from secondary school, 15 years old, becomes the starting point for reflection on their experiences, and the pupils' meaning-making gets expressed in their narratives about the relationship between then and now. The pupils emphasise that the past is based on the conditions of today. 'It is hard to understand exactly how life was but one understands that the punishments were much harder than now' (Gustafsson and Pros 2013: 16). Definitely, it is better nowadays if you compare in Sweden (Gustafsson and Pros 2013: 19).

The time traveller implies that the past was worse and life was harder than today. The pupils express the difference between now and then, and the sense of distance to the past is clear. At another historic site, Kronobäck the thirteenth-century hospital, and a time travel back to year 1899, a pupil expresses the following sentiment. 'We got the chance to apprehend life in the past. Nowadays it is mostly not that way; we don't have to clean the stairway, we don't have to graze potatoes or wash our clothes by hand. But we could experience life then and it was rather fun to see how they lived then. But it was unfair that we had to wait for them all the time' (Lund 2000: 97).

The pupils put the narratives about the past as a contrast to the situation today. They describe the past as different, unfair and mostly worse than their own lives. The participants dissociate themselves from habits and laws in the past. However, if the past is experienced as too different from the pupils' own lives, the past appears less valuable from the present position and reinforces the critical image of the past. The pupils' reflections show a critical narrative where the past can be interpreted like an isolated time dimension that differs from the present. This is expressed in the quote that follows in which two pupils, 11–12 in age, are talking about the time travel back to 1936 and where their reflections start in the present:

> L: [Now] we kind of say . . . if someone says 'will you do the dishes? Mmm, yes, if I get my pocket money, you do it for the money'.
> H: Then, they didn't do it for the money, because they had to do it, otherwise they were beat up or something like that. They did it to get food . . . yes to survive.
> (Gustafsson 2002:156)

During a day of time travels and historical experiences at Eketorp castle, the visitors found themselves right in the middle of acts of war. Ammert (2009:9–10) describes it:

> Men in historic clothes use bows, fence with heavy swords and look threatening. After a while the fight subsides. However no visitor knows what the fight was all about, who fought who or how it ended up. One of the combatants says: "Now we have a break until two o'clock". Of course spare-time soldiers must have a break, but for the visitor it is confusing whether the soldiers want to picture the medieval age or 2005. It can be perceived somewhat confusing to visitors if the staging of time travel does not take into account a sense of authenticity or to involve participants in the drama. A lasting impression is then that the participants are unsure about what the time travel or the role play says. One of the visitors expresses that "it is awesome, but what is it all about?"

How a time travel is staged affects the participants' meaning-making in the sense that the time travel can estrange the participants' perceptions of the past and thereby enhance prejudices about the life that was lived in the past. The staging can prevent the participants from seeing the relationship now and then. The past then appears as such a critical narrative, and it becomes a distanced relief to the present (Figure 5.3).

The times they are a-changing – genetic narrative
Further examples from the time travel at Kalmar castle with pupils who are 15 years old pronounce the relationship now and then. At the same time they include

Figure 5.3. The battle of Eketorp, July 2005 (Photograph by David Bergström, Barometern).

reflections of the future: 'when you study what has happened in the past, you will get a better overall view of what perhaps is to come', and 'you may get a better opinion of how punishment was different in the past. At the same time it tells you something about the punishments today' (Gustafsson and Pros 2013: 18).

The pupils express awareness of change. It stresses the present time as a changing point between the past and the future. In a genetic narrative the pupils reflect on our current setting, in relation to the past as well as to the future. The pupils discuss official punishments such as when a person was singled out, and the public despised and spit on her. Afterwards this person could never come back to town. The time travel is a carrier of a narrative that opens for a reflection and comparison to our time, where people risk being singled out on Facebook and in other social media (Gustafsson and Pros 2013: 19). They see the relations between the present and the past and the future as something that can enable empathy, interpretation, understanding and a historical overview. The pupils connect the past to the present and show in their examples and arguments what they find important and what creates meaning.

At another time travel event at Eketorp castle, which includes adult participants in the role play, the following statements were expressed:

F: This is my life. I like the friendship and . . . kind of bonding amongst us, and I feel like I belong; I feel at home in the past.
R: Because of your interest, your values or?
F: Yes, and it's a way for me to handle everyday life. My life is richer and I am not that stuck in current and paltry issues.
R: Could you give an example?
F: Material things, we have too much of everything. When you live as at medieval time here at Eketorp or other places, you see what is necessary. We have to change that in the future, we must learn to live without all the technical stuff and all the terrible modern weapons. Here we fight with bows and swords.
(Ammert 2009: 12).

This can be interpreted as an example of a genetic narrative where the participators feel that the medieval time is a unique epoch that opens for reflections about the present time. Values from another time get embedded in present time when the participator is questioning our time and its hunt for *material things*. A time travel means an inter-temporal journey with clothes and props, but most importantly it is a mental journey that creates existential reflections about the participant's own life.

Conclusions

Time travel is an exciting educational method full of possibilities. It has a potential to create experiences, genuine feelings and an understanding of relations between the past and the present. In this chapter our aim was to analyse how the time travel participants perceived the time travel and how meaning-making is expressed in their reflections.

Reality is not a narrative, but it is told as a narrative and so is the past (Ricœur 1984). Separate occasions are brought together in narratives, which represent contexts and create meaning (Ankersmit 2012). Besides, when we insert our own interpretations in wider narratives and contexts, they become more relevant, and they may deepen our meaning-making. In that way there are contexts of meaning – or a uniting order – which, if we recall Charles Taylor, is crucial for individuals as well as for societies. Participants create and experience meaning during time travels. Meaning is made by challenge but also by recognition. The expressions for meaning can be identified when the participators describe and reflect on time travels in terms of how they have been stimulated or trigged. The participants' interpretations of the past can be understood as a message from the past, and at the same time it gives perspectives on the future. We interpret and make meaning from our understanding of the connection of the past to the present and occasionally to the future – through narratives with signs of a traditional, exemplary, critical or genetic ways of interpreting. In a time travel the participants interact with people 'in the past' as with themselves. By this inter-temporal, sociocultural meaning-making, participants use their own references in encounters framed in wider contexts (Öhman 2008, 26).

In view of the time travel, participants' statements, and with Rüsen's analytical categories presented as different historical narratives, our intention was to deepen the discussion on how time travel can be perceived and ultimately how it can raise some issues as a consequence of the way it is perceived. In the participators' reflections we have identified that they stress issues of certain importance, often personal or societal. Reflections and reactions based on ethical values are frequent. We interpret the reflections as expressions for meaning that say something about what is important for the participants. When the participators reflect upon the time travel as a traditional narrative, it offers glimpses of a different life at a different time. The messages from the past bridge connections and recognition over time. In an exemplary narrative the participators express that moral and ethical directions in life get perceived. There is a risk that the time travels overemphasise an exemplary narrative where the message performs as moral lessons. Then the past time can be used as a unidirectional tool to persuade people. In the participators' critical narratives the contrasts shed light on the present, and the past appears as a time dimension that differs from the present. There is a risk to be too critical and dismiss the past from a present point of view and emphasise differences rather than similarities. Neither of the alternatives have a mutual connection over time. The genetic narrative is the educationally most interesting because the participants place themselves in the centre of the historical transformation, and a reflection on their current position takes place. By entering a specific character within the time travel, the participant can 'walk in someone else's shoes' and his or her own life thereby can be mirrored in the meeting with 'the Other'. Such a reflection can contribute by challenging the time traveller's understanding of oneself and the surrounding world. According to Taylor (1991) and Brown (1987) such a process is important. Within a society immersed by individualism, self-understanding and contextualized 'world views' there is a need to question. In a time of diversity and ambiguity educators have to face this with a mission to strengthen the individual's critical and self-critical ability (Bauman 2001). The time travel confrontation with the unfamiliar time, story and culture can become such an encounter between different conceptual worlds in which the limits of one's own conceptions can be challenged.

This statement leads to a challenge when it comes to staging time travels. Due to previous research, pupils at school often highlight the practical chores and activities during the time travel more than the content and the message. Pupils regard the time travel as a pleasant and funny alternative to the ordinary work at school. A consequence is that the time travel may end up as a 'happening' without substance. There is a risk that the multi-perspective experiences, in which the participants reflect on their current position, may not get considered. Previous research has also shown that organisers of time travels are busy conducting the time travel and show less reflection upon their continuing role when it is completed (Fritzén and Gustafsson 2009).

When the time travel is completed it is, from our perspective, important to start a critical reflection together with the participators, a dialogue with an interest to take part in the participants' interpretations and simultaneously challenge the common assumptions that get expressed. It is a question of organising a critical dialogue that creates a situation of new meaning-making. When arguments and the taken-for-granted get placed in a new light the participators' meaning-making' get challenged. According to Taylor (1991) we face a challenge to care about diversity, polyphony and uncertainty that reflect the present we live in. And for this mission we argue that both the organisers of time travel and the schools need to take responsibility for such a mission through such meaning-making dialogues.

Acknowledgements

The authors of the previous studies, Lena Fritzén, Stefan Lund, Daniel Sundberg, Linda Pros and David Gustafsson, have given their oral consent for our use of empirical data from their reports. We sincerely appreciate their accommodating.

References

Almqvist, Jonas, Kronlid, David, Quennerstedt, Mikael, Öhman, Johan, Öhman, Marie and Östman, Leif. 2008. Pragmatiska studier av meningsskapande i *Utbildning and Demokrati* 17(3):11–24.

Ammert, Niklas. 2009. Do You Want Me to Kill You Now? Ett historiedidaktiskt nedslag vid Eketorps fornborg. Kalmar, Högskolan i Kalmar.

Ankersmit, Frank. 2012. *Meaning, Truth and Reference in Historical Representation*. Ithaca, Cornell University Press.

Bauman, Zygmunt. 2001. *The Individualized Society*. Cambridge, UK, Polity Press.

Biesta, Gert and Nicholas Burbules. 2003. *Pragmatism and Educational Research*. Lanham, Rowman and Littlefield.

Brown, Richard Harvey. 1987. *Society as Text: Essays on Rhetoric, Reason and Reality*. Chicago, The University of Chicago Press.

Cicero, Marcus Tullius. 1862. *De oratore*. Leipzig, B. G. Teubner.

Fritzén, Lena and Gustafsson, Birgitta. 2007. Now and then: The similar and the different. Time travels bring schools and museums together. In Agrita Ozola (ed.), *Time Travels. Innovative and Creative Methods of Historic Environment Education in Modern museums*: 31–45. ICOM Latvia, Muzeological Library.

Gadamer, Hans Georg. 1989. *Truth and method*, 2nd ed. London, Sheed and Ward.

Gustafsson, Birgitta E. 2002. Upplevelsen som grund för lärande. In Peter Aronsson and Erika Larsson (eds.), Konsten att lära och viljan att uppleva: Historiebruk och upplevelsepedagogik vid Foteviken, Medeltidsveckan och Jamtli. Centrum för kulturforskning, Växjö universitet, Rapport nr 1.

Gustafsson, Birgitta E. 2008. Att sätta sig själv på spel. Om språk och motspråk i pedagogisk praktik. Växjö, Växjö University Press.

Gustafsson, David and Linda Pros. 2013. *Brott och straff – nu och då: En studie av hur elever i årskurs 8 upplever en historisk upplevelsedag*, Examensarbete, Institutionen för pedagogik, psykologi och idrottsvetenskap, Kalmar and Växjö, Linnéuniversitetet.

Janik, Allan. 1991. Cordelias tystnad. Om reflektionens kunskapsteori. Stockholm, Carlssons.

Karlsson, Klas-Göran. 2010. Europeiska möten med historien: Historiekulturella perspektiv på andra världskriget, förintelsen och den kommunistiska terrorn. Stockholm, Atlantis.

Lund, Stefan. 2000. Rollspelsdagen – Södra bruket i Degerhamn 1899. In Peter Aronsson, Per Gerrevall and Erika Larsson (eds.), *Att resa i tiden: Mål och medel i mötet mellan museum, skola och elever*. Växjö, Växjö universitet, Centrum för kulturforskning, Rapport nr 1.

Öhman, Johan. 2008. Erfarenhet och meningsskapande. In *Utbildning och demokrati* 17(3):25–46.

Ricœur, Paul. 1984. *Time and Narrative*, Vol. 1. Chicago and London. University of Chicago Press.

Rogoff, Barbara. 1995. Observing sociocultural activity on three planes: Participatory appropriation, guided participation and apprenticeship. In James Wertsch, Pablo del Rio and Amelia Alvarez (eds.), *Sociocultural Studies of Mind*: 139–164. Cambridge, Cambridge University Press.

Rüsen, Jörn. 2000. Historical objectivity as a matter of social values. In Joep Leersen and Ann Rigney (eds.), *Historians and Social Values*: 57–68. Amsterdam, Amsterdam University Press.

Rüsen, Jörn. 2004. Berättande och förnuft: Historieteoretiska texter, Göteborg, Daidalos.

Rüsen, Jörn. 2005. History: Narration – Interpretation – Orientation. New York and Oxford, Berghahn Books.

Schlink, Bernhard. 1999. *The Reader*. New York, Vintage Books.

Sundberg, Daniel. 2000. Upplevelsedagen – vid Kronobäcks kloster 1490. In Peter Aronsson, Per Gerrevall and Erika Larsson (ed.), *Att resa i tiden: Mål och medel i mötet mellan museum, skola och elever*. Växjö, Växjö universitet, Centrum för kulturforskning, Rapport nr 1.

Säljö, Roger. 2000. Lärande i praktiken. Ett sociokulturellt perspektiv. Stockholm, Prisma.

Taylor, Charles. 1991. *The Ethics of Authenticity*. Cambridge, Massachusetts, Harvard University Press.

van Boxtel, C., Klein, S. and Snoep, E. (eds.) 2011. *Heritage Education: Challenges in Dealing with the Past*. Amsterdam, The Netherlands Institute for Heritage.

Commentary

Forming Bridges Through Time Travel

Cecilia Trenter

The two chapters in Part 2, one by Ebbe Westergren and the other by Niklas Ammert and Birgitta E. Gustafsson, describe how time travels form bridges between contemporary time travellers and historical contexts, which are communicated in narrative as complex stories in order to make sense of history, to mobilize norms of today and to create identities. South Africa and Serbia, from the prehistoric age, to the renaissance and the industrial era, are the objects of the time travels described in the two articles. The historical settings are quite different epistemological spaces, and the didactic uses are, according to the disparities, also diverse. In Westergren's study, time travels are tools for learning about environmental sustainability, reconciliation and tolerance. Ammert and Gustafsson's chapter focusses on experiencing meaning in a broader perspective transmitted by narrative types such as traditional, exemplary, critical and genetic. The time travellers are pupils of primary school. While Westergren gives deep and extensive description of time travels from the organiser's viewpoint, Ammert and Gustafsson present how the participants interpret the historical destination of time travel in relation to the present. Although the chapters' approaches differ from each other, the didactic potentials of time travels are convincingly highlighted and make way for further discussion on practical methods and the epistemological approaches of time travel as a tool for learning.

The past is not a narrative but is communicated by narratives, write Ammert and Gustafsson, referring to the postmodern discourse on the ontological status of plots and stories and the past. The past as a larder full of potential parts to build bridges between now and then is an inescapable point of view when planning or analysing time travel. History inevitably becomes an object despite the fact that the past consists of complex contexts, and the experiences of the past differ. Westergren discusses the ethical aspects that must be taken into account when choosing representative events and contexts. The need for objectification might be the reason why the organizer of the time-travel described in Ammert and Gustafsson presents the settings as *wie es eigentlich gewesen*, or 'how it really was'; it has to be an epistemologically defined starting point before the interactive travel takes over.

That is, the objectification of the past is necessary. I would argue that one could advance the objectification further by discussing the opposite temporal space in the mediation model, namely the present, in likewise heuristic types. If the idea of the past is interpreted in different narratives, should the present, in which time travel takes place, as well be understood in terms of the Webern ideal types of traditional, exemplary, critical and genetic narratives, despite the characterization of contemporary life as the site for multiple identities, according to Charles Taylor (1991)? Do people actually get into time travelling without any more solid structures than the postmodern pluralism of their identities, or is it possible to understand people's comprehension of nowaday's society in terms of historical narratives?

From which perspective of the present does the time traveller depart? When it comes to the time travels, the intentions and identity are in some respects pronounced. In Westergren's study, the aim of the time travel is well defined as a wake-up call for ethical standpoints of today. Apartheid and civil war are politically loaded historical events and contexts that in their own rights signal values of human rights and the need for tolerance. The time travellers are well aware of the overall aim when participating in time travels in Serbia and South Africa. The aim of time travels in the cases of Ammert and Gustafsson's study are not that specifically defined, except from the claims of authenticity (the traditional narrative). On the contrary, the exemplary narrative such as underlining the consequences of xenophobia, is interleaved in the settings.

It is much more difficult to define the narrative starting point of each single person than to describe the intentions of the organizer. It would take a huge effort to map every epistemological starting point of the individuals who participate in time travel, but one could learn more about how time travel affects people's understandings of the present and the past by combining different time travels in a learning process. One could get inspired by research on re-enactment in which bleed effects refer to when the players let their identities transfer to their characters in the role play, or the inverse relationship as when the players allow the character in the role play to influence their personalities. An arrangement of a series of time travels would create opportunities to examine how different narratives affect the travellers and how the experiences from previous time travelling might affect the next encounter with the past. How would a pupil, who felt that the harsh punishment in the early modern period was more reasonable than the current humanitarian punishment, respond to time travel in South Africa or Serbia? Would the pupil's understanding of the modern penal system's supposed softness alter, or would the pupil perceive that Apartheid's brutality is not comparable with the punishment and crime in the distant pre-modern society and today's society in Sweden? Or would pupils think of civil war in Serbia and Apartheid in South Africa as present time in comparison with early modern time or even prehistoric time that is 'real' history?

The question could be pushed further. Are the Weberian ideal types competing views, or are they complementary narratives in a long learning process? If the critical narrative creates a distance to the past, a gap that creates space to reflect on present time, how does this reflection actually change views of today? The types might reflect stages of a wider perspective of the learning of meaningfulness. For example, how does a critical narrative work to give way to a traditional narrative? To rally around common knowledge of misrepresentations of history such as the national romantic heritage of the horn Viking helmet, puts focus on the misuses of history but implies a traditional narrative (in which the Vikings did not wear horned helmets).

The two articles show unequivocally the potential of time travel tools for learning about the present and the past. The results raise questions about how the perspectives can be widened. The proposal that has been presented here involves a cohesive learning process where several kinds of time travels are carried out by the same individuals. The focus is on the present where heuristic narrative types are communicated, and the examples ultimately elucidate how these narrative types of the present and the past interact with each other.

References

Taylor, Charles. 1991. *The Ethics of Authenticity*. Cambridge, Massachusetts, Harvard University Press.

Part Three

Living the Distant Past

Chapter 6

Performing the Past
Time Travels in *Archaeological Open-air Museums*

Stefanie Samida

Abstract

Historical and archaeological topics have been very popular for many years. This is witnessed by a variety of events and developments, as for example by time travel formats on television as well as by such performances at historic sites or at open-air museums. These historical performances and affective adoptions – bodily and sensual experiences that serve as a medium to the past – attract a large audience. This chapter is devoted to these historical performances and their impact as an educational tool in archaeological open-air museums, especially in Germany where their use is still in its infancy. The first part of the chapter deals with the phenomenon and development of historical performances, while the second focusses on potentials and limits of recent time travel performances in German archaeological open-air museums on the basis of interviews with performers and museum curators. The analysis looks at both the benefits and limitations of living history performances. On the one hand, time travels offer benefits because they stem from the haptic nature of the experience and the ability of the viewer to interact with history through their senses. On the other hand, time travels can, for example, create stereotypical presentations of the past. A look back at the roots and the analysis of contemporary living history performances illustrates that time travels tell us more about the time they are practiced than they do about the past.

Keywords: Living history, reenactment, open-air museums, prehistory, experience, performance.

Introduction

For many years, the public has become increasingly aware of historical and archaeological topics. Large-scale and well-attended exhibitions, an ongoing success of historical television documentaries and a booming market in specialised books and magazines give ample proof of this interest. Since the end of the 1990s there has been a trend towards a more experience-oriented presentation of historical topics, especially in open-air museums. In addition, a growing number of people dream of travelling to past worlds. These historical performances and affective adoptions of the past – in terms of bodily and sensual experiences that serve as a medium to past environments or as a projection screen for interpretations of the past – are well known as 're-enactments', 'living history' or 'time travels' and are seen as a 'global phenomenon not necessarily confined to autochthonous events nor even to factual ones' (Agnew 2004:328). Yet, even though the impact of time travels as an educational tool in archaeological open-air museums – especially in Germany – is still in its infancy, the affective adoption and staging of history is not a new phenomenon. There is a long tradition of performing the past, starting with medieval passion plays and historical pageantries. During the 1970s, there was also a 'resurrection' of similar performances in US open-air museums that spread to Europe during the 1990s. Today, many museums frequently rely on these performances or 'museum theatre events' to increase attendance.

As an educational tool, however, time travels offer potentials beyond the traditional museum exhibit with its showcases and 'mute' objects. These benefits stem from the haptic nature of the experience and the ability of the viewer to interact with history through their senses. In this way, museum visitors can internalise the experience and are more likely to learn or absorb the ideas conveyed in the time travel. However, there are challenges or limitations that require archaeologists, museum directors, re-enactors and visitors to avoid persistent stereotypical presentations of the past through lack of quality standards and self-reflective discussions. The main objectives here are to critically assess the benefits and limitations of living history performances for disseminating scientific knowledge in the context of educating the public and to assess whether time travels tell us more about the time they are practiced than they do about the past.

To achieve this, I draw from the research project 'Living History: Re-enacted Prehistory between Research and Popular Performance' (Centre for Contemporary History Potsdam and University of Tübingen), which lasted from 2011 to 2016. This project focussed on television documentaries, open-air museums, historic sites and 'themed walks' (Samida 2012a; Willner *et al.* 2014). Within this context, my own research was directed at the interactions between professional archaeologists, performers and visitors (scholars, actors and recipients) in selected German open-air museums and historic events. Data used here were collected through interviews in 2012 with re-enactors and museum curators. To provide a historical setting for the discussion of modern-day time travels, I chronicle the phenomenon and development of historical performances and affective adoptions of the past. Here, early acting phenomena are outlined. I then discuss and analyse potentials and limits of recent time travel performances in archaeological open-air museums in Germany.

Historical performances

Beginnings and development

The tradition of performing the past goes back to ancient times. Widely ignored in the discussion of living history's precursors is their similarity to the presentations known as *naumachiae* that were very popular during the Roman Empire. *Naumachiae* can be described as re-enactments of historical naval battles performed by gladiators and people who were sentenced to death. For these spectacles, artificial lakes, amongst others, were created specifically for this purpose. One of the most famous *naumachia* in Roman times was probably the re-enactment of the Battle of Salamis (480 BC), which was staged under Emperor Augustus in the year 2 BC. Moreover, *naumachiae* were not only popular in ancient times but also during the Baroque era (*c.* 1600–1770). For example, at Castle St. Georgen (Bayreuth/Germany), on various occasions, naval battles were staged on the man-made lake surrounding the castle.

Religious or spiritual plays – common in many cultures and confessions – constitute another root of historical performance. They represent a mode of ritual performance and were and are usually carried out at specific times of the year. The most famous Christian plays besides *Krippenspiele* (Christmas pageants) are surely passion plays, which emphasise the suffering and death of Jesus. They were first staged in the Middle Ages and are still performed as the well-known Oberammergau Passion Play (Germany), which was organised for the first time in 1634. Since 1680 this world-famous passion play, in which only the inhabitants of Oberammergau may take part, has been held every ten years. During the play in 2010, each performance lasted more than five hours. Quite as popular as the passion plays is the Roman Catholic procession on the Via Dolorosa in the Old City of Jerusalem (Israel), which takes place annually on Good Friday. According to religious tradition, Jesus had to carry his cross on this path to the Mount of Golgatha where he was crucified. The procession – usually headed by a priest or monk – follows this route and commemorates Jesus's sufferings at nine Stations of the Cross. During this procession, the pilgrims pray and chant. Currently, re-enactments also take place in which people in historical costumes re-enact Jesus's sorrowful path.

Here it might be important to observe that all Christian plays have two things in common: they emerged in medieval times, and the organisers of these 'festivities' were generally towns. These festivals were not reserved only for specific classes but were festivals for all residents independent of their social background. The performers in these festivals, which often lasted hours and even days, usually were and are not clerics but lay people. Thus, a town could have transformed itself into

Jerusalem and the spectators into the townspeople of Jerusalem for the duration of the play (Fischer-Lichte 2012:15). In doing so, the assembled community saw itself as a Christian community, and through the regular repetition of these plays it again and again affirmed this common spirit. By performing such festivals, the participants tried to conquer the fear of pain, suffering, violence and death (Fischer-Lichte 2012:20). Moreover, the participation, whether as a passive observer or an active performer, had a sacramental character, because the Church quite often granted the indulgence. The collective participation in the performance thus gave everyone a sense of community as well as redemption, the forgiveness of sins.

In addition to religious or spiritual plays, another form of historical performances evolved in the last third of the 19th century: *Historische Festzüge* (pageants) were an expression of the emancipation process of the middle class. Their aim was to present the past in a historical procession and at the same time to thereby educate the public. These public pageants, which are sometimes called 'costumed' or 'artistic' pageants, are characterised by their physical involvement and affective experience (embodiment) because they involve 'being there', that is 'experiencing'. For this reason, the pageant and other forms of performing the past are, as Meghan Lau (2011:268) put it, 'powerful tools for the representation of history because they work not simply through reason but through emotion, the body and memory'.

On the one hand, the pageants mainly aimed to renew and to consolidate the potentates' leadership claims, and on the other hand, they were a means of self-expression and of creating identity as a nation, town, village or guild. Thus, the pageants had an identifying function. Furthermore, they can be viewed as an expression of cultural and social progress. Re-enacting the past was to illustrate that history leads to something better (Fischer-Lichte 2012:49).

In 1886 about 1500 costumed actors performed the triumphal procession of a ruler of the Attalid Kingdom, most likely of King Attalus I (Figure 6.1). The pageant, held in the German capital city of Berlin, presented the victorious Hellenes and the defeated Galatians (or Celtic Galatians). What at first glance looks like an entertaining performance was nothing less than an allegory for German history because the Prussians defeated France in the Franco-Prussian War of 1870/1871; and, as a result, the unified German Empire was founded shortly thereafter. Numerous newspapers of that time reported on the pageant in detail and with pictures. Amongst them were, for example, the family magazine *Gartenlaube*, which was popular and widely read in the 19th century, and the *Illustrirte Zeitung*, which was published weekly in Leipzig (see the articles in *Gartenlaube* 1886, No. 31, 540 ff.; *Illustrirte Zeitung* [Leipzig], 10 July 1886).

Figure 6.1. Greek Festival in Berlin, 1886
(Illustrierte Zeitung, 10/7/1886, No. 2245).

But while re-enactments of the ancient world were not very common in German pageants, exceptions are those mentioned above and the one in honour of German Emperor Wilhelm II at the Saalburg at a totally reconstructed Roman fort, the re-enactments of the so-called 'Germanic Prehistory' were rather popular in the early 1900s (see Hartmann 1976). Such anniversary celebrations were held at different places in 1909 to remember the famous Varusschlacht (Battle of the Teutoburg Forest or Varian Disaster) between Roman legions under Varus and Germanic tribes under the leadership of Arminius of the Cherusci (Herman) which took place in AD 9. The largest festival involved several hundred participants in a Germanic pageant that was held in Detmold, a city at the edge of the Teutoburg Forest where a monumental bronze statue of Herman as the liberator of 'Germany' has been standing since 1875.

While Germanic warriors were portrayed in animal skins as oversimplified and stereotyped for a long time, by the beginning of the 20th century the public began to see these early warriors as freedom fighters and as representative of a common nationalistic pride. In this way, the narrative had changed, and a transformation took place even though the re-enactment itself had not been modified. People brought their own experience into it and began to perceive the story differently. The pageants, thus, are an, albeit slight, expression of a metamorphosis that can be ascribed to more overall movements such as nationalism.

Approximately at the same time, the so-called *Pfahlbauern* (lake dwellers) were celebrated in Switzerland. In 1854 Ferdinand Keller (1800–1881), Swiss archaeologist and founder of the Antiquarische Gesellschaft Zürich, discovered the first lake dwellings at Obermeilen (Lake Zurich). The residents of these Neolithic lake dwellings were considered to be ancestors of Swiss history and 'pioneers of civilisation' (see Gramsch 2009). Moreover, they offered the contemporaries in the young Swiss province, established in 1848, an identity in opposition to that of mountain farmers in the Alps and the Swiss national hero Wilhelm Tell.

Such historical pageants, however, were not only popular and widespread in nineteenth-century central Europe, we find a similar phenomenon in Great Britain and the USA in the early years of the 20th century. British artist Louis N. Parker (1852–1944) established the 'pageant movement' by initiating the first event – The Pageant of Sherborne – in 1905. At that time he was invited to produce a celebration of the 1200th anniversary of the founding of Sherborne. The outdoor spectacle involved hundreds of performers who re-enacted scenes from the town's history before a huge audience, and it was a big success (Lau 2011:270). Afterwards it was hardly surprising that he produced a series of pageants; examples are those in Warwick (1906) and Dover (1908). Parker's rather apolitical approach to pageantry was simply to re-enact scenes from local history in order to celebrate the common past of a town's history and to create a social experience. He claimed, as Lau (2011:271) points out in her interesting article, that the open-air plays are a 'great incentive to the right kind of patriotism; love of hearth; love of town; love of county; love of England' (Parker 1928:279).

A closer look at the pageant movement shows that it was a reaction to the consequences of industrialisation and urbanisation as well as a protest against them or, to put it briefly, modernity. The new age brought with it a certain loss of solidarity and a social collapse, as observed in a growing individualism (Fischer-Lichte 2012:24). Thus, like the historical pageants and passion plays, these pageants were to strengthen the sense of community – thought to have been lost – of a town, a district or a village. Another characteristic of pageantry is its claim of authenticity, which is a claim based on the fact that the performance was held at the historical site with which the presentations are most closely connected. The performance at the historical site promised and guaranteed the 'celebration' of townspeople's continuity (Fischer-Lichte 2012:27; see also Parker's comments in his autobiography 1928:278–303). Above all, Parker emphasised the educational aspect in an interview given to *The Star* (Christchurch/New Zealand) in September 1909 in which he stated the following:

> Thousands of boys and girls have had a new interest in history awakened. I have been able to show them the actual occurrences in history, re-enacted on the actual place where they occurred, by people dressed exactly as the actual actors were dressed, and in many cases by their actual descendants, bearing the same names. I have made history a living thing where it was dead, and I have enabled the people of a number of towns to realise what a splendid history they were heirs to.

In the USA the pageants were adopted quite quickly and attracted enormous interest until the end of World War I in 1918. The first event took place in Philadelphia in 1908. But unlike the British pageants, the American performances were generally much less intent on glorifying the past and were rather oriented towards the future (for more details on US pageantry see Glassberg [1990]).

Thus, historical performances have a long history with the body as the core of performative acts. The sensual experiences – mediatised by the actors through costuming, music, ritual and ceremonial acts – affect the audience and lead to a sense of community. Hence, pageantries, as a mode of performance and historical representation, are quite obviously a form of affective history (Lau 2011:266–267). While these historical performances mostly have a religious or ritual origin and try to strengthen identities, historical performances in open-air museums have a more educative goal.

Living history museums

Skansen, the first open-air museum in the world (for more details see Rentzhog 2007:4–32), served as a model for contemporary living history museums. It was founded in 1891 near Stockholm by Artur Hazelius (1833–1901). From the very beginning, the museum, which was dedicated to Swedish folk culture, included 'living models' like craftsmen, musicians and other 'performers' who were to 'enliven' the museum. Hazelius's concept also integrated the local fauna and flora (e.g. reindeer) in the exhibition in order to convey a complete impression. As Nils-Arvid Bringéus (1974:14) stated, Hazelius's 'intention was not only to entertain, but to create traditions that would never be abandoned'. Although Skansen presented the visitors a romantically idealised and quite patriotic view, this museum was still a novelty whose concept spread all over Europe.

In Germany the Urgeschichtliche Forschungsinstitut in Tübingen (south-western Germany), which was founded in 1921, played a particularly important role in the 1920s *Ästhetisierung der Vergangenheit* (aestheticism of the past). Markedly well-preserved lake dwellings in the Federsee area revived a 'living past', which was animated by actors and recorded in movies in a romanticised and glamorised form ([Figure 6.2] for more details see Strobel [1999:95–109]). Thus, the distant past provided a vast projection screen for the ideals and dreams of the society of the Weimar Republic, which was traumatised by its defeat during World War I (Strobel 1999:96). The Nazis' takeover in Germany in 1933 then also affected the young discipline of prehistoric archaeology, which was quite quickly exploited.

Figure 6.2. Photography of the movie Das Leben der Pfahlbauern *([c. 1920] Institute of Pre- and Early History and Medieval Archaeology, University of Tübingen).*

The adaptation of the dominant ideology led to *Germanophiler Volksbildung* – a Germanophile popular education, not only within the discipline but also in museums. At this time, the open-air museums above all saw a boom in many new establishments such as Oerlinghausen (Paardekooper 2012:41–42; Schmidt 1999; Sénécheau and Samida 2015:108–113). As prehistorian Hans Maier (1936:652) at that time proclaimed, 'every German could be visually impressed by the multi-millennia history and heritage of his homeland'. At Oerlinghausen as well as at other German open-air museums, Germanic cultural superiority and the continuity of Germanic settlement were pointed out.

As already alluded to, the US open-air museums above all played a crucial role in establishing living history as we encounter it today in museums and at historical events. It is here that new concepts that attempt to convey and experience the past through 'theatrical representations' were developed. At that time, these groundbreaking forms of mediatisation greatly promoted the popularity of many historic sites since this mode of representation went far beyond that which was familiar in museum exhibitions until then – artefacts, texts, true-to-the-original reconstructions and historic buildings. In the USA Colonial Williamsburg and Plimoth Plantation belong to the earliest American historic sites that integrated living history in their exhibitions (for a detailed history see Rentzhog 2007:135–151). Thanks to the financial support of John D. Rockefeller Jr. (1874–1960), the capital of the British colony of Virginia was reconstructed in the 1920s and 1930s as the biggest 'living history museum'. Colonial Williamsburg gives its visitors insight into a North American town of the 18th century – a town brought to life through actors in historical costumes. Here you can meet craftsmen, merchants, politicians, judges, soldiers and slaves. They all act like persons of the 18th century and thus simulate the past. Another example, Plimoth Plantation, shows the first settlement of the Plimoth Colony (Rentzhog 2007:245–254), which was founded in 1620 by English settlers – the so-called pilgrims – who travelled on the Mayflower to America and arrived on the coast of Massachusetts. The main objective of Plimoth Plantation, established in 1947, was to show the life of the pilgrims in the year 1627 in a reconstructed historical setting based on existing archaeological and historical sources – mainly written sources such as passenger lists, letters and church and court records. The presenters in the settlement therefore only communicate in a way that gives 'visitors the impression of actually meeting a person of that era' (Carlson 2000:241).

Thus, the attempt to imitate the past is neither a new nor exclusively postmodern phenomenon. Rather, it has played an important role for many different social groups with quite different functions for a long time. Hence, living history or time travelling has many roots and cannot be traced solely to the historic pageants of nineteenth-century central Europe or to the development of open-air museums in North America. But today, and this must be pointed out, the reasons why people want to travel back in time are different. Therefore one can agree with Vanessa Agnew (2004:327), who said that the contemporary boom can be seen in the 'winning combination of imaginative play, self-improvement, intellectual enrichment and sociality'.

Time travel as living history

A look back at the roots of living history has shown that the phenomenon is not new. However, time travels into prehistoric times and specifically in museums and archaeology tourism as well is a recent phenomenon. This is particularly true in Germany, as a trend to a more experience-based orientation in German archaeological open-air museums has only been noticeable since the 1990s. Further, since the start of the new millennium, open-air museums are no longer conceivable without it.

As far as the German discussion in archaeology is concerned, the scientific discussion of what constitutes time travels and what possibilities and dangers are inherent in it has just begun (e.g. DASV 2011; Keefer 2006; Mölders 2008; Samida 2012b, 2014a; Schöbel 2008; Sénécheau and Samida 2015). This must be emphasised because Anglophone research on this topic, mainly on terminology, has a long tradition. One of the pioneers of living history research, the American folklorist Jay Anderson (1982:291), defined it as 'an attempt by people to simulate life in another time'. In his well-known and fundamental book *Time Machines: The World of Living History* (1984:12–13), he distinguished three types or dimensions of living history that are relevant for us. First, living history can be part of 'research'. According to Anderson this means, for example, that through 'experimental' living history, archaeological hypotheses about specific questions such as technology could be tested. Second, living history could serve as a tool for interpretation as a means of disseminating knowledge about the past. And finally, living history could be conceived of as 'play'. In doing so, it could serve as a 'recreation' where one could 'participate in an enjoyable recreational activity that is also a learning experience' (Anderson 1982:290–291).

Anderson's classification, however, has led to a certain dilution of the concept and a blurring of the academic, professional and public – non-professional – spheres, which inevitably causes misunderstandings from multiple sides. Furthermore, as Scott Magelssen (2007: xx–xxi) emphasised, the term *living history* is unfortunate because it implies on the one hand that there are forms of history, which are 'dead' and, on the other, 'that one can bring history back to life by way of performance'. Magelssen's remark shows that the term living history is ultimately contradictory. Similarly, the differentiation between living history on the one hand and re-enactment, on the other, can hardly be maintained in everyday usage; both are often used interchangeably. To be sure, the term *re-enactment* refers to the replay of concrete historical events (often battles), whereas living history generally implies an attempt to simulate in the present other living conditions of the distant past.

Wolfgang Hochbruck, a specialist in American studies, has also repeatedly called attention to these inconsistencies and ambiguities. Specifically, he emphasises the need to differentiate between various kinds of living history (e.g. 2009, 2013). Instead of living history he uses the term *history theatre* and differentiates between what he called re-enactment and *museum theatre* as modes of history theatre. While the first stands generally for re-enactments as costumed plays for leisure activity, the latter describes a special form of living history or history theatre including a didactical concept that is solely performed in museums (Hochbruck 2009:216–218). This is without a doubt an important suggestion that ought to be taken up in future research.

The term 'time travel' is used as well (e.g. Fenske 2009; Holtorf 2007, 2010). Quite different than in H. G. Wells's famous science fiction novel *Time Machine* (1895), in which the leading character travels into an unknown future, our contemporaries travel into a seemingly well-known past. Hence, the term *time travel* – unlike the concepts presented here so far – also implies a journey into the future. Cornelius Holtorf (2010:33) put it as follows, 'time travel is an experience and social practice in the present that evokes a past (or future) reality'.

Anderson's classification has – as already mentioned – led to equating experimental archaeology with living history, respectively time travel. However, experimental archaeology is a special subject of archaeology, which by means of repeatable and controlled scientific experiments, attempts to gain deeper insights into certain pre- and protohistorical phenomena (e.g. Eggert and Samida 2013:56–57; Outram 2008). Strictly speaking, experimental archaeology is not a form of living history or time travel at all because experimental archaeology is not a social practice that evokes a past reality. Experimental archaeology is an archaeological method (like dating, classification, ethnoarchaeology, etc.) that provides analogies for interpretation based on measurable scientific results (e.g. Mathieu 2002). For sure, there is overlap; time travels and experimental archaeology, for example, deal with objects and how they were produced and used in former times. But I agree with Christopher Hawkes (1954) of more than 60 years ago and others in recent times (e.g. Eggert 1993, 2003) that a concept of a humanistic experimental archaeology as Bodil Petersson and Lars Erik Narmo (2011) proposed it cannot deliver insights into the social and religious conceptions – the immaterial sphere – of prehistoric humans. This does not mean that research going on with a focus on living experiments in, for example, houses and an overall understanding of the living conditions in past times are disqualified in general. We can probably get some ideas – which might also be gained by means of ethnoarchaeological studies – of how people in ancient times might have behaved – no more, no less.

Taking all this together and according to Roeland Paardekooper (2010:67), with whom I agree, one could say, that living history can be seen as 'focusing on people and stories, while experimental archaeology focusses more on artefacts and techniques'. Magelssen (2011:6), who mentions that the 'very notion of performance as a practice of *creating* history is an essential issue today' or Holtorf (2010:31) who emphasises that time travel goes along with storytelling, argue similarly. Living history tries, and the quotations again clearly show this, to tell stories about past environments in an affective way because performances allow for quite different opportunities to 'tell' stories than are possible by means of text; 'It can encourage considerations of the gestural, the emotional, the aural, the visual and the physical in ways beyond print's ability to evoke or understand them' (Canning 2004:230; see also Handler and Saxton 1988:248). Not only time travellers themselves recognise this, but now so do many directors of open-air museums, who tend to base their programmes less frequently on artefacts and more often on activity-based interactions. The key words of archaeological open-air museums are then, as Paardekooper (2010:62) stresses, education, presentation, experiment, commerce and time travel. Thus, archaeological open-air museums should be considered as a form of living history.

Potentials and limits of archaeological time travels

As already mentioned, my own research is directed at the interactions between professional archaeologists, performers and visitors in selected German open-air museums and historic events. Various interviews, which I conducted with curators of archaeological open-air museums as well as with performers in 2012, will serve as the basis for the following critical analysis of potentials and limits of time travels.

One museum director emphasised that there is, of course, always a constant search for new didactic possibilities such as multi-media shows and living history. Precisely living history has the advantage because it stresses the haptic even if one cannot, of course, prevent the 'nostalgic moment' that comes along with such an affective presentation.[1] However, the balancing act between education and entertainment, which accompanies, for instance, the inclusion of living history performances, is seen particularly problematic by German curators (e.g. Schmidt 1999) and is described as *Disneyfication*. This term, primarily used in a pejorative overtone in discussions about the intersection of cultural heritage and tourism, is encountered quite often. Critical depictions decry trivialisations of culture and history and reduce these developments to Disney theme parks (see Bryman 2004:5–10).

---

[1] Interview with R. B., 28/11/2012; translation by author.
'There is the difficulty – we do not have any gold, gems that sparkle, but it is # it is the prehistoric buyback centre which has been preserved. There is nothing which is really attractive, and so one of course looks for new didactical concepts in order to communicate it. And then there are the multimedia shows, that's one thing – and the other is this haptic thing, off # – that is the exact opposite – away from the modern world of computers into this haptic thing: to touch something again, back into the past, and, of course, there is a bit of nostalgia involved in order to essentially simulate the past. '
In order to make the translated interview clippings more legible, the interviewer's questions and expressions (e.g. affirmations) as well as interjections (e.g. hm), stammering and overlappings were eliminated. Notations: (.) – (. . .) = 1 to 3 second pause; # = partial words or sentences, speaker restart; [...] = ellipsis.

One of my interviewees adverts to the increasing competition within the leisure market. The interviewee asserts that climbing parks, with their extraordinary experiences, put pressure on museums. Thus, on the one hand, the open-air museum has to participate in the modern leisure market, which is in the end defined by the visitors of the so-called *Erlebnisgesellschaft* (experience society) and their frame of expectations. On the other hand, there are limitations since there are aspects that cannot be performed affectively for ethical reasons (e.g. aspects of the archaeology of religion and ritual such as a child's immolation).[2] Moreover, it was underscored by this curator that, from a museum's perspective, 'stagings in the form of time travels does not make representations of the past more credible and more scientifically precise'.

Quite the contrary, in most cases, the popular scientific performance introduces problems with its bodily and affective presentation because the presented images make a much stronger statement and have a much stronger effect than perhaps texts.[3] One could say that by means of staging performances, interest in the past is aroused in an entertaining manner; whereby, the mediated images and living environments make an extraordinary impression on the audience because of their emotive approach to the past, which actively involves both parties (i.e. the time travellers and the audience). Thus, there is a certain danger that such performances create not only false but also misleading images of the past. This concerns primarily visitors who give museum presentations particular credence because they 'tend to believe what they see and experience is "authentic" and close to what they conceive of as "historic truth"' (Oesterle 2010:171). The danger, as Carolyn Oesterle (2010:171) continues, is the 'uncritical absorption and internalisation of sanitised versions of history that may be based on privileged knowledge, prevalent stereotypes, or worse, outright propaganda' (similarly Tivers 2002:189). Just think about clichés and stereotypes such as Celtic Druids cutting mistletoes, instrumentalisations by esoteric groups, neo-pagan religions as well as right-wing extremist circles (see e.g. Banghard 2009; Mölders and Hoppadietz 2007).

---

[2] Interview with R. B., 28/11/2012; translation by author.
'Yes. Yes, certainly. Museum # participates in the modern leisure market, if you want to call it that. And this market is ultimately (. . .) defined by the visitors and their expectations. Or at least # or what one subliminally ascribes to visitors' expectations – well, that's propaganda, too. But the, the # for sure, museums, that want to generate visitors, certainly need to move somewhere on this platform together with other institutions – whether this is a climbing park or what have you. And so, the museum of course also changes. And then not always for the better. [. . .] There is in the end # That's difficult # also limits to archaeological communication as far as experiences are concerned. I cannot stage everything experientially. [. . .] And then we just had two exhibitions – one was about aspects of an archaeology of religion and ritual and then there was the exhibition with M., where we focussed on child murder, if you wish. Or on the sacrifice of a child (.) to be more precise. In this case, of course, it is difficult to set up a fitting theme in an open-air venue. And here, we are forced – and this is of course sometimes also quite difficult – to mesh the interior with the exterior.'

[3] Interview with R. B., 28/11/2012; translation by author.
'But living history performances do not make the past more credible or more scientifically precise but rather the whole thing is only – how shall I say? – produced quasi-scientifically anew with a new factor. And that's, of course, where the problems already also begin.'

In order to avoid such stereotypical presentations in general, quality standards have to be negotiated with all involved parties (museums, time travellers and academics). To this end, first discussions and suggestions were made (see Hochbruck 2011). But besides expertise, didactical and pedagogical concepts as well as acting qualifications, the will for integration and communication of all parties must be the first step to less stereotyped and more accurate presentations of the past. Just like all presentations of the past, time travel performances have a responsibility, that is to say that they first have to encourage an understanding of the past in the context of the present (Tivers 2002:198–199). Additionally, visitors should be informed as to how archaeologists achieve their conclusions and models and on what facts the presentations and performances are based (Schmidt 1999:154). For sure, some observers could be disappointed, but 'we cannot please everyone, nor should we aim to' (Schmidt 1999:154–155).

The re-enactors also consider bodily experience and haptic aspects to be a central advantage in their performances. One actor expressed this very succinctly: 'we are the "answer showcase" that can be touched' (Interview with A. W., 24/7/2012). Along with it, however, the experience, particularly when it concerns the visitor, is also repeatedly moved into the foreground. The spectator has to 'live' and vividly experience the past and how people lived then precisely because that which is experienced leaves a deeper impression:

> Okay, I want to show this late robe, I want that normal people somehow experience this, I want that they experience how it is to talk to someone to, to # to stand in front of somebody like that, I also want to experience that myself and then perhaps give a report about my experience, a bit like in experimental archaeology. (Interview with C. E., 23/7/2012)

One can recall something that one experienced much more readily than something that one simply read on an information board. In order to have the 'correct' experience, emotions again play an important role. One re-enactor uses this element quite consciously in order to draw in the audience and to provoke an experience.

> With whatever you connect an experience, that's what you remember forever. If I cried during a play, this scene I remember till the end of my life, yes. But what I have read on some information board is possibly forgotten two hours later. And so I use strong emotions as a hook. So, it is like casting a fishing line in order to try to catch fish. People take the bait, and children also bite but adults also still take the bait. (Interview with C. E., 23/7/2012)

However, the question remains as to what extent the past can actually be experienced or relived at all because many time travellers are aware that one cannot immerse oneself in or enter into the past. One is, for example, not an ancient Celt, but one only attempts to play one.[4] The Australian historian Alexander Cook (2004:489) came straight to the point when he said, '*We* can never be *Them*'. He emphasised that time travels do not perform a spectacle of the past but rather are a spectacle of people who try to explore the past (Cook 2004:494). Cook is not the only critic; in fact, there is a broad consensus that time travels, and thereby living history, ought rather to be understood as a social practice in the present (Holtorf 2010:33). Vanessa Agnew (2004:235) is even more radical since she refuses re-enactment's epistemological claim that experience furthers historical understanding. Moreover, she stresses that 'body-based testimony tells us more about the present self than the collective past' (see also Cook 2004:494; Fenske 2007:87).

Is time travelling therefore only a play that tells us nothing about the past and only holds up a mirror of the present? Is history just another event in our experience society? The answer remains 'yes, but'. Time travels can certainly evoke effects, which have already been mentioned such as stereotyping and they surely promise too much because there are aspects that cannot be performed affectively. From an academic viewpoint, time travel is an ambivalent social phenomenon. Its problems as presented here are by all means well known (e.g. stereotypical presentations of the past, the static mode of the representations and lack of re-enactors' self-reflection), but what is sometimes forgotten is its potential. Time travelling as living history must be seen in a very positive sense as a form of 'history from below'. It should be welcomed because even though history is an academic field, it should be open to everyone who is interested. Although this form of public history does not always deliver a scientific view of the past, time travel often addresses quite different questions about the past, as one of my interviewees underlines.

> But the contribution is, as stated, a) to expose, uncover questions, gaps, where one could make new research. The second is, to some extent, a long-term experience. If you namely are on the road with your equipment for ten years, to be sure not every day, but often, then you recognise what works and what does not. (Interview with A. W., 24/7/012)

He and others give examples such as long-term tests of clothes and equipment or technical aspects of processes of production. While wearing or reconstructing costumes, new questions to the material and its condition emerge like 'do the Romans really wear this sword during their campaign in that way? It's not really comfortable – they should have worn it in a different way'. Thus, one has to agree with Cook (2004:495) who states 'reenactment can offer no answers' but it certainly 'raises questions' (similarly also Willmy 2010).

---

[4] Interview with D. A., 24/7/2012; translation by author.
Okay, that's how it could have been, but we do not know the rest. This [the past] is really unknown to us. We cannot immerse ourselves there. Never.

Re-enactment – one of the most currently important tropes for historical engagement that can be found in nearly all media and forms (de Groot 2009:104) – is a phenomenon that, at least in central Europe, is best paraphrased with the Latin expression *in statu nascendi* (under construction). In view of its popularity, scientific discussions of it have to be intensified because living history raises many questions concerning education, ownership and authenticity that have remained unanswered while also being under-theorised by both historians and archaeologists as Jerome de Groot emphasises (2009:103). The impact of time travels as an educational tool in archaeological open-air museums – especially in German open-air museums – is still in its infancy. This is due to a general scepticism by German museum directors who understand museums still as educational institutions where entertaining and experience-oriented presentations are widely dismissed. Many argue that education and entertainment do not go hand in hand (e.g. Schmidt 1999; my interview partners). Time travel performances also pose the question of ownership in the sense of 'who owns the past?' As a form of 'history from below' it competes with the academic history, which often discredits such forms of history presentations. Here something has to change in the future because dismissive polemics are not the appropriate way to engage with alternative histories or archaeologies; understanding and dialogue on both sides are necessary (see Holtorf 2005). Furthermore, the aspect of 'authenticity' in time travels as a currency 'that confers status both within the re-enactment community and on its relations with cultural institutions and wider audiences' (Gapps 2009:398) is also under-theorised. What does authenticity or 'authentic experiences' mean in the context of time travelling? By whom and how is authenticity created? Why does authenticity play such an important role for actors and observers? (e.g. Samida 2014b) Finally, the aspect of personal and group identity within living history (e.g. Goodacre and Baldwin 2002:167–199), which also needs further analyses in the future, plays an important role because living history activities can 'foster and develop "memories" which can contribute to the identity of individuals and groups' (Goodacre and Baldwin 2002:196). They can also 'powerfully affect the way in which we identify ourselves and others' (Goodacre and Baldwin 2002:197). So if, as Vanessa Agnew (2007:309) declares, 're-enactment is to gain legitimacy as a historical genre', it will be necessary 'to do for re-enactment what has been done for other forms of history writing', that is to establish systematic source-criticism and self-reflectivity.

Conclusion

The main aim of this chapter was to illustrate the development of time travel performances and second to present potentials and limits of such performances in present-day archaeological open-air museums. The historical survey shows that time travels are not a postmodern or new phenomenon of our times. They have a long and changeable tradition and diverse roots that go back to the ancient world.

While in Roman times ancient battles were re-enacted, the reversion to Christian plays were of particular importance in the Middle Ages. Time travels – illustrated in the short historical overview as well – had and still have at all times and in varied contexts quite different functions. The re-enactment of history in medieval times must be seen within a spiritual and religious context, while pageants of the 19th century must be considered as a reaction to an increasing industrialisation and urbanisation and an instrumentality for nationalistic purposes. Since the emergence of open-air museums at the end of the 19th century, time travels have been considered to be a mode of stimulation where historic living environments can be presented quite vividly. In this context, time travels serve as a method to communicate knowledge; therefore, they play an increasing role in present-day open-air museums. However, this form of historical performance has not only advantages but also disadvantages. As noted above, the problems lie in the potential to perpetuate and create stereotypical presentations of the past. Moreover, time travelling cannot constitute a process but is a much more static mode of representation. Quality standards as well as a self-reflexive discussion of the mostly non-academic actors of these performances, are often absent. Besides these limits, time travels certainly do have positive aspects and advantages over other presentations of history. The actors 'experience' the past especially through objects, so the haptic moment has to be seen as one of the important experiences in this case. In addition, the emotive approach to the past also involves the spectator who can be taken 'along for the ride' and enmeshed in the performance. The past is no longer displayed in a showcase but can be touched. However, it must be remembered that the past is bygone and cannot be repeated. To phrase it more positively, one could say: 'the actor cannot really recreate a moment in history, nor can the spectator travel in time, but provoked by the performance, the spectators' imaginations can transport them to another reality, a liminal one that feels real' (Hughes 2011:146). Thus, the past is just simulated – imagined – and in doing so the past usually tells us more about the present than the past itself.

Acknowledgements

The research presented here was supported through a fellowship at the Berlin Excellence Cluster *Topoi: The Formation and Transformation of Space and Knowledge in Ancient Civilizations* as well as the *Volkswagen Foundation*. Many thanks are given to Ruzana Liburkina (Berlin) who did the transcription of the interviews that I conducted. I am grateful to Cornelius Holtorf and Bodil Petersson for inviting me to this publication and their critical comments on an earlier draft of this paper. Finally, I would like to thank Herma Moschner (Clearwater, USA) who corrected my English, which was definitely no easy undertaking – thank you very much. All German quotes in the text were translated by the author.

References

Agnew, V. 2004. Introduction: What is re-enactment? *Criticism* 46(3):327–339.

Agnew, V 2007. History's affective turn: Historical re-enactment and its work in the present. *Rethinking History* 11(3):299–312.

Anderson, J. 1982. Living history: Simulating everyday life in living museums. *American Quarterly* 34(3):290–306.

Anderson, J. 1984. *Time Machines: The World of Living History*. Nashville, American Association for State and Local History.

Banghard, K. 2009. 'Unterm Häkelkreuz'. Germanische Living History und rechte Affekte. Ein historischer Überblick in drei Schlaglichtern'. In Hans-Peter Kilguss (ed.) *Die Erfindung der Deutschen. Rezeption der Varusschlacht und die Mystifizierung der Germanen. Dokumentation zur Fachtagung vom 03. Juli 2009*: 29–35. Köln, NS-Dokumentationszentrum der Stadt Köln.

Bringéus, N-A. 1974. Artur Hazelius and the Nordic museum. *Ethnologia Scandinavia* 5–16.

Bryman, A. 2004. *The Disneyization of Society*. Los Angeles, Sage Publications.

Canning, C. 2004. Feminist performance as feminist historiography. *Theatre Survey* 45(2):227–233.

Carlson, M. 2000. Performing the past: Living history and cultural memory. *Paragrana* 9(2):237–248.

Cook, A. 2004. The use and abuse of historical re-enactment: Thoughts on recent trends in public history. *Criticism* 46(3):487–496.

Dachverband Archäologischer Studierendenvertretungen (DASV) E. V. (ed.) 2011. *Vermittlung von Vergangenheit. Gelebte Geschichte als Dialog von Wissenschaft, Darstellungen und Rezeption*. Weinstadt, Bernhard Albert Greiner.

de Groot, J. 2009. *Consuming History: Historians and Heritage in Contemporary Popular Culture*. London, Routledge.

Eggert, M. K. H. 1993. Vergangenheit in der Gegenwart? Überlegungen zum interpretatorischen Potential der Ethnoarchäologie. In M. Augstein and S. Samida (eds.), Waxmann, *Retrospektive: Archäologie in kulturwissenschaftlicher Sicht*, 63–70. Münster, Waxmann.

Eggert, M. K. H. 2003. Das Materielle und das Immaterielle: Über archäologische Erkenntnis. In M. Augstein and S. Samida (eds.), *Retrospektive: Archäologie in kulturwissenschaftlicehr Sicht*: 183–220. Münster, Waxmann.

Eggert, M. K. H. and Samida, S. 2013. *Ur- und Frühgeschichtliche Archäologie*. Tübingen, Basel, A. Francke.

Fenske, M. 2007. Historische Doku-Soaps als Handlungs-, Diskussions- und Erlebnisräume. In A. Hartmann, S. Meyer and R-E. Mohrmann (eds.), *Historizität. Vom Umgang mit Geschichte*: 85–105. Münster, Waxmann.

Fenske, M. 2009. Abenteuer Geschichte. Zeitreisen in der Spätmoderne. Reisefieber Richtung Vergangenheit. In W. Hardtwig and A. Schug (eds), *History Sells! Angewandte Geschichte als Wissenschaft und Markt*: 79–90. Stuttgart, Franz Steiner.

Fischer-Lichte, E. 2012. Die Wiederholung als Ereignis. Re-enactment als Aneignung von Geschichte. In J. Roselt and U. Otto (eds.), *Theater als Zeitmaschine: Zur performativen Praxis des Re-enactments. Theater- und Kulturwissenschaftliche Perspektiven*: 13–52. Bielefeld, Transcript.

Gapps, S. 2009. Mobile monuments: A view of historical re-enactment and authenticity from inside the costume cupboard of history. *Rethinking History* 13(3):395–409.

Glassberg, D. 1990. *American Historical Pageantry: The Uses of Tradition in the Early Twentieth Century*. Chapel Hill, The University of North Carolina Press.

Goodacre, B. and Baldwin G. 2002. *Living the Past: Reconstruction, Recreation, Re-enactment and Education at Museums and Historical Sites*. London, Middlesex University Press.

Gramsch, A. 2009. Schweizer Art ist Bauern Art Mutmaßungen über Schweizer Nationalmythen und ihren Niederschlag in der Ur- und Frühgeschichtsforschung. In S. Grunwald, J. Koch, D. Mölders, U. Sommer and S. Wolfram (eds.), *Artefakt. Festschrift für Sabine Rieckhoff zum 65. Geburtstag*, 1:71–85. Bonn, Habelt.

Handler, R. and Saxton, W. 1988. Dyssimulation: Reflexivity, narrative and the quest for authenticity in 'living history'. *Cultural Anthropology* 3:242–260.

Hartmann, W. 1976. *Der historische Festzug. Seine Entstehung und Entwicklung im 19. und 20. Jahrhundert*. München, Prestel.

Hawkes, C. 1954. Archaeological theory and method: Some suggestions from the Old Word. *American Anthropologist* 56:155–168.

Hochbruck, W. 2009. Belebte Geschichte: Delimitationen der Anschaulichkeit im Geschichtstheater. In B. Korte and S. Paletschek (eds.), *History Goes Pop. Zur Repräsentation von Geschichte in populären Medien und Genres*: 215–230. Bielefeld, Transcript.

Hochbruck, W. 2011. Geschichte dramatisch nachbessern? Wissenschaftlicher Anspruch und Performativität im Museumstheater. In DASV 2011:77–87.

Hochbruck, W. 2013. *Geschichtstheater: Formen der 'Living History'. Eine Typologie*. Bielefeld, Transcript.

Holtorf, C. 2005. Beyond crusades: How (not) to engage with alternative archaeologies. *World Archaeology* 37:544–551.

Holtorf, C. 2007. Time travel: A new perspective on the distant past. In B. Hårdh, K. Jennbert and D. Olausson (eds.), *On the Road. Studies in Honour of Lars Larsson*: 127–132. Stockholm, Almqvist and Wiksell International.

Holtorf, C. 2010. On the possibility of time travel. *Lund Archaeological Review* 15/16:31–41.

Hughes, C. 2011. Is that real? An exploration of what is real in a performance based history. In S. Magelssen and R. Justice-Malloy (eds.), *Enacting History*: 134–152. Tuscaloosa, University of Alabama Press.

Keefer, E. (ed.) 2006. *Lebendige Vergangenheit: Vom archäologischen Experiment zur Zeitreise*. Stuttgart, Theiss.

Lau, M. 2011. Performing history: The war-time pageants of Louis Napoleon Parker. *Modern Drama* 54(3):265–286.

Magelssen, S. 2007. *Living History Museums: Undoing History through Performance*. Lanham, Scarecrow Press.

Magelssen, S. 2011. Introduction. In S. Magelssen and R. Justice-Malloy (eds.), *Enacting History*: 1–9.Tuscaloosa, University of Alabama Press.

Maier, H. 1936. Das erste germanische Freilichtmuseum im Teutoburger Wald. *Nationalsozialistische Monatshefte* 7(76):651–653.

Mathieu, J. R. 2002. Introduction - experimental archaeology: Replicating past objects, behaviours and processes. In J. R. Mathieu (ed.), *Experimental Archaeology: Replicating Past Objects, Behaviours and Processes*: 1–11. Oxford, Archaeopress.

Mölders, D. 2008. Archäologie als Edutainment. Können Re-enactment und Living History historische Lebenswelten erklären? In I. Benková and V. Guichard (eds.), *Gestion et présentation des oppida. Un panorama européen*: 155–164. Glux-en-Glenne, Bibracte: Institut archéologique de Bohême centrale.

Mölders, D. and Hoppadietz, R. 2007. 'Odin statt Jesus!' Europäische Ur- und Frühgeschichte als Fundgrube für religiöse Mythen neugermanischen Heidentums? *Rundbrief Theorie-AG* 6(1):32–48.

Oesterle, C. 2010. Themed environments – performative spaces: Performing visitors in North American living history museums. In J. Schlehe, M. Uike-Bormann, C. Oesterle and W. Hochbruck (eds.), *Staging the Past: Themed Environments in Transcultural Perspectives*: 157–175. Bielefeld, transcript.

Outram, A. K. 2008. Introduction to experimental archaeology. *World Archaeology* 40(1):1–6.

Paardekooper, R. 2010. Archaeological open air museums as time travel Centres. *Lund Archaeological Review* 15/16:61–69.

Paardekooper, R. 2012. *The Value of an Archaeological Open-Air Museum in its Use: Understanding Archaeological Open-Air Museums and their Visitors*. Leiden, Sidestone Press.

Parker, L. N. 1909. The pageant maker: Louis N. Parker, creator of a new art. In *The Star* (Christchurch/New Zealand), 11 September 1909.

Parker, L. N. 1928. *Several of My Lives*. London, Chapman and Hall.

Petersson, B. and Narmo, L. E. 2011. A journey in time. In B. Petersson and L. E Narmo (eds.), *Experimental Archaeology: Between Enlightenment and Experience*: 27–48. Lund, Lund University.

Rentzhog, S. 2007. *Open Air Museums: The History and Future of a Visionary Idea*. Stockholm, Carlssons.

Samida, S. 2012a. Re-enacted prehistory today: Preliminary remarks on a multidisciplinary research project. In N. Schücker (ed.), *Integrating Archaeology: Science - Wish - Reality*: 75–80. Frankfurt a.M., Römisch-Germanische Kommission.

Samida, S. 2012b. Re-Enactors in archäologischen Freilichtmuseum: Motive und didaktische Konzepte. *Archäologische Informationen* 35:209–218.

Samida, S. 2014a. Moderne Zeitreisen oder Die performative Aneignung vergangener Lebenswelten. *Forum Kritische Archäologie* 3:136–150. DOI: 10.6105/journal.fka.2014.3.10

Samida, S. 2014b. Inszenierte Authentizität: Zum Umgang mit Vergangenheit im Kontext der Living History. In M. Fitzenreiter (ed.), *Authentizität. Artefakt und Versprechen in der Archäologie*: 139–150. London, Golden House.

Schmidt, M. 1999. Reconstruction as ideology: The open air museum at Oerlinghausen, Germany. In P. G. Stone and P. G. Panel (eds.), *The Constructed Past: Experimental Archaeology, Education and the Public*: 146–156. London, Routledge.

Schöbel, G. 2008. Erfahrungen und Erkenntnisse eines Filmprojektes. Die ARD/SWR Filmdoku, Steinzeit – Das Experiment. Leben wie vor 5000 Jahren' aus Sicht des Pfahlbaumuseums Unteruhldingen. *Experimentelle Archäologie in Europa* 7:111–130.

Sénécheau, M. and Samida, S. 2015. *Living History als Gegenstand Historischen Lernens: Begriffe – Problemfelder – Materialien*. Stuttgart, Kohlhammer.

Strobel, M. 1999. Zur Ästhetisierung der Vergangenheit während des Nationalsozialismus. In C. Kümmel, N. Müller-Scheeßel and A. Schülke (eds.), *Archäologie als Kunst: Darstellung - Wirkung - Kunst*, 65–117. Tübingen, Mo Vince.

Tivers, J. 2002. Performing heritage: The use of live 'actors' in heritage presentations. *Leisure Studies* 21:187–200.

Willmy, A. 2010. Experimentelle Archäologie und Living History – ein schwieriges Verhältnis? Gedanken aus der Sicht eines Archäologen und Darstellers. *Experimentelle Archäologie in Europa* 9:27–30.

Willner, S., Samida, S. and Koch, G. 2014. Archaeological Live Interpretations, Docu-Soaps, and Themed Walks: Similarities and Differences. *EXARC Journal* 14(2). URL: http://exarc.net/issue-2014-2/int/archaeological-live-interpretations-docu-soaps-and-themed-walks-similarities-and-differences.

Chapter 7

Being There
Time Travel, Experience and Experiment in Re-enactment and 'Living History' Performances

Mads Daugbjerg

Abstract

This chapter investigates practices of time travelling and the striving for historical 'experience' in the context of historical re-enactment and 'living history' performances. It is based on ethnographic fieldwork amongst American Civil War re-enactors and draws on previous studies of Danish heritage institutions. These modern heritage practices are discussed in relation to the methodology of experimental archaeology and the epistemological status of the experiment as a source of trustworthy knowledge. This discussion includes a pondering on the common roots and contemporary relations between the two key terms 'experiment' and 'experience'. In contrast to positivist historians' and archaeologists' condemnation of experiential approaches to learning about the past, this chapter pays special heed to the interplay and grey zones between experimental and experiential activities as spaces of productive creativity. It is argued that, despite a still-widespread black-and-white rhetorical distinction between (scientific) experiments and (unscientific) experiences, it is exactly the blurred in-between territory that holds promise for a nuanced understanding of the human fascination with history and with the possibilities of cross-temporal mobility.

Keywords: Re-enactment, time travel, experience, experiment, archaeology

Introduction

What kind of knowledge is produced in and through historical re-enactment? In what senses and by what means do such activities include time travelling? Can these endeavours in immersion and experience be regarded also as 'experimental' activities? These are the main questions to be addressed in this chapter. They are thus epistemological at their core but will be investigated here through a theoretically informed analysis of material derived from ethnographic fieldwork conducted amongst American Civil War re-enactors and Danish heritage institutions.

To archaeologist Alan K. Outram (2008:3), this field, in which costumed amateurs (often labelling themselves 'living historians') seek to revive elements of past battles, episodes, craft activities or other so-called 'period' life, is not to be confused with experimental archaeology, as they are 'clearly not, in philosophical and research terms, experiments'. Further, he states: 'It is perhaps unfortunate that the boundaries between experimental archaeology (a research tool), experiences and demonstrations (educational and presentational tools) and re-enactment activities (a recreational pursuit) have become blurred in the minds of many' (Outram 2008:3).

This is undoubtedly the case when these activities are viewed from the positivist perspective. Yet, it is precisely this blurred territory that I wish to explore here. True, the activities undertaken by the hobbyists of my studies were rarely driven by strict hypotheses or conducted under highly controlled conditions. Nevertheless, besides their 'recreational' aspects, the ambitions, ideas and motivations for participants were often (though not always) surprisingly similar to those of the experimental archaeologist.

Indeed, as we shall see, the boundaries between experts and laymen in this field can be very hard to maintain. It is not easy to draw the lines, as material reconstruction and rigorous testing seem to continuously 'spill over' into less controlled scenarios and atmospheric (re-) stagings. Experiment and experience seem almost impossible to keep apart in today's heritage landscape. Instead of condemning this conflation, with Outram and others, here I openly investigate such grey zones and overlaps – between experience and experiment, between science and non-science, between expertise and amateurism, and between producers and consumers of historical knowledge – as arenas of human creativity and curiosity.

My approach is thus less categorically dismissive than much previous academic work on re-enactment in which the phenomenon is sometimes taken to almost generically 'distort' or 'falsify' history or heritage (e.g., Agnew 2007; Cook 2004; Kaufman 2006; Walsh 1992). I align myself, instead, with scholars devoted to exploring the affective aspects and performative potentials of re-enactment and to a detailed unpacking of the dynamics of specific events or cases and their epistemologies (e.g., Crang 1996; Kalshoven 2012; Magelssen 2014; Schneider 2011). Performance theorist Rebecca Schneider (2011:38), in her inspiring book *Performing Remains*, critiques the 'long Western corridor binarizing history (composed in document) and memory (composed in the body)' and contends that 'the space between is layered with anxiety about verity, authenticity, falsity, theatricality, truth, and claim'. One way to describe my aims in the following pages is to say that it is an exploration of this very 'space between' documents and bodies, including anxieties, truth claims and the possibilities of temporal mobility.

Experiment, experience and the in-between

Outram (2008:3–4) states that 'from an academic point of view, it is clearly beneficial to maintain a clear distinction between what is "experimental" and what is "experiential"'. A closer look at the relationship between *experiment* and *experience* constitutes a useful starting point for my discussion. The two terms share etymological roots. In fact, says anthropologist Robert Desjarlais (1994:887), 'the modern English word "experiment" best preserves the original meaning of "experience"'. They both stem 'from [the Latin] *experiri*, a compound verb formed from the prefix *ex-* ("out") and a prehistoric base *per-* ("attempt, trial") that meant "to try, test"' (Desjarlais 1994:887, drawing on Ayto 1990). From this sprang the idea of having 'actually observed phenomena in order to gain knowledge from them,' which in turn evolved into a more subjective 'condition of having undergone or been affected by a particular event' (Ayto 1990, quoted in Desjarlais 1994:887). In other words, an earlier meaning revolving around observation and knowledge has, at least partly, given way to another one stressing subjectivity and affective transformation. Experience thus 'evolved from a verb denoting an external engagement with or testing of one's surroundings to a template marking a person's subjective awareness of that engagement' (Desjarlais 1996:73). We thus note two distinct, though related, dimensions of experience, perhaps better captured by the two different German translations of the English term: *Erfahrung* and *Erlebnis*. While Erfahrung conveys the cumulative and 'temporally elongated notion of experience based on a learning process' (Jay 2005:11), Erlebnis expresses the 'inner' or 'lived' experience of the individual and 'generally connotes a more immediate, pre-reflective, and personal variant of experience' (Jay 2005:11).

This last variant, connected to momentary, sensorial impact and rush, is particularly central for my purposes. This is especially so given the strong current in the contemporary museum and heritage sector towards stressing bodily, tactile and emotional engagement. This is often done precisely in the name of experience, a term invoked extensively across the cultural and leisure industries, and prominently so in the heritage sector (Daugbjerg 2011; Edensor 1997; Falk and Dierking 1992). Opinions are divided, with a number of heritage and museum analysts upholding a sceptical view of the widespread celebration of these trends (e.g., Handler 1994; Kirshenblatt-Gimblett 1998; Lowenthal 1998) while others, conversely, stress the learning potentials and promises in embracing experiential currents in various ways (e.g., Hall 2006; Landsberg 2004:111–139; Prentice 2001). Such studies are but fragments of a much broader literature on the ubiquity and power of experience, often lauded as a sphere of new commercial potential (Boswijk *et al.* 2007; Knudsen *et al.* 2014; O'Dell and Billing 2005; Schulze 1992). The so-called *experience economy*, a concept coined by marketing professors Joseph Pine and James Gilmore (1998, 1999), has become a particularly influential rallying point. Pine and Gilmore regard experience as 'an existing but previously unarticulated *genre of economic output*' (Pine and Gilmore 1999:ix, emphasis in original) and describe the experience economy as the fourth step in a ladder of 'natural progression' of economic value (Pine and Gilmore 1999:5). In contrast to *commodities*, *goods* and *services* – emblems of previous and allegedly outmoded economical regimes that the experience paradigm is argued to replace and supersede – 'experiences are inherently personal, existing only in the mind of an individual who has been engaged on an emotional, physical, intellectual or even spiritual level' (Pine and Gilmore 1998:99). As a consequence, in the new millennium, 'manufacturers must *experientialize* their goods' (Pine and Gilmore 1999:16, italics in original).

But this is not merely about making money. It is about recognising the broader 'value', in a more-than-economic sense, of experiential approaches to understanding conditions of the past. Several academics, including archaeologists, have been less rigid and dismissive than Outram. Izumi Shimada, in a useful overview of the state of experimental archaeology at the turn of the millennium, is less critical of the blurring of experimental (or 'research') and experiential (or 'educational') contexts, describing them merely as 'two poles of the stated aims of experimental archaeology' (Shimada 2005:614). In Western European open-air museums in particular, he notes, 'the experiential and public educational aspects of experimental archaeology are emphasized as much as scholarly concern with testing of hypotheses about the past' (Shimada 2005:612). Embracing rather than confronting this hybridity and the entanglement between experiment and experience, Shimada suggests that 'experimental archaeology is a means by which available archaeological knowledge and understanding are translated into a careful reconstruction of the past, during the process of which our ideas (those both of the public and the archaeologist) are tested and refined' (Shimada 2005:613). In a related vein, Bodil Petersson and Lars Erik Narmo (2011) have sought to soften positions by opposing positivist legacies and tendencies in experimental archaeology. In their call for a 'humanistic' experimental archaeology, they argue for a more liberal approach to experimenting that opens towards emotional, experiential and what they call 'action-mediated' methodologies in order to 'free ourselves from the control need, the need for repetition, in favour of individual approaches' (Petersson and Narmo 2011:34; see also Flores and Paardekooper 2014).

'Chasing that period high': Time travel and magic moments in re-enactment

In 2010, I conducted five months of ethnographic fieldwork in and around Gettysburg in Pennsylvania, USA, in which I studied various parts of the heritage debates and tourism dynamics that revolve around the traces of the American

Civil War (1861–1865). As part of my fieldwork, I joined one of the many groups of history enthusiasts who revive the conflict through costumed re-enactment, during which they invest a lot of both spare time and money in their hobby. Amongst these men, the so-called 'magic moment' has a special and almost mythological status. Also known as 'Civil War moments' or 'period rush', such rare and often brief occurrences constitute especially dense or even 'sublime' experiences in which a particularly strong sense of temporal connection with the 1860's – of 'being there' – can allegedly be felt or sensed.

Dave, the first sergeant of my company of re-enactors, insisted he had only had two or three such moments since his coming into the hobby three years earlier. He told me about one of them:

> I remember coming out on the field for the Sunday battle. And the way the smoke hung in the air, there were so many muskets firing you couldn't hear the individual shots. You couldn't distinguish them in your ear. It was just a roar, and you could see the battle flags waving in the breeze, with everyone yelling and screaming. And in the background there's a band playing *Dixie* over it all. Just for a split second it was a surreal moment.[1]

There is a deliberate suspension of disbelief involved, and a strong desire for these rare experiences, which are described in almost revelatory terms by some of my informants. Steven Cushman has succinctly described this as an urge in re-enactors 'to lose track of time, to fool themselves, to experience a mystical moment when the seemingly impermeable boundary between the present and the past suddenly dissolves' (Cushman 1999, quoted in Amster 2008:21). This was indeed the case for my American comrades-in-arms. Dave described his own urge in terms of addiction. He said, 'I try to go to every event I can, trying to get that experience again, it's like . . . almost like a heroin addict that does heroin the first time. And it's the greatest thing in the world. Then they keep chasing the dragon, so to speak, chasing that high. It's like you chase that period high'.

The moment of battle confusion described by Dave was a favourite motive often highlighted by the men of my company (and one found in largely similar accounts in previous studies; see e.g., Amster 2008:20; Handler and Saxton 1988:245). It takes its power from the immersion in the 'fog of war', and entails a lack of overview and often a misty or smoky haze in which temporal registers are felt capable of blurring. Another popular activity particularly ripe with time travelling opportunity, according to my informants, is the long military march. My company sometimes ventured on half- or full-day marches as part of commemoration, preservation or charity events or as an element of a specific

---

[1] All personal names in this article have been changed for purposes of anonymity. All quotes from informants are from recorded or videotaped interviews.

battle scenario. Billy, a veteran of the group, said he loved marching more than anything else in the hobby, although he had some difficulties putting this fascination into words:

> How to explain it? I just love marching. I don't know why [laughs] . . . . It's just a good feeling. And you sort of lose yourself into the period. You know, we get out there with no modern things around; you're all marching. You see all the troops there, all looking authentic, with their good clothing and everything. And it just puts you right back to that period, and you think 'this is how they did it'.

Such a purported 'losing of oneself' in the discipline and the rhythm of the draining march, and of the joint experience of brotherhood and shared purpose, has evident resemblances with certain aspects of pilgrimage (Coleman and Eade 2004). The elevation is connected to a holistic and supremely bodily sense of being, which cannot be reduced to factual learning about the past. Although Billy, like most re-enactors, possessed a keen historical interest, it was entirely unscholarly. 'I don't retain knowledge', he told me. 'It sort of goes in one ear and out the other with me. It's always been that way, and there's nothing I can do about it.' Others in the group were adamant that their hobby had taught them much more 'real' history than the US school system, which many held in disdain as presenting a 'whitewashed' or outright false version of Civil War history. Mark, a young fellow, insisted that he had 'learned more about history, and more about the Civil War, by re-enacting it' than he ever did in school. We were hanging out in the sizzling Pennsylvanian summer heat in the Confederate army's camp (Figure 7.1) during the Gettysburg 2010 Annual Re-enactment and were surrounded by 'period' tents (Figure 7.2), smouldering bonfires, Confederate flags and grey-clad, largely like-minded, white Americans. Taking in the scenery and the atmosphere of sweat, gunpowder, smoke and horse dung (Figure 7.3), Mark elaborated on what he saw as the differences between these two modes of learning:

> When you're in a classroom, and you're in this hard little desk, and you're watching a teacher sit up there at the chalkboard and drone on and on and on, you can't help but lose interest. When you're out on the battlefield, in your jeans cloth, and you're sweating, and you have black powder in your teeth, and you can smell the smoke in your nose, and you see the banners flapping, and the glint of the metal, and . . . the whole scene is . . . [gesticulating with both arms as if embracing the surrounding countryside] playing out before your eyes; you feel that you're part of it. And you start to feel you can *understand* what it must have . . . been like for them.

Again, we see a celebration of the experiential possibilities in the immersed midst of 'battle', conceived in holistic and multi-sensory fashion. The participatory factor – feeling 'that you're part of it' – was crucial, amounting to a sense of 'having a say' or 'having a go' in the making or revision of history (see also Daugbjerg 2014a:732; de Groot 2009:109; Thompson 2004:181).

Figure 7.1. Cooking in the Confederate army's camp during the Annual Gettysburg Civil War Battle Reenactment, 2013.

Figure 7.2. Re-enactor's bivouac set up at Spangler's Spring, near Gettysburg, 2010.

Figure 7.3. Mounted Union officers taking in the scene prior to battle, at the Annual Gettysburg Civil War Battle Reenactment, 2010.

First Sergeant Dave, broadening perspectives slightly from the rare and addictive magic moments to a more general argument on re-enactment as a form of 'escapism', explained to me that the hobby to him was very much about putting 'all the things of the modern world [aside], like having to worry about paying your bills on time, problems at work, maybe relationship problems. You leave all that behind, you leave the century, so to speak, come out and hang out and see the buddies.' There is, of course, not much room for 'leaving the century', or for a 'mystical' dissolving of the kind suggested by Cushman (quoted above), in a conventional Western conception of history and being. When re-enactors nevertheless insisted on the power of such experiences, these insistences thus implied a challenge to rational thought, and to the black-and-white, common sense distinction between being there and not actually being there (and between supposedly 'rational' experiments and purportedly 'irrational' experiences). They sought, in some cases even craved, the experiential enjoyment derived from occupying the grey zone in-between now and then. Schneider (2011:29) proposes that re-enactment can be said to contest 'tightly stitched Enlightenment claims to the forward-driven linearity of temporality'. In her suggestive phrasing, 'a re-enactment *both* is *and* is not the acts of the Civil War. It is *not not* the Civil War. And, perhaps, through the cracks in the "not not," something cross-temporal, something affective, and something affirmative circulates. Something is touched' (Schneider 2011:43, italics in original).

Chasing the 'period high' for American Civil War re-enactors is certainly both affective and affirmative. It requires a certain experiential openness, an attitude not opposed as such to written history, school-based learning or chronological museum displays, but one which nevertheless embraces what is viewed as a possibility of reaching *beyond* such authorised renderings of the past. As Jonathan, the captain of my re-enactment company, said when I asked him about his initial motivations for joining, 'I wanted what the books couldn't give me'. He elaborated:

> I started studying the American Civil War when I was in middle school, and I just automatically got hooked and read everything I could get my hands on. Ken Burns came out with his Civil War [television] documentary at the same time I was getting into it. And as I am reading it, and seeing it, I am always wondering, "what was it like, what was it like," you know, walking a mile in somebody's shoes? And when I found out they did re-enactments, I was like "I gotta try that. I gotta do that." And then I found the first local re-enactment. unit in my area . . . and I joined them. And it was really amazing to really walk a mile in their shoes and to get that experience.

This perceived clash between bookish knowledge and lived experience is typical of my informants' attitudes. This corresponds well with Richard Handler and William Saxton's (1988:243) earlier findings that although they are almost by definition keenly committed to history, 'living historians explicitly devalue written history, history as it is found in books' (see also West 2014:163). Still, I found that my informants' relationships to written history were not as purely negative as this may suggest; indeed, many of them, like Dave and Jonathan, consumed vast amounts of historical literature. But such theoretical knowledge was regarded as insufficient in grasping 'what is was like', in Jonathan's words. They wanted more; they wanted to move beyond history as text. As we shall see below, such a stance is not restricted to amateur hobbyists.

From experiments to legends and 'enthrallment'

If, as we saw earlier, there is no clear scholarly consensus on the degree to which experimental archaeology should *in principle* abstain from dabbling with 'experience', it is safe to say that *in practice*, the experiment/experience distinction is largely obscured across much of the heritage sector, and perhaps increasingly so. Consider the case of the Historical-Archaeological Experimental Centre at Lejre, Denmark, which Shimada (2005:613) points out as an exemplar of what he calls the 'open-air research laboratory'. The centre, the first of its kind worldwide, has experimented with historical and archaeological reconstruction and craft since its opening in 1964 under the tutelage of ethnologist Hans-Ole Hansen, and is widely regarded as a pioneer on the experimental archaeology scene (e.g. Rasmussen 2007).

I had the pleasure to meet Hansen several times back in 2006 during my studies at another institution founded on his visions, the Dybbøl Battlefield Centre in Southern Denmark (see Daugbjerg 2011, 2014b), to discuss the role of history and historical interpretation with him.[2] While Hansen was clearly driven by a desire to experiment, rebuild and materialise past structures, this experimental drive included an essential corporeal, multi-sensory and experiential dimension. It was evident that what mattered was not merely bringing these historical milieus into sight, visually, but bringing them into *mind*, so to speak. For instance, when discussing a specific artillery experiment at Dybbøl, in which four historical cannons had been continuously fired at maximum frequency over a ten-minute period, Hansen stressed the physically felt thumps of the big guns, the roars of which had literally shaken the ground, and the confusion and lack of orientation brought about by the thick cover of the resulting smoke. He explained to me how at that particular exercise, the audience – including museum academics initially sceptic towards reconstruction and re-enactment – was 'enthralled' as they stared 'into something horrible, some of the horrible realities that are hard to communicate' conventionally. These kinds of activities, he argued, had the potential to provide historical insights non-derivable from traditional, academic historical or archaeological studies.

Should such initiatives be lumped under experimental or experiential labels? In cases like this one, they evidently overlap; arguably, they are inseparable. Interestingly, Hansen's old Lejre site, originally called the Lejre Historical-Archaeological Experimental Centre, was renamed in 2009 and is known today as *Lejre: Land of Legends*. As insignificant as this particular case of relabelling might seem, it is exemplary of the general experiential turn in tourism and heritage already outlined. It seems that the experimental ventures of yesteryear, when tests, facts and scientific rigor were higher on the public agenda, have today merged with, and to some degree been superseded by, vaguer but also perhaps more alluring and individualistically pitched invitations to immerse oneself in landscapes and milieus of experience, legend and fantasy.[3]

The moments of 'enthrallment' that Hansen and his assistants worked to facilitate on the basis of experiments were clearly seen to encompass more than positivistic measuring and controlled testability. This intangible 'more' is not unlike the re-enactors' striving for something that 'the books couldn't give' them, as discussed above. It is also, in a more theoretical vein, close to what historian and

---

[2] In this particular case, and as an exception, I have not anonymised the interviewee. Excerpts are my translations from Danish.
[3] The English names provided here are officially endorsed translations devised by the centre. It opened in 1964 under the Danish name *Lejre Historisk-Arkæologisk Forsøgscenter*. In 2009 this was changed to *Sagnlandet Lejre* (http://www.sagnlandet.dk/en/. Accessed 25 May 2015). On the changes at the Lejre site and the invocation of experience, also see Holtorf (2009, 2010).

historiographer Eelco Runia (2006) has tried to grasp in his writings on what he calls 'spots of time', moments in which the past 'forces itself' upon the present, often involuntarily. Such a presence of the past – the 'living on of the past in the here and now', Runia (2006:310) writes, 'is strikingly undramatic, very elusive and impossible to isolate. You can experience it, but you can't document it. It can move you, but you can only tell from its wake that it has been there'. Such glimpses or spots are clearly related to the (lay) theories on 'magic moments' and 'period highs' I found amongst the American re-enactors. In addressing these desires for a different kind of knowing, overwhelmingly sensorial and kinaesthetic, the work of Runia as a theoretical historiographer thus resonates both with Hansen's practical-experimental stance and with the immersive urges of the hobbyists of my American fieldwork. Each in their own way, they all seek to create a space that allows such a 'more' to creep in, something that goes beyond positivistic experimentation and strictly bound chronologies. While academics of a more conventional schooling may want to protest against Runia's phenomenological suggestions, he insists that these experiences of what he calls a 'mysterious surplus' are in fact familiar to all historians:

> How else to explain a phenomenon that I think every historian recognizes: that suddenly our sweating away at some historical "object," our rummaging and nitpicking, our plodding and tinkering, suddenly yields to a kind of luminosity, a luminosity in which the past comes to our assistance and supplies our work with the life we ourselves couldn't provide. You may call it "inspiration," an "Aha-Erlebnis," or just plain "insight," but the point is that it is a kind of gift from regions whose existence we normally do not recognize. (Runia 2006:310)

Scripted battles and tactical experimentation

While Runia is primarily concerned with the involuntary experiences that the past, according to him, in some cases 'imposes upon' the present, the American re-enactors I fell in with worked intensively to enable or actively *provoke forth* such moments of temporal connection. They were rare and never guaranteed, as we have seen already, but there was a conscious effort to 'get there' different from Runia's focus on mostly coincidental and unintentional rushes.[4] Although the hobby historians in my field thus worked ceaselessly to optimise the probabilities for 'period' moments – including serious bodily, material and financial investments – their stagings and preparations could hardly be compared to the controlled premises of the classic scholarly experiment. Still, I would insist, re-enactment as a phenomenon concerns not merely personal or collective experience, but also aspirations of an experimental kind. A brief discussion of a key empirical distinction

---

[4] In this, Runia is explicitly inspired by the seminal writings of Marcel Proust and Walter Benjamin on personal and involuntary memory.

in the field of battle re-enactment can set the scene for this final discussion of mine. It concerns the difference between what is called 'scripted battles' and 'tacticals'. As their name suggests, the first type of engagements are governed by adherence to an already agreed upon script modelled over the events of a specific historical battle. That is, the scripted 2010 battle of New Market, Virginia, was meant to be a reconstruction of the original 1864 battle of New Market, with manoeuvres, tactics, casualties and outcomes decided in advance and in relative accordance with the historical record. Scripted battles were usually staged to an audience, fenced off from the events by rope or sometimes, in the case of the largest events, situated on grandstands next to the field.

As was inevitably the case, *in practice* a long list of elements had to be adapted and altered, or they simply failed, so that the final show ended up being not in line with the historical record at all – often to the dismay of many re-enactors – but the *principle* of the scripted battle is nevertheless to remain faithful to the course of the historical battle. Thus, the scripted battles I took part in were by nature largely unsurprising and predictable in their outcomes (except for the inevitable mess-ups of the script), and were also often characterised by a less energetic and exhilarating atmosphere than the so-called tacticals. While in a certain sense of the word, the scripted engagements were certainly (meant to be) more 'authentic' in relation to their historical precedents, in terms of their experiential content they often felt less genuine than the tactical ones.[5] The main reason for this was the pre-inscribed knowledge we held of the battle's outcome, which was obviously different from the confusions, fears and thrills of the soldiers of the 1860's (see also Kelly 2009:8.6–8.7). This necessarily 'fixed' feature of the scripted battles lent them an artificial quality of temporal overview and reassurance that differed from the relative openness and insecurities inherent in the tactical.

In the case of these latter confrontations, typically performed out of sight of the public, a much more liberal perspective on 'historical fact' was upheld. The main idea was that, while remaining observant of historical structures and logistics of battle organisation, order giving, military manoeuvring and so on, the officers in charge were given more of a free reign to steer and 'fight' the battle as they wished. Sometimes this was phrased as a chance for commanders to test their own tactical abilities and 'see what they would have done' in a specific case that might or might not be modelled over a historical episode.

---

[5] The concept of (and controversies over) 'authenticity', while central to the re-enactment scene, will not be discussed in detail here, as it is covered intensively in the literature already. Classics on authenticity concerns in heritage and tourism include Bruner (1994), Cohen (1988), Handler and Saxton (1988), MacCannell (1973), and Wang (1999). For a useful, broader overview of the significance of authenticity, see Lindholm (2008).

Thus, the tacticals were arguably experimental in the (liberal) sense that they allowed re-enactors a large degree of freedom in performing tweaked versions of historical events, and to approach – if always in piecemeal and unsystematic fashion – some of the hundreds of 'what if' questions surrounding the Civil War. Such questions were always pertinently present anyway, for instance in small talk and discussions around the campfires at night or on the Internet fora that constitute vital communication nodes in the dispersed communities of the hobby.[6] What if, during the Battle of Gettysburg, (Union) Colonel Joshua Chamberlain had hesitated and not issued the bayonet counter-charge in defence of Little Round Top? Or what, on the other hand, if (Confederate) General Thomas 'Stonewall' Jackson had still been alive and in command at Gettysburg? What if, in this or that engagement, the cavalry had been allowed to advance farther before the infantry was deployed, or what if a particular skirmish formation had been abandoned earlier? The list is endless.

Such constant speculation and reflection was, admittedly, highly unsystematic business. This trying out of various tactics and scenarios, through chat and discussion when in camp, but also corporeally in the format of the tactical battle, did *not* mean that my informants imagined themselves able to perform laboratory-style experiments in counter-factual history and come up with scientifically proven tests or responses. What they did allow for, however, was a curious, playful and – crucially – *embodied* and *felt* reflection of tiny snippets of experience, concerns or moot points of the Civil War as imagined by these enthusiastic, non-academic but supremely 'living' and experimental historians.

As such, the battle re-enactments I have taken part in are clearly not fully comparable to the rigorous open-air research laboratories hailed by Shimada so much as imaginative events in which less structured and more explorative scenarios and ideas could be tried out. In their work on the place of 'place' in tourism, Simon Coleman and Mike Crang (2002:10) have argued for an unfinished, 'progressive' sense of place, 'where space is an eventful and unique happening more to do with doing rather than knowing, less a matter of 'how accurate is this?', than 'what happens if I do it?' (see also Massey 1993). This curious and explorative stance – paradoxically, perhaps, in a subculture otherwise so bent on authenticity and verisimilitude – captures an important quality of re-enactment, especially relating to the 'tactical' battles in which results are not predetermined.[7]

---

[6] The main re-enactment web fora frequented by my American informants were http://www.authentic-campaigner.com, http://www.re-enactor.net/ and http://www.cwre-enactors.com.
[7] In an earlier article I have discussed this 'unfinished' element of re-enactment as a key attraction for participants in some detail (Daugbjerg 2014a; see also de Groot 2009:108–09; Schneider 2011:33).

While it is poorly suited to address the kind of strictly controllable research questions that have traditionally occupied experimental archaeologists, the curiosity and the creativity inherent in these re-stagings seem to offer something else: a testing, if you will, well aware of its own limitations, but nevertheless permeated by a belief that a certain amount of creative liberty may enable a partial and enriching contact with the realities of former times.

Conclusion: What kind of science is this?

In this chapter, I have explored the grey zones and temporal attractions in-between experiential and experimental practices in re-enactment and living history settings on the backdrop of concerned academic voices from more conventionally inclined experimental scientists. I have shown how, despite continuing insistences in some quarters on the importance of upholding a sharp and impenetrable barrier between experience and experiment, in practice these types of activities overlap and blur. Certainly, this blurring – increasing, if anything, across a heritage sector aligning itself more and more with experientially driven economies and tendencies – calls for nuanced scholarly reflection. Whereas some prefer to uphold rigid lines between them, I have opted instead for an immersed perspective focussing on common ground and historical and contemporary conflations between positions. I have argued, in essence, that experience and experiment are two sides of the same coin.

I doubt that my unfolding of blurred spectacles, 'enthralling' events and 'magic moments' will have done much to satisfy the school of experimental archaeologists still inclined to devalue any kind of trialling that does not qualify as laboratory-style experiments of a controllable, repeatable and falsifiable nature. However, it may be worth recalling that the ideals underpinning this veneration for the positivist experiment are not naturally (or divinely) given but are themselves products of historical processes, negotiations and intense power struggles. In a short but intriguing essay entitled 'What Kind of Science is Experimental Physics?' historian Otto Sibum (2004:60) has outlined the early modern (late 18th to early 20th century) scholarly debates and doubts surrounding 'the artificial technological character of experiment'. In particular, he points out, it was the human and physical manipulation of objects in laboratories that served to initially cast the then new experimental procedures and principles into long-lasting suspicion. Could these man-made installations be trusted – as opposed to the scholarly 'experience' gained from traditional unobtrusive observation of nature – to provide trustworthy knowledge about the world? Of particular interest to my own discussion is Sibum's recounting of the emergence of a new controversial position of middleman – a 'third man', as it was termed in the mid-18th century – who 'was sought to bridge the divide between theorists and practitioners' (Sibum 2004:60). These new experimentalists would, it was hoped, 'unite science and art' (experiment, being 'artificial', held to belong to the latter category), even though, initially, they were shunned by both traditional theorists and conventional practitioners. 'Like bats, they were difficult to classify. Did their studies of nature, practiced with head and hand, lead to a specific form of knowledge? And did this knowledge qualify as scientific?' (Sibum 2004:60).

Since these early modern headaches, the reservations towards the epistemological status of experimental research have largely vaporised. As Sibum (2004:61) notes, by 'the turn of the 20th century, the art of experiment had been developed to the most powerful art of knowing within science'. Still, the questions on the suspicious but potentially useful 'third man' utilising both head and hand constitute a useful historical reminder. Today, it seems to me, the scientific traditionalists, no longer apprehensive of 'experiment', have instead directed their scepticism towards 'experience' in its particular twenty-first-century guises. The conceptual suspicion has thus in a certain sense been reversed.

There may be several specific and in some cases sound reasons for such scepticism, some of them related to the various instrumentalist causes, commercially, ideologically or otherwise, for which 'experience' is often enlisted nowadays. Still, given that bodily, emotional and experiential approaches to history keep gaining ground both in amateur and professional circles, it would seem that a nuanced and theoretically well-founded discussion of possibilities and problems inherent in such approaches would be of more value than an outright rejection. Indeed, this chapter can be seen as a small-scale contribution to initiating such a discussion. Perhaps it ought not be thought controversial to insist that those several layers of historical reality that lab-style experiments indisputably ignore in their identification and isolation of a few 'controllable' variables *also* contain a value that remains unaccounted for when they are peeled off; perhaps, even, that in some cases, it may be exactly these peeled-off layers that constitute what Runia called the 'mysterious surplus' of historical insight. At the very least, we need to acknowledge – but also, obviously, to critically assess and discuss – the efforts of the 'third men' of today, amateurs as well as professionals who seek to capture this elusive surplus.

References

Agnew, V. 2007. History's affective turn: Historical re-enactment and its work in the present. *Rethinking History* 11(3):299–312.

Amster, M. 2008. A pilgrimage to the past: Civil War re-enactors in Gettysburg. In Claire L. Boulanger (ed.), *Reflecting on America. Anthropological Views of U.S. Culture*: 15–27. Boston, Pearson/Allen and Bacon.

Ayto, J. 1990. *Bloomsbury Dictionary of Word Origins*. London, Bloomsbury.

Boswijk, A., Thijssen T., and Peelen E. 2007. *The Experience Economy: A New Perspective*. Amsterdam, Pearson.

Bruner, E. 1994. Abraham Lincoln as authentic reproduction: A critique of postmodernism. *American Anthropologist* 96(2):397–415.

Cohen, E. 1988. Authenticity and commoditization on tourism. *Annals of Tourism Research* 15(3):371–386.

Coleman, S. and Crang M. (eds.) 2002. *Tourism. Between Place and Performance*. New York and Oxford, Berghahn Books.

Coleman, S. A. and Eade, J. (eds.) 2004. *Reframing Pilgrimage: Cultures in Motion*. London and New York, Routledge.

Cook, A. 2004. The use and abuse of historical re-enactment: Thoughts on recent trends in public history. *Criticism* 46(3):487–496.

Crang, M. 1996. Magic kingdom or a quixotic quest for authenticity? *Annals of Tourism Research* 23(2):415–431.

Cushman, S. 1999. *Bloody Promenade: Reflections on a Civil War Battle*. Charlottesville, University Press of Virginia.

Daugbjerg, M. 2011. Playing with fire: Struggling with 'experience' and 'play' in war tourism. *Museum and Society* 9(1):17–33.

Daugbjerg, M. 2014a. Patchworking the past: Materiality, touch and the assembling of 'experience' in American Civil War re-enactment. *International Journal of Heritage Studies* 20(7–8):724–741.

Daugbjerg, M. 2014b. *Borders of Belonging. Experiencing History, War and Nation at a Danish Heritage Site*. Oxford, Berghahn Books.

Desjarlais, R. 1994. Struggling along. The Possibilities for Experience Among the Homeless Mentally Ill. *American Anthropologist* 96(4):886–901.

Edensor, T. 1997. National identity and the politics of memory: Remembering Bruce and Wallace in symbolic space. *Environment and Planning D* 29:175–194.

Falk, J. H. and Dierking, L. D. 1992. *The Museum Experience*. Washington, D.C., Whalesback Books.

Flores, J. R. and Paardekooper, R. (eds.) 2014. *Experiments Past. Histories of Experimental Archaeology*. Leiden, Sidestone Press.

de Groot, J. 2009. Historical re-enactment. In *Consuming History. Historians and Heritage in Contemporary Popular Culture*, 105–123. London and New York, Routledge.

Hall, M. 2006. The reappearance of the authentic. In I. Karp, C. A. Kratz, L. Szwaja and T. Ybarra-Frausto (eds.), *Museum Frictions: Public Cultures/ Global Transformations*: 70–101. Durham and London, Duke University Press.

Handler, R. 1994. Lessons from the Holocaust Museum. *American Anthropologist* 96(3):674–678.

Handler, R. and Saxton, W. 1988. Dyssimulation: Reflexivity, narrative, and the quest for authenticity in 'living history'. *Cultural Anthropology* 3(3):242–260.

Holtorf, C. 2009. On the possibility of time travel. *Lund Archaeological Review* 15:31–41.

Holtorf, C. 2010. Meta-stories of archaeology. *World Archaeology* 42(3):381–393.

Jay, M. 2005. *Songs of Experience. Modern American and European Variations on a Universal Theme*. Berkeley, University of California Press.

Kalshoven, P. T. 2012. *Crafting the Indian. Knowledge, Desire and Play in Indianist Re-enactment*. Oxford, Berghahn Books.

Kaufman, W. 2006. *The Civil War in American Culture*. Edinburgh, Edinburgh University Press.

Kelly, V. 2009. Ghosts of the past. Breaker Moran and re-enactment. *History Australia* 6(1):8.1–8.14.

Kirshenblatt-Gimblett, B. 1998. *Destination Culture. Tourism, Museums, and Heritage*. Berkeley, CA, University of California Press.

Knudsen, B. T., Christensen, D. R. and Blenker, T. 2014. *Enterprising Initiatives in the Experience Economy: Transforming Social Worlds*. London and New York, Routledge.

Landsberg, A. 2004. *Prosthetic Memory. The transformation of American Remembrance in the Age of Mass Culture*. New York, Columbia University Press.

Lindholm, C. 2008. *Culture and Authenticity*. Malden, Blackwell.

Lowenthal, D. 1998. *The Heritage Crusade and the Spoils of History*. Cambridge, Cambridge University Press.

MacCannell, D. 1973. Staged authenticity: Arrangements of social space in tourist settings. *The American Journal of Sociology* 79(3):589–603.

Magelssen, S. 2014. *Simming. Participatory Performance and the Making of Meaning*. Ann Arbor, University of Michigan Press.

Massey, D. 1993. Power-Geometry and a progressive sense of Place. In J. Bird, B. Curtis, T. Putnam and G. Robertson (eds.), *Mapping the Futures: Local Cultures, Global Change*: 59–69. London and New York, Routledge.

O'Dell, T. and Billing P. (eds.) 2005. *Experiencescapes: Tourism, Culture and Economy*. Copenhagen, Copenhagen Business School Press.

Outram, A. K. 2008. Introduction to experimental archaeology. *World Archaeology* 40(1):1–6.

Petersson, B. and Narmo L. E. (eds.) 2011. *Experimental Archaeology. Between Enlightenment and Experience*. Lund Acta Archaeologica Lundensia Series in 8, Vol. 62. Lund, Lund University Department of Archaeology and Ancient History.

Pine, B. J. and Gilmore J. H. 1998. Welcome to the experience economy. *Harvard Business Review* (July–August):97–105.

Pine, B. J. and Gilmore J. H. 1999. *The Experience Economy: Work is Theatre and Every Business a Stage*. Boston, Harvard Business School Press.

Prentice, R. 2001. Experiential cultural tourism: Museums and the marketing of the new romanticism of evoked authenticity. *Museum Management and Curatorship* 19(1):5–26.

Rasmussen, M. (ed.) 2007. *Iron Age Houses in Flames. Testing House Reconstructions at Lejre* (Studies in Technology and Culture Vol. 3). Lejre: Lejre Historical-Archaeological and Experimental Centre.

Runia, E. 2006. Spots of time. *History and Theory* 45 (October 2006):305–316.

Schneider, R. 2011. *Performing Remains. Art and War in Times of Theatrical Re-enactment*. London and New York, Routledge.

Schulze, G. 1992. *Die Erlebnis-Gesellschaft. Kultursoziologie der Gegenwart*. Frankfurt and New York, Campus Verlag.

Shimada, I. 2005. Experimental archaeology. In H. D. G. Maschner and C. Chippindale (eds.), *Handbook of Archaeological Methods*: 603–642. Lanham, Altamira Press.

Sibum, Otto H. 2004. What kind of science is experimental physics? *Science* 306 (Oct 1, 2004):60–61.

Thompson, J. 2004. *War Games. Inside the World of 20th-Century War Re-enactors*. Washington, D.C., Smithsonian Books.

Walsh, K. 1992. *The Representation of the Past: Museums and Heritage in the Post-Modern World*. London and New York, Routledge.

Wang, N. 1999. Rethinking authenticity in tourism experience. *Annals of Tourism Research* 26(2):349–370.

West, B. 2014. Historical re-enacting and affective authority: performing the American Civil War. *Annals of Leisure Research* 17(2):161–179.

Chapter 8

Face-to-Face with the Past
Pompeii to Lejre

Cornelius Holtorf

Abstract

Archaeology has long been considered and portrayed as the discipline par excellence of things and material culture. Most valued by archaeologists and their audiences have been those sites and artefacts that are best preserved and thus seemingly allowing direct glimpses of past realities. Throughout the history of the discipline of archaeology ancient artefacts never left centre stage, although the way in which, according to the archaeologists, their significance emerged in the present has changed considerably over the decades and centuries. In this chapter I argue that over the past decade or so an alternative framework for interpreting the past and its remains has been gaining ground in contemporary society. Staged performances, scripted or improvised play and virtual simulation now allow many people face-to-face encounters with the past without the need of preserved things from antiquity. The significance of things in archaeology has changed as bodily sensations and evocative narratives are substituting for tangible evidence and hands-on experiments. Objects still play a significant role though; as props they facilitate storytelling and contribute to holistic time travel experiences. A case in point for this significant development is provided by the changing character of visitor experiences at archaeological open-air museums where the past is brought to life. This chapter is based on fieldwork at Land of Legends, Lejre, Denmark.

Keywords: Immersion, material culture, reconstruction, story-telling, things

Introduction: Wonderful things

Archaeology has long been considered and portrayed as the discipline par excellence of things and material culture. Most valued by archaeologists and their audiences have been those sites and artefacts that are best preserved and thus seem to allow direct glimpses of past realities. Well-preserved ruins, like those in Pompeii (Figure 8.1) and Herculaneum, and complete bodies, like Egyptian mummies and Northern European bog bodies (Figure 8.2), have fascinated people since even before the full emergence of a scientific archaeology, as they provided a sense of an immediate encounter with the past in the present (Sanders 2009:219–233). Characteristic for the visceral experience provided by these ancient objects is Stendhal's account of a visit of Pompeii from 1826 (cited after Blix 2009:54, 84): 'one has the sense of being transported into antiquity and so long as one has the habit of trusting only one's eyes, instantly knows it better than any scholar . . . it's a great pleasure to see this antiquity face-to-face.'

At the heart of the archaeological experience, though not always realised, was from its beginning not the absence of a living present and the fact that the people of the past are missing, as Lucas (2010) argued, but their magical presence. This presence resembles the way in which ghosts can be perceived as present in haunted buildings and are accessible to a medium through a psychical deployment of the senses so that "you can just feel the history here" (Hanks 2015:128, 145).

Subsequently, the discipline of archaeology developed out of collections containing artefacts that had been found at archaeological sites. One of the most elementary frameworks of prehistory, the Three-Age System of Stone Age, Bronze Age and Iron Age, was the result of the Danish antiquarian Christian Jørgensen Thomsen (1788–1865) studying the collection of the National Museum of Denmark in Copenhagen. The main principles behind his classification and chronological organization of the artefacts are still being used today for making sense of the distant past, even though archaeologists now ask a wide variety of questions about the societies and social changes behind the patterns directly discernible from studying ancient technologies.

Figure 8.1: Transported into antiquity in the surprisingly well-preserved Roman town of Pompeii, Italy (http://commons.wikimedia.org/wiki/File:Pompeii-Street.jpg).

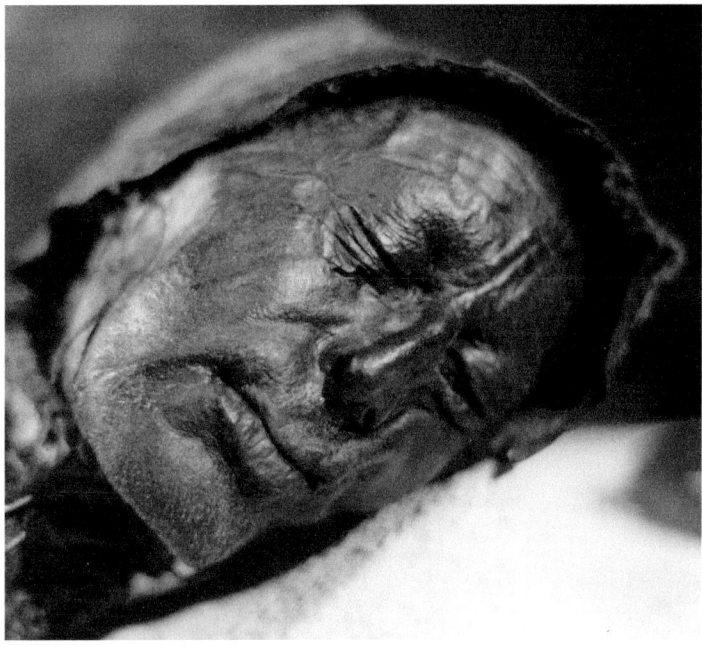

Figure 8.2: Face-to-face with Tollund man, a bog body from the pre-Roman Iron Age in central Jutland, Denmark (http://commons.wikimedia.org/wiki/File:Tollundmannen.jpg).

When the English Egyptologist Howard Carter (1874–1939) several generations later discovered the tomb of Tutankhamun, the fascination of archaeologists and their broad audiences with well-preserved objects had long been self-evident. It manifested itself clearly when curious onlookers asked Carter what he could see at the very moment of discovery. His famous answer was: 'Wonderful things!' Here, as at Pompeii, the splendid material remains of the past allowed archaeologists and others a kind of magical operation that almost effortlessly resurrected the past in the present (Blix 2009:87). It was as if the recovery of past things alone could unlock the past, an idea that is still present today in some popular perceptions of archaeology (Figure 8.3).

Subsequent generations of archaeologists presented evermore detailed ways of dividing artefacts into categories and of analysing and interpreting them in the context of wider spatial and temporal patterns reflecting (pre-) historical change and development (Eggers 2006). As the discipline of archaeology thus matured, things and material culture remained central, but the character of encounters with the past shifted from a visceral sensation in the stomach to a challenge for the mind. More skills were needed for archaeological reasoning than what it took to recover wonderful things and trusting one's eyes.

Figure 8.3: Unlocking the past; how wonderful things connect people, past and present. (Book cover of University Press of Florida, using an oil painting by Martin Pate, Newnan GA, courtesy of Southeastern Archeological Center, National Park Service, USA)

The theoretical debates that started during the late 1950s lifted the significance of theoretical and methodological issues in the discipline. Revealingly, the anthropologist Robert Braidwood (1958:734) at that time described the aim of North American archaeology as discovering 'the Indian behind the artefact'. Material culture, increasingly seen in terms of scientific data, remained however central to the acquisition of archaeological knowledge about past societies even during the high days of the so-called New Archaeology in the 1960s and 1970s. This significance of things continued also subsequently during the 1980s and 1990s when a series of new theoretical paradigms and new agendas were proposed for the discipline of archaeology. For example, Christopher Tilley, one of the key representatives of the post-structural archaeology developed at Cambridge in the United Kingdom, edited a programmatic study entitled *Reading Material Culture* (1990) exploring the complex relations between things, social reality and powerful interpretive frameworks offered by structuralism, hermeneutics and post-structuralism. According to the blurb on the book's back, 'central to any understanding of the significance of material objects, whether contemporary or prehistoric, is a discussion of the very nature of interpretation itself: how we "read" artefacts and inscribe them into the present' (see also Chapter 3 in Olsen 2010). Things were to be read and interpreted like texts.

In recent years, both in archaeology and throughout the humanities and social sciences, a return to things as such has been proclaimed. Archaeologist Bjørnar Olsen at Tromsø, Norway, is one of the main advocates of an archaeology that 'is first and foremost a concern with things' (Olsen 2010:2). He draws, among others, on the work of his colleague Michael Shanks at Stanford in California, who has long been arguing that archaeology, more than anything else, is about caring for things: 'archaeologists do not discover the past; they work on what remains. Archaeology is about our relationships with what is left of the past' (Shanks 2014). This so-called return to things can be seen as a response to some of the more brainy discussions in theoretical archaeology of the past two decades. In reality, it re-affirmed what arguably always was present in the discipline of archaeology: a notable preoccupation with things and the sites where they were found. It can be said that throughout the history of the discipline of archaeology ancient artefacts never left centre stage, although the way in which, according to the archaeologists, their significance emerged in the present has changed considerably over the decades and centuries.

In this chapter, I argue that over the past decade or so an alternative framework for interpreting the past and its remains has been gaining ground in contemporary society, although some of the roots of this process are much older. This paradigm of bringing the past to life emerged largely in popular culture and daily life. It has only very recently started to be recognised in academia that such popular time travels in fact constitute a challenge to the foundations of our archaeological and perhaps also historical thinking (Holtorf 2007 and chapter 1 in this volume; McCalman and Pickering 2010; see also de Groot 2009; Hjemdahl 2002; Melotti 2011). Staged performances, scripted or improvised play, and virtual simulation now allow many people face-to-face encounters with the past without the need of preserved things from antiquity. The past has become something of a contemporary lifestyle choice and travelling destination. A case in point for this significant development is provided by the changed visitor experiences in one particular kind of archaeological collections and museums, the archaeological open-air museum.

Bringing the past to life at Lethra

Archaeological models and reconstructions in open-air museums are intended to bring the past to life. Throughout Europe they have long been succeeding better than ordinary museums in attracting visitors and stimulating interest in the past. But behind their continuing viability lies a change in character that archaeological open-air museums have gone through in recent decades (Paardekooper 2012; Petersson 2003; Petersson and Narmo 2011; Rentzog 2007). Based on fieldwork published elsewhere (Holtorf 2014), I argue that this transformation is connected with a change of both the significance of things and the role of storytelling and sensual experiences.

Founded in 1964 by Hans-Ole Hansen, the archaeological open-air museum at Lejre, Denmark, now called Land of Legends, has inspired many other centres and museums and is something of a type-site of its genre but is continuously developing ([Figure 8.4] Holten 2014; Meldgaard and Rasmussen 1994; Petersson 2003:140–142). Originally known as *Historical-Archaeological Experimental Centre* (Centre), the open-air museum was intended as a scientific field station for archaeological experiments and reconstructions using prehistoric technologies. The material culture present on the site thus served experimental purposes as heuristic devices allowing cognitive inferences about a past reality. This purpose followed naturally from the idea that one of archaeology's main aims is to gain cerebral knowledge about prehistoric living conditions, based not only on archaeological finds and features but also on ethnographic analogies and on contemporary experiments (Rasmussen 2011:149; see also Keefer 2006). The issues investigated ranged from techniques of manufacturing and using ancient types of tools to functional reconstructions of Iron Age buildings, and from daily life under conditions of the distant past to taphonomic processes that inform archaeological methodology.

At the same time, the Centre has always been pioneering public interpretation and education in archaeology, bringing to life the Danish Iron Age for a large public invited to visit the site, study the reconstructions and observe scientific experiments in progress. There was always an ambition to foster dialogue between craftspeople and researchers, students and teachers, professionals and amateurs, and between visitors and their ancestors (Meldgaard and Rasmussen 1994:129). In this context, the material culture in the open-air museum had the additional function of illustrating both prehistoric living conditions and scientific hypotheses about the past (Rasmussen 2011).

Since 1974, during the summer months, ordinary families have been inhabiting Lethra, Lejre's full-size model of the Iron Age village. Staying one week at a time, they were both to gain experiences about prehistoric technologies and to perform life in the past for curious visitors. The role and perception of prehistoric families has changed fundamentally over the years. This change reveals a larger transformation.

Figure 8.4: Face-to-face with the Iron Age in the full-size reconstructed village of Lethra at Lejre, Denmark (Photograph: Cornelius Holtorf 2011).

The families were initially considered part of the experiment of a complete village as it were and to be contributing to answering research questions in relation both to the full-scale models of Iron Age houses in Lethra and the living conditions in and around them. The family members conducted their own practical experiments and formed an integral part of the experimental character of the village at large (Rasmussen 2011:159–60; Steenstrup 1999:29–30). From around 1980 the families in their own right began to be seen as tourist attractions and learning possibilities for visitors (Steenstrup 1999:21–22, 31). They were consequently considered as staff and stayed for free on a full board basis (Steenstrup 1999:38). In 2015, the families paid 1975 DKK (c. € 265) per adult per week. What can account for this development?

Today, the full-scale models and most other material culture at Lejre are facilitating embodied and narrated performances through which the prehistoric past is staged (see Chapter 4 in Steenstrup 1999). The Centre, which once had pioneered a modern way of researching, teaching and presenting the past for large audiences, has to some extent turned into a modern theme park providing themed experiences that are meaningful and attractive to visitors in contemporary society (see also Hjemdahl

2002). This new strategy, based on extensive market research, involved not only a rebranding and name change from *Historical-Archaeological Experimental Centre* to *Land of Legends Lejre* but also the foregrounding of time travel experiences and storytelling. This is, more than anything else, a change of emphasis; whereas previously the Centre educated visitors about the past in an appealing way, now it offers visitors appealing stories that also educate about the past.

The new strategy meant that previously important historical accuracy gained by tightly controlled scientific experiments and manifested in full-scale models and reconstructions was complemented by a new significance of sensual evocations of the past brought about by applying 'creative imagination' and 'the magic of make-believe' (Hjemdahl 2002:116). Visitors and prehistoric families alike are more than willing to experience Lethra 'as if' it was something other than the patchwork of various assumptions and interpretations by several generations of archaeologists, which it actually is (Rasmussen 2011:162–163). As the social anthropologist Kirsti M. Hjemdahl (2002:116) found in her research about a Norwegian open-air museum, 'dirty butter, logs, bonfires and pancakes with honey are completely uninteresting in terms of objects of the past – yet the grime, toil, smoke and stickiness nevertheless give rise to dreams and thoughts about life in another era' (see also Figure 8.6 below). The prehistoric families seek that special holiday experience of a camping holiday based in the past (Warring 2015). Indeed, although you do not notice it on site, the smell will stick to your clothes and travel with you for hours after you have left Lethra, prompting memories of living in another era. The demand for such a package holiday is high, and few of those selected to live in the past are taken aback when they realise that they are paying in parts for the privilege of performing for other paying visitors to the open-air museum.

By the same token, perceptions and experiences of the material culture in Lethra appear to have become much more important than the chronologically accurate skills required for their manufacture and proper use. During my stay in Lethra in 2011, a staff member, assisting the Iron Age families during opening hours, happily declared one morning that today she was actually wearing shoes inspired by Viking age originals. She went on to suggest that, really, it made no difference to the overall experience of the Iron Age. Material culture remains, therefore, highly significant in the village but in another way than before: it evokes perceptions and reinforces storytelling on a theatrical set. Time travel is thus not facilitated by accurate reconstructions necessarily based on comprehensive expert knowledge about life in another period but by an assortment of things sufficiently tightly associated with the intended travel destination in the past.

For the visitors to be able to feel 'as if' they are in prehistory, the houses have to provide a suggestive stage-set, the objects present on site need to function as props evoking the past, prompting certain stories and behaviour, and crucially, the actors on stage need to offer plots that engage the visitors. When the visitors begin to understand prehistory with all their senses and through their own bodies they effectively perceive what has been called 'performative authenticity', that is an empathetic understanding of something 'other' through bodily experiences (Knudsen and Waade 2010, see also Brædder 2015). The human body is thus no longer merely a tool employed to witness and learn about past practices, but it has turned into a medium through which the past is staged and felt. That past is not of a certain datable age but of a certain degree of pastness which is the contemporary quality of something to be 'of the past' (Holtorf 2013).

The models of Iron Age houses have turned into stage-sets in front of which the prehistoric past is performed by families in appropriate costumes (Steenstrup 1999:56). Whereas back in the 1970s the prehistoric families wore modern sweaters and rubber boots (Holten 2014:273), now it is deemed essential that they wear garments considered broadly appropriate for the Iron Age. The families, in their period outfits, tell stories to the visitors, using the props they have ready to hand. Most suitable to tell stories are the 'Iron Age' clothes and shoes the families are wearing, the tools they are using in their daily activities and the pots and dishes used during meal times. For example, once I employed my modern outdoor knife to carve an ad hoc bow for my son, after vaguely remembering what I had played with as a child (Figure 8.5). The resulting weapon and its amazing capacity to distribute flying twigs around the village and among the geese initiated several conversations with interested visitors who clearly admired our apparent survival skills. The bow was not significant for how it had been made and how it could be used but for the contribution it made to the larger stories being told at Lethra about past and present. The object qualities operative here were not any physical characteristics of the bow but its potential to act as a potent prop onstage and to contribute to evoking a holistic sense of the presence of the past. In that sense, objects can become subjects: they speak to us as we use them or see them in use (Hjemdahl 2002:116); they can transform the quality of a given situation (Kobiałka 2013).

Visitors typically also asked what we were eating, whether the clothes were scratching on the skin, whether we were freezing in the houses, which beds we each were sleeping in and whether they were soft enough. The visitors, in turn, told stories too, for example about their own holidays in Africa where they had seen similar objects in use. Many visitors were also keen to hear where each of us was coming from, how long we were staying and why we were here. They wanted to hear *our* Iron Age stories rather than stories about the Iron Age that no longer is. This became very notable when my son was wearing a modern bandage over his thumb after he had injured himself with his modern knife and been treated at the local hospital; many visitors enquired about this, full of empathy and interest in just *that side* of our Iron Age lives.

Figure 8.5: A modern time traveller's toolkit: gadgets bought on the internet (our knives), poorly executed home-made imitations (our dried shoes) and pure childhood fantasy ([my son's bow and arrows] Photograph: Cornelius Holtorf 2011).

In the eyes of the visitors, somehow, meeting the time travelling families, and speaking to them, authenticated the village and its objects rather than vice versa. Through such encounters and associated storytelling the visitors are being touched by a different kind of performed authenticity, one that arises from a particular affect inside themselves and that connects to the world at large, not to prehistory (Knudsen and Waade 2010).

The transformation of the village of Lethra from a scientific field station to a theme park went hand in hand with a changing perception and engagement of both the visitors and the prehistoric families with the things surrounding them. As I have discussed, material culture turned into a device facilitating embodied human experience in the present rather than a tool to gain cerebral insights about the past. At the same time, the objects present at the site ceased to be perceived predominantly as working models to test abstract hypotheses about prehistoric living conditions and instead began to function as a stage-set facilitating contemporary experiences and storytelling. This change has been aptly described by Mads Daugbjerg (this volume, p. 164) who wrote, with reference to Lejre but in the context of larger trends in heritage and tourism, that 'the experimental ventures of yesteryear, when tests, facts and scientific rigor were higher on the public agenda, have today merged with, and to some degree been superseded by, vaguer but also perhaps more alluring and individualistically pitched invitations to immerse oneself in landscapes and milieus of experience, legend and fantasy'. At Lejre, as elsewhere, evidently, there is a growing desire by people to immerse themselves in experiences of other ages. They are effectively bringing the past back to life and entering it fully embodied with all their senses (see also the other papers in the present volume and Hjemdahl 2002).

The past coming to life

Lethra may be a splendid Iron Age village, but it does not feature any 'wonderful things' in the way that Tutankhamun's grave did. Unlike in Pompeii, in the Danish countryside without well-preserved remains the visitors simply trusting their eyes is not sufficient for the past to become present. Instead, the sense of a presence of the past derives from a number of factors linked to the overall experience of the site in the present. As I discuss in the introduction to this volume (see also Holtorf 2010), particularly important for creating the perception of being immersed in the past is the extent to which

- the past reality presented is consistent and understandable;
- the audience is familiar with the medium and willing to suspend any disbelief;
- the audience's senses are persuaded through rich and vivid impressions;
- pre-understandings and expectations of the audience are matched; and
- the audience is involved and engaged in a meaningful way. (inspired by Lombard and Ditton [1997])

These criteria can easily be exemplified at Lethra, and this accounts for the strength and quality of the audience's experience of being in the Iron Age.

Iron Age life is certainly relatively consistent, especially during the Land of Legend's opening hours (10am–5pm) when the prehistoric families are onstage and instructed to keep up appearances. Having said that, there are many modern objects in the village that visitors never see. These include not just various fire and first-aid equipment but also the inhabitants' sleeping bags, modern shoes, swim vests, secret food supplies both of individual families and for the entire group, an electric socket, a water cooker, cameras, various modern tools such as steel knives and toilet supplies, amongst other items (see also Steenstrup 1999:60–64). Since all this is hidden, the Iron Age remains consistent and therefore understandable.

Broadly speaking, contemporary audiences are also familiar with the medium of full-size models and the concept of living history so that the question of whether or not the houses are two millennia old or why the families are wearing those ancient-looking clothes does not arise, and it is relatively easy for many to suspend disbelief.

Rich and vivid experiences contribute to creating a sense of immersion into a different reality. As in theme parks, Lethra offers much detail including features of the natural building materials used and the flora and fauna in which it is enmeshed. There are also distinctive sensations of smell (the log fire), taste (food), touch (artefacts from organic materials), bodily posture (low entrance doors to the houses) and loads of things to discover visually.

In addition, the audience is already familiar with representations of the Iron Age, not only from school education but also from TV documentaries and popular culture such as Asterix and Obelix. Insofar as Lethra therefore matches some of the audience's expectations of an Iron Age village, it becomes credible as an Iron Age village (see Hjemdahl 2002:117). Audiences are pre-programmed from conventional representations that the Iron Age village is to a large extent about basic routines of daily life, which is exactly what Lethra offers and thus contributes to its pastness.

The families are easily instructed and engaged in the various necessary tasks, and even visitors happily get involved when possible, so that both, although to a different extent, can feel at home in the Iron Age village and perceive the presence of the past (Figure 8.6).

*Figure 8.6: At home in the Iron Age, Lejre, Denmark.
Photograph: Cornelius Holtorf 2011.*

Conclusions: Experiencing the past itself

I have been arguing that throughout much of the history of archaeology the sense of experiencing the past face-to-face has derived from an encounter with well-preserved ancient material culture. Over the course of decades, the nature of that encounter changed gradually from a visceral sensation in the stomach to a challenge for the analytic mind. But in recent years the presence of the past has increasingly become the outcome of a particular feeling again. At places like Lethra encountering antiquity face-to-face no longer requires well-preserved objects from the past. The sensation of experiencing the past is evoked differently; perceived pastness is independent of inherent age (Holtorf 2013).

I am arguing therefore that archaeology has ceased to be the discipline par excellence of things and material culture. The significance of things in archaeology has changed as bodily sensations and evocative narratives are substituting for tangible evidence and hands-on experiments. We are no longer dependent on material devices that help us to unlock the past, whether by marvelling at their sheer presence after all those centuries or as a result of detailed study and expert analysis. The role of the experts has changed to facilitating an experience for their audiences. However, objects still play a significant part; as props they facilitate storytelling and contribute to holistic time travel experiences (Daugbjerg 2014; see also Chapter 4 in Petersson 2003). They have the potency to assist transforming a contemporary scene into one of the past (Kobiałka 2013).

Perhaps more than ever before, archaeology today is about experiencing the past itself, face-to-face as it were. The quality of that experience is ultimately down to the audience's ability to suspend disbelief and let themselves in for an embodied encounter with a different time and its inhabitants. Freeman Tilden (2007 [1957]:102), the American pioneer of heritage didactics, once formulated a challenge for the professionals working in this field: 'the ruin must somehow manage to convey the notion to the visitor that the ancients who lived there might come back this very night and renew possession.' By now, for many audiences in our time the ancients evidently have returned and taken ruins, reconstructed villages and other sites firmly back into their possession.

Acknowledgements

Some of the research discussed in this paper derived from empirical work conducted as a prehistoric family in Lethra, Lejre, in 2011 (fully published in Holtorf 2014). I would like to thank the other prehistoric families at the time as well as Lars Holten, Director, and Henrik Schilling, then Head of Communication, at Land of Legends Lejre for their support. An earlier version of this paper was presented immediately before my visit in Lejre as part of the session 'The Archaeology of Time Travel', co-organised with Bodil Petersson for the *11th Nordic-TAG* conference held in 2011 at Linnaeus University in Kalmar, Sweden. I am grateful to Bodil Petersson for comments on the penultimate version of this paper.

References

Blix, G. 2009. *From Paris to Pompeii. French Romanticism and the Cultural Politics of Archaeology.* Philadelphia, University of Pennsylvania Press.

Brædder, A. 2015. Kroppen som medium til 2. verdenskrig. In T. Kruse and A. Warring (eds.), *Fortider tur/retur. Reenactment og historiebrug*: 67–89. Frederiksberg: Samfundslitteratur.

Braidwood, R. J. 1958. Vere Gordon Childe 1892–1957. *American Anthropologist* 60(4):733–736.

Daugbjerg, M. 2014. Patchworking the past: Materiality, touch and the assembling of 'experience' in American Civil War re-enactment. *International Journal of Heritage Studies* 20(7/8):724–741.

De Groot, J. 2009. *Consuming History. Historians and Heritage in Contemporary Popular Culture.* London and New York, Routledge.

Eggers, H. J. 2006. *Einführung in die Vorgeschichte.* 5th edition [first published 1959]. Schöneiche: scrîpvaz.

Hanks, M. 2015. *Haunted Heritage. The Cultural Politics of Ghost Tourism, Populism, and the Past.* Walnut Creek, California, Left Coast.

Hjemdahl, K. M. 2002. History as a cultural playground. *Ethnologia Europaea* 32(2):105–124.

Holten, L. 2014. Engaging experiments. From silent cultural heritage to active social memory. In J. Reeves Flores and R. Paardekooper (eds.), *Experiments Past. Histories of Experimental Archaeology*: 269–283. Leiden, Sidestone.

Holtorf, C. 2007. Time travel: A new perspective on the distant past. In B. Hårdh, K. Jennbert and D. Olausson (eds.) *On the Road. Studies in Honour of Lars Larsson*: 127–132. Stockholm, Almqvist and Wiksell.

Holtorf, C. 2010. On the possibility of time travel. *Lund Archaeological Review* 15–16(2009–2010):31–41.

Holtorf, C. 2013. On pastness: A reconsideration of materiality in archaeological object authenticity. *Anthropological Quarterly* 86:427–444.

Holtorf, C. 2014. The time travellers' tools of the trade: Some trends at Lejre. *International Journal of Heritage Studies* 20(7–8):782–797.

Keefer, E. (ed.) 2006. *Lebendige Vergangenheit. Vom Experiment zur Zeitreise.* Stuttgart, Theiss.

Knudsen, B. T. and Waade, A. M. 2010. Performative authenticity in tourism and spatial experience: rethinking the relation between travel, place and emotion. In B. T Knudsen and A. M. Waade (eds.), *Re-Investing Authenticity. Tourism, Place and Emotions*: 1–19. Bristol et al: Channel View.

Kobiałka, D. 2013. The Mask(s) and transformers of historical re-enactment. Material culture and contemporary Vikings. *Current Swedish Archaeology* 21:141–161.

Lucas, G. 2010. Triangulating absence: Exploring the fault lines between archaeology and anthropology. In D. Garrow and T. Yarrow (eds.), *Archaeology and Anthropology*: 28–39. Oxford and Oakville: Oxbow.

McCalman, I. and Pickering, P. A. 2010. From realism to the affective turn: An agenda. In I. McCalman and P. A. Pickering (eds.), *Historical Reenactment. From Realism to the Affective Turn*: 1–17. Basingstoke and New York, Palgrave Macmillan.

Meldgaard, M. and Rasmussen, M. 1994. Historisk-Arkæologisk Forsøgscenter i Lejre. 30 års forsøg med fortiden. *Naturens Verden* 4–5:121–129.

Melotti, M. 2011. *The Plastic Venuses: Archaeological Tourism in Post-Modern Society.* Newcastle upon Tyne, Cambridge Scholars Publishing.

Olsen, B. 2010. *In Defense of Things. Archaeology and the Ontology on Objects.* Lanham, Altamira.

Paardekooper, R. 2012. *The Value of an Archaeological Open-air Museum is in Its Use.* Leiden, Sidestone Press.

Petersson, B. 2003. *Föreställningar om det förflutna. Arkeologi och rekonstruktion.* Lund, Nordic Academic Press.

Petersson, B. and Narmo, L. E. (eds.) 2011. *Experimental Archaeology. Between Enlightenment and Experience.* Lund, Department of Archaeology and Ancient History, University of Lund.

Rasmussen, M. 2011. Under the same roof. Experimental research and interpretation with examples from the cof House Models. In: B. Petersson and L. E. Narmo (eds.), *Experimental Archaeology. Between Enlightenment and Experience*: 147–166. Lund: Department of Archaeology and Ancient History, University of Lund.

Rentzog, S. 2007. *Open Air Museums – The History and Future of a Visionary Idea.* Östersund: Jamtli and Stockholm: Carlssons.

Sanders, K. 2009. *Bodies in the Bog and the Archaeological Imagination.* Chicago and London: University of Chicago Press.

Shanks, M. 2014. Michael Shanks – archaeologist at Stanford. Webpage at http://documents.stanford.edu/michaelshanks/Home (accessed 10 Feb 2015).

Steenstrup, J. 1999. Jernalderen – en legeplads i nutiden. Et studie af nutidige familier i en rekonstrueret jernalderby. Specialerække no. 137 (Masters thesis). University of Copenhagen, Deptartment of Anthropology.

Tilden, F. 2007. *Interpreting Our Heritage.* 4th edition [first edition 1957]. Chapel Hill, University of North Carolina Press.

Tilley, C. (ed.) 1990. *Reading Material Culture. Structuralism, Hermeneutics and Post-Structuralism.* Oxford, Blackwell.

Warring, A. 2015. At rejse i tid – fortidsfamilier i Sagnlandet Lejre. In T. Kruse and A. Warring (eds.), *Fortider tur/retur. Reenactment og historiebrug*: 43–66. Frederiksberg, Samfundslitteratur.

Commentary

The Power of Time Travel

Roeland Paardekooper

Time travel is a powerful and inclusive method to reach knowledge and experience relating to the past. Arguably, the success of time travel (the number of performers is increasing rapidly and the shows are ever more popular with the public) has to do with the haptic nature and the experience involving all the senses, which fits so well with present society. The three chapters by Samida, Daugbjerg and Holtorf all share a vision on time travelling in open-air stages.

The motivation for the actors in time travels can range from learning to teaching, from escapism to immersion, between rationalism and irrationalism. What makes something of value to the public depends on these motivations, both from the performer and from the public. A single activity can have a multitude of purposes; some goals are better reached with a certain part of the public than with another. While re-enacting the Battle of Hastings, one can still collect experimental data fit for a scientific publication – not every experiment needs to be executed in an indoor or outdoor laboratory. Artefacts and archaeological data are to be interpreted to learn about the people behind the artefacts we excavate and experiment with. This is exactly the humanistic experimental archaeology Daugbjerg mentions.

The staging of a battle re-enactment is however very different from the preparation for a semi-controlled field experiment. The re-enacted Battle of Hastings, for example, is about acting out a battle to chase the magic moment of the 'period high' Daugbjerg mentions, not a deep analysis of one controllable variable. Such multi-sensory performances also are ways for both the storyteller and the public to escape from the present and immerge into a fantasy world.

But the storyteller always has a responsibility to grosso modo stick to what is known from the period, which is re-enacted. The experience should not just be fun, but the audience should also learn a simple lesson or two. Holtorf mentions, however, that time travel does not necessarily need to be accurate and authentic but needs to be a suggestive stage-set, engaging the visitors. This means that if the public or the performers are not hindered by small inauthentic details, it should not be an issue. Visitors are still experiencing a kind of pastness (Holtorf), a generic feeling of being away in the past.

Are performers in museums, open-air museums and at historical events conveying archaeology to tell a story, or are they telling a story to convey archaeology?

The question is if centres like Lejre in Denmark manage to keep that balance, or whether they emphasise appealing stories over education about the past. Samida suggests that it is a problem to repeat stereotypical presentations in time travels. I would argue, however, that a more holistic approach is required. But when you want to bring a message to your public, you have to meet them at their level of information; you have to meet their interests. Visitors will want to know how people ate and slept – and their stereotyped image of, for example, cavemen is a great start for a story on Stone Age life. A storyteller mixes facts with fiction in order to get a complete story – but is it important that the public, like a true scientist, discerns between archaeological dry facts and the imagined details? Performers have a great responsibility in making the audience question everything they experience. A good storyteller balances education and entertainment. Having 'authenticity police' around makes life for performers difficult, but good performers will do enough of their own research so their show is in tune with what we think we know about the past.

Samida focuses her research on the interactions between professional archaeologists, performers and visitors (scholars, actors and recipients) in selected German open-air museums and at historic events. The three groups Samida mentions are different roles adopted by the same people at different times. A professional archaeologist can be a visitor, just like an actor can be. A performer can learn so much about archaeology that she becomes a teacher; an archaeologist in turn can learn so much about performing that she becomes an actor. It is exactly this blurring of roles (as Daugbjerg also mentions) that leads to more successful time travelling. Just think of the prehistoric families in Lejre (Holtorf). The recipients who first were a part of the experiment have become actors and function as "tourist attractions and learning possibilities for visitors" (Steenstrup 2000:21–22, 31). The boundaries between experts and lay people blur when a blacksmith is performing and a person witnessing is saying "my grandfather was a blacksmith," and then starts telling stories.

An important goal for museums and the academic world is to make current research as widely available as possible. The desire for communication should bring performers and academics together (Samida), like it used to be in Lejre where there was an ambition to foster dialogue between crafts people and researchers, students and teachers, professionals and amateurs, and between visitors and their ancestors (Meldgaard and Rasmussen 1996:129). The change in emphasis in Lejre from research through education to storytelling is an important development. Personally, I see archaeological open-air museums like Lejre not as research centres but as focused on storytelling in all ways one can imagine. The (re)constructed houses and their artefacts become a stage where professionals, as actors, perform serious but entertaining stories.

The experience society is changing into an augmented reality society where virtual experiences follow each other in high pace, in short bursts of attention. The typical long-read of the past seems to be gone. Short performances embedded in story telling may become very successful. More than before, good time travel will offer the possibility of interaction between performers and the public. In other words, the story itself is merely a tool to pass on a message. As long as this message has some kind of accuracy, authenticity does not have to be the main priority of time travelling. The experience of travelling in time is the very reason for its present success.

References

Meldgaard, M., and M. Rasmussen, 1996. Arkæologiske eksperimenter i Lejre, København, Historical-Archaeological Experimental Centre.

Steenstrup, J., 2000. Fornemmelser for fortiden, blandt fortidsfamilier i en rekonstrueret jernalderlandsby i Lejre Forsøgcenter, Forsøg med Fortiden, no. 7. Lejre, Historisk-Arkæologisk Forsøgscenter Lejre.

Commentary

Mediated and Embodied Pasts – A Comment

Carsten Tage Nielsen

The three papers in this section discuss different ways of 'time travelling' and history as a performed practice. Stefanie Samida focusses on the 'benefits and limitations' of living history performances at archaeological open-air museums in Germany; Mads Daugbjerg focuses on 'experiment and experience' in re-enactment and living history performances; and Cornelius Holtorf on face-to-face encounters with the past at Land of Legends, Lejre, Denmark. The authors' agendas are to promote and critically discuss more affective and bodily ways to get in 'contact' with a particular past. My comments are based on my own study of medieval re-enactment in Denmark and my constructionist position within the study of the uses and memory of history.

The past as a time different from the present has to be retrieved and mediated into the present to be present, as otherwise it would not be present. Semantically, the past is a time different from the present, and that's why we need tools or technologies to retrieve it because it is not here automatically. If we feel that the past is present in our lives, it is because we mentally make it alive. This is of cause a constructionist way of comprehension, and others might say that the past is present per se without any human action. The chapters in this section deal with 'living history' and 're-enactment' as vehicles of time travelling. The question is, could we, as human beings, get closer to a specific past through experiments and experiences?

Technologies of time travelling are however not enough to bring a past alive. To be present, a past must also be perceived as relevant and usable by the people involved in the history-making activity whether it is as a performer of a particular past or as an audience to a past performed and represented by someone, by means of something. Otherwise the 'connection' between that past and present will not be established. Any past is not present at any time, only those pasts that people in the present perceive as relevant and important, and that changes over time.

The authors in this section are generally positive towards methods involving the body and the senses, and they discuss different positions of outspoken scepticism and resistance. Such positions are not marginal within historical disciplines and can't just be ignored. In Samida's chapter the antagonists are those who fear stereotypical or 'Disneyfied' representations of the past lacking any source-criticism and self-reflectivity, lacking the hallmarks of academic history. But re-enactment and living history are not academic genres like the peer reviewed article or the dissertation and ought not to be measured with academic standards. By saying so I might imply, that re-enactment and living history can't be methods within historical disciplines – on the contrary. To 'feel' the past or to 'be there' as though I am beamed back in time might be pure imagination and suggestion. But sensorial and affective approaches are not alternative views but complementary approaches to the past enabling us to comprehend and understand other aspects of past lives and realities that we can't achieve by reason and pure logic. To deny the body and the senses in historical disciplines is to reduce the field of interest in past lives and realities. If historians are reluctant to deal with materiality – and many are – they will cut off a considerable proportion of past – and present – life. Imagine your life and your world without things. No smart phone, no forks and knives, no cloth, no cars and so on. In Holtorf's chapter the antagonists are those archaeologists who insist on the primacy of things and material culture. Imagine your life and your world without feelings. No joy, no sorrow, no love, no hate and so on. In Daugbjerg's chapter the antagonists are not addressed explicitly but are in general traditionalist- and positivistic-thinking scholars. I will come back to them below. The authors argue for more plural approaches to the past but do not take on any decisive ontological battles with their antagonists.

To feel or to imagine does not necessarily exclude reflections. Re-enactors typically use their bodies to test equipment and clothing, and they make iterations according to what their bodies tells them in order to achieve authentic replicas. They do what the American educationalist Donald Schön (1983) conceptualized as 'reflection in action'. Mind and body is not separated as the antagonists might think but is co-working according to Schön. The division of body and mind does not make sense from a constructionist point of view.

What seems to disturb and worry some scholars is a presumption that lay people in general are naïve or easy to manipulate. Lay people are assumed to confuse representations with what they represent – taking a reconstruction for an original, an amusement park for a museum, a movie for the reality – unless an authority intervenes telling them the 'truth'. If worried scholars tried to conduct audience research they would however be surprised. Roy Rosenzweig and David Thelen (1998) did such research in *The Presence of the Past: Popular Uses of History in American Life*. Their conclusion was not that lay people are naïve users of history. Instead, they turned out to be perfectly able to differentiate and evaluate among different types of representations and genres. They do not lack critical and reflective thinking.

The antagonists' problems are in my opinion their dualist ways of thinking. By thinking in dualisms, the body is separated from mind and cognition, object from subject, part from hole; what comes together is comprehended as opposed to each other or even seen as something that threatens each other. Concepts like 'embodied minds' or 'embodied cognition' (see e.g. Wilson and Foglia 2016) are based on the opposite assumption and allow us to engage with the questions raised in the three chapters without reluctance or embarrassment. We might be asking questions like how body and mind are working when we engage with past times and making past times come alive in our present when we, for example, dress up in historical clothing and use historical tools on a medieval fair. What roles do metaphysics play in a presumably rational world for our understandings and actions? In a dualist world we all walk around as half-persons. Imagine that literally!

Dualism and positivism are mental barriers when it comes to recognition of experience as one of more ways to 'get in contact with' the past. If history is seen as 'uses of pasts' that do not equal 'the past' per se, the focus will shift from the past in itself to the many ways and forms in which history is made and produced, and from such a perspective it should be entirely uncontroversial to include experiment and experience as proper ways in which people (we) engage with particular pasts.

Now I have come to an even more profound question. How is mental time traveling possible at all? What kind of human instances do support such processes? Memory researchers such as Endel Tulving (1983) or Hans J. Markowitsch and Harald Welzer (2005), pointed out that our so-called autobiographical memory is the neurological basis for mental time travelling. This is the ability to differentiate time in the past, present and future and to combine and relate the different time dimensions. It is not a natural memory, but one which is developed in our brain in a bio-psycho-social-process since our third year of living and fully developed in the early adulthood. According to memory researchers like Markowitsch and Welzer, history is something involving both body and subjectivity.

'Authenticity' is another concept used in the three chapters. It is stressed that authenticity is something both academics and other history-makers strive for. But what is actually meant by the concept 'authenticity'? Authenticity is a multi-layered concept. In some contexts authenticity means original or genuine such as a historical artefact behind glass in a museum showcase. In other contexts authenticity means trustworthy or likely, for example the replica of a sword or garment crafted by people in a re-enactment group. Authentic is also used to characterize a character or an attitude such as 'the authentic self' and 'the authentic teacher'. Authenticity may also be associated with what is authorized, certified or legally valid, like a Donald Duck figure with a printed mark on the back confirming that the trademark of the Walt Disney Corporation indicates it is an authentic Donald Duck figure. As the three chapters illustrate, authenticity is an open question and something that is negotiated.

Most people are very well aware that a one-to-one reconstruction or retrieval of a particular past is neither possible nor even desirable. It is not everything from a particular past that is re-enacted in a re-enactment group or at a living history museum. Illness, murder and genocide are obvious examples. Every representation of a particular past is therefore a reduction. Whether a representation of a past is too simplistic or sufficiently complex is a matter of negotiation. It can't be fixed once and for all. What kind of approach to a past is preferred or chosen must rely on what kind of knowledge and experience we want to retrieve from that particular past and why we want to do it. No methods can per se be excluded as irrelevant or improper.

References

Markowitsch, Hans J. and Walzer, Harald (2005). Das autobiographische Gedächtnis. Stuttgart, Klett-Cotta.

Rosenzweig, Roy and Thelen, David (1998). *The Presence of the Past. Popular Uses of History in American Life*. New York, Columbia University Press.

Schön, Donald (1983). *The Reflective Practitioner. How Professionals Think in Action*. London, Temple Smith.

Tulving, Endel (1983). *Elements of Episodic Memory*. Oxford, Claredon Press.

Wilson, Robert A. and Foglia, Lucia (2016). Embodied Cognition. In Edward N. Zalta (ed.), *The Stanford Encyclopedia of Philosophy*. Spring 2016 edition. Available at http://plato.stanford.edu/archives/spr2016/entries/embodied-cognition/ (accessed 19 August 2016).

Part Four

Time Travel on Screen

Chapter 9

Waterworld
Travels in Time between Past and Future Worlds

Bodil Petersson

Abstract

In the future-oriented action film Waterworld *(1995) the world has been flooded for centuries because of melted ice caps due to environmental destruction. This film gives an opportunity to explore the materiality of both past and future worlds as the film-makers create the world anew in an explicitly material sense, with several connotations of our present that have been transformed into a distant past. On top of what aspects of a material past do they construct this future world? The text explores aspects of materiality in a fictive future setting. The conclusion is that film is a cheap way to get to other places and times. It is also an easy way for film-makers to create another universe where it is possible to invert values and intentions, to draw conclusions of our own way of life here and now and bring us to the probable future world to get us to see the consequences of our actions now. It is sometimes a laughing mirror to take the edge off the rhetoric. You can laugh at certain situations and consequences even if time travel goes to Dystopia.*

Keywords: Archaeology, materiality, time travel, film, climate change

Departure

Travelling in time with the aid of film is probably both the easiest and most efficient way to access other eras. In today's cinemas you get immersed in alternative worlds of experience, and you can get astonished by surroundings you never knew before. In very recent times it has also become possible to experience films in 3D, and this further enhances the experience of other worlds.

In the future-oriented action film *Waterworld* (1995) the earth has been flooded for centuries because of melted ice caps due to environmental destruction. Actor and director Kevin Costner presents the film *Waterworld*, which at that time was the most expensive Hollywood film production in history. This film gives the viewer an opportunity to experience materiality of both past and future worlds as the film-makers create the world anew in an explicitly material sense with several connotations to the present. Upon what material past do they construct this future world for viewers to experience and understand? In this text, I explore aspects of materiality that we encounter when we are immersed in this fictive future world. It is obvious that there is a very close connection between materiality of the past (our time) and the construction of future worlds. It is also obvious that one important device used to generate travel in time is truly material: to load the surrounding material objects with good or evil connotations relating to the past world in the film's plot line.

The climate threats and the future

At the beginning of the film, there is a very special transformation of the earth as the logo of Universal Studios is seen from space today. Suddenly the ice caps melt, and the land slowly disappears below the rising sea level. Soon there is only water left covering the earth's surface. For us, from the perspective of our time, the scenario is both frightening and familiar. In this fast-forward development we see one suggested effect of our own lifestyle projected onto a future world scenario.

Let us start with a short time travel back 20 years to 1995. The climate threat defined as global temperature rise is recognised and highly debated. Since 1988 the United Nation's IPCC ([Intergovernmental Panel on Climate Change] http://www.ipcc.ch reports on the effects of climate change, accessed 28 December 2014) has been studying climate change, and in 1992 it published a report on climate changes and how they affect global temperatures. The cause of melting polar caps are intensely studied, and the thoughts on consequences of human action on the global state of our environment also affect themes in the world of films.

The story of *Waterworld*

In short *Waterworld* is about the few remaining people on planet earth, who, after the great future deluge, try to survive even though the sea level has risen to incredible levels. Climate changes have totally melted the polar ice caps, and no land can be seen. Only in myth do surviving ideas exist about how it once was to live on land, and in myth this area is called Dryland.

People fight bravely in this world of water and evil. The star of the film, Kevin Costner, portrays the sailor Mariner (Figure 9.1). In his daily life he lives alone on board an advanced trimaran raft. Now and then he visits floating trading stations; in the film they are named *atolls*, where it is possible to trade valuable goods. Together with a woman and a girl who has a map tattooed on her back, he searches for the mythical Dryland.

Mariner has discovered a way to use a primitive diving bell to sustain himself underwater. While diving, he finds traces of the flooded world that existed 600 years ago, which everyone above water already seems to have forgotten in their daily struggle for life. Under the surface are, among other things, the remains of cities

Figure 9.1. Kevin Costner, the director of Waterworld, in the role as Mariner (© Everett Collection/IBL Bildbyrå).

with skyscrapers and a sunken submarine. The lost civilisation appears as a sunken Atlantis. During his visits to this underwater world from times gone by, Mariner collects certain items, which he trades with at the atolls. Other factors become keys to the understanding of the bygone world and represent pure sensory experiences of the past. What these objects and experiences represent I return to later on.

A Hollywood film is not a Hollywood production unless it contains elements of struggle between good and evil. The film's sinister characters are called 'Smokers', who are small-scale polluters who indulge in the consumption of a residual layer of oil, and like pirates they travel the sea on water scooters plundering and ravaging. For unclear reasons, they also have good access to both tobacco and alcohol, which they consume in large quantities. The film's basic story is thus built up around the conflict between these evil Smokers and ordinary people striving to survive in a cruel and hard, aquatic world.

Future past

I am interested in how we imagine the past and the ways in which we choose to reconstruct it, bring it to life and make it comprehensible in our own time (Petersson 2003, 2009a, 2009b; Petersson and Narmo 2011). After exploring notions of the past I have also become interested in ideas about the future. It is obvious that attempts to reach the future, for example through time travel in films or reconstructions, is not a movement in a single direction. Travelling goes to the future as well as back to the present in shifting intervals. If you travel to the future, as in the movie *Waterworld*, the destination is influenced by the present, just as is the case when travelling back in time, because the present is always the basis for interpretation of a hypothetical future. The imagined future also has a past to look back on, and imagination must be put in motion to create the future past in partial decay.

The interpretations made of present and future times are also a depiction of our self-understanding, and through this connection comes an unbroken line between our interpretation of the past, our lives today and our conception of the future. Travelling to and fro ties together our self-understanding in an interesting way. Materiality is of interest, since the depiction of how we as humans relate to and are affected by the things surrounding us shows how we look at things, how they matter in our lives and how they affect us (cf. Miller [2005] for a discussion on materiality and its meanings and Hodder [2012] for an archaeologist's view of materiality).

The cinema presents good opportunities to show how we create our material surroundings, how they affect us for generations and how matter continues to also mean something in a not-so-well-known future. In films about the future it is common that new technologies are displayed based on the latest technology available in the present. If this technology is retrieved, for example, from the 1970s, it is easy to recognise elements such as physical form and choice of colours as they appear in 1970's aesthetics, even if the time represented is supposed to be hundreds of years ahead of this period of time. In films like *Waterworld*, which instead look back on the remains of material culture from a bygone era (in this case our own present time), it is easy to recognize the parts that constitute comprehension of material culture; but the selection of objects is unique, because it is about the film-maker's valuation of what part of our contemporary material culture is possibly unique in the future. As archaeologists, with trained understanding of the material world and of the role of materiality in our lives, it is easy for us to recognize and analyse the perception of the material world then, now and in the future, and even put ourselves into a fantasy about how the material world that surrounds us affects people over time.

Film as portrayal of history and future

Historians have analysed cinematic representations of historical events and developments, and a particular focus of our time is on questions of identity and history: that is, how people react to the storytelling of various historical phenomena in films and then use ideas as confirmation of our own construction of identities in the present (e.g. Jönsson 2004; Zander 2006). One historian who has focussed on Hollywood films of history and identity formation today is Ulf Zander. In the introduction to his book *Clio at the Movies* (2006; author's translation, in Swedish: *Clio på bio*) he notes that historical films succeed best if the film's narrative is linked to the 'ideological preferences and prevailing scientific ideals' of the times (Zander 2006:17). To relate to a film's identity-building role is perhaps the most obvious perspective when historians consider how we see ourselves and our world then and now. But for this text, I have chosen a slightly different point, namely the presence of the physical world, its activity and connotations for the observer, in theoretical contexts now often referred to as *materiality*. As an archaeologist, it is a way of viewing things' meanings close at hand. I have also chosen to base the analysis on a future setting instead of a past one, but as we shall see, this has less importance as the result nevertheless relates clearly to a study of the past.

Past materiality in a future setting

Independent of *Waterworld* and its qualities as epic narrative, I find the film interesting based on how future relics of the past constantly pop up and are given compelling roles in the film's plot. Although the theme of the film is basically dismal and dark, as in most films about the future of humanity, it is within this futuristic scenario that there is also room for sparks of hope. The hope as well as the darkness the past represents is clearly expressed in the material world that viewers glimpse in the film.

Communication through the senses

A film is evidently made primarily for the sense of sight, and most situations experienced through cinema are intended for the eye. But hearing is also an integral part of the experience. Even the other senses are involved through the film, because indirectly smell, touch and taste are also present. Through our imagination, we can thus use all our senses in a film experience. This is a fact that the creators of *Waterworld* have used well in the film's production.

In a direct parallel to the world of archaeology, the film displays characteristics of what is called *contemporary archaeology*, which focusses on the recent past, for example the years from 1950 and onwards into our own time. Most archaeologists appreciate the distant past more than the recent past, so therefore a specific argument is needed to highlight the importance of contemporary perspectives on materiality of the recent past. One argument is how experiencing objects from the past involves our senses and evokes memories and through this re-awakening makes us reflect existentially on our being in the world. Archaeologists of contemporary times are philosophical and existential (e.g. Burström 2007:87ff.), something that is not so usual when it comes to archaeological reflections on more distant pasts. Usually the distant past is instead presented in a more scientific and technical manner: nutrition or building techniques, just to mention a few approaches.

In the film *Waterworld* we are confronted with objects as symbols of a lost world. These symbols are material objects filled with connotations relating to the past: that is, our own times. These objects tell us important stories about how time travel affects inherent meanings of material objects, but they also give us a clue as to why it is important to know the context of objects. Otherwise we can really get lost in interpretation. The objects in this sense become a laughing mirror intended for archaeologists, since we here can discern a critique towards our professional way of handling objects from the past as relics that we do not understand the dimensions of anyway. If we were not able to travel in time in the world of film, we would not be able to decode our feelings relating to the chosen objects, and the objects' inherent second meanings would definitely get lost in the story. For us to understand this effect of time travel to future worlds, I have picked some examples of relations to materiality – the meaning and communicative aspects of the material world – from *Waterworld* to illustrate the phenomenon.

The rear-view mirror

In an early scene in the film Mariner entertains some children by using a rear-view mirror to reflect sunlight. Given that the earth has been flooded for hundreds of years, the mirror he uses must be a truly odd relic to the living people on this water planet, perhaps even something unknown. A mirror such as this one gives us time to reflect. We are given the possibility to relate to the past world through an object we are very familiar with, but we realise at the same time that this object has lost its original meaning in this future situation. It is of course also possible to consider a deeper meaning in the use of a rear-view mirror, when the fact is that the film evolves around consequences of human actions in the past. To have a look in the mirror can reveal a lot about one's own time. The expression itself, to look in the rear-view mirror, is something that we use today when we look back at something that happened in the past, so the mirror metaphor is a good starting point for time travel.

Desired dirt

Mariner, who is a kind of travelling salesman, arrives at an atoll to sell dirt in a jar. It isn't clear where he got the dirt, but he has probably picked it up during one of his secret visits underwater. It is obvious that dirt has become scarce, and is now much sought after. Everyone is willing to pay a lot of money for it. Soil, which for us here and now is ever present albeit polluted, exploited and artificially fertilized, is in Waterworld a much-sought-after rarity.

Entering the new world with old prestigious boots

In another early scene Mariner has been below the sea surface and among other things has picked up a pair of ski boots from the 1990s. He puts them on his feet and uses them during his visit to the atoll. The boots obviously impress the surrounding people at the atoll. Just as in the case of the rear-view mirror the viewer experiences something eye-opening with the message inherent in the material: the impossibility in this world of skiing in the sparkling white snow on a cold winter's day. This experience has become something quite impossible and has even been forgotten in the new situation for planet earth. We are made to reflect on the existential matter that ice and snow are melting very fast from the earth's surface in present times, and maybe future generations will not able to experience this phenomenon with their senses, just as it has become the case in the film.

Newsprint paper

In a jar on his raft Mariner keeps some wrinkled papers from National Geographic magazine. Both the text content and the outstanding natural images in the magazine, depicting the earth and trees as well as the smell of the paper when the lid of the jar is opened is a relic for Mariner and others that see this artefact. The magazine shown in the film is an issue from December 1995; maybe it was also a question of advanced product placement? The journal focuses on images of people, animals, nature and on earth and its survival. This focus makes National Geographic a good choice as an example of material remains in this particular film. The magazine carries the message of the importance of preserving and saving the global environment with all the plants, animals and humans that inhabit our world (http://www.nationalgeographic.com/, accessed 6 January 2015).

The crayons

The child in the film, a girl named Enola who has a tattooed map on her back that supposedly leads to the mythical Dryland, finds crayons on Mariner's raft. She uses these crayons to draw pictures that tell the stories she carries with her. In this way, the crayons become bearers of a message of a bygone civilisation when she draws images emanating from her early childhood memories. In the end of the film it becomes evident that she once lived on dry land. These crayons give Enola the opportunity to present a visual story about mythical Dryland.

Exxon Valdez

The most striking, largest and humorous 'artefact' throughout the film is the rusty tanker Exxon Valdez, which for many recalls a major oil disaster that once took place in our real world in 1989 off the coast of Alaska. In the film the wreck of this oil tanker has come to new use as the villain Deacon's ship where he retrieves the remains of the oil to fuel his team of gangster Smokers. The oil tanker is powered as a giant galley with the help of slaves. A scaled model of the ship, made for the movie, was until recently placed at the Mojave Air and Space Port near Los Angeles in California, USA (http://mojaveairport.com, accessed January 6, 2015). Some scenes of the movie were filmed at this location, but the props in the form of a scaled model of the Exxon Valdez moved in the summer 2014 to a private person (http://www.parabolicarc.com/tag/exxon-valdez/, accessed September 26, 2015).

The oil

The oil, a fossil fuel that once contributed to the flooding that is portrayed in the film, is the ultimate evil artefact of them all, and now it is in the possession of the evil villain who uses it to loot and reign terror. Here are the connotations of materiality following a well-known pattern in which desired dirt and newsprint paper consistently stand for goodness, while this sticky, black substance – used excessively by the evil side – stands for an ideology that once destroyed the world. As much as we use oil today, it also stands for now as well as in the imagined future everything that is evil and destructive.

Tobacco and booze

In Waterworld the addictions of our own time such as smoking and alcohol have become pure attributes of evil. The evil boss, Deacon, and all the other Smokers, smoke all the time (but where do they grow their tobacco?), and they drink booze all the time too. (Where does it come from?) All in all, it is really a question of 'dark matter' similar to the oil managed by the evil ones (Figure 9.2).

Missing high-tech

Unlike some other cinematic images of future life, there are no real high-tech components in Waterworld. In total devastation everything has been reversed to a basic mechanical technology without computers, mobiles, microchips and nanotechnology. Admittedly, there is a few years between 1995 and today, but technological developments were certainly advanced even in the 1990s. In this imagined future world heavy scrap iron technology is applied. It is not a question

Figure 9.2. Dennis Hopper in the role as the villain Deacon (© Everett Collection/IBL Bildbyrå).

of tailoring art at a high level; fish skin is used as a material as suggested by at least Mariner's outfit. As an archaeologist, it is easy to recognize the dream of a 'low-tech' lifestyle that often exists among archaeologists and others, and that gives the exercise of low-tech knowledge from past times high status in certain contexts (Petersson and Narmo 2011:27ff.). However these future peoples are primarily forced to live low-tech, but they are also very inventive, and this can be seen, for example, in the construction of Mariner's trimaran and the artificial atolls built by the survivors in this new world.

Discussion on matter and related phenomena

Now we have reached the phase of discussing the topic of materiality of the past in the creation of future worlds and how our cinematic time travel to this future world makes us reflect on how materiality affects us in both small and big issues. But besides a purely material approach, I also discuss more abstract phenomena such as religion and evolution since some expressions of these are also made explicitly tangible in the film. These more abstract phenomena actually transforms into tangible 'matter' in a way that is similar to other kinds of matter in the presentation above.

Good and evil matter

Exactly in the same way as Kevin Costner and Dennis Hopper portray the film's good and evil sides of humanity, it becomes obvious that there are good and bad materiality throughout the film. On the good side is paper, crayons and soil. On the evil side is oil, booze and tobacco. This parallelism between the behaviour of people and inherent actions of materiality is intriguing to ponder. Do we consider the world of matter as evil or good when we judge it? Or is it human actions that load it with evil or good? The film offers no obvious answer to that question, and our own judgement of the issue in our time is probably not entirely unambiguous.

Abstract phenomena become tangible

More abstract phenomena also appear in the film. These are the concepts of evolution and religion. In the world of this film they are portrayed in ways that makes them sensory perceptible, and it clearly shows that these phenomena have become material in their expression and meaning.

Evolution

Although the time frame of the movie Waterworld is only about 600 years, it is clear that evolution has begun to affect some people's physical appearance, which is surprising considering how slow evolution works in reality. The hero Mariner, for example, has had time to develop both webbed feet and gills. It has not happened in the same way with the people who live on the atolls, they have not had to adapt to water in the same way. Just because Mariner has evolved, he has become an oddity and an outcast. It is likely that he wears the bulky ski boots on his feet when he enters the atoll to keep his webbed toes undiscovered. The boots effectively conceal the evolutionary impact on his body from the people there. But what he has done is to adapt to the circumstances, while the rest have resisted and not wanted to give up the idea of life on land. In the end of the film, after the actual discovery of Dryland, Mariner leaves for the sea again because he begins to suffer from land sickness, a parallel to seasickness. Physically, he needs to get close to the sea again to feel good. In this evolutionary perspective there is also hope connected to the flooded film world, namely the fact that people have an ability to adapt to new circumstances.

Religion

There are also religious aspects of life in Waterworld. Our own time has already, after only 500 or 600 years, become mythical. Apparently all documentation about the prior 600 years has been destroyed. A document in the film that relates to any kind of belief based on an environmental approach is how dead bodies are 'recycled' on the atolls. After death the bodies are lowered down into a muddy mess that bubbles and boils. During the movie it is not clear what this muddy mess is used for, but probably it goes to some kind of cultivation and in the end nourishment of the population. In addition to 'recycling' dead bodies, it is also possible to be sentenced to 'recycling in the customary fashion' if you have done something criminal. This penalty is about to happen to Mariner, who, however, manages to escape at the last second.

The materiality of the past in the future

In the film there is an obvious relation between past and future materiality. The material culture of our time has been transformed into relics that confuse people of the future, as the objects relate to a bygone world about which little seems to be known. It is exciting to watch the film and guess what fragments are, where they come from and how they are used again by these peoples of the future.

The resurrected Garden of Eden

The analogy to the deluge is obvious. Even though the water that has flooded the planet is a disaster, it has also washed away some of our contemporary woes, and the world is made ready to begin anew. Towards the end of the film the Smokers end up dead on the bottom of the sea together with their oil tanker wreck. The heroes, the good guys, find their way to Dryland, which strangely looks like the Garden of Eden. Dryland seems almost untouched, clean and unharmed, and the good people may here begin their lives anew.

Concluding remarks

By analysing our visions of the future through time travel that our contemporary film directors create for us, we, who inhabit today's Western world, might gain insight into ourselves and our view of our contemporary times, as viewed through the staging of today's material world as something past. Films like Waterworld tie together the past, our own times and the future through materiality. The individual objects and their meaning for us now, then and in the future show how materiality can be pieced together for us to understand our own self-image. Through analysis of how we perceive good and evil matter throughout the film, we can distinguish our contemporary classification of good and evil. (Soil, paper and crayons are good matter, while oil, alcohol and cigarettes are bad matter.) Simplification and sharpening is a part of the film's rhetoric. Instead of considering other worlds and times through 'physical' time travels, we are presented with a completed interpretation, which we may support or reject. But in this world of stories told, materiality is shown to play at least the same role of importance as the props used in all physical reconstructions made of other worlds.

Travelling in time with the aid of film is a cheap way to get to other places and times. It is also an easy way for film-makers to create another universe where it is possible to invert values and intentions, to draw conclusions of our own way of life here and now and bring us to the probable future world to get us to see, then and there, the consequences of our actions now. This kind of time travel has both moral and ethical aspects. There is a kind of educational tone in these films, often relating to how we manage the world today and how we ought to manage it to avoid the future scenarios presented in the film.

It is also a kind of laughing mirror to take the edge off from the rhetoric. With the aid of humour and somehow comic situations, you can also laugh at certain situations and consequences even if time travel goes to Dystopia.

Acknowledgements

Thanks to Jes Wienberg, Cornelius Holtorf and Jerryll Moreno for constructive feedback on this manuscript. Special thanks are also due to Hainska Stiftelsen who made it possible for me to develop these thoughts.

References

Burström, M. 2007. *Samtidsarkeologi. Introduktion till ett forskningsfält*. Lund, Studentlitteratur.

Hodder, I. 2012. *Entangled. An Archaeology of the Relationships between Humans and Things*. Malden, Massachusetts, Wiley-Blackwell.

Jönsson, M. 2004. *Film och historia. Historisk Hollywood Film 1960-2000*. Lund.

Miller, D. (ed.) 2005. *Materiality*. Durham, Duke University Press.

Petersson, B. 2003. *Föreställningar om det förflutna. Arkeologi och rekonstruktion*. Lund, Nordic Academic Press.

Petersson, B. 2009a. Den hälsovådliga resan i tiden. In B. Petersson, K. Jennbert, and C. Holtorf (eds.), *Arkeologi och samhälle*: 97–111. Acta Archaeologica Lundensia Series in 8 No. 58. Lund.

Petersson, B. 2009b. Runristare idag. Om vikingatida identitet. In S. Edquist, L. Hermanson, and S. Johansson (eds.), *Tankar om ursprung. Forntiden och medeltiden i nordisk* historieanvändning: 341–365. The Museum of National Antiquities, Stockholm, Studies 13. Stockholm.

Petersson, B. and Narmo, L. E. 2011. A Journey in Time. In B. Petersson and L. E. Narmo (eds.), *Experimental Archaeology - Between Enlightenment and Experience*: 27–48. Acta Archaeologica Lundensia Series in 8, No. 62. Lund.

Zander. U. 2006. *Clio på bio. Om amerikansk film, historia och identitet*. Lund, Historiska Media.

Chapter 10

A Cup of Decaf Past
An Archaeology of Time Travel, Cinema and Consumption

Dawid Kobiałka

Abstract

Time travel is a certain social practice that evokes experiences about past or future realities (Holtorf 2010). The Archaeology of Time Travel awakens and resurrects the past and introduces ways to make the past relevant in the present. However, the Archaeology of Time Travel addresses archaeology that not only approaches the past in the present but speaks even more generally about archaeology in contemporary popular culture. Additionally, the phenomenon of time travel confronts archaeology with theoretical problems that are worth close attention. As it will be argued in this chapter, if we took away the fictional elements in archaeological representations such as those expressed through time travel the authentic aspects would also vanish. That is why there is no real archaeology without fictional elements – there is no archaeology without time travel fantasy.

Keywords: Archaeology, public archaeology, time travel, historical re-enactment, fantasy

Introduction

It seems to be unproblematic from an archaeological point of view to criticise films about Indiana Jones and Lara Croft. They have nothing to do with academic archaeology. Of course, Indy and Lara misrepresent archaeology. But first of all, we should ask ourselves a crucial question: does a film represent any reality, in this particular case, an archaeologist's reality?

Much recent research indicates that Indiana Jones and Lara Croft are the most famous archaeologists in the world (Holtorf 2007; Paynton 2002; Ramos and Duganne 2000). That is why today's popularity of archaeology is based on fictional heroes rather than real archaeologists. But what do archaeologists think about their popularity built upon fictional heroes? Most of us, I think, are ready to criticise films about Indy and Lara. Archaeology has nothing to do with the adventures and tomb robbery seen in these films. Archaeology is a scientific practice. For an archaeologist one correct ^{14}C date is more important than all of the gold that Indy ever found. Ironically, no one other than Indy himself in *Indiana Jones and the*

Last Crusade (1989) perfectly describes what archaeology seems to be truly about: 'Archaeology is the search for fact. Not truth. If it's truth you're interested in, Dr Tyree's philosophy class is right down the hall. So forget any ideas you've got about lost cities, exotic travel, and digging up the world. We do not follow maps to buried treasure, and "X" never, ever, marks the spot!'

However, the question that needs to be posed is the following one: what if such an academic critique of 'pop archaeology' (Paynton 2002) is right in its falsity? That is to say, without any doubt academic archaeology has nothing to do with Indy and Lara. But why is such a relation between archaeology and fictional heroes presupposed in the first place? The aim of the archaeologist as a scientist is not a reactionary deed, in this case, a naïve criticism of popular culture. The aim of archaeology as a scientific practice is something quite the opposite: to show how obviousness is not so obvious and to make familiar the unfamiliar (e.g. Buchli and Lucas 2001).

Archaeology, mimesis and simulation

How, then, is archaeology presented in popular culture? The archaeologist is usually identified as an adventurer, detective or person making profound revelations and taking care of ancient sites and finds (Holtorf 2007). Another strong cliché is the one of the archaeological, evil-minded scientist. Most of these clichés focus upon the figures of Indy and Lara. Indy looks for artefacts with a detective's precision. Looting of cultural heritage does not stand in opposition to breathtaking adventures. And all of these are done on behalf of science.

But what do archaeologists, who are very critical of Indy and Lara, share with those who deeply appreciate fictional heroes (e.g. Holtorf 2007; see also Marwick 2010)? One can claim that both groups presuppose that film mirrors reality, in this case, the archaeologist's reality? Does a film really represent reality? Above-mentioned questions are especially reverent in the context of archaeology because, as it was already indicated (e.g. Holtorf 2007; Paynton 2002; Ramos and Duganne 2000), cinema and TV are the main source of today's archaeological popularity. Additionally, a lot has been written about archaeology and cinema, or more properly, about archaeology in cinema (e.g. Ascherson 2004; Fagan 2006; Fowler 2007; Jordan 1981). All this calls for a closer consideration of the role of cinema in archaeology. No less important, another argument for a closer look at the relations between archaeology and different kinds of time travels (Åkesson 2010; Holtorf 2010; Narmo 2010; Paardekooper 2010; Petersson 2010; Sandström 2010; Westergren 2006) is the fact both of them are very often used in various TV series and Hollywood's films (Kobiałka 2013a).

Paradoxically as it may sound, at the most elementary level, the aim of a film is not to represent reality (see also Zander 2006). Film is not usually an attempt to give a true objective representation of the world. In other words, film does not follow Aristotle's principle of mimesis, which a Greek philosopher described in *Poetics*. Mimesis is, to put it succinctly, the attempt to give the true account of reality. In this way, art is about mirroring reality as it really is. However, film seems not to follow such logic. Film rather simulates reality. This means, film retroactively changes what we call reality as being very unreal (Žižek 1997). In what follows, I discuss a few examples of how simulation works.

In the 'good old days' of the Cold War, soviet KGB agents had orders to watch films about James Bond. Supposedly, in some cinemas in the UK there were more KGB agents coming to see James Bond films than ordinary people. What did a typical KGB agent think before watching James Bond? Before watching the film the world was an ordinary place: cars were to drive, pens to write, and so on. Having watched the film, the perception of the world changed entirely, it was not the same place any longer. In other words, the normal world becomes very unreal, a strange place. The film retroactively changes the agent's entire perception of the world. A perfectly ordinary writing implement following a viewing of James Bond could be a secret camera, microphone or filled with explosive materials. The same concerns cars. A car is never just a car in James Bond films. Recall a famous shot from *The Spy who Loved me* (1977) where James Bond's car changes into a kind of submarine. This is the very reason why James Bond's adventures were the cause of true paranoia for the entire Soviet Union. Film makes day-to-day reality very unreal. Not only did it force the KGB agents to observe their surroundings attentively, but the KGB agents had to rethink their past as well. To provide an example known by most archaeologists, what about *The Mummy* (1932) directed by Karl Freud? Let us ask ourselves, who of us after visiting an archaeological museum has not had a moment of spontaneous question: 'what if the mummy were to wake up?' The coldness, peacefulness and passivity of the mummy appear to be just an illusion. It is as if the mummy would wake up and slowly begin to walk as in the famous scene in Karl Freud's masterpiece.

A very similar effect is experienced when one considers more closely *The Matrix* (1999) directed by the Wachowski brothers (see also Kobiałka 2013a). Before watching the film, the world was – more or less – a normal place. But the first questions after watching *The Matrix* must be what if my world is just an illusion, or what if my life is the same as Neo's? And what if I am part of a computer program? This film changes not only the future, but the very past is rethought, and what was normal so far is no longer so. And in this ability to simulate reality, rather than simply mirroring it, lays the art of cinema.

Therein, perhaps, resides the ultimate lesson of the dialectical tension between documentary reality and fiction: if our social reality itself is sustained by a symbolic fiction or fantasy, then the ultimate achievement of film art is not to recreate reality within the narrative fiction, to seduce us into (mis)taking a fiction for reality, but, on the contrary, to make us discern the fictional aspect of reality itself, to experience reality itself as a fiction. We are watching on screen a simple documentary shot in which, all of a sudden, the entire fantasmatic depth reverberates. We are shown what "really happened", and suddenly, we perceive this reality in all its fragility, as one of the contingent outcomes, forever haunted by its shadowy doubles. (Žižek 1997:77)

If one considers film more as simulating reality rather than simply mirroring it, then one can put social imaginations about archaeology on another level. And this level of cinema, film as simulation, has been deeply underestimated so far by archaeologists. There is nothing complicated about criticising films about archaeology. Such a critique is obvious. But science, and archaeology as science, should do something different. That is to say, archaeology as scientific practice has to show how obviousness is not so obvious. Film as mimesis, film as representation of the world (in this case, the archaeologists' reality) is such obviousness. When one considers cinema as simulation of reality we do something quite the opposite, the non-obviousness of obviousness itself is highlighted. To put it simply, instead of only telling how Indy and Lara obscure archaeological reality, archaeologists should indicate the fields that can be made unfamiliar (Buchli and Lucas 2001) by using films and popular culture as well. The point to make then is that instead of criticising popular culture, archaeologists should use popular culture to show how both archaeology and popular culture are complex, multi-levelled cultural phenomena.

As it was noticed by Cornelius Holtorf (2010) and Bodil Petersson (2010), one of the recently most popular ways the past and archaeology in general is used is time travel. Time travel phenomenon is a child of postmodern times. No wonder then that it is crucial to take into consideration what philosophers, sociologists and so on say about present times. Although relying upon concepts such as the *experience economy* or the *dream society* is – unquestioningly – a useful approach, it nonetheless does not give us a full account of why archaeology is seen and used in the way it actually is. What cannot but stagger one is the fact that probably the first deeply archaeological film – The Mummy – was released in 1932. However, what has to be mentioned here is that the first films where archaeology is part of the plot are: *La Fuite en Égypte* (1898) directed by Alice Guy, *Cléopâtre* (1899) directed George Mélies, and *The Haunted Curiosity Shop* (1901) directed by Walter R. Booth.

The previously mentioned film, *The Mummy*, provides a typical storyline. The plot takes place in Egypt. Archaeologists discover a mummy of a priest. The mummy returns to life (travels in time!) when a reckless archaeologist casts an ancient life-giving spell. Of course, when Imhotep does not want to go back to the other world, archaeologists have to do their best to save this world. The film discloses all the features that characterise the contemporary understanding of archaeology. We can see a great discovery. Archaeologists are adventurers and detectives who take care of ancient sites and finds. When archaeologists appear, then the plot of the film refers, more or less, metaphorically to time travel. So, my point is not only that contemporary archaeology is misperceived. In a way, from the very beginning archaeology was understood in the way it is also perceived today.

An even more fascinating story built upon archaeology and time travel is that of *Hawkman*. Hawkman is a comic book hero who first appeared in *Flash Comics* in 1940. Carter Hall, the main character, is an American archaeologist who conducts excavation in Egypt. (The coincidence of Carter Hall's name with a famous Egyptologist, Howard Carter, is, of course, not accidental.) Once upon a time while conducting an excavation, Carter Hall finds the embodiment of an ancient Egyptian prince – Khufu. In short, Carter discovers the so-called 'metal Nth' is not subject to gravity. Having possessed special powers and reinforced with archaeological artefacts, he embarks on the fight for justice. Once more the vision of the archaeologist as a detective of the past who makes profound discoveries and takes care of artefacts (and by the way the whole world), proves to be the pillar of the entire story. When Carter discovers he is an embodiment of the past, he is nothing more than a kind of time travel. Such images of the archaeologist as detective, adventurer, time traveller and so on perfectly fit a Lacanian reasoning of fantasy, as Slavoj Žižek (2002) highlights.

The ontological paradox, scandal even, of fantasy resides in the fact that it subverts the standard opposition of "subjective" and "objective". Of course, fantasy is by definition not "objective" (in the naïve sense of "existing" independently of the subject's perceptions); however, it is also not "subjective" (in the sense of being reducible to the subject's consciously experienced intuitions). Fantasy rather belongs to the "bizarre category of the objectively subjective – the way things actually, objectively seem to you even if they don't seem that way to you. (http://www.lacan.com/interpassf.htm)

The fantasmatic dimension of archaeology could be the very reason why it is so problematic to understand people's thinking about archaeology and contemporary popularity of time travels. No such ways of thinking are objective if we compare them with how academic archaeology really looks. Nor they are simply subjective if we take into account the fact that archaeology, for more than a century, has been seen within more or less similar categories.

Decaf archaeology

One way of analysing the popularity of archaeology and archaeological time travels is to take a closer look at more general conditions of contemporary culture and society. Philosophers, sociologists and economists write in a similar way about contemporary times. On the one hand, some claim that we live in a world that loses its materiality but is filled with the torrent of signs, copies and simulacrums (Baudrillard 1994). Others describe our times referring to consumption (Bauman 1989) or post-industrial contexts (Bell 1974). On the other hand, Rolf Jensen (1999) writes about the dream society, and Joseph Pine and James Gilmore (Pine and Gilmore1999, 2007) focus on the experience economy. What links all of these perspectives? I would risk some simplification that at the most elementary level all the above-mentioned, except the premises that desire for experience and pursuit of signs, are crucial constitutive elements of the contemporary world. The consumption of experiences and signs, or in other words, pursuit of dreaming paints our social picture. That is why today's popularity of archaeology can be understood through the concepts of the dream society and experience economy. Indeed, the *Archaeology of Time Travel* inherits much from today's economics (Holtorf 2010).

One of the conclusions to be drawn from the experience society could be that changes of the society demand the change in a way of doing and popularising archaeology. The Academy is not a proverbial 'ivory tower', and every discipline does not stand for itself. Archaeology has to face the problems of contemporary times and try to act out its social role in a new social context. The appearance of archaeology – so-called archaeo-appeal (Holtorf 2005) – is the result and part of popular culture. As many commodities, it can be claimed that archaeology is also goods for sale, for consumption and experience to be used as time machines into the past. To live today means literally to consume; consumption is the condition of the postmodern man ([liquid modernity, in Bauman's terms] Bauman 1989).

Many archaeological festivals seem to be precisely about time travelling and consumption of the past (e.g. Pawleta 2010, 2011): for example, the Slavs and Vikings Festival organised by the Slavs and Vikings Centre Wolin Jomsborg Vineta in Wolin (Poland) or in Scandinavia, the very popular Viking Week at the Foteviken Museum. On the one hand, places where archaeological festivals take place look like they are from a different period. On the other hand, the archaeological festivals are a context in which a more mythical past is staged (Figure 10.1). Some events promote themselves as being quite literally time machines, as was the case of II Historical Picnic organised by the Historical Museum in Gdańsk (29 October 2012, Poland).

Figure 10.1a, 10.1b. Two versions of the same 'consumption' of the past (Grzybowo 2012, author Dawid Kobiałka).

But, what if the things are more complex? Let us briefly focus on the other side of contemporary consumption. Žižek (2004) in many places makes a similar point apropos today's consumption, as the Slovenian philosopher claims.

On today's market, we find a whole series of products deprived of their malignant property: coffee without caffeine, cream without fat, beer without alcohol.... And the list goes on: what about virtual sex as sex without sex, the Colin Powell doctrine of warfare with no casualties (on our side, of course) as warfare without warfare, the contemporary redefinition of politics as the art of expert administration as politics without politics, up to today's tolerant liberal multiculturalism as an experience of Other deprived of its Otherness (the idealized Other who dances fascinating dances and has an ecologically sound holistic approach to reality, while features like wife beating remain out of sight.(http://www.lacan.com/zizekdecaf.htm)

Such logic, which can be called, *the logic of decaf coffee*, perfectly illustrates the problem of misperception of archaeology by the public. When some archaeologists (Fagan 2006; Fowler 2007; Kristiansen 2008; Russell 2002) claim that archaeology has nothing to do with Indiana Jones, Lara Croft, and so on, what they effectively want is a 'decaf archaeology'. This popular misperception (understood as something subjective) of archaeology is part of the very process of perception of archaeology itself. Without caffeine, coffee is not real coffee. In the same vain today, without Indiana Jones or Lara Croft as well as different archaeological time travels there is no archaeology as such. What seems to be an obvious error according to archaeologists about their profession is in reality a deeply unobvious social process.

The fascination of time travel and historical re-enactment can be the result of the very same process. When people travel in time, let us say, to the Early Middle Age, what they experience is an experience without experience. The experienced past is deprived of its malignant property. For example, great and fearless warriors who fight a 'life-and-death' struggle use blunt weapons (Figure 10.2). Here we have a Middle Age's fight without fight, without blood and corpses, which, let me risk the following hypothesis, were frequently encountered during the Middle Age's battlefields.

It is interesting to use a *decaf logic* in relation to the history of archaeological thought as well – to make the familiar unfamiliar. To simplify, contemporary academic archaeology consists of three ways of doing archaeology: culture-historical archaeology, processual archaeology, and post-processual archaeology. The first basically relies on positivism, the second on modernism and the third on postmodern thought. Whereas culture-historical and processual archaeologies do not pay close attention to how interpretation of the past is connected to the present, in post-processual archaeology it is one of the main problems (Shanks and

Figure 10.2. Decaf past – a contemporary Viking (Photograph by Tomasz Marciniak).

Tilley 1987). In addition, the problem of how the past is mixed with the present is a distinctive feature of post-processual archaeology. However, this point needs a short clarification.

Culture-historical and processual archaeologies, of course, approach the present. From ethnoarchaeology, and the so-called ethnographical analogy, to Micheal Schiffer's works (e.g. 1991), the present observations of people's beliefs, actions and thinking have been used as a way to approach the past in more detail. What is so crucial is the fact that the present is not important for itself. The role of the present for itself is, however, precisely what is characteristic for contemporary archaeologies (e.g. González-Ruibal 2013) and the *Archaeology of Time Travel* too.

However, it is culture-historical and processual archaeologies that are *more* postmodern than post-processual archaeologies. The past without the present is nothing else than another version of coffee without caffeine, a version of a product that is deprived of its essence. That is why *truly traditional* archaeologies are post-processual archaeologies. Only here archaeologists dare to drink a cup of true coffee, the coffee full of dangerous caffeine, the past with the present. This is what the *Archaeology of Time Travel* is about (e.g. Holtorf 2010; Kobiałka 2013a; Petersson 2010; Sandström 2010).

Reality or illusion

Let us now consider in more detail *The Matrix*. Although the film is not about archaeology, there is one scene that is very significant in relation to the *Archaeology of Time Travel*. Take into consideration the moment when Morpheus asks Neo about his will to exit the matrix. Neo must choose between a blue and a red pill. By taking the blue one, he would return to the illusion created by the matrix. If Neo chose the red pill, then he would see the reality beyond the matrix.

Žižek interprets this scene in the documentary *The Pervert's Guide to Cinema* (2006). The Slovenian philosopher points out that the Morpheus's proposition is deeply false. The choice between the illusion and the reality is not a true choice because the matrix as an illusion already structures what we see and experience as reality. In other words, there is no reality without illusion, or beyond illusion. That is why the question that really needs to be asked is *not* 'what is the truth and what is the falsity in human life', but rather how the reality is already an illusion. This would be a third way, the third pill which Žižek demands in *The Pervert's Guide to Cinema*.

Wolfgang Petersen's *The NeverEnding Story* (1984) is an even more evocative example than *The Matrix*. The plot is about a young boy named Bastian who is basically lost in his life. His mother died in a car crash. The young boy has problems with his father and is terrorised by school bullies; whilst fleeing their pursuit, he hides in a bookstore. He gazes at the books and sees one book is not for sale. Bastian steals the book, hides in school and begins to read it. The book is about a young boy who tries to save the world called Fantasia from an evil force, the *nothing*. At first glance, the world of the book is just an illusion. As the plot goes on, Bastian discovers that he himself is the only hero who can save Fantasia. But Fantasia has to be saved not only for itself. If Bastian had failed, not only Fantasia but his own reality would have fallen into decline. There is a wonderful dialogue in the film between Bastian (in Fantasia his name is Atreyu) and a very bad wolf called G'mork.

> G'mork: Foolish boy. Don't you know anything about Fantasia? It's the world of human fantasy. Every part, every creature of it, is a piece of the dreams and hopes of mankind. Therefore, it has no boundaries.
> Atreyu: But why is Fantasia dying, then?
> G'mork: Because people have begun to lose their hopes and forget their dreams. So the nothing grows stronger.
> Atreyu: What is the nothing?
> G'mork: It's the emptiness that's left. It's like a despair, destroying this world. And I have been trying to help it.

As one can see, this film for children says something of extremely theoretical importance: without fantasy (illusion) there is no reality. The same goes for the

Archaeology of Time Travel. There is no real archaeology without fictional elements. In other words, there is no archaeology without time travel fantasy.

The same problem that Žižek sees, as far as *The Matrix* is concerned, is the same one we encounter in *The NeverEnding Story*, and (of course) in archaeology as well. One of the consequences of archaeology's popularity is its presupposed simplification and misrepresentation by the public. Some archaeologists' have reservations (e.g. Fowler 2007; Kristiansen 2008; Russell 2002) that mass media, and generally society, incorrectly perceive archaeology and miss the point. There is no chance to distinguish clearly what is true and what is false in people's idea of archaeology. Such opposition reflects a more general metaphysical duality of the reality-fiction. The basic assumption of this way of thinking is that between reality and fiction there is a clearly distinguished border. The premise is that if we take away fictional archaeological heroes (Indy, Lara, etc.), or contemporary fantasies of time travelling (e.g. historical re-enactment events) into a mysterious past, the true archaeology will remain. However, a more probable scenario is the following one: as in the case of *The NeverEnding Story*, if we took away fiction about archaeology, the true archaeology would also loss its social relevance in the present. That is to say, there is no true archaeology without fiction. So, instead of trying to distinguish reality and illusion from each other (what is truly a *neverending story*) one should take a closer look at the reality of archaeological illusion itself. And this is what the *Archaeology of Time Travel* could be about, amongst other things.

What is so paradoxical about illusion is the fact that illusion can be more real than ordinary, day-to-day reality. That is why Žižek claims in the very last words in *The Pervert's Guide to Cinema*: 'In order to understand today's world, we need cinema, literally. It's only in cinema that we get that crucial dimension which we are not ready to confront in our reality. If you are looking for what is in reality more real than reality itself, look into the cinematic fiction.'

Is it not also the truth of archaeologists' reality? If one would look for what is in archaeological reality more real than archaeological reality itself, look into cinematic fiction, films can say something about archaeology and time travels. Illusion is never just illusion. It has its own material dimension that can say something about contemporary times. *The archaeological* lies also in the form, not only in the content of a film (e.g. Marwick 2010; Shanks and Pearson 2001). An instructive example is *Wall-E* (2008), an American cartoon directed by Andrew Stanton. At first sight, it is a story about the future where people live on cosmic ships because the Earth sunk in garbage produced by human beings. There is not even one clear reference to archaeology. Nonetheless, as Ben Martick (2010) wonderfully showed, the film is about relations between material culture (garbage) and human behaviour. And this is something very archaeological. Accordingly, the

American archaeologist shows through popular culture (*Wall-E*) the relevance of archaeology in the present.

Something very similar might be the *Archaeology of Time Travel*. Time travelling is a widespread social and cultural phenomenon nowadays. Archaeology will be important to people when it delivers fascinating stories about the past in the present. As long as there is no past without the present, there is no present without past as well.

Conclusion

Back to the Future (1985) is an American blockbuster directed by Robert Zemeckis. The film indicates a wonderful idea. It seems that one can go back to the things from the past. Following such reasoning, one can travel in time by watching a film, visiting an archaeological festival, or looking at an historical re-enactment event, amongst other things. However, what the film presupposes is the fact that paradoxically one can go *back to the future* as well. There might be things that still await a closer consideration that could belong the future. What this entails is that there are situations in which doing new things, going to the future, demands first of all returning to the past (Kobiałka 2013b:17–18).This is the very reason why one can claim that the *Archaeology of Time Travel* is very traditional and in this is its novelty. What it approaches is not the past without the present – a postmodern logic of decaf coffee – but, on the contrary, the past with the present, the past in the present. This is precisely the logic of coffee *with* caffeine. And in this way one could say that the *Archaeology of Time Travel* is its own travel in time. Being, in a way, very traditional, is more progressive than many others' archaeologies. Indeed, here archaeologists *go back to the future of archaeology*.

To indicate the complexity of archaeological investigations into time travel phenomenon, I took a five-step approach. Firstly, by references to such 'archaeological' film heroes as Indiana Jones and Lara Croft on the one hand, and James Bond on the other, I highlighted the fact that an archaeological critique should always go beyond repeating social clichés, to show how obviousness is not so obvious, or, as Victor Buchli and Gavin Lucas (2001) would have said, to approach how the familiar is unfamiliar.

Secondly, this fascination with unobviousness allowed me to look at archaeo-appeal (Holtorf 2005) beyond a standard distinction between reality-fiction or true-false. Psychoanalysis teaches us that social fantasies cannot be reduced to objective or subjective statements. Fascination with archaeology, of which one of the embodiments is time travel phenomenon (e.g. archaeological festivals, historical re-enactment events, to mention only a few), goes beyond the distinction. As Žižek points out, social fantasies are a *bizarre category of the objectively subjective*.

Thirdly, social processes analysed by, amongst others, archaeologists are often very sophisticated and paradoxical. This is the case of different time travels and, what is closely linked to it, consumption of the past. Once again, it seems obvious that contemporary society consumes archaeological stories (e.g. archaeological festivals, historical re-enactment events, etc.). As long as such perspective is not wrong, it nonetheless obliterates, in my opinion, a much more interesting process: how consumption of the past is becoming its own opposite nowadays, which is a loss by contemporary society of what truly defines consumption. To truly consume is to take positive and negative aspects of any object. Archaeological time travels are usually only about the former. That is the reason why fascination with the past by contemporary people can be referred to as *a decaf archaeology* (*decaf time travel*).

Fourthly, the implication of the previous point was an idea that there are no such things as a 'true archaeology' and 'false archaeology'. Coffee is only coffee when it contains caffeine. The same has to be said, as I argued above, there is no real archaeology without fictional elements/time travel fantasy. In other words, no fiction in archaeology means more or less no archaeology at all.

Last but not least, I believe that the success of archaeology lies in its broadening. The archaeological is also in the form not the content alone. There is no reason to claim that Steven Spielberg's *Raiders of the Lost Ark* (1981) is a more useful and inspiring film than *The Matrix*, *The NeverEnding Story* or *Back to the Future* for an archaeologist. By broadening the archaeological interest in popular culture, archaeology cannot but only strengthen its position as science that is of relevance for the present and future societies.

And finally, a short anecdote for the end: once Bertolt Brecht was visited by a young student. The student said more or less the following: 'Dear master, I have many great ideas, and I can write a very good story but I do not know how to begin'. Brecht answered: 'Very easily, begin from top left-hand corner of the sheet'. One should take Brecht's lesson very seriously. Instead of a hasty critique of popular culture, how the phenomenon of time travelling simplifies an objective historical and archaeological reality, we should begin from the top left-hand corner of the sheet. This means, first of all, to ask the question: do films and generally popular culture represent any reality? Only after answering this question can one start analysing the role of the past in the present and begin to write a very good story.

Acknowledgements

This publication was produced during my scholarship period at Linnaeus University, thanks to a Swedish Institute scholarship. This chapter relies loosely on my two texts already published in Polish (Kobiałka 2011a, 2011b). I would also like to express my warmest thanks to Tomasz Marciniak for providing Figure 10.2.

References

Åkesson, L. 2010. Waste and garbage as time travel. *Lund Archaeological Review* 15–16:95–98.

Ascherson, N. 2004. Archaeology and the British media. In N. Merriman (ed.), *Public Archaeology*: 145–158. London, Routledge.

Baudrillard, J. 1994. *Simulacra and Simulation*. Translated by S. Glaser. Ann Arbor, University of Michigan Press.

Bauman, Z. 1989. *Globalization. The Human Consequences*. Cambridge, Cambridge University Press.

Bell, D. 1974. *The Coming of Post-Industrial Society. A Venture in Social Forecasting*. New York, Basic Books.

Buchli, V. and Lucas, G. (eds.), 2001. *Archaeologies of the Contemporary Past*. London, Routledge.

Fagan, G. 2006. Diagnosing pseudoarchaeology. In G. Fagan (ed.), *Archaeological Fantasies: How Pseudoarchaeology Misrepresents the Past and Misleads the Public*: 23–46. London, Routledge.

Fowler, P. 2007. Not archaeology and the media. In T. Clark and M. Brittain (eds.), *Archaeology and the Media*: 89–107. Walnut Creek, California, Left Coast Press.

González-Ruibal, A. (ed.) 2013. *Reclaiming Archaeology: Beyond the Tropes of Modernity*. London-New York, Routledge.

Holtorf, C. 2005. *From Stonehenge to Las Vegas. Archaeology as Popular Culture*. Lanham, Altamira Press.

Holtorf, C. 2007. *Archaeology is a Brand. The Meaning of Archaeology in Contemporary Popular Culture*. Walnut Creek, California, Left Coast Press.

Holtorf, C. 2010. On the possibility of time travel. *Lund Archaeological Review* 15–16:31–41.

Jensen, R.1999. *The Dream Society. How the Coming Shift from Information to Imagination will Transform your Business*. New York, McGraw-Hill.

Jordan, P. 1981. Archaeology and television. In I. Evans, B. Cunliffe and C. Renfrew (eds.), *Antiquity and Man. Essays in Honour of Glyn Daniel*: 207–213. London, Thames and Hudson.

Kobiałka, D. 2011a. Matrix, czyli iluzja w archeologii. *Archeologia Żywa* 53(1):28–29.

Kobiałka, D. 2011b. Społeczny wizerunek archeologii – o rzeczywistości w fikcji. In A. Marciniak, D. Minta-Tworzowska and M. Pawleta (eds.), *Współczesne Oblicza Przeszłości*: 133–148. Poznań, Wydawnictwo Poznańskie.

Kobiałka, D. 2013a. Time travels in archaeology: Between Hollywood films and historical re-enactment. *AP: Online Journal in Public Archaeology* 3:110–130, available at http://www.arqueologiapublica.es/index.php, accessed 15 August 2016.

Kobiałka, D. 2013b. On (very) new and (extremely) critical archaeologies, or why one may remain forever eighteen years behind the truly new. *Forum Kritische Archäologie* 2:15–22, available at http://www.kritischearchaeologie.de/fka/article/view/26/25, accessed 15 August 2016.

Kristiansen, K. 2008. Should archaeology be in the service of 'popular culture'? A theoretical and political critique of Cornelius Holtorf's vision of archaeology'. *Antiquity* 82:488–490.

Marwick, B. 2010. Self-image, the long view and archaeological engagement with film: An animated case study. *World Archaeology* 42(3):394–404.

Narmo, L.E. 2010. Handcraft as time travel. *Lund Archaeological Review* 15–16:43–60.

Paardekooper, R. 2010. Archaeological open air museums as time travel centres. *Lund Archaeological Review* 15–16:61–69.

Pawleta, M. 2010. 'The Past Industry': Selected aspects of the commercialisation of the past and products of archaeological knowledge in contemporary Poland. *Sprawozdania Archeologiczne* 63:9–54.

Pawleta, M. 2011. Encounters with the past: The significance of archaeological festivals in contemporary Poland. In A. Arnberg and T. Stjärna (eds.), *Communicate the Past – Ways to Present Archaeology to the Public*: 57–76. Västerås, Stiftelsen Kulturmiljövård Mälardalen.

Paynton, C. 2002. Public perception and 'pop archaeology': A study of current attitudes toward televised archaeology in Britain. *The SAA Archaeological Record* 2(2):33–36.

Petersson, B. 2010. Travels to identity. Viking rune carvers of today. *Lund Archaeological Review* 15–16:71–86.

Pine, J. and Gilmore, J. 1999. *The Experience Economy. Work is Theatre and Every Business a Stage*. Boston, Harvard Business School Press.

Pine, J. and Gilmore, J. 2007. *Authenticity: What Consumers Really Want*. Boston, Harvard Business School Press.

Ramos, M. and Duganne, D. 2000. *Exploring Public Perception and Attitudes about Archaeology* prepared by Harris Interactive Inc. for The Society for American Archaeology.

Russell, M. 2002. No more heroes any more: The dangerous world of the pop culture archaeologist. In M. Russell (ed.), *Digging Holes in Popular Culture. Archaeology and Science Fiction*: 38–54. Oxford, Oakville Oxbow Books.

Sandström, E. 2010. Visiting the Middle Ages. *Lund Archaeological Review* 15–16:87–94.

Schiffer, M.B. 1991. *The Portable Radio in American Life*. Tucson, University of Arizona Press.

Shanks, M. and Tilley, C. 1987. *Re-constructing Archaeology: Theory and Practice*. Cambridge, Cambridge University Press.

Shanks, M. and Pearson, M. 2001. *Theatre/Archaeology. Disciplinary Dialogues*. London-New York, Routledge.

Westergren, E. (ed.) 2006. *Holy Cow. This is Great! Report from a Symposium on Historical Environment Education and Time Travels in Vimmerby, Sweden, November 2004*. Kalmar, Kalmar Läns Museum.

Zander, U. 2006. *Clio på bio. Om amerikansk film, historia och identitet*. Lund, Historiska Media.

Žižek, S.1997. *The Plagues of Fantasies*. London-New York, Verso.

Žižek, S. 2002. The interpassive subject. *The Symptom* 3, available at http://www.lacan.com/interpassf.htm, accessed 15 August 2016.

Žižek, S. 2004. A cup of decaf reality. *lacan.com*, available at http://www.lacan.com/zizekdecaf.htm, accessed 15 August 2016.

Commentary

On Time Travelling and Cinema

Laia Colomer

Beside its basic entertainment aim, the fiction film industry could be interestingly analysed from a time travelling perspective, noticing the connection between the present and what we imagine of the past, and the future. The film industry is where imaginative worlds get real. Screenwriters know that they first need to build up a story because a great story is what makes a great film; then, they pitch a character because a compelling character can extend across a series of sequels; and finally, they define a world (in the past, the present or the future), since a world can support multiple stories, involving multiple characters across multiple landscapes. Yet, world-building is central to a great deal of any genre fiction plots because it is more interesting, for both the director and the audience, to build and explore worlds and stories than dealing with individuals (Borràs and Colomer 2008).

Many films take history, memory, archaeology or heritage as main elements in their plots, or include archaeologists or historians as their main characters. There are films interpreting history from a patriotic or critical view (e.g. *Battleship Potemkin*, Sergei M. Eisenstein [1925]; *The Battle of Algiers*, Gillo Pontecorvo [1966]). There are films where their humanistic stories are set in particularly relevant historical backgrounds (e.g. *Paths of Glory*, Stanley Kubrick [1957]; *Aguirre, the Wrath of God*, Werner Herzog [1972]). There are films that use the past to reflect on today's events, so time span gives freedom to the film director's voice (e.g. *Twelve Monkeys*, Terry Gilliam [1995]; *Agora*, Alejandro Amenábar [2009]). There are films where a particular future is the direct result of a conflict present (e.g. *The Planet of Apes*, Franklin J. Schaffner [1968] and Tim Burton [2001]; *Mad Max*, George Miller [1979]). Other films reveal how particular actions of the past conform to events in the present (e.g. *Peggy Sue Got Married*, Francis Ford Coppola [1986]; *Eternal Sunshine of the Spotless Mind*, Michel Gondry [2004]) or picture the future to change the present (e.g. *It Happened Tomorrow*, René Clair [1944]; *Time Lapse*, Bradley King [2014]). Further, there are films where people collect objects or experiences so they do not lose their roots and identities (e.g. *Everything Is Illuminated*, Liev Schreiber [2005]). There are films where time, memory and time travelling are the plots (e.g. *Memento*, Christopher Nolan [2000]; *The Infinite Man*, Hugh Sullivan [2014]). And there are films where collecting material culture turns out to be relevant for building sustainable futures (e.g. *Wall-e*, Andrew Stanton [2008]). No list of time travel films would be complete without, at least, featuring the father of time travel fiction himself, H. G. Wells, and the films recreating his novel, *The Time Machine* (George Pal [1960] and Simon Wells [2002]). And, of course, there is the blockbuster *Back to the Future* I, II and III (Robert Zemeckis 1985, 1989, 1990).

What makes all of these films interesting here is that they act as a time travel experience for an audience seated comfortably in a cinema palace, and that all of them (no matter where they are set in time and place) talk either about the human condition or today's views. In this context, the papers written by Bodil Petersson and Dawid Kobiałka certainly provide imaginative examinations of fiction films as a time travel methodology. As these authors point out, more interestingly is the discussion about whether the image of the past portrayed in fictional films is rigorous enough; that is, analyzing to which extent these films portraying particular visions of the past, are actually referring to interested views of the present. This interest runs parallel to post-processual academic analysis on the use and abuse of archaeology and cultural heritage practices for the interest of political agendas (e.g. Harrison 2013; Smith 2006). Using fictional films as another materiality of this image of past history in contemporary time adds a new critical dimension in public archaeology (see also Hall 2004; Russell 2002).

Bodil Petersson's article is an example of how futuristic films could also be used to understand how we visualise our present and address our future. Here, it is not the past that mirrors the present but the future. The future is constructed upon our views of the present by selecting certain current elements and performances that we acknowledge as relevant. However, what makes Petersson's article more interesting is that she does this hermeneutic exercise following archaeological principles of context and material analysis. Both the production's context and the film's props are used to interpret what kind of present Kevin Costners' *Waterworld* (1995) portrays, a production that in the 1990s aimed to come across with an ethical-ecological message about global climate change. By focussing on the film's props, objects introduced as coming from the past, that is the 1990s (i.e. a rear-view window, dirt in a jar, ski boots, crayons and images in an old *National Geographic* magazine), Petersson takes the film's props as synonymous with "material culture", that is the archaeological materiality of a present meaningful for a particular future. Semiotically, the message is clear; interpreting this materiality, the main characters understand their past and their present, while the audience acknowledges that the way ecologically the earth is managed today will address us to an apocalyptic future. Accordingly, Petersson's chapter moves interestingly from being a cinematography review to an archaeological material culture review of a Hollywood film. Material culture and the context are used thus to understand the past, the present and the future, both by the characters and the audiences.

Following this operation, I would like to add that Kevin Costner's *Waterworld* might allow us to exercise another analysis, now regarding heritage practice. Petersson shortly notices how the props included in the film are "relics of a past" in a watery world. Precisely, most of these objects are debris that become treasures in this future world. As most of today's archaeological objects, Mariner's treasures have lost their original meaning but gain new significances, either because of new uses by society or a new symbolical context. In this sense, it would be possible to step further and see Mariner as a treasure hunter of contemporary relics in a future world. Following this argument then, the film director is like a museum curator, selecting those relics/props that contain sufficient emotional and ideological connotations to deliver the ecological message to an audience from the 1990s. From a time travelling perspective on heritage practice itself, the film may also be taken as an example of Western notions of cultural heritage and traditional museology, specifically on both the art of recovering collective memory and object's collection management, and its significance today in delivering messages to society (after Pearce 1993; Hooper-Greenhill 2000).

David Kobiałka's chapter provides us with a Lacanian analysis on the relation between film industry and archaeology, particularly the tweeted relationship between reality and illusion. His main argument is that fiction could not exist without reality, but also reality could not exist without fiction. Indeed, fiction literature, theatre and cinema are the perfect arena for imagined scenarios, either of the past, the present or the future. These imagined scenarios are always designed from the present time, its experience, perceptions and expectations. And accordingly, no imagination is fully invented from nothing. Our imaginaries grow up from our reality, both from its more dark ghosts and our positive wishes to change. The film industry is, more than any other fictional media, a case study for this tweeted relationship between reality and illusion because films provide concrete, powerful and likely images of these imaginaries. It is in this film creative process that the references to our present are strongly evident to all of us. The *Star Wars* saga, for example, portrays military strategies and equipment that resemble more the epics of WW II than any society technologically centuries ahead from us. If the film would have been produced today, the screenwriters may have imagined that future war scenario resembling the clean, even opaque, war encounters facilitated today by military drones. Unless, of course, they still want to add the patina of glory, loyalty and companion that men used to like to add in war action films.

At the beginning of this section, I mentioned several examples of how the past and the future are set in films aiming for different goals, from political to entertainment. This is not a new issue to add neither to film studies nor public archaeology. However, what Petersson and Kobiałka have added is an archaeological review on film's materiality and the validity of any scientific falsity. Equally important for the time travel is that this fictional world (either set in the past or in the future) does not picture the present, but it represents this present according to our own interests, agendas or perceptions of our current debates. As Petersson points out, it exists as an unbroken line between the interpretation of the past, our perceptions of today events and our projections of the future. And in this process, archaeologists, heritage managers, film-makers and film art designers operate similarly; they interpret the past and design the future according to what they perceive is relevant to our present. We may drive a parallel line between the history of academic archaeology and a critical history of cinema, assuming that both archaeology and cinema operate according to present times. There is a similar path between, on one hand, the decision process on which historical topics are chosen in the film industry, how their plots are focused and what ideological meaning portrays the stories on scene, and, on the other hand, how traditional, processual and post-processual archaeologies define their research topics, interpret data, and give relevant meaning to particular issues. For example, we can 'sequently travel' from classic films portraying the Bible as *The Greatest Story Ever Told* (George Stevens 1965), encounter after processual versions of the Bible in *Jesus Christ Superstar* (Norman Jewison 1973) or *Monty Python's Life of Brian* (Terry Jones 1979) and finally experience a post-modern interpretation of the Book with *The Last Temptation of Christ* (Martin Scorsese 1988). Or we can exemplify the inclusion of an indigenous perspective in archaeology and heritage studies by confronting how the same event is portrayed differently in films such as *They Died with Their Boots On* (Raoul Walsh 1941) and *Little Big Man* (Arthur Penn 1970). This parallelism, which is nothing other than evidence of how far human creativity and inquiry is contextually defined, is what makes fiction films interesting for the time travelling methodology and the public archaeology in general.

References

Borràs i Vidal, J. and Colomer i Puntés, A. 2008. *El guió del gènere de ficció per a televisió i cinema*. Barcelona, Editorial Universitat Oberta de Catalunya.

Hall, M. 2004 "Romancing the stones: Archaeology in popular cinema", *European Journal of Archaeology* 7(2):159–176. DOI: 10.1177/1461957104053713.

Harrison, R. 2013. *Heritage. Critical Approaches*. London, Routledge.

Hooper-Greenhill, E. 2000. *Museums and the Interpretation of Visual Culture*. London, Routledge

Pearce, S. 1993. *Museums, Objects, and Collections. A Cultural Study*. Leicester, Leicester University Press.

Russell, M. (ed.) 2002. *Digging Holes in Popular Culture: Archaeology and Science Fiction*. Oxford, Oxbow Books.

Commentary

A Cup of Decaf Past and Waterworld

Niklas Hillbom

The two chapters, referred to here as 'Decaf' and 'Waterworld', analyse films, archaeology and time travel experiences. Although they deal with the same or similar subjects, their approaches and methods divert. Decaf presents a theoretical analysis of the interaction between fiction and archaeology, using examples from various films. Meanwhile, Waterworld focusses on one particular film and provides numerous down-to-earth examples of archaeological time travels. The articles also have some common features such as their discussions on how time travel experiences mediated in films can shed light on contemporary values/ideals as well as on how archaeologists examine the changing views of their own discipline.

There are several ways to define archaeological time travel. When teaching, I use the concept of time travel mostly as a method of increasing our understanding of the past. Several techniques can be combined to create as much time travel experience as possible. Reconstructions, augmented reality, quotations, plans, eyewitness testimonies, recreations, experimental archaeology and so on work together to increase the understanding of the past. In addition to hard facts, all senses are stimulated to generate a stronger time travel experience in which history 'comes alive'. Films and TV are two of several such building blocks.

The chapters at hand have made me aware of other ways to define and use the concept of time travel, including deeper levels of analysing the present as well as the connection with post-processual archaeology.

During the last two decades, a period of the so-called 'Gladiator effect', the analyses of archaeological and historical films have shifted from (the often pointless) critiques of what is historically correct or not, to analysing the contemporary world and values. In my field, antiquity, several new books have appeared, (e.g. Hammar and Zander 2015) with numerous interesting chapters on how films on ancient Greece and Rome tell us a lot about our own time and in what ways we today consume history and time travel.

In Decaf, Kobialka takes the discussion one step further and examines how fiction interacts with the current development of the discipline of archaeology. One of the main conclusions is that 'there is no real archaeology without fictional elements – there is no archaeology without time travel fantasy'. The author divides his conclusions into five sections. In step one he describes how 'an archaeological critique should always go beyond repeating social clichés', and in the second he looks at 'archaeo-appeal beyond a standard distinction between reality-fiction or true-false'.

The perhaps most interesting and groundbreaking sections are the third and fourth ones. Here Kobialka highlights the phenomenon of filmmakers choosing some aspects of history while ignoring others. The archaeological time traveller chooses positive aspects of history, a decaf archaeology or a decaf time travel. The author demonstrates in an excellent way how one of the main problems in post-processual archaeology is to study how the interpretation of the past is connected to the present. The conclusion that all interpretation of the past needs the fictional elements used in time travel is thoroughly convincing. 'No fiction in archaeology means more or less no archaeology at all'.

The last section argues that all sorts of films that present other worlds and periods can be equally inspiring for an archaeologist and broaden the archaeological interest in popular culture. I, however, think that films that specifically focus on archaeology and history – such as Indiana Jones, Lara Croft or Gladiator – play a more important role in this type of analyses. There are many fascinating examples of alternative realities such as *The Matrix*. But if too many kinds of movies/illusions are included, we risk a too-broad perspective and then the analysis is watered down. Perhaps we sometimes exaggerate the impact films have on our view of the world. Most people do not see the world as a much different place after watching a movie. And perhaps we sometimes underestimate the internal, ironic references within a movie. When Indy, in *Indiana Jones and the Last Crusade*, tells his students that "X" never, ever marks the spot' of archaeological discoveries, this can of course be analysed as a reference to what archaeology is all about (in fiction or in reality influenced by fiction). But it is also just a direct, internal joke in the film itself – pointing forward to the scene in Venice where a very large 'X' indeed does mark the spot of the discovery.

In her analysis of Kevin Costner's *Waterworld* Petersson uses quite a different approach. The discussion is less theoretical and focusses on concrete examples, from one film, on how the materiality of the past is present in a future world, and what this tells us about our own period. It is an appealing examination of the film, with numerous details concerning objects and references to the past I did not notice when I first saw it some years ago. When I watched the film again, the text by Petersson opened my eyes on many new such details.

The chapter starts off with a discussion/presentation of how the film shows us that there is 'a very close connection between materiality of the past (our time) and the construction of future worlds'. From the viewpoint of a classical archaeologist an interesting parallel (and a possible future discussion) can be found in the classicism and neo-classicism movements. After the discoveries of Herculaneum and Pompeii in the 18th century the neo-classicists used the material remains of antiquity to create new forms of literature, architecture, visual arts, theatre and so on. This was indeed a true and new construction of the world, and its values, based on the materiality of the past.

What kind of objects we choose, and do not choose, when collecting the bits and pieces from a lost world is interesting, regardless if the collector is a neo-classicist in Pompeii or diving down to the skyscrapers of a twentieth-century Atlantis. In the tough future world of water where survival is everything, the use and trade of practical objects is essential. It is therefore striking that so many of the objects collected by Mariner are purely decorative artefacts without any practical use. Especially in his (museum-like) collection below deck there are many such objects. My favourite is his necklace made of an old microchip. Symbols and symbolic interpretations of a lost paradise indeed. Re-use and old objects with new functions are of course common challenges when analysing archaeological artefacts.

As Petersson points out, objects out of context become 'a laughing mirror intended for archaeologists, since we here can discern a critique towards our professional way of handling objects from the past as relics that we do not understand'. The mirror Mariner gives to the children is another odd relic that has lost its original meaning. It is a nice example of how to reflect on archaeological interpretation of objects of disputed function. I am, however, not sure that the filmmakers deliberately used specifically a rear-view mirror to symbolize the looking at the past.

The discussion on good and bad materiality is interesting. Paper, crayons and soil vs. oil, tobacco and alcohol. As the chapter Waterworld demonstrates in a clear way, the producers have created polarized sets of symbols throughout the film. I think there are many levels of possible symbolic interpretation on the use of these objects, both the 'good' and the 'bad' ones. Before the girl, Enola, gets the colourful crayons, she makes drawings with charcoal. These drawings show her 'vision' of the last surviving part of paradise – the mythical Dryland. The style of these early drawings strongly resembles that of the earliest drawing of mankind; prehistoric cave paintings and rock carvings. The animals and hunting scenes could be taken straight from an archaeological publication.

The cigarettes used by the bad guys, the Smokers, are not just cigarettes. They are prestige, a symbol of wealth and power as well as an economic tool when controlling the masses. These cigarettes are actually handed out to the people by the evil boss, Deacon, while riding in the last car on earth. The 'High Priest' gives alms to the subordinate. He even completes the picture of ritual by repeating a 'sacred' phrase: 'Growth Is Progress'.

The article points out that cinematic time travel makes us reflect on how materiality affects us in both small and big issues, including abstract phenomenon such as religion. To interpret the function or meaning of artefacts and symbols connected to religion and ritual is a difficult task for any time traveller or archaeologist. The film has some nice examples that can inspire us to a critical look at archaeological interpretations of unknown rituals. The portrait of the twentieth-century captain of the *Exxon Valdez*, Joseph Hazelwood, has changed into a 600-year-old icon of 'Old Saint Joe'. The villains pray to this Saint Joe and ask him for support.

The skeletons on Dryland are full of flowers and surrounded by valuable objects – possible grave gifts. The new arrivals, coming from a world where bodies are 'recycled' in some sort of organic mud, reflect different types of funerals and beliefs: 'Maybe we should put them under the dirt, I think it was their way.' Once again, it's all about the difficult task of interpreting the rituals of other cultures and time traveling on several levels.

All the ancient symbols – of good vs. bad, old vs. new, technology vs. nature – are summarized by the (old, understandable?) sticker on the car of the villains: 'NUKE THE WHALES!'

Both Decaf and Waterworld clearly demonstrate that film is one of the most important tools when creating a time traveling experience. The articles also show that it is important to include all senses to make this experience as powerful as possible. One task I give students of archaeology and time travels is to compare how this plays out in two TV series: *I, Claudius* (1976) and *Rome* (2005). While the first one is elegant and witty, theatre-like and very British, the second is full of colour, smells, dirt, sex, blood and vivid outdoor mass-scenes. Obviously, Rome communicates more forcefully by engaging the senses more and thereby creates a stronger time traveling experience. Most movies analysed in Decaf and Waterworld use these techniques in a good way, as many modern films do, and are thus well-chosen examples. The past truly comes alive.

Both chapters show us that there are several levels of time traveling and that these mental journeys tell us a lot both about our own time, and the ever-changing discipline of archaeology itself. The discussion on fiction and the archaeological illusion is inspiring. If future studies included the other platform for such fiction/illusion – computer games – and compare them with films, this could be very rewarding. Another comparison can naturally be made to literature. An interesting step would be to test the discussion on illusion, time travel and decaf consumption on books as well. There are, to my knowledge, no films yet that have used as many aspects of archaeological time travel as some books have. Jack McDevitt and Isaac Asimov write most elaborately on the archaeology of the future, and include more views on time travels and on the past as present than any film. Imagine if any of these books were made into epic movies, followed up by interesting analyses, like the ones at hand, from the fascinating viewpoint of archaeological time travel.

Reference:

Hammar, I. and Zander, U. (eds.) 2015. *Svärd, sandaler och skandaler - Antiken på film och i tv.* Lund, Studentlitteratur.

Part Five

Time Travel and Contemporary Society

Chapter 11

History as an Adventure
Time Travel in Late Modernity from the Perspective of a European Ethnologist

Michaela Fenske

Abstract

In Western societies, 'histotainment' is currently very much in demand. A wide and constantly changing offer of time travel involves willing 'travellers' in different ways. What do people look for by using these offers? And what are the implications of the popularity of the past for the different branches of historical scholarship? In addressing these questions, the present chapter draws on ethnographic field research in Germany. In the framework of entertainment studies, it profits from both heritage and knowledge studies conducted in the context of European ethnology. The essay develops three arguments. First, time travels are interpreted as new spaces of action and experience. This new space allows post-modern individuals to share new experiences while also constituting a space in which the values and rules of post-modern societies are negotiated. Second, the current boom of time travel demonstrates a large interest of post-modern actors in new forms of learning in which not only the mind, but also the body is included. In other words, time travellers are not only looking for an intellectual experience but also a sensual one. And third, for scholars of history the wide-spread interest in histotainment constitutes an invitation to negotiate their interest in the past as well as interpretations and representations of the past with different public actors.

Keywords: Applied history, histotainment, living history, senses, tangible history

A thirst for travel – direction: The past

Ever since the 1960 film adaptation of H. G. Wells's science fiction classic *The Time Machine*, originally published in 1895, the theme of time travel has been popular.[1] While Wells's protagonist travels to a gloomy future, today's post-modern time travellers prefer to choose the opposite direction; they travel to the past. In contrast to the Wellsian future, they imagine this past as mostly positive. The

---
[1] This contribution is a slightly revised and enlarged translation of my essay 'Abenteuer Geschichte: Zeitreisen in der Spätmoderne. Reisefieber Richtung Vergangenheit', In Hardtwig, Walter, and Alex Schug (eds.), 2009 *History Sells! Angewandte Geschichte als Wissenschaft und Markt*: 79–90. Stuttgart, Steiner. The translation has been prepared by Philip Saunders.

possibilities of time travel appear unlimited; there is the imaginary journey readers of popular historical novels take while participating in historical docu-soaps, such as *Schwarzwaldhaus 1902* (Black Forest House 1902)[2] or *Abenteuer Mittelalter* (The Adventure of the Middle Ages).[3] There are visits to medieval fairs and knights' festivals, flights with the legendary *Rosinenbomber* (Raisin Bomber) over Berlin,[4] a 'country pleasure-weekend' in eighteenth-century style,[5] Biedermeier-markets[6] and, more recently, urban history festivals, such as the *Historiale*.[7] The wide range of offers caters to all tastes and budgets. The active involvement of travellers also varies; it ranges from reading or watching TV to so-called 'living history', (i.e. the actual attempt to relive the historical experience). For some participants, time travel even becomes a semi-professional passion. While many participants occasionally choose from a wide range of constantly changing offers, members of re-enactment societies often spend considerable periods of their spare time re-enacting the 'lifelike' presentation of past realities.

While Wells's hero always remained in the same place, today's time travellers change both time and place. Even so, the dramatics of late-modern time travel work similarly to the journey of the Wellsian protagonist. Now, 'time-gates' such as a coach or a train take over the task of the Wellsian 'time machine' in transporting the willing traveller into a historical or historicised environment. The device's role is to carry the travellers into both an alien time and an alien world that is far from their usual experience in terms of period as well as locality. The involvement of experts, including both historians and experienced re-enactors, vouches for the 'authenticity' of the historical experience, for almost all offers of time travel claim to convey historical truth. As simple as the offers may seem, time travel is a highly complex product. It connects fact and fiction, and it involves technical expertise (e.g. the experience of experimental archaeology, professionally operated re-enactments and depictions of everyday culture in museums) as well as emotionalisation, personalisation and dramatisation. This type of entertainment as a form of both experience and knowledge orientation has been labelled histotainment (Maase 2006:52). The demand for this form of entertainment is considerable. The numbers of sales and of visitors are multi-digit, and the amount of consumers watching performances on TV is high.[8] The different

---

[2] SWR Fernsehen Baden Baden, zero südwest in Baden-Baden and Heise, Volker (Director), Schwarzwaldhaus 1902 1–4, original broadcast 2002.
[3] MDR, Arte, ARD, and Aernecke, Susanne (director), Abenteuer Mittelalter: Leben im 15. Jahrhundert (Adventure Middle Ages. Life in the fifteenth century): 1–5, original broadcast 2005 (DVD, UAP Video GmbH, 2006).
[4] See http://www.yatego.com/yamando/p,47d9155695c8f,446332efd6b158_1,rosinenbomer-zeitreise, accessed 6 July 2008.
[5] See http://www.lumieres-event.com, accessed 6 July 2008.
[6] See e.g. the market in Werben/East-Germany (http://www.werben-elbe.de/biedermeier/biedermeier-in-werben), accessed 17 July 2014. See also Fenske (2013).
[7] See http://www.lumieres-event.com, accessed 7 July 2008.
[8] See, e.g. the information in Philipp, Marc J., Geschichte in den Medien. Tagungsbericht. (History of Media. Proceedings.) http://hsozkult.geschichte.hu-berlin.de/tagungsberichte/id=1074, accessed 7 July 2008. This

markets at which the time travel providers aim include the media, tourism industry and manufacturers of historical costumes and tools.

The thirst for travel to the past is part of the general boom of history that has engulfed late-modern contemporaries. The editors of a volume on the subject of cultural heritage even mention a current 'obsession with history' (Hemme *et al.* 2007:9). History is used in numerous instances as a resource serving economic, political and social interests. Currently, popular time travel is part of the vast and highly differentiated single field of 'applied history'. Some experts sharply criticise time travel. Because it mixes fiction and fact, it produces, in the view of those experts, speculative imaginings, or 'pseudo-historical utopias of the present'. In short, it runs the risk of teaching 'false history' (e.g. Fischer and Wirtz 2008; Fraund 2007; Hardtwig 2005; Kaiser 2008; Schwellenbach 2007; Wolf 2005, 2008). In this manner popular time travel perfectly documents the tension between the various requirements of history as an interpretation of past experience (i.e. the various requirements voiced by research, education, entertainment and the market).

Which function does history fulfil in time travel, and which requirements are actually met? Which representations of history and historical images come to fruition? Which challenge does the current popularity of history pose to the special branches of scholarship? The following essay addresses these questions on the basis of empirical studies conducted by European ethnologists particularly in Germany. Theoretically, the article is set in different contexts that touch on the demands of entertainment research, heritage and ethnological knowledge research. The present chapter is primarily concerned with historical docu-soaps and non-professional re-enactments. It is complemented by preliminary interviews with providers of tourist travel and the results of research on the realistic historical novel (definition according to Nünning 1995). The chapter is understood as an attempt to highlight key characteristics of time travel from an ethnological perspective. Even though time travels vary widely with regard to their claims, their content, manners of execution and the media used, they are comparable in their fundamental concerns. These concerns constitute the phenomenon of time travel – at least where they are popular. Time travel opens up new agendas with particular qualities of experience for today's actors.

---

is well documented for the historical docu-soaps. For example, the first docu-soap broadcast in Germany 'Das Schwarzwaldhaus 1902' reached an average of over six million viewers. cf. Das Erste: Report/Documentary: Schwarzwaldhaus 1902 – Leben wie vor hundert Jahren (Life like a hundred years ago). Neues von den Boros (News from the Boros). 18.04.2003, http://www.daserste.de/doku/030418.asp accessed 7.7.08; in the programme 'Windstärke 8' (Wind Force 8) there was casting for over 5,000 people, Windstärke 8, Das Casting (Wind Force 8 – The Casting), http://www.wdr.de/tv/w8/60_projekt/content/61_casting.phtml, accessed 7 July 2008.

History as a new space of action and experience

Swedish ethnologist Lotten Gustafsson (2002) has labelled the space that opens up through historical performances as *enchanted zones*. Enchanted zones are areas of action in which late-modern actors encounter new experiences, enabling them to test themselves (and maybe others). Here, the new spaces of action offer experiences that are not possible in contemporary everyday life. In her study of medieval re-enactors in southern Lower Saxony, Germany, European ethnologist Annemike Meyer interviewed a participant who stated: 'You come to represent someone, a fictional personality and how that personality might have lived in the Middle Ages. Often, a new freedom opens up in areas of your personality. It is an interaction, similar to the conviviality that is attributed to the campfire' (Meyer 2003:53).

In a similar manner, the reference to a satisfying social interaction is also encountered among other time travellers (Drieschner 2005). The person acting as a maid in the historical docu-soap *Adventure 1927* also mentions the potential of self-awareness as a motivation for her participation in the programme: 'The offer to travel back in time is something unique. . . . I also wanted to know whether I could work or live under such conditions. Furthermore, I found it interesting to "try" a completely different life, to take on a different role and to live in a way that has nothing to do with my real life.'[9]

Participants also look for experiences on the edge. They want to find out whether they can live under alien conditions (Schwellenbach 2007:47). From the researcher's perspective the result of this experience might initially be startling. For example, some travellers explicitly value the hard physical labour faced in their time travel and their inferior position within social hierarchies. In some ways, the new experience appears to facilitate their lives. As a one-time traveller explained: 'What was really positive, however, was having so much to do and not really having to act independently. You had a lot less to worry about. I had so much to do that I did not have the time to really think about my life and the meaning of life' (Fenske 2007:99–100).

Given the complexity of their late-modern everyday life and considering their search for existential meaning, particularly young participants conspicuously may opt for the positive sides of a supposedly simple hierarchical order of historical societies – or what they take this order to be. The new space offers the option to reconsider traditional gender roles (Figure 11.1). Gender makes a key difference in many offers of time travel (Maierhofer 2005).

---

[9] Unpublished questionnaire, digitally located by Esther Heckmann, Göttingen, June 2008. The author would like to thank Esther Heckmann for this information.

Time travels also offer the experience of nature, and they reflect the alienation of the modern city dweller vis-à-vis natural living conditions. These are themes to which docu-soaps and the leisure re-enactor or visitor to sites of historical heritage respond (Kirshenblatt-Gimblett 1995). History turns into a space of experience and an 'adventure playground' (Svensson 1998) for a society that has largely been alienated from a tangible forest, from meadows, fields and agricultural food production.

At a first glance time travels have an affirmative, conservative framework. They offer the simplicity of high and low suggested by the 'historical' hierarchy, the clear separation between men and women, the perception of natural life, the close contact with other living beings from which the participants are not alienated. These are central points that participants experience as a contrasting enrichment of their own lives. At a second glance the 'conservative closure' (Klaus 2006:102) does not succeed. Even in well-organised media productions the travellers use the new space of experience not only in an affirmative manner, but also in contradiction to the conservative framework. For instance, performers protest against rules of conduct they perceive as unfair (Fenske 2007:100). And while re-enactors might use the time travel to perform historical gender roles as an alienated experience, they do not intend to reinstall these orders in their everyday lives (Figure 11.2). On the contrary, they enjoy exactly the diversity of experiences in time and space (Fenske 2013b). By these and other practices the travellers use time travels to discuss the present time, their contemporary environment and their current values and orders (Fenske 2013a).

The individual motivations for time travel vary. Some travellers take advantage of the experience after finishing high school or before impending marriage or retirement to reflect their changing position in society. Others aim to share an extraordinary experience in the company of family members. Almost all participants want to immerse themselves in previously unknown experiences and feelings (Fenske 2007:95–97). In this manner, history, as a presumed experience of the past, opens up new agendas and opportunities while allowing for self-awareness and self-discovery. The experience of alterity is required in order to enable re-enacted history to become an adventure. Therefore, it is no coincidence that the Middle Ages enjoy a particularly large popularity. Temporal distance and the supposed alien experience turn the journey to the 'exotic Middle Ages' into a long-distance trip of a special kind (Althoff 1992; Groebner 2008). Meanwhile, the 'lived experience' of the past that time-travel propagators provide and that is expected by time travellers assumes certain forms of presentation as a given.

Figure 11.1. Time travellers into the German Biedermeier, Werben, 2009 (Photograph by Michaela Fenske).

Figure 11.2. Time travellers into the German Biedermeier, Werben, 2009 (Photograph by Michaela Fenske).

History as an Adventure 247

Figure 11.3. Jadis flyer for time travelling (Reproduction in public domain obtained by Michaela Fenske 2008).

Smell, taste, feel – tangible history

According to a promise that many time travel offers make, history should include a physical and a sensual experience. An example of how this can work in practice is the concept of *Jadis*, a tour operator of time travel aimed at members of the upper middle class.[10] The tour operator, at the turn of the present millennium, offered time travel to different epochs under the guidance of a person educated as a historian. Seasonally and scenically adjusted, the travellers visited hotels with bygone flair and enjoyed luxuries, such as horse racing or summer getaways, in a historic setting that was formerly reserved for members of the upper class. The focus was the sensual physical experience that the organisers achieved above all by means of historical dress as well as historical dining and table culture (Figure 11.3).

The advertising promised a 'papillae expedition', as the way to a man's heart as well as a historical experience goes through the stomach.[11] In historical docu-soaps

---

[10] Unpublished questionnaires digitally collected by Michaela Fenske, Göttingen, in March 2008. The author thanks Ms. Meißner for being available for an interview, as well as for providing various promotional material
[11] Mit Reifrock & Chapeau Claque, brochure of the Agentur für Reisen in die Vergangenheit (Travel agency for travel to the past), Kristina Meißner, undated.

or re-enactments, the experience of history is also virtually centred on one's own body. The dramaturgy of the experience is structured by scratchy clothing, hard beds, the pungent smell of animals, fellow actors struggling with unusually hard physical work and the strange taste of unfamiliar foods (Fenske 2007; Meyer 2003). Since the feeling, sensing and smelling appear to be a silver bullet to the past, it is a matter of course that the past itself is made of a perfume. The perfume, Library of Fragrance, promises such 'memories in bottles' (Hemme 2010).

Experts have labelled the history at stake in time travel as 'everyday cultural history'. Inasmuch as this is, at the same time, the 'story of the many', the offer also pertains to the self, such as the history of our own ancestors. Members of the middle class might experience a certain contradiction between their normal lives and the offer to live the bygone culture of the upper classes as a traveller with Jadis or to re-enact the so-called lords in docu-soaps. Even so, this contradiction embodies a strong 'recreational value' for the people concerned insofar as the individual experience of multiple layers of diverse and alien sensations enables them to go on a 'vacation from their own egos'. The crucial point is the experience of past lives. At the same time, the promise of being able to experience historical worlds by means of time travel and to participate in the everyday life of past ancestors implies a certain paradox. The offers are directed at a wide audience, most of whom do not possess detailed historical knowledge. Consequently, the culture of everyday life experienced in a (presumed) historical setting is contemporary and tainted with the backdrop of late modernity.

The details of how a person would have moved in the Middle Ages, which gestures and facial expressions he or she might have had, how he or she might have spoken – in short, the sum of cultural practices representing the everyday past, is at best painstakingly learned and appropriated by talented actors or re-enactors.[12] 'Normal' participants in historical time travel do not usually have this knowledge. They remain, therefore, inevitably excluded from the experiences of people who lived during an earlier period. In consequence, critics judge time travel as tantamount to 'role play'. Whether historical novel, re-enactment or docu-soap, many offers share an ahistorical view of humanity in that the cultural shaping of human life is excluded, at least in the dominant narrative. While historical and ethnological scholarship convey insights into the cultural structuredness of

---

[12] It is worth reading, in this context, Natalie Zemon Davis's description of shooting the film version of her study about the true story of the return of Martin Guerre (2004). The book was first made a film in 1982 (Le Retour de Martin Guerre/The Return of Martin Guerre. DVD Freemantle Media [1982]), starring Gérard Depardieu and Nathalie Baye. Davis described how Depardieu tirelessly practiced gestures and facial expressions of the sixteenth century in order to arrive at the final result that, in her opinion, was quite impressive. The subsequent filming by Sommersby (DVD Regency Enterprises/Le Studio canal [1993]) with Richard Gere and Jodie Foster in the lead roles was also far more popular than the first. This is also probably because the Zemon Davis story was here spun as a romantic love story without reference to the paraphrased original.

emotions and experiences, the message of time travel implies that the physical experiences of people remain eternally unchanged.

If one follows David Lowenthal's (1986) characterisation, fiction displays a particularly powerful effect in the representation of history. In terms of reception and acceptance, it is much more sustainable than scientific representations of the past. Similarly, historian Bodo von Borries (2007:208) pointed to the powerful effect of historical representations in television. It is not the historically known features of a Luther, Napoleon or Hitler that remain in people's memory, but the features of the respective actors. Against this backdrop the critics' concerns of popular time travel offers gain additional momentum. Even if one assumes that many time travellers are less interested in the past than in self-awareness and the discussion of the actual problems of their time, time travel shapes contemporary views of history. Considering this aspect, where are the breaks and inconsistencies, the quiet moments that constitute everyday cultural history as a story of the many? What about the history of the losers? Tracy Chevalier's story of the *Girl with a Pearl Earring* (1999), interpreted as a romantic love story between the maid Grit and the artist Vermeer, was devoured en masse as a novel, and many people watched the movie starring superstar Scarlett Johannson in the title part.[13] However, historical portrayals of a bygone woman's life would probably expect, even in the best case, only a four-digit number of readers (Blaschke and Schulze 2006; Langewiesche 2008).

In fact, a story like that of the Ansberger seamstress Anna Vetter, whom literary scholar Eva Kormann (2004) portrayed in her misery and oppressive constriction without any emotionalisation or dramatisation, does not invite the audience's individual identification; in short, it is not entertaining. The sensuous experience of such a life would be anything but pleasant – although it would certainly be instructive. Consequently, we may wonder whether a complex history of the many with all its facets and contradictions is suitable for a popular treatment. Critics point out that history as treated in time travel is essentially reduced to beloved stereotypes. It would treat the glamour of historic seaside resorts, aristocratic manors or the supposed uncivilized Middle Ages in linear and closed accounts (Uka 2003). Time travel, therefore, thematises to a large extent what the audience already knows. Moreover, it has to do this – at least if you follow the argument of British cultural theorist John Fiske (2003), who recognizes familiarity as a prerequisite for popularity and, thus, the economic success of the entertainment offer.

Meanwhile, time travel contains extremely important messages as far as the representation and medium of history is concerned. By promoting 'experience' rather than 'reading', in other words by turning history into a sensual experience, both the participants and the makers of time travel meet core needs. While one might

---

[13] Concorde Video, Webber; Peter (Director), 2003.

be inclined to dismiss the mix of entertainment and education as a convenience for a pleasure-drenched mass audience (Heidtmann 2001), the massive commitment to a 'tangible history' can also be interpreted as a vehement plea for other than traditional forms of mediation. In academic learning, the head and brain are expected to 'learn', while the body is at disciplined rest. Here, the whole body, all the senses, should 'feel' the sensual experience of 'earlier' life. Time travel documents the need for a tangible history. In addition, time travel as a special arena for action and interaction offers yet other issues; it sparks discussions about history. It discusses responsibilities, interpretations and 'truths' as well as possible ways of presentation.

History in dialogue

In recourse to post-modern theories in the social sciences, empirical cultural researcher Lioba Keller Drescher (2007) has reminded us that history is somehow always 'made'; it is constantly changing in the process of inexorable reconstructing and constructing. Therefore, reconstruction and construction coincide. History, understood as an interpretation of past worlds or historical traditions, is part of a constant process of negotiation between different actors. If one agrees with the suggestions of recent knowledge research (Gibbons *et al.* 1994; Nowotny *et al.* 2001; Weingart 2005), this process of negotiation is no longer just part of scholarship because it is now posited in between actors from the more scientific and the more public spheres (because these spheres are not clearly separated from each other). When referring to knowledge production as a cultural practice, it is important to understand the different actors and practices in addition to the contents of knowledge. If one aims to do so, an open concept of knowledge as propagated by anthropologist Fredrik Barth (2002) helps. Barth and others understand knowledge and its transfer as an open, multi-dimensional process that is not concerned with right or wrong, top or bottom, experts or lay public. Instead, they see it as a complex negotiation of various assumptions, interpretations and opinions. In this sense, to understand the principles of time travel, we first and foremost need to understand the underlying principles of its design. The task, therefore, is to understand the needs and the imminent discussions of contemporary society that are linked to the current inflationary interest in history and its production. Time travel aims rather less at reconstructing the past than at providing answers to the burning questions of today, such as alienation from nature, the threatening experience of the complexity of social systems and so on. Simultaneously, time travel as an interpretation of history constitutes a serious phenomenon because it is enthusiastically shared by many participants. It is a contribution in the process of negotiating history in the consciousness of present societies. History as an interpretation thus basically evolves from dialogue, and the only open question is the extent to which the so-called 'experts' (i.e. the academic historians) want to engage in this dialogue.

The adventure of travelling to foreign countries

'The past is a foreign country.' This dictum is often used by practitioners of history to express the strangeness of past worlds. They employ the motto to emphasise the cultural formation and shaping of the human experience (Lowenthal 1986; Stark 2008). The wording resonates with a certain love of travel and adventure, a love that the practitioners of history share with many late-modern contemporaries. Meanwhile, the currently popular time travel has actually little to do with history as (re-)construction or with history as an interpretation of historical ways of life. Time travel is a cultural construct of the present, it mainly documents today's needs and necessities. To modern participants, time travel opens up new realms of action and experience that offer them, among other things, the possibility of determining their position within a complex society under the conditions of globalization. At the same time, it allows for the negotiation of various roles, values and standards. With its range of specific and standardised alienation, time travel contributes to relaxation, fun and pleasure, and so also to the regeneration of the travellers. The enthusiasm for time travel documents an interest in history as a phenomenon that is closely linked to the present and the future of the people now alive. Although the promise of a truly 'lived' history is hardly valid, time travel satisfies at least the need for sensual and, therefore, direct experience. Here, an important task presents itself for practitioners and researchers of history. They have to be both at the same time, analysts of popular uses of history and advocates of history as an interpretation of past life-worlds. They must not only add their respective interpretations of the past to the dialogue, but they must also negotiate with other members of the society in appropriate ways of communicating their knowledge to wider audiences. Concerning these aspects academic scholars may learn a lot from time travellers and other people engaged in history. For instance, they may learn how to teach not only with letters and words, but also with body language, the senses and direct physical experiences. In exchanging ideas about what people today need concerning the past, academic scholars may expand not only their methods of communication, but also their research questions and topics. In addition to historical research in archives, with objects such as material culture or oral history, the dialogue with actors from different parts of our societies and the related negotiations constitutes a further adventure for historians and other students of the past.

References

Althoff, Gerd (ed.). 1992. *Die Deutschen und ihr Mittelalter: Themen und Funktionen moderner Geschichtsbilder vom Mittelalter* (The Germans and Their Middle Ages: Themes and Features of Modern Perceptions of the Middle Ages). Darmstadt, Wissenschaftliche Buchgesellschaft.

Barth, Fredrik. 2002. An anthropology of knowledge. *Current Anthropology* 43:1–18.

Blaschke, Olaf and Schulze, Hagen (eds.). 2006. *Geschichtswissenschaft und Buchhandel in der Krisenspirale? Eine Inspektion des Feldes in historischer, internationaler und wirtschaftlicher Perspektive* (History and Bookshops in a Crisis Spiral? An Inspection of the Field in an Economic, Historical and International Perspective). München, Oldenburg.

Borries, Bodo von. 2007. Historischer, Spielfilm' und Dokumentation': Bemerkung zu Beispielen (Historical 'feature film' and 'documentary': Comments and examples). In Christoph Kühlberger, Christian Lübke and Thomas Terberger (eds.), *Wahre Geschichte – Geschichte als Ware: Die Verantwortung der Historischen Forschung für Wissenschaft und Gesellschaft* (True History – History as a Commodity: The Responsibility of Historical Research to Scholarship and Society): 187–212. Rahden, VML.

Chevalier, Tracy. 2003. *Das Mädchen mit dem Perlenohrring*. Munich, List (English Original: Girl with a Pearl Earring [1999]). London, Harper Collins.

Drieschner, Carsten. 2005. Living history als Freizeitbeschäftigung: Der Wikingerverein 'Opnn Skjold e.V.' in Schleswig (Living history as a leisure activity: The Viking club 'Opnn Skjold e.V.'). *Kieler Blätter zur Volkskunde* 37:31–61.

Fenske, Michaela. 2007. Geschichte, wie sie Euch gefällt: Historische Doku-Soaps als spätmoderne Handlungs-, Diskussions- und Erlebnisräume (History as you like it: Historical docu-soaps as late-modern arenas of action, discussion and experience). In Andreas Hartmann, Silke Meyer and Ruth Mohrmann (eds.), *Historizät. Vom Umgang mit Geschichte* (Historicity: How to deal with history): 85–105. Münster, Waxmann.

Fenske, Michaela. 2009. Abenteuer Geschichte: Zeitreisen in der Spätmoderne. Reisefieber Richtung Vergangenheit (The adventure of history: Time travel in late modernity). In Hardtwig, Walter, and Alex Schug (eds.), *History Sells! Angewandte Geschichte als Wissenschaft und Markt* (History Sells! Applied History as Scholarship and Market): 79–90. Stuttgart, Steiner.

Fenske, Michaela. 2013a. Making the new by rebuilding the old Werben: Histourism in Werben, Germany. *Anthropological Journal of European Cultures* 22:5–23.

Fenske, Michaela. 2013b. Vom Hobbyhandwerker zur feinen Dame: Doing Gender in spätmodernen Zeitreisen. In Elisabeth Cheauré, Sylvia Paletschek and Nina Reusch (eds.), Geschlecht und Geschichte in populären Medien (Gender and History in Popular Media): 283–298. Bielefeld, Transcript.

Fiske, John. 2003. *Lesarten des Populären* (Modes of Reading the Popular). Vienna, Turia+Kant.

Fischer, Thomas, and Rainer Wirtz (eds.). 2008. *Alles authentisch? Popularisierung der Geschichte im Fernsehen* (Everthing Authentic? The Popularisation of History on Television). Konstanz, UKV-Verlagsgesellschaft.

Fraund, Philipp. 2007. Popularisation of history on television – Consequences for the science of history? 19.09.2006-22.09.2006, Konstanz, *HSoz-u-Kult*, January 9, 2007, (http://hsozkult.geschichte.hu-berlin.de/tagungsberichte/id=1201)

Gibbons, Michael, Nowotny, Helga and Scott, Peter (eds.) 1994. *The New Production of Knowledge: The Dynamics of Science and Research in Contemporary Societies*. London, Sage.

Groebner, Valentin. 2008. *Das Mittelalter hört nicht auf. Über historisches Erzählen* (The Middle Ages do not end. About Historical Narrative.). München, Beck.

Gustafsson, Lotten. 2002. *Den förtrollade zonen: Lekar med tid, rum och identitet under medeltidsveckan på Gotland* (The Enchanted Zone: Playing with Time, Space and Identity during the Medieval Week in Gotland.). Nora, Nya Doxa.

Hardtwig, Martin. 2005. Geschichte als Seifenoper? Über den Boom der Populärgeschichte (History as a Soap-Opera? About the Boom of Popular History), deutschlandradio Berlin, February 6.

Heidtmann, Florian. (2001). *Geschichtsbilder und Nutzung von Geschichte, dargestellt an ausgewählten Mittelaltermärkten* (The Perception and Use of History, Presented by Discussing a Selection of Medieval Markets). Hannover.

Hemme, Dorothee. 2010. Harnessing daydreams: A library of fragrant fantasies. *Ethnologia Europaea* 40:5–18.

Hemme, Dorothee, Markus Tauschek and Regina Bendix (eds.) 2007. *Prädikat 'Heritage': Wertschöpfung aus kulturellen Ressourcen* (The Label 'Heritage': Creating Value from Cultural Resources). Berlin, Lit Verlag.

Kaiser, Andrea. 2008. Die Billigen und die Willigen: Neue Fernsehsendungen fingieren die Wirklichkeit, Das Gefälschte ist vom Echten nicht mehr zu unterscheiden (The cheap and the willing: new TV show feigns reality, the fake is indistinguishable from the real). *Die ZEIT online*. http://www.zeit.de/2003/35/Reality-TV. accessed 7 July 2008.

Keller-Drescher, Lioba. 2007. Die Fragen der Gegenwart und das Material der Vergangenheit: Zur (Re)Konstruktion von Wissensordnungen (The questions of the present and the materials of the past: The (re)construction of systems of knowledge). In Andreas Hartmann, Silke Meyer and Ruth Mohrmann (eds.), *Historizät: Vom Umgang mit Geschichte* (Historicity: How to Deal with History): 57–68. Münster, Waxmann.

Kirshenblatt-Gimblett, Barbara. 1995. Theorizing heritage. *Ethnomusiocology* 39:367–380.

Klaus, Elisabeth. 2006. Grenzenlose Erfolge? Entwicklung und Merkmale des Reality TV (Success without borders? Development and characteristics of reality TV). In Brigitte Frizzoni and Ingrid Tomkowiak (eds.), *Unterhaltung:*

Konzepte – Formen – Wirkungen (Entertainment: Concepts – Shapes – Effects): 85–106. Zürich, Chronos.

Kormann, Eva. 2004. *Ich, Welt und Gott: Autobiographik im 17. Jahrhundert* (I, The World and God: Autobiography in the Seventeenth Century). Cologne, Böhlau.

Langewiesche, Dieter. 2008. Geschichtsschreibung und Geschichtsmarkt in Deutschland (Historiography and the history market in germany). In Nikolaus Buschmann and Ute Planert (eds.), *Zeitwende: Geschichtsdenken heute* (A Turning Point in History: Historical Thinking Today): 9–17. Göttingen, Vandenhoeck und Ruprecht.

Lowenthal, David. 1986. *The Past is a Foreign Country*. Cambridge, Cambridge University Press.

Maase, Kaspar. 2006. Grenzenloses Vergnügen? Zum Unbehagen in der Unterhaltungskultur (Unlimited pleasure? The discomfort in entertainment culture). In Brigitte Frizzoni, and Ingrid Tomkowiak (eds.), *Unterhaltung: Konzepte – Formen – Wirkungen* (Entertainment: Concepts – shapes – Effects): 49–67. Zürich, Chronos.

Maierhofer, Waltraud. 2005. *Hexen – Huren – Heldenweiber: Bilder des Weiblichen in Erzähltexten über den Dreißigjährigen Krieg* (Witches – Whores – Heroines: Images of the Feminine in Narrative Texts about the Thirty Years War). Cologne, Böhlau.

Meyer, Annemike. 2003. '*Die Wochend-Ritter ...': Streifzüge durch die Mittelalter-Szene, Eine kulturwissenschaftliche Betrachtung des Phänomens* ('The Weekend Knights ...'. Wanderings in the Medieval Scene, A Cultural Analysis of the Phenomenon). Master's thesis, Georg-August-University, Göttingen.

Nowotny, Helga, Peter Scott and Michael Gibbons (eds.). 2001. *Re-Thinking Science: Knowledge and the Public in an Age of Uncertainty*. London, Polity Press. (German Translation [2004], *Wissenschaft neu denken: Wissen und Öffentlichkeit in einem Zeitalter der Ungewissheit*, Weilerswist: Velbrück).

Nünning, Ansgar. 1995. *Von historischer Fiktion zu historiographischer Metafiktion* (From Historical Fiction to Historiographical Meta-fiction), vols. 1–2. Trier, WVT.

Schwellenbach, Judith. 2007. 'Geschichte light' zum Mitmachen? Das TV-Format Living History am Beispiel der Serie 'Windstärke 8 – Das Auswandererschiff' ('History light' to Join in? A Discussion of the TV Format Living History, Taking the Series 'Wind Force 8 – The Emigrant Ship' as an Example). Master's thesis, Münster, 58–65.

Stark, Laura. 2008. Premodern concepts of self and body in Finnish magic narrative, Public Lecture, Göttingen, July 2.

Svensson, Birgitta. 1998. The nature of cultural heritage sites. *Ethnologia Europaea* 28:5–16.

Uka, Walter. 2003. Historie (History). In Hügl, Hans-Otto, (ed.), *Handbuch populäre Kultur: Begriffe, Theorien und Diskussionen* (Handbook of Popular Culture: Concepts, Theories, and Discussions): 240–248. Stuttgart, Metzler.

Weingart, Peter. 2005. *Die Wissenschaft der Öffentlichkeit. Essays zum Verhältnis von Wissenschaft und Öffentlichkeit* (The Science of the Public: Essays on the Relationship between Science and the Public). Weilerswist, Velbrück.

Wolf, Fritz. 2005. Trends und Perspektiven für die dokumentarische Form im Fernsehen: Eine Fortschreibung der Studie 'Alles Doku – oder was?: Über die Ausdifferenzierung des Dokumentarischen im Fernsehen' (Trends and Perspectives for the Documentary Form on Television: A Continuation of the Study 'Everything Docu – or What?: On the Further Specification of the Documentary on Television). Düsseldorf. http://www.mediaculture-online.de/fileadmin/bibliothek/wolf_dokuform/wolf_dokuform.pdf (accessed February 9, 2013)

Wolf, Fritz. 2008. Alles Doku – oder was? Über die Ausdifferenzierung des Dokumentarischen im Fernsehen: Zusammenfassung und zentrale Expertise der Ergebnisse (Everything Docu – or What? On the Differentiation of the Documentary on Television: Summary and Key Expertise of the Results). http://64.233.183.104/search?q=cache:-WPRFRbs3RQJ:www.lfm-nrw.de/downloads/allesdoku-zusam.pdf+Fritz+Wolf+Alles+Doku&hl=de&ct=clnk&cd=2&gl=de&client=firefox-a. accessed 7.7.2008

Zemon Davis, Natalie. 2004. *Die wahrhaftige Geschichte von der Wiederkehr des Martin Guerre* (The True Story of the Return of Martin Guerre), Berlin: Wagenbach (French Original: Le Retour de Martin Guerre [1982]. Paris, Robert Laffont).

Zemon Davis, Natalie. 1998. Ad me ipsum, in: Zemon Davis, Natalie, Lebensgänge: Glikl, Zwi Hirsch, Leone Modena, Martin Guerre, Berlin: Wagenbach: 75–104.

Chapter 12

Time Travel to the Present
Interview with Erika Andersson Cederholm

Cornelius Holtorf and Bodil Petersson

Biography
Erika Andersson Cederholm is Associate Professor in sociology at the Department of Service Management and Service Studies, Lund University. Her research interests embrace the intersection between culture, economy and social interactions, including service encounters and experiences in tourism and hospitality contexts. Her recent research focusses on the commodification and organisation of intimacy and emotions in hospitality contexts, lifestyle enterprising in the rural experience economy, and the boundary work between economic and non-economic life spheres in various service contexts.

Keywords: Authenticity, experience economy, experience society, lifestyle migrants, tourism

The interview

Cornelius:
Let us talk about time travel! Erika you are a sociologist and a tourist expert. How would you study the phenomenon of time travel that is quite popular these days in society from a sociological perspective?

Erika:
I am not a historian so I do not really have a historical perspective in my research, but I am interested in how people view history or people's ideas of the past and what they do with the past, for instance in different kinds of tourism activities, which I have been studying. So I am interested in actually how people think about past and pastness and what they do with the past and also a bit why it is interesting for people to engage in the past. But I think the why question is quite complex because I think it is many different kind of factors today that make people be interested in the past. Mainly I have been interested in what people associate in the past and what they actually do with it.

Bodil:
You also have this other affiliation to service management, which is part of the name of your Department. Is that also affecting your approach here together with sociology?

Erika:
Yes, definitely, I think so. My training is as a sociologist, and I took my PhD in sociology at the department of sociology at Lund University. But since then I have been working and doing research in a more interdisciplinary environment at service management and service studies at the campus in Helsingborg, and I think that has affected my research and my way of thinking. I have been interested in the interdisciplinary area of service studies and tourism studies. When I was doing my PhD in sociology I was interested in tourism as a phenomenon and touristic experiences (Andersson Cederholm, 1999). In the last few years I have also become more interested in some economic aspects of tourism, but as a sociologist. There is often a tension between economic aspects and other, experience-oriented aspects. I am interested in these kinds of tensions. So my interest in the economic aspect is also related to the fact that I work in an interdisciplinary environment encompassing both service studies and the service industry and so on.

Cornelius:
Is there a particular larger trend in society today which could explain why people are so interested in experiencing the past? Would you connect this phenomenon to bigger movements or trends in society?

Erika:
This is the why question. Why are people so interested in this kind of thing today? It is always complex and there are many different kinds of aspects involved. But one particularly important aspect is, I think, the search for identity and the idea of belonging and participating with other people in doing things. A key concept here is the idea of authenticity. People are longing for authentic experiences in various forms. Why is that so important? I think it is not new that people are longing for authentic experiences, but there is now a new aspect of it. The longing for authentic experiences today is also to a certain extent commodified as an industry around authenticity which makes this interesting for me.

Cornelius:
Is this connected to what some people have called the Experience Society?

Erika:
Yes. It is more generally the idea of the experience society and the experience economy. It is not only about a new form of economy, it is also about cultural movements, new ideas and a new focus on certain issues which have more to do with new ways to searching and confirming identities. So yes.

Bodil:
As a sociologist you have been exploring travelling in some of your work (Andersson Cederholm 2004, 2009). I wonder if you see a huge difference or rather similarities between travels in space and travels in time, if you approach them as a sociologist?

Erika:
Yes, they are related to each other. I think people experience that quite a lot. For many tourists, travelling in space is an important part of the tourist experience; but for many people travelling in space is also associated with travelling in time, as both are about visiting 'other' cultures, 'other' places and the notion of the 'other'. I think people also associate that when doing a certain kind of time travel. In my research I have been interested in rural tourism: people going to the countryside to experience, for instance living or staying on a farm as part of a tourist experience doing activities connected to nature and the rural context (Andersson Cederholm and Sjöholm 2014). In this example urban people travel in space, but there is also an idea of travelling in time because for many people the rural context is associated with nostalgia, with a past of local communities and a sense of belonging. So I think there is a time dimension in the way people experience space in tourism; that there is a move to another place but also another time.

Cornelius:
So that might support the view that the past is a foreign country?

Erika:
Yes, and no. It could be literally but also symbolic, that is in the way it is framed. You go to a certain place which is framed in time and space.

Cornelius:
To what extent would you say that the experience of the past in what we call time travel and pastness is a way of engaging with the social world around us? Is it a medium or a resource which we draw on in order to achieve certain aims in society? How does that work in a sociological perspective?

Erika:
As I mentioned before, I think that the notion of authenticity is very important here. But if you use authenticity as an analytical concept it is important to define what you mean by authenticity. One aspect of authenticity is what I and other authors have been calling existential authenticity (Andersson Cederholm 1999; Wang, 1999). It could be a sense of the past, a sense of belonging, a sense of authenticity. That doesn't necessarily have to do with what is actually authentic in an objective meaning.

One dimension of this existential authenticity is a heightened feeling of presence and of being present here and now, also with other people. I think that that is something that people search for in various ways. A heightened sense of presence actually might sound paradoxical but I think that both the past and the future could be a means of reaching a sense of presence. Whether it is about ideas of the future or ideas of the past, time is a medium for reaching a sense of presence. People long for this in many ways. Tourism experiences are just one way of trying to reach a heightened sense of presence. For example, a tourist going to rural places and staying on a farm or having 'nature' experiences such as horse riding could be associated with the local context and ideas of the past. But sometimes a holiday is also more, a medium for reaching that kind of sense of existential authenticity – being there, being there with other people, being in nature. It could be with other people, but it could also be by yourself.

Bodil:
You describe this kind of existential authenticity very much in terms of a subjective experience and maybe a shared subjectivity between different individuals, but is there a collective side to it as well?

Erika:
Yes. There is always a collective side to it and there is always also an individual and subjective side to it. There is one tourism researcher called Ning Wang, and he has been writing a lot about this existential authenticity concept (Wang 1999). Wang makes a division between what he calls intra-relational existential authenticity and inter-relational existential authenticity. The intra-relational experience could be the very subjective flow-like experience of being totally absorbed in a particular activity. If you climb a mountain or you are alone in a sailing boat surrounded by nature – that is a subjective, individual experience. But then there is also inter-relational existential authenticity which is more focussed on sharing things. So in that meaning you can make a distinction between this very subjective side and the collective social side of it. Of course there is always a collective, social aspect in the very idea of time travel and authenticity; the very idea and the way we talk about it is socially constructed which is a collective dimension. It is also an expression of our time and our society today that we are so interested in time and time travel. So in that sense it is always a cultural, collective social phenomenon.

Cornelius:
Where does all this actually come from? The fact that we are interested in our time in these particular expressions, these forms of time travelling, is that to do at all with media and wider trends in popular culture such as film or literature? Or are these larger social issues? We were talking about identity searching earlier,

is that something which perhaps has changed in character compared to previous generations, even though it is not entirely new?

Erika:
I think it is not entirely new. The historical perspective of the time travel itself is interesting. The idea of time travel comes and goes in history. But why do we think that it is so interesting today? There are many inter-relating factors here. I think the media are a catalyst in the process, and popular culture could be also a very important interesting catalyst. But it is not a cause, it is more one aspect of everything. The industry around experiences, the experience industry and tourism is also one part of it but you can't say that it is a cause either. I think it is something that accentuates the speed and the flow of information around the idea of time travel. There are so many interrelated aspects to why people are interested in searching for experiences and knowledge.

Bodil:
I would like to turn to the material aspects of travelling in space or time. Can there be catalysts of a very material kind? When you perform handicrafts, when you take care of animals or when you make something with your hands, you will get tangible outcomes of that as well. Have you seen a lot of relationships with the material world in your studies?

Erika:
In my studies of tourist experiences and producer perspectives, people start different kinds of tourist-oriented enterprises in the rural context in order to provide experiences for tourists and visitors. One important aspect is that when they try to create experiences they take into consideration all these material things, and they are very important. People have at least an idea and I think also a sort of longing for this important experience of doing things. That could also be a more sports-oriented kind of recreational type of activities like riding horses. I have a project specifically on horse farms. It is very clear in that context that the animals play an important role, not only in the traditional meaning of riding a horse for sport or recreation but also regarding the emotional and embodied experience of being with the animals and doing things with animals (Andersson Cederholm 2014). You can relate that to other kinds of activities such as being engaged in traditional handicraft. One part of a tourist experience is the offering or taking part in traditional craftsmanship, like 'we are making traditional cheese at our farm and as part of your experience you can participate in making cheese in the traditional way', that kind of thing. So that is also a part of that idea of existential authenticity, being there with all your senses and doing things. The material aspects are very important here: things, artefacts, and also other kinds of

mediums like animals. The material side and the sense of authenticity that people get from it are very important indeed.

Cornelius:
One of the characteristics of society is that it is dynamic, that it is constantly changing and that it is difficult to predict in which way it will go. To the extent that time travelling is a social phenomenon, what sort of dynamics would you see affect these various processes, for example in tourism? What sort of conflicts are there, what sort of breaking points may we see that things are changing into something else because not everybody likes this sort of tourism and not everybody is perhaps in favour of it? Some people may not like that tourism commodifies the countryside and commodifies the past and maybe caters for certain kinds of tourists and not for others, and maybe is not sustainable either. How would you describe the significance of these tensions?

Erika:
I think it is a field full of tensions, different kinds of tensions which is interesting in itself. We have the more general tension between the process of commodification and people's experiencing of over-commodification. That is one aspect of searching for authenticity. Many people perceive that if it becomes too commercialised, too commodified, it loses a sense of authenticity. We can see that quite clearly in tourism. For instance, if a place becomes too crowded then people go somewhere else. Searching for the unique is often an important aspect of the tourism experience. But there is a tension because people also want to have confirmation. People want other tourists to be there in order to confirm that this is a good tourist experience; but then on the other hand they also want to go to places where there are no other tourists. So this classic tension in tourism has to do with people's ideas of the unique and the authentic and the idea that a certain type of commodification undermines authenticity.

In heritage tourism we can see that same tension quite clearly, which also has to do with different ideas of what is authentic. For instance, if you are a heritage institution you have a certain obligation of preserving and conserving the authentic objects. From that a conflict with the tourist industry can arise, and also with people's ideas of experiencing the more sensual aspect of authenticity, the existential authenticity. People want to have a *sense* of authenticity, and that is more valuable than the experience we find in the authentic objects sometimes. At the same time, for a tourist it is very important to see the authentic objects. In order to understand this dynamic and this tension it is important, analytically, to make a distinction between different perceptions of authenticity; if you mean the objective authenticity that is immanent *in* certain objects and artefacts or if you are referring more to the experience of the authenticity, the existential authenticity.

There are also other kinds of tensions which are connected to ideas of sustainability and to the idea of time and rhythm: for instance, slowness versus speed, mobility versus embeddedness in the community. People travel all over the world today. There is so much mobility and yet there are also increasingly ideals that you shouldn't travel so much due to sustainability problems. So we have also got emerging trends towards slow travel and near tourism. You shouldn't go to the other side of the world, but go to your nearby village instead and experience something of that village or of your own town. That is another tension.

Cornelius:
Heritage doesn't always have to provide exclusively positive experiences. There is another heritage: dark heritage, connected to the terrible parts of history which you can also visit and experience. People appreciate that too, when they visit concentration camps, for example, or prisons and places like that.

Erika:
Yes we have this idea of dark tourism. It is a very wide concept actually because everything is included, from visiting concentration camps or historical battlefields to foreign nuclear power plants. Dark tourism is a wide range of different kinds of experiences, even including the heritage associated with disaster and death. There are interesting moral issues and debates going on. What is a proper site; where to go as a tourist or where not to go; what is possible to commodify, and what should not be commodified? There are continuous negotiations of what is appropriate and not appropriate; what is good tourism and what is bad tourism; what is the good past and the bad past; what can we show to people, and what can we not show to people.

Bodil:
If you apply a time aspect to this then maybe more darkness is permissible when you go farther back in time. Do you have this time filter which makes it easier to approach disasters and death in the past?

Erika:
Yes. That is an interesting aspect. When a certain time has passed, such sites become more acceptable to visit. It is interesting to know the limit. How long back is it possible, or how close in time is it not possible to visit? When you want to define something as acceptable, this also is connected to how you define cultural heritage. There is also a time aspect, how far back in time do you have to go in order to call something heritage. So that is all part of negotiations. For a sociologist, it is interesting to see how people negotiate here; how they draw the boundaries between what belongs to the past and what belongs to the present, what is good and what is bad, what is authentic and what is not authentic, what is okay to

commodify and what is not okay to commodify. It is actually very much about boundary work, a concept that I use very much in my research. It is a constant making and remaking of these boundaries.

Cornelius:
To stick with this notion of boundaries for a bit longer, what do you say about time travel as a way of transgressing the boundary of our society in a way of leaving our society? Is a time travel a statement against the ruling conditions in some form, a desire to find an alternative to our way of life? Is it an escape from something that one experiences as imperfect, to say the least, or outright negative?

Erika:
I think that time travel is experienced by many people as an escape. It is important for people to draw boundaries in order to have this heightened experience. For instance, if you go as a tourist to a nearby village, you are very familiar with this village. But in order to create a special experience, you need to frame it in time and in space. Establishing a boundary to your ordinary life makes it an extraordinary experience. It is one essential aspect in tourism – and also in the sort of construction of experiences in general – that you need this sort of bubble that you go into, this 'frame', even if you travel nearby, in a 'staycation'. I don't know if you are familiar with that concept, it is a sort of a mix between staying and going on vacation. In order to appreciate this staycation experience as a tourist you need to have clear boundaries established. The escapist aspect of tourism is always there. You want to go somewhere else or to another place or time or to go into this bubble. These boundaries are very, very dynamic; they are remade all the time. We are continuously pushing the boundaries of what is considered as an appropriate tourist experience. It is not only a psychological aspect. I am interested in the more collective and the social construction of these boundaries. It is not only about one individual creating a bubble, a time-space bubble if you like. We always have a collective idea of doing this; that it is okay for us to go on this kind of holiday or go on a staycation or go somewhere else. There is always a social process involved in this kind of defining and making boundaries.

Cornelius:
There are some people today who decide to live permanently on the other side of the boundary as it were: people who don't escape for a while but decide to live permanently as tourists, so to speak, perhaps offering certain experiences to other tourists. How do they fit in? How can you transgress these boundaries permanently? Are new boundaries maybe created as a result?

Erika:
I think that is a very interesting aspect. I am doing research on people who may be so-called lifestyle migrants, that is people leaving an urban environment and careers moving out to the countryside, perhaps in order to start a small business. They've always dreamed, for instance, about starting a small bed and breakfast, or about having a horse farm for tourists. They can share their life dream with other people and also sell this idea to tourists. This is very interesting because on the one hand they are tourists but on the other hand the tourist experience becomes everyday life for them after a while. They live their daily lives there, and they have their work, and their children go to school, and it can become a grey everyday life, like for everybody else. But at the same time, their lifestyle, which is part of why they have been moving there in the first place, that lifestyle is also attractive to other people. Visitors are attracted to go there, not only to spend a few nights in that particular bed and breakfast, but also to experience the host's lifestyle. So in a way they don't just sell a conventional service product in hospitality, food and accommodation, but they also sell their lifestyle. People go there and they consume their host's lifestyle. It is important for these lifestyle migrants, in order to sell their product, to market their lifestyle, live in this bubble, in order that other people will be attracted to it. It is interesting to see how they maintain these boundaries around their world and their lifestyle without being drawn back into that everyday grey life. They do a lot of work to maintain that boundary. For instance, they do storytelling and marketing on their websites. They tell the story of how they left the urban lifestyle and started a new life in the countryside. They often emphasize these personal aspects by telling all the names of their family members and the cats and the dogs and so on. That storytelling is one part of creating an image: 'We live the perfect lifestyle here. We are a happy family. We are offering experiences to you to come here and be happy at least for those two days that you stay with us.' One tool that they use is storytelling and marketing. Having said that, I don't think that these people often consider themselves as very skillful marketers. They do this more or less unconsciously. They have a feeling that people are attracted to come there because of them.

But there are different ways of trying to create this boundary. Another strategy is emphasizing the small scale of the production. For instance, if they have food production, it is presented as handicraft, a craftsmanship-oriented type of traditional production. The visitors can partake in the production process. This often includes animals, and the hosts are offering different kinds of animal experiences. All these are lifestyle migrants who are both living their dream and also selling their dream. They are an interesting case. They are both tourists and non-tourists at the same time.

Cornelius:
In a way their dream is, of course, part of the urban world today. We understand immediately what you mean because it's familiar to all of us. Lifestyle migrants may find that their neighbours came from a different city. So they are not really leaving the city but still bound up in a set of norms and values that we urban folk can all relate to.

Erika:
Yes, caught in the norm of the rural idyll and the countryside. Today, the boundaries between the urban and the rural are very blurred. What is rural, really, and what is urban? It is very much interconnected. But it is in the interest of these tourist businesses that the boundaries and distinctions are maintained in order to sell the rural dream or the ideal. Everything that is associated with the rural – with the local community, sense of belonging and all these ideas of the authentic – is important for people today.

Bodil:
All this is about leaving the urban lifestyle for the rural one. Are there other tendencies today, approaching other lifestyles than the rural one? For example, we are told sometimes that we live in a post-industrial society and that there are movements towards commodifying the industrial era. Can you see that tendency in society?

Erika:
Yes, well in tourism there is quite a large trend of visiting industrial heritage. Industrial heritage tourism is an important industry and that includes not only the old mining industry but also newer industries that are no longer working. This is definitely something that seems to be emerging. Going to other places and other times, really takes so many different shapes. It could be the rural, it could be the industrial heritage, it could be going to very far places and other cultures. The idea of the 'other' is important, and there is often both a cultural and a temporal distance connected to that. The idea of other people or other places is very abstract; but as long as it is something 'other', there is some attractiveness in that.

Cornelius:
There seems to be, at least in my superficial view, a certain sense that the 'self' needs the 'other' to define itself. It is not the case that you need to find other selves who are more or less similar. Instead you need to contrast that. You need to experience something that is different, whether that is in time or in space or some other transgression of experience. I wonder if that existed in all previous periods or exists similarly in other parts of the world today.

Erika:
I think the romantic idea of the other has a history. But there are many forms of 'others' today. The supply of otherness is so large. You can choose a large variety of otherness in different ways. There is an industry of otherness. This is a new aspect today. It is so interesting to contrast ourselves with the 'other', both seeing the similarities and the differences. They are just like us, and they are different. We have both these aspects and each could come out in many ways.

Cornelius:
So the best time travel offers the prospect of experiencing the 'other' without leaving your own country?

Erika:
Yes, you can say that, because you can find the other next door. You can find the other everywhere. It is easier to find the other today than it was before. I mean the other in that abstract meaning; not in the essential meaning of someone who is 'the other', but the object of otherness as it changes all the time. But we live in a global society and globalisation contributes to all these different aspects. It is important to consider globalisation and the cultural variety that we have. It is easy to find the other everywhere.

Bodil:
Could you say that time travel is a more sustainable way of travelling?

Erika:
Yeah, because the temporal aspect is there in the idea of 'the other'. If you have an idea of even a contemporary other, you can see some pastness in this contemporary other that you can see in your own society. It could be more difficult and maybe not so attractive, to look for the past in your own local society – you can see the past best through other people. There is always this attraction of the idea of searching for the past.

Cornelius:
When you refer to the past and to pastness then you are not talking about detailed chronologies in the way a historian might do but you are referring to a particular experience. How important are the senses and emotions in that?

Erika:
I think they are very important. Going back to this notion of existential authenticity, which is a wide concept, the essential aspect is that you are there with your whole mind and body. This is very important, triggering all your senses. The tourist industry has hooked onto this, too. Maybe the reason for this demand

is an experience of lack, a lack of something essential. People are perhaps searching somewhere else for the existential experiences they are missing in their ordinary lives. Or maybe they need organised forms of existential experiences. Or maybe you need the organised forms so you will be able to talk about existential experiences. I don't know. Of course, you have existential experiences all the time. You are always there or here with all your feelings and emotions. You can't really divide emotional or cognitive aspects. These more organized forms of existential experience allow us nevertheless to speak of an ideal or even a norm that you should experience with your whole body and feeling. This emergence in something bodily and emotionally can take the form of tourism or it can take the form of going to the gym or to a dance class.

Cornelius:
So on one level, one thinks that the senses are something very personal and very subjective: 'only I know what I like, and it is just up to me'. On another level, you prove the opposite: that it is all determined by the social context in which we find ourselves. When we follow certain trends, we often follow more general trends and norms. How do the subjective and the collective go together in this?

Erika:
I look very much at the collective – indeed, the very idea of the subjective is also a collective idea. The idea of being there with yourself and as a subject is a socially constructed idea. This is my sociological mind. I can't really escape from that. I always see everything in this social aspect. But of course I can't deny that there is an individual dimension too. There is a constant tension between the two. This is a classic tension in social science between the actor and the structure – the individual and the collective. There is an emphasis on the subjective and the individual experience in our society, which is due to our historical context. There is a very strong cultural ideal which emphasizes the individual and the subjective. That is also visible when it comes to the experience industry. The subjective experience and the individual experience are very important and also sensual. You should be there with all your senses and experience, but it is always connected to social norms on how you should express your individuality and your subjectivity. Is it okay to go on a time travel to this place or to that place? There are always norms. So in that sense it is always social. The social structures emphasise the individual and subjective experience in our society.

Cornelius:
Can you see a tendency of different social groups choosing different ways not of time travelling but of experiencing?

Erika:
Definitely, I think there are different kinds of social groups preferring different kinds of experiences. You can see it from an economic perspective and talk about

different types of consumers who prefer different kinds of experiences. But I think it also has a wider sociological meaning. You can see differences based on class, gender and ethnicity; and all these aspects are also related to how we want to experience things. If, for instance, we really enjoy experiencing the past through nature, or the idea of going to the countryside, I think there is a cultural aspect to that. At the same time, it is not something that everybody wants to do, but it is also to a certain extent class related. In Sweden, for instance, there is a long history of the urban middle class going to the countryside in order to recreate. I don't know how much similar behaviour is class-related today, but there certainly is a history of the urban middle class wanting to go to experience the countryside. There are definitely different groups having different kinds of norms and ideals.

Cornelius:
In a way you could maybe say: 'tell me which past you want to travel to, and I tell you who you are'.

Erika:
Well that is a dream for marketers. I think there is a lot of truth in that statement, although it is always a bit more complex than that.

Cornelius:
In all the examples you gave and then the points you made, you always came back to the point that as time travellers we are travelling to the past, but really we are travelling to our own time. On one level we are leaving the present but on another one, at the same time, we are returning home.

Erika:
Yes, I think so. I think that is a very good conclusion. I think that we are travelling to ourselves in many ways; or we want to reconfirm our sense of identity, our cultural norms and our ideals through something that is 'other'. That could be another time, another place, but I think we need that in order to confirm our identity. So in that sense, time travel is about us. Even if it is about going somewhere else, it is very much about us and our time.

Cornelius:
By going somewhere else we can stay where we are.

Erika:
Yes, but we nevertheless change a little bit along the way.

Cornelius and Bodil:
Thank you for talking to us!

Acknowledgements

The interview was conducted on 15 January 2015 in Hässleholm. For help with the transcription we are grateful to Sarah May.

References

Andersson Cederholm, E. 1999. Det extraordinäras lockelse - luffarturistens bilder och upplevelser: Arkiv förlag.

Andersson Cederholm, E. 2004. The use of photo-elicitation in tourism research - framing the backpacker experience. Scandinavian Journal of Hospitality and Tourism, 4(3):225–241.

Andersson Cederholm, E. 2009. 'Being with others': The commodification of relationships in tourism. ATLAS Reflections 2009: 31–43. The Netherlands: Association for Tourism and Leisure Education.

Andersson Cederholm, E. 2014. Hosts, guests and horses – triadic relationships in horse-based hospitality. In Björck, Lönngren, Jennbert, Andersson Cederholm (eds.), *Exploring the Animal Turn*. The Pufendorf Institute for Advanced Studies, Lund University.

Andersson Cederholm, E. and Sjöholm, C. 2014. Att leva och sälja sin dröm - livsstilsföretagaren mellan familjeliv, marknad och politisk retorik. Sociologisk Forskning, 50(2):33–52.

Wang, N. 1999. Rethinking authenticity in tourism experiences. Annals of Tourism Research, 26:349–370.

Commentary

Time-Travelling Tourism
Reflections on the Past as a Place of Fascination as well as Refuge

Thomas Småberg

Throughout recorded history, the landscape of the past has always been a fascination and at times an obsession for individuals, as well as societies. For instance, in Western Europe during the Middle Ages, the captivation with the mythology surrounding King Arthur led to the re-enactment of famous battles and tournaments, and to knights and ladies dressing up during courtly feasts as King Arthur, Guinevere, Lancelot and other popular Arthurian characters. In modern times, the use of history for entertainment, education and for influencing the present has continued in similar form in Western Europe, for example through the re-enactment of battles such as the *Battle of Visby 1361* being performed on the island of Gotland, Sweden, in recent years or via medieval festivals held all over Europe. In a modern, digital era, it should not surprise anyone that computer games, TV shows, movies and Facebook groups makes use of a perceived past and allow visitors and users to experience long-gone days.

For the last few decades a common form of experiencing the past has been through the pedagogical tool called time travel. Time travel can be defined as being immersed in an era, frequently the Viking Age or the Middle Ages, by means of dressing up in era-authentic clothing, watching or participating in re-enactments by professional or semi-professional actors, or by eating and drinking what is called authentic cuisine. This form of histotainment has proven to be very popular and has spawned re-created villages, festivals, merchandise and a whole tourism industry.

The contributions by Michaela Fenske (History as an Adventure) and Erika Andersson Cederholm (Time Travel to the Present) to this anthology both concern the phenomenon of time travel, which is a much studied field (Warring 2015). The authors discuss the modern preoccupation with the past and reflect on the causes from, respectively, an ethnological and sociological perspective. Explanations for this trend of time travel tend to range quite widely in scholarly work from a genuine interest in history to a post-modern reaction to a complicated present, a new wave of civilizational critique or a deep seated, almost existential need to experience the past through the senses, to taste, smell and live the past. Fenske and Andersson Cederholm both contribute to the field of time travel and delve into several interesting areas such as existential authenticity, the past as present, body and participation. In this commentary, however, I shall restrict myself to discussing the term authenticity, which both authors reflect on extensively.

Authenticity is an ambivalent term, as for instance Andersson Cederholm discusses. Authenticity is imagined and perceived differently by professionals such as archaeologists, historians and cultural heritage pedagogues than by visitors to time travel experiences or museums. It is also important to underline the fact that varying degrees of authenticity exists, for example when it comes to actors participating in time travel. Some actors strive for the recreation to be as historically correct as possible right down to the way their garments were made. Others mix and blend historical eras in their clothing and in their recreations, sometimes even including fantasy themes as well. This is equally true for those professional or semi-professional actors who recreate the past, as well as for those who merely visit the recreated past (Egberts 2014).

Time travel as it is used today tends to explore the borderline between fact and fiction, making authenticity negotiable. A term frequently used to define this grey area is histotainment, history as entertainment, a key word against which authenticity must be measured. A case in point is the exhibition 'Power Play: A Costume Drama at the Royal Armoury' ('MAKTSPEL – ett kostymdrama i Livrustkammaren') at the Royal Armoury of Sweden in Stockholm. Here, three individuals, two real, King Erik XIV of Sweden and Queen Elisabeth I of England, and one fictional, Joffrey Baratheon from *Game of Thrones*, met visitors wishing to experience history. The Royal Armoury, it should be noted, is an institution steeped in historical authenticity, with the actual armours, clothing and carriages of Sweden's royalty on display. In this exhibition, however, authenticity was negotiated and ambivalent with historical, as well as fictional characters' clothes, and this ambivalence was further underscored by the fact that the displayed clothes of Elisabeth were not the historical Queens own, but instead those worn by Cate Blanchett in two Hollywood movies (Gyllenberg 2014). Further, one Royal Armoury web page stated: 'Many of the events in *Game of Thrones* can be linked to historical events' (Livrustkammaren 2014). This exhibition is thus clearly a form of histotainment. One likely purpose behind this exhibition was to get more people interested in history, but this use of history is fraught with danger. The question of what is fictional and what is historical was blurred in the exhibition, and it is reasonable to expect that a visitor might have problems telling the difference. One provocative question is, does it matter? My answer is a resounding yes. Fiction such as *Game of Thrones* has influenced many peoples' perception of the past such as the American artist Snoop Dogg who apparently believes *Game of Thrones* portrays a historical past (*BBC Newsbeat* 2015). He is an idol for many young people; his ideas will influence many. And since our understanding of the past influences how we perceive our society and ourselves, this matters.

There are numerous other examples of histotainment in museum exhibitions. The most famous Swedish example is the huge impact of a fictional character, Arn Magnusson, on the tourism industry in Västergötland, Sweden, in the 1990s and early 2000s. Arn was the hero of a series of books, later made into films, by Jan Guillou, in which Arn was portrayed as the perfect medieval knight. Arn and his equally fictional wife Cecilia Algotsdotter were heavily exploited by museums and cultural heritage sites as well as by entrepreneurs who for example sold journeys to authentic sites connected to Arn in the books. These journeys were frequently marketed under the slogan 'I Arns fotspår' (In the footprints of Arn) to which Västergötlands museum published a travel guide (Forsell 2000). At Gudhem monastery, where Cecilia was incarcerated in the books, the visitor centre displays finds from the medieval monastery as well as backdrops from the movie (Gudhems kloster 2016). These marketing strategies fuse fact with fiction and authenticity is once more negotiated. Labelled 'Arntourism', this industry attracted huge numbers of visitors over the years; in one year almost 400,000 visitors are said to have travelled to various sites and museums in Västergötland. A report states that almost half of the day tourists who visited the authentic medieval sites mentioned in the books did so not for an interest in the history of the Middle Ages but because of the books (Arnturismen 2004).

Several museums had exhibitions where Arn was the centrepiece (Artsman 2003). Västergötlands museum, for instance, had exhibitions on medieval history, both local and national where fact met fiction. A visitor would meet portrayals of Arn as an almost actual, historical figure, which was bolstered by quotes from the author where Jan Guillou stated that Arn not only had existed, he should be considered the founder of Sweden (Renander 2006). Jan Guillou himself has stated that the quote should be interpreted in context with a reference made by him to a stone relief at Forshems church and not directly to Arn himself (Guillou 2004). However, the wording and the context in which Västergötlands museum placed it is certainly misleading for visitors (Renander 2006). It is an example of post-modern nationalism that historians generally have abandoned as genuine research for over a hundred years. In this context, however, it becomes the norm, and fiction becomes historical fact while constructing an image of the past. Here lies the danger when fusing fact with fiction and allowing popular culture to come to the forefront and to overcome critical reflections of the past. There is an assumption in many circles, that by using popular culture in historical exhibitions professional archaeologists, historians and cultural heritage pedagogues can educate the public, and that this is a gateway to a genuine interest in history for many who otherwise would not have been interested. Another assumption in connection with this seems to be that the past is too dull and too dusty to be interesting, and that we must make histotainment in order to captivate people's imaginations.

History is not merely the past; it is not only bygone days that no longer concerns us and now must be made to entertain us. History is a battlefield that present-day actors mould for their own purposes. The use of fiction and of fictional characters can in some exhibitions and time travel experiences be examples of a trivialisation of history as a means of disarming serious examination of history by the broader population rather than an attempt at education. Seen as a modern trend, it most certainly is so. Instead of museum exhibitions and time travels centred on critical reflections of the past, authenticity and the way the perception of the past forms our present and shapes the direction of the future, actors produce histotainment as bread and circus for the masses (Linderborg 2005). Many of today's time travels with a focus on experience, body and senses are merely the equivalent of the soap operas of television, entertainment devoid of content. If time travel is the trend as well as the future of experiencing the past we need to take the public's obvious interest in history and make use of modern technology, living history and the remnants of our past in order to reflect on our own society.

References

Arnturismen 2004. 2004. Rapport/Turismens utredningsinstitut. http://www.vastsverige.com/Documents/vastsverige/2004_Arnturismen.pdf (accessed 3 March 2016).

Artsman, Margareta. 2003. Västergötlands museum söker nya hjältar efter Arn. *Svenska dagbladet.* 23 December. http://www.svd.se/vastergotlands-museum-soker-nya-hjaltar- efter-arn (accessed 3 March 2016).

BBC Newsbeat. 2015. Snoop Dogg seems to believe Game of Thrones is historically accurate. *BBC Newsbeat.* 11 May. http://www.bbc.co.uk/newsbeat/article/32688956/snoop-dogg-seems-to-believe-game-   of-thrones-is-historically-accurate (accessed 3 Marach 2016).

Egberts, Linde. 2014. Experiencing the Past. Introduction to Experience, Strategies, Authenticity and Branding. In Linde Egberts and Koos Bosma (eds.). *Companion to European Heritage Revivals*: 11–30. Heidelberg: SpringerOpen.

Forsell, Håkan. 2000. Var ligger Sveriges vagga. *Dagens nyheter.* 4 August. http://www.dn.se/arkiv/kultur/var-ligger-sveriges-vagga (accessed 3 March 2016).

Gudhems kloster. 2016. http://www.gudhem.se/14/1/gudhem/ (accessed 3 January 2016).

Gudhems kloster. 2016. Kulisserna från Arn-filmen. http://www.gudhem.se/4/92/arns- kulisser/ (accessed 3 March 2016).

Guillou, Jan. 2004. Jan Guillou tillbakavisar anklagelser om sakfel. *Nättidningen Svensk Historia*. 8 March. http://svenskhistoria.se/jan-guillou-tillbakavisar-anklagelser-om- sakfel/ (accessed 9 March 2016).

Gyllenberg, Eva-Karin. 2014. 'Game of Thrones' blir utställning i Stockholm. *Dagens Nyheter*. 12 March. http://www.dn.se/kultur-noje/game-of-thrones-blir-utstallning-i- stockholm/ (accessed 28 February 2016).

Linderborg, Åsa. 2005. Medeltiden och hotet mot framtiden. In Anders Högberg and Håkan Kihlström (eds.). *Medeltid på tevetid: en dokusåpas historiedidaktik*: 31–44. Malmö, Malmö Kulturmiljö,.

Livrustkammaren. 2014. Temavisning - 'Game of Thrones på riktigt'. Livrustkammaren. 20 August. http://livrustkammaren.se/sv/temavisning-game-thrones-pa-riktigt/ (accessed 28 March 2016).

Renander, Carina. 2006. Finns Arn? Jan Guillous historiska romanserie i svensk historiekultur 1998-2005. In Klas-Göran Karlsson, Eva-Helen Ulvros and Ulf Zander (eds.). *Historieforskning på nya vägar*: 135–148. Lund: Nordic Academic Press.

Warring, Anette. 2015. At rejse i tid – fortidsfamilier i Sagnlandet Lejre. In Tove Kruse and Anette Warring (eds.). *Fortider tur/retur: reenactment og historiebrug*: 43–66. Frederiksberg: Samfundslitteratur.

Commentary

Time Travels as Alternative Futures

Britta Timm Knudsen

In the chapters in this section, time travels are understood as enchanted zones and framed "bubbles" that inhabitants of the late modern world enjoy visiting because they present alternatives to a contemporary lifestyle in the information society. With a focus on experiencing and learning through the body in a more or less staged historical environment such as the Viking Age, the Iron Age or the Middle Ages time travellers re-enact something that is *not* not the past, borrowing a formulation from Rebecca Schneider (2011). The learning potential in the embodied experiences of former production forms, types of dwelling, war technologies, dress codes, ways of transportation and family life is unquestionably huge. We can thus state that one can learn something of former periods through time travelling, but first and foremost this activity offers escapes and refuges from contemporary life. That is fine and is something – apparently – that contemporary dwellers in late modernity need.

However, I have three points, which I would like to make in the following short text. The first one concerns the very hegemonic monologue that time travels appear to be when we understand them as enchanted zones. Secondly I would like to position time travelling further in the experience economy as an ontological turn that touches upon all spheres in society (Knudsen et al. 2014). Thirdly, I would like to look at time travelling as a critical activity enhancing the present with virtual possibilities eventually opening new futures.

What troubles me here is neither that the past is always seen through the lens of a present frame, nor that past times are seen as an inventory of ways of living that contemporaries can pick and choose from – points with which Lowenthal has made us familiar since 1986. What troubles me is the lack of agency that the past is given in this solely social constructivist framework. Because the past talks back, it refrains us from actions and it makes us perform other actions. It attracts us and it repulses us. Whether the past takes the form of sociocultural customs, vestiges in the forms of buildings, political institutions, artefacts in museums, landscapes, cultural memory mediated and remediated by global, national and social media, it is important to enter a dialogue with the past, to listen to the voices of the past and to understand the past in the present as inherited without being deterministic and without losing a socially constructivist perspective. Contemporaries thus have the possibility to increase their knowledge of the present, enhanced by past life, and to connect morally and ethically to the past by listening to testimonies, vestiges, landscapes, animals, plants and so on. In this perspective, time travelling is not just bubble makings for exhausted middle class knowledge workers or for kids, time travelling needs to connect contemporaries morally and knowledge wise to the past. The obligation towards the past could free us as contemporaries from the burdens of free choices and endless identity-constructions, but it co-exists with our ethical obligation of caring for the voices and vestiges of the past.

History as an adventure and time travel to the present strongly emphasise the embodied, sensuous and experience-oriented and authenticity-hungry dimensions of time travelling due to the fact it appeals to contemporary cultural consumers. I believe that these points are very important component of the success of time travelling as a way of experiencing the past nowadays. Hans Ulrich Gumbrecht (2003) has called it a production of presence and points to the shift from hermeneutics to embodied doing as one of the consequences of this experiential or affective turn as we could name it. We need to feel the past in order to fully embrace it; or in order to engage in and mobilize around the past, our senses, affects and emotions need to be attuned. This shift has two consequences that we have to bear in mind. Time travelling as the bodily recording of time through space thus has become an important constituent of any heritage management. Very often the most used pasts are the very iconic ones of former national glory or mythical greatness, and in that way, standardized views on the past are just confirmed; but sometimes local collections on subaltern groups in society gets attention. A few weeks ago I visited the first welfare museum in Europe situated at Svendborg, a smaller town in Southern Denmark. It is an in situ site consisting of a poorhouse – closed down only as late as 1982 – with several exhibitions, including orphanages not only as we knew them in the 1950s but also in present day. This exhibition likewise makes use of time travelling in its design in order to engage audiences. The in situ place offers the relics and the material vestiges as an immersive environment; the various digital enhancements give voice to testimonies and imagined destinies from the past; and the actual framing is in the form of a current court case in which the Danish State is accused of not taking proper care of the children at the orphanages up until the 1970s.

Time travel can also be an overtly critical tool and something that responds to grand challenges in societies. If transitory societies are marked by wars, ethnic, religious and political tensions, regime change, civil wars and genocide, time travelling in the form of re-enactment, testimony narratives and multi-perspectival views on heritage could have healing effects. Some museums that practice active socio-museology reach out to minorities, subaltern groups of any sort (e.g. the County Museum of Jämtland in Sweden that works with boys tired of school in order to engage them in an education track), and in that sense we can say that time travels ideally become an instrument to realize a more equal, just, inclusive and sustainable society.

Conclusion

Chapter 13

Anachronism and Time Travel

Bodil Petersson

Abstract

It is often argued that well-prepared time travels, for example those through re-enactment and reconstruction, represent some kind of gained truth about the past. There is a striving for authenticity in detail, sometimes with a need to fill a few gaps here and there where information is missing. Anachronism on the other hand is generally banned and seen as something that should not appear at all in settings where authenticity is required. I argue, from my own experiences with research and from examples throughout this book, that the driving force behind all time travels is anachronism at its very core, and that conscious use of anachronism is an important and essential method for developing new approaches to and understanding of ourselves as well as of past societies being (re)created in the present.

Keywords: Anachronism, time travel, authenticity, re-enactment, method

A sinful practice

Do archaeologists and historians ever sin? Maybe it is an odd thing to ask. I wasn't aware of the possibility to value the theme in these words until I read a book by a Finnish historian touching upon anachronism in relation to history (Syrjämäki 2011). I knew that anachronism had not been highly valued in the daily practice of archaeology and history; however, this was the first time I was confronted with anachronism in combination with the concept of sin. It made me curious. As a consequence I started to explore the question and realised that anachronism is a fruitful and elucidating tool for understanding past times. The conscious use of anachronism within archaeology and history, especially when it comes to time travel, results in a better understanding of ourselves in relation to the past that we try to (re)create. Before presenting this tool for a new and better understanding, I outline the framework of this approach (Figure 13.1).

The elephant in the room

There is a constant feeling of an 'elephant in the room' regarding anachronism. As can be seen from the above example, which points out anachronism as a sin, it is usually conceived of as something genuinely bad. Anachronisms ought therefore to be highlighted and reduced so as to avoid the introduction of bias from our

Figure 13.1. A local knight in the reconstructed medieval children's setting Salvestaden, close by Kalmar castle, Sweden. The image immediately caught a sense of balancing between past and present, and therefore I chose it as cover for my book (Petersson 2003) on reconstruction and re-enactment (Photograph by Jes Wienberg 2002).

present time into the interpretations of the past (cf. Skinner 1969; Syrjämäki 2011). To move past the feeling that something is wrong and instead become aware of the positive consequences of embracing and even forming anachronism as a method for understanding ourselves in relation to the past, we need to consider the unconscious use of anachronism when people (re)live or (re)create history as it once might have been.

The unconscious use of anachronism that I refer to is, for example, about not noticing that props, materials or expressions are used in a historical context where they have not yet appeared. The interesting thing is that we cannot get around the fact that we are present-day humans with an impossible task as we aspire to avoid everything that is not contemporary with the epoch in question. Some things we see as obvious anachronism; others we don't notice at all, and therefore we might feel content with the result. As literature historians Catherine Butler and Hallie O'Donovan put it: 'Any modern representation of the experiences of those who lived in the past must necessarily be a ventriloquistic performance, given in terms designed to be understood by a modern audience' (Butler and O'Donovan 2012:73). Here is an explanation of the obvious and active use of anachronism. It is described as the skilled translation between past and present, and for a good translation it needs to be adapted to the audience, in this case a modern one.

Historian Bernard Eric Jensen provides an interesting glimpse into traditions amongst professional historians and their ways to either engage with or avoid re-enactment (Jensen 2015). He presents, in addition to others, historian Raphael Samuel, whose work *Theatres of Memory* (2012 [1997]) shows an alternative approach to re-enactment compared with how most other historians see these activities. Samuel's approach allows several voices, embraces popular culture and different uses of heritage, and understands the inevitable link between past and present. Interestingly, Samuel's approach to history also includes the view that community involvement should be an ingredient in all history work.

A strong direction among historians today is steered by the wish to avoid being influenced by the senses in interpretations of history. To 'live the past' is often seen as dangerous to authenticity. The senses (except sight) are seen as enemies to keep out at any time. There is a development, though, more generally within academia; the senses have been more valued within research such as the humanities and social sciences in recent years. Still, the scepticism remains. The primary reason is the supposed deceptive character of the senses that have the potential to mislead our critical minds (Howes 2005). But is it so?

Re-enacted past

In this text I argue for a conscious use of anachronism in reconstructions of the past. Anachronism functions as a means of confronting and understanding both the past itself, and ourselves in relation to the past in new ways (cf. Cornelius Holtorf's introductory chapter in this volume for a definition of time travel in relation to archaeology). Topics that are discussed and elucidated in the following pages concern the perceived danger of anachronism, how anachronism appears in time travel today, including examples throughout this book, and finally what we can gain from a conscious use of anachronism.

Around the world today we see several examples of time travelling in the form of reconstructions and re-enactment of past societies, buildings, traditions and habits (Kruse and Warring 2015; Magelssen 2007; Paardekooper 2012; Petersson 2003; Rentzhog 2008). The explicit ambition at reconstructed sites and museums and within some re-enactment organisations is often to be true of archaeological or historical sources that are being used for interpretation (Petersson 2003; http://exarc.net, accessed April 8, 2014). The purpose is to try to avoid the most obvious anachronisms to protect the authenticity of the experience for the spectator/participant. One way to be true to the sources is not to fill in the gaps in the story being told. Unfortunately the result often becomes an unfinished and incomplete version of the past, perceived of as primitive and poor. This has been discussed for example in relation to reconstructions of prehistoric buildings, exterior and interior, in which some things are archaeologically known, while other details that must have been present in one way or another are not so well known or not even discernible in the archaeological record due to preservation conditions (cf. Björhem and Säfvestad 1987:42f.). Instead of persistently trying to avoid explicit references to the present within different kinds of time travel, I argue that references to the present would be a good way both to reach the past and to be conscious of how we form the interpretation of the past (see Petersson and Narmo 2012:27ff.). The embarrassment should be replaced by embracement.

'Welcome to the current Middle Ages!' proclaims the Society for Creative Anachronism ([SCA] www.sca.org, accessed 8 April 2014; Cramer 2010:xi). I couldn't agree more upon the strategy expressed in this declaration. Instead of hiding away the unavoidable, this creative society has explicitly embraced the fact that interpretations of past societies are influenced by the present. The SCA's strivings for authenticity are combined with the insight that we live our lives in the present (cf. Cramer 2010:173). A specific example of an inspiring anachronism within the current Middle Ages genre is the use of modern music, for example in the film *A Knight's Tale* (2001) where rock music accompanies a medieval tournament (Cramer 2010:x). The atmosphere suddenly becomes more intense and somehow explained through this anachronistic translation.

The conscious use of anachronism makes explicit that regardless of how we interpret the past – or the future – it is formed by the present. This fact concerning the use of history is extremely evident around us. We continuously see new perspectives on history emerging, perspectives that change the past in favour of our own views, thoughts and wishes (Wilk 1985). For example in our age we often look for evidence of female power, queer perspectives, diversity, sustainability and the role of children and healthcare in the past. All aspects are highly relevant and/or debated in today's society and therefore also seen as relevant to our interpretations of the past. Research does not stop at a mere comment on conditions in the past; there often follows an idealization of the past as more equal, sustainable, caring and diverse than the present. This is an explicit way of handling the past in research by using perspectives that are of interest to us today. We are constantly acting in this way within museum exhibitions, re-creations and research alike. In museums such as the National Historical Museum in Stockholm, Sweden, the contemporary is in focus when family constellations in the past are being discussed. Examples of family structures in the present are brought into the discussion on family structures in the past. And we tend not to be particularly embarrassed about the presence of the present in museums, only in other contexts such as research and reconstruction where a scientific ambition is cherished and temporal contamination ought to be avoided.

Anachronism and authenticity

The word *anachronism* comes from ancient Greek and is composed of *ana-*, meaning 'against', and *chronos* meaning 'time'. Anachronism thereby refers to something being 'against time'. Amongst archaeologists and historians, an anachronism is almost always conceived of as wrong, but within other areas such as art and literature anachronism is a method used to get an audience/reader to relate the past to his/her present time and experience (cf. Martindale [2005] on relations to the past in Shakespeare's plays). The creation of such a relation is, as I conceive of it, a very explicit goal with historical presentations.

There is even such a thing as 'future anachronism'. This branch of anachronism relates to visions of the future, in which, for instance, the level of technology and the look of people show not to be the same as how the future develops in reality. One such explicit example is interior design, dress and technical equipment from the science fiction original TV series *Star Trek* (1966–1969 [Figure 13.2]). When seen several years afterwards, the technology, hair styles, makeup and dress used in 1966 that was pretending to be in the future 2260s are in fact dating the series to the late 1960s and placing it in the Western world and the United States (see a comment in Claeys [2011:194] on *Star Trek* and the attempts to extend the American way of life into the universe). It shows how hard it is to predict future materiality; still there is an obvious interest in doing these predictions in film and literature. A counter-argument would be that the possibility of tracing materiality back to our own times

Figure 13.2. A picture from the TV series Star Trek, 1966–1969, showing future technology and future dress codes (Photograph: Hollywood Pictures © IBL).

is part of the meaning of the film and its being in the present, since it – through its materiality – actually relates us directly to an interpretation of the future.

Closely connected to the concept of anachronism is *authenticity*. The word emanates from Greek and means 'original', 'genuine' or 'reliable'. Where authenticity is seen as the righteous interpretation of the past, anachronism is seen as an interpretation that went wrong. But, if anachronism is a condition, authenticity is an ambition. What I mean by this is that we cannot escape the inherent anachronism since we always carry with us the present, and it will affect every single one of our interpretations of the past whether we wish it or not. When it comes to authenticity, this is not an absolute entity but an endeavour towards something that we wish for, a goal in relation to representing the past.

In attempts to represent the past, different paths are chosen. Concepts used to explain ways to approach the past can be *(re)construction*, *(re)creation* and *replication*. These expressions signal that ambition is to be more exact in representation and mostly relating to objects and physical matters. Other expressions such as *re-enactment* and *living history* signal a desire to make things, people and environments come alive. There are also reconstruction activities relying on new techniques such as *3D representations* and digitally constructed worlds through *virtual reality*. Here the span is the same, from reconstruction of objects to attempts to live the past. All these activities have in common that they are used within the realm of (re)creating past times and thereby are parts of what I would call *methodical anachronism*.

Methodical anachronism

Places where methodical anachronism might be performed are within traditional museums, open-air museums, museum centres and so-called educational centres as well as at archaeological and historical sites sometimes named heritage sites. Methodical anachronism might also appear in books and other publications either scientific or popular. Arrangements and activities can also relate to historically inspired events. These arrangements can be markets, theatres, games and tournaments. They can be arranged by for example schools, universities, non-profit organizations, societies, gaming communities and web communities. It can also be the practice of ancient handicrafts with old-fashioned tools and methods. A specific branch of re-enacting the past is named *first-person interpretation*. This is when a person is acting in a recreated environment as if every subsequent time has not yet happened (cf. Roth 1998).

It is said that conscious anachronism such as it is performed for example by the SCA is in essence a postmodern practice (Cramer 2010:xiv–xvi). This statement is related to the fact that SCA performs an eclectic interpretation of the Middle Ages with elements from different epochs mixed in one representation. But on closer examination it can be stated that anachronism, a practice from long before any postmodern time during the 20th and 21st centuries, has deeper roots in human practice, both conscious and unconscious. It can thus be interpreted as a human practice of translating between times and thereby an effect of human awareness of time.

The experience from craftsmen of today, who try to reproduce past times in craftsmanship, is very often based on anachronisms. In an ongoing study of Viking Age shipbuilders, I have noticed that, especially in Norway, they have had a tradition of building wooden boats in historic times and preserving this knowledge to the present. The traditional boatbuilding has also influenced later decades' intense production of Viking ships. Even if craftsmen try to avoid being anachronistic, the leap of more than a thousand years can be very difficult to make. The boatbuilders instead take themselves step by step into the past via old techniques and thereby bridge the past with the present (cf. Planke and Stålegård 2014).

Another area of performing the past where time travel is used is connected to new techniques. To travel in time can be to take a virtual tour in reconstructed ancient Pompeii in a 3D setting (Dell'Unto *et al.* 2015:18). Sometimes it is even possible to take a tour of a reconstructed site by flying around and above it with the aid of a drone equipped with a 360-degree camera. It can also be a digital experience that allows us to take part in a specific ritual, as in the museum setting in southern Sweden presented in this volume (Ljungar-Chapelon), with his/her own movements through a motion capture system. These virtual performances align themselves on an unofficial scale from 'authentic' to 'experiential', and it is always the experiential part that is most closely linked with anachronism, depending on involvement of senses perceived of as deceitful and incorrect as tools for objective judgement. The deceitfulness is probably an effect of the close link of our senses with the present – thus anachronism again.

In this latest example the anachronism is obvious, since it is a new technique that allows the experience of past times to happen. If it weren't for this technique it would have been impossible even to come this close to notions of the past. But we can be fairly sure that these ideas of the past are deeply rooted in the present. Who in the distant past would even think of the possibility to take an air ride to see an ancient town, or room, from above? This represents our time and its strivings to get an overview, not in an ancient way but in a very modern way. This is in essence a kind of creative anachronism.

Anachronism in artistic work, theatre and literature

Artists have through time made active use of anachronistic references, crossing periods at different levels of awareness of this practice: unconscious, semi-conscious and fully conscious use of anachronisms. In church paintings from the medieval period in Scandinavia (*c.* 1050 onwards) and throughout the Middle Ages, people depicted are dressed in clothes contemporary with the painter for recognition by the audience, in this case visitors to church ceremonies (Figure 13.3). In another example from Swedish painting tradition somewhat later, from the 1800s, there is a depiction of Christ being taken down from the cross (Figure 13.4). This was a pedagogical trick to make history relevant to the general public by showing the circumstances as if they were actually present there and then. The content of the stories were brought closer to the people experiencing the story.

Two genres that make active and conscious use of anachronism are theatre and literature. Plays are often transformed into contemporary settings. For example Greek dramas or Shakespearian plays are remodelled into the twenty-first-century society of Western Europe, or opera plays such as Mozart's *The Magic*

Figure 13.3. A church painting with people from a biblical story obviously dressed up in medieval clothing, here from the Old Testament about the prophet Jonah, soon to enter the stomach of the whale. Painting from Härkeberga church in Sweden (Photograph by Bodil Petersson 2010).

Flute (*Zauberflöte* in German) are reshaped for more recent, present or even future settings. The stories are constantly being reinterpreted and modernised. This can give renewed actuality and credibility to important thoughts and actions in plays and texts from the past, even if they were created and performed many hundreds, or even thousands, of years ago. As archaeologists and historians we should, instead of fearing anachronism, do more like theatre and literature by using anachronism as a tool for creating actuality through time. When important thoughts are put in contemporary settings, their actuality and relevance are accentuated instead of destabilised.

Areas of practice with special interest in the phenomenon of anachronism relating to authenticity include historic music and the use of language in literature, film and theatre (Haynes 2007; Lowenthal 2006). The strivings here are not so much to use as to avoid anachronisms. The ambition is often to try to avoid more recent soundscapes or words/languages/expressions in favour of ancient and thereby 'authentic' ways of using sound and language. It might be

Figure 13.4. Example from folklore painting, here from a specific painting tradition in the Swedish landscape of Dalecarlia, where biblical stories were painted as if they actually took place in the year of the painting, which in this case is 1799. Dresses and houses are familiar to this region (Photograph: © Wikimedia Commons License).

very disturbing for an audience to hear modern language spoken within a setting supposed to be Roman or Viking. In this genre the efforts are more related to those within archaeology and history, in which the goal is to avoid 'inauthentic' interpretations that are too dependent on present circumstances. However, even here it is possible to have a playful attitude towards the effects of anachronism and to compare authentic interpretations with those not so authentic. It is easy to find differing interpretations through time of books and plays, especially ones that are old or translated and still in use, and of music performed and/or recorded with different requirements of sounds and instruments.

Perceived dangers of anachronism

There are some obvious traps that descendants of the 20th century are aware of in re-enacted or recreated interpretations of the past. This is usually when it comes to interpreting the past with politically unacceptable lenses or premises (cf.

arguments against World War II re-enactment in Slayton [2011]). This includes neo-Nazi interpretations, fascist or racist interpretations, wartime conflicting interpretations and on the whole interpretations that go against a paradigm of tolerance, multi-culturalism and peace. In fact this latter approach is a Western European paradigm based on a UN vision of the world, where the past becomes a tool for peace, equality and tolerance. However even the UN vision can be questioned and contested by some. Whenever the past is re-enacted, it might also be used in different and disputable ways. Especially in areas of conflict and with ongoing or recently ended wars, the past and its representations become a renewed arena for conflict and negotiation. In this fact is a perceived danger relating to anachronism.

Another possible danger is the deceptive character of arranging settings with contemporary traits that makes the present integrated in the past so much that it really feels familiar and understandable. In this case it can be questioned if something new is at all appearing, or if it is just a theatrical setting where we put ourselves and adapt the environment after our own needs. Then the reconstructed past is just as a mirror of the present and has no purpose of being anything else.

It is further also a risk that anachronisms aren't recognized as such at all. Then all ideas of conscious anachronism is in vain. But as I see it, this risk is constantly there, and we can only see anachronisms that are elucidated by our own knowledge of the past. Therefore a prerequisite required for methodical anachronism is knowledge about both past and present conditions.

Anachronism in this volume

Examples of time travel and the anachronistic appearances that go with them in the chapters of this book are now highlighted to strengthen my point concerning the benefits of using anachronism as a conscious approach. Several time travels performed in different settings have been presented, each combining the past with the present in different ways, to reach an understandable interpretation that relates to past circumstances as well as to present-day experiences and issues of interest. The settings are defined in the parts of the book with the topics of virtual time travel, educational time travel, living the distant past, time travel on screen, and time travel in contemporary society.

Virtual time travel and anachronism

Technical equipment offers great advantages when it comes to immersion and partaking in environments and activities relating to present interpretations of the past. With technical gear it is possible in a 3D format to experience outdoor as well as indoor environments; architectural traits can be elucidated, and the use of space can be tested. Illumination and sound can also be interpreted in these (re)created digital environments. The text by Nicoló Dell'Unto, Ing-Marie Nilsson and Jes Wienberg, and the text by Magali Ljungar-Chapelon in this volume both show the possibility to clarify space, sight, movements and ritual aspects of activities in the past. In the article by Dell'Unto *et al.* it is primarily spatial and visual aspects that are developed further such as how many people could gather within the church and how visual communication was possible. Ljungar-Chapelon's attempts to put present-day people in an unusual setting related to the past, just to see how present-day individuals' experiences interact with and are affected by the created environment, its sounds and movements. This experimental approach using motion capture as an ingredient has something to do with the past, but is not an obvious interpretation step by step from known sources. It is a mix of now and then, it is not possible to tell exactly which part is past and which part is present. What we can be sure of is that the technique used is from the present, and thereby the experience is fully and consciously anachronistic.

Educational time travel and anachronism

When the approach is educational, it is obvious that the relationship with authenticity and sources of interpretations are in focus. With an aim to educate, to start with, there seems to be a need for authenticity. This approach is also present in the text by Niklas Ammert and Birgitta Gustafsson. At the same time the authors are also extremely explicit with what really is the essence of time travel, namely its relation to the present. As the authors clearly state, the 'meaning-making entails being able to relate oneself to the events of the time travel' (Ammert and Gustafsson, this volume). When we are brought back in time with the aid of Kalmar County Museum and their specific strategy for educational time travel (Ebbe Westergren in this volume), it is the present that is immediately in focus. You are actually supposed to remain in yourself and through this self actively confront issues raised when performing a travel back in time to a specific historical or archaeological event. This method relies on the present experience and shows in an explicit way how present times are intimately intertwined with our ideas of the past. The method is anachronistic in its very core.

Living the distant past and anachronism

In relation to educational time travels, the re-enactment sector and the archaeological open-air museums experience a struggle with authenticity and anachronism. Here it is more about 'a feeling of' authenticity conveyed through performance or structures such as houses, villages and other physical environments either reconstructed or using existing old buildings and environments. The point here is that it is you yourself that form the anachronism by seeking and partaking in activities. The confrontation takes place within our own bodies. In a way similar to how technology can make us believe the environments are real, the environments are actually there, and you can feel the surroundings with all senses; you can wear clothes, taste food, touch buildings and meet people dressed up as in other times. It is the most full-potential use of senses that can be presented to us today. It gives a possibility to be 'swept away' by an interpretation. Mads Daugbjerg in this volume chooses an understanding approach – not rejecting the experiential part of time travel and re-enactment as not being knowledge. He argues that the activities are worth considering as method for understanding the past. However there is a critique of the genre that is more about the present than about the past. Stefanie Samida's critique in this volume covers the aspect of time travel and re-enactment being too stereotypical when it comes to representing life in the past. She states that 'the past is bygone and cannot be repeated' (Samida, this volume). Cornelius Holtorf (this volume) describes in his text 'Face-to-face with the Past' how archaeology in recent years has been strongly affected by the development and impact of popular culture and this has even resulted in an alternative framework of interpretation. Staged performances and reconstructions of different kinds have strongly affected the role of storytelling and experience both within and outside the discipline and has at the same time reduced the role of material culture. Objects are still needed, but are often reconstructed and used as props to enhance the experience of the past in a sensory way. Archaeology has become more experiential and sensory in approach. Reflecting on these three rather different approaches to time travel, is there any way to soften attitudes towards the stand that reconstruction, re-enactment and time travel actually contain knowledge of the past, even if it is filtered through the present? For better or worse the approaches are anachronistic bodily experiences in the present of a constructed past.

Time travel on screen and anachronism

When it comes to time travel and films, the immersion of the spectator into another epoch is clearly temporary. You go to the cinema or view the film through another medium for a specific amount of time, then you return to the present at the end of the film. You are not part of the film, but you can still get strongly emotionally involved in the story. The time travel experience in film relies on the effectiveness of storytelling. In most cases the film-maker has a specific purpose with the film, as described in my presentation of the film *Waterworld*, where environmental destruction and catastrophe is the reason a global flood occurs. This future situation is used to understand the consequences of the past (i.e. our present) and to form the vision of a better future. In Dawid Kobialka's discussion we see another argument develop: the need of fiction for the maintenance of authenticity within archaeology. The argument is that there is a need for excitement and fascination with archaeology to strengthen the authentic parts of the subject. A conclusion relating to the use of film as a means of transport in time is that the speed in moving between past and present strengthens the possibilities to consider time as direct consequence of the medium itself. Kobialka's argument draws on how a practice in the present influences the feelings of authenticity regarding the past part of that practice.

Time travel in contemporary society and anachronism
Perhaps it is in the obvious mix of past and present that the danger of anachronism is most emphasized. The texts in this part concern the role of time travel in present-day settings. It reveals how well suited the past is to engage the senses and to fit with contemporary matters such as the shaping of identity. Michaela Fenske discusses 'histotainment' in the text, and this mix of history and entertainment is often seen as something bad and also explicitly anachronistic within the genre of archaeology and history. But Fenske instead emphasises the possibilities of engaging with the past with all senses. In the interview with Erika Andersson Cederholm the impact of the contemporary world is made explicit. Identity, belonging and authenticity are factors held forth in this discussion, and interestingly enough authenticity becomes more interesting as the past becomes more dubious or distant. One possibility is actually that the more we relate the past to the present, the more we discuss the topic of authenticity, probably because we feel how past and present are intertwined in an explicitly anachronistic way, and we therefore need to uphold a feeling of distance between them.

After showing that all forms of time travel, reconstruction and re-enactment are anachronistic in their very core, it is time to point at what is good about a conscious use of anachronism.

What we can gain from a conscious use of anachronism

With a conscious use of anachronism we can more easily move between the past and the present in a way that we are destined to by our actual being. We may associate freely and make use of the past today. The past has an effect on societies when it comes to claims for land and also for the 'resurrection' of lost traditions. What is then not taken into account is the 'low-key' use of archaeology and history. Examples here could be inspirations from food tradition with the 'stone age food' trend in recent years (cf. Durant and Malice 2013). Even if some take this reference to the Stone Age literally, it is a way of using experiences from knowledge of the past in the present. Is this use good or bad? Right or wrong? Beyond direct politics, this anachronistic use is a matter of taste. And if we find today's lifestyle too stressing and bad for health, the past ways can stand as an alternative for inspiration (Petersson 2008). It actually provides the possibility to look back for solutions.

Conclusion

Apart from the fact that we no longer need to feel bad because we have sinned when present lives affect the past we create, we can learn to make active use of the past in present-day society. From the examples in this book it is clear that every interpretation of the past in the present constitutes a mix of eras that in the end is anachronistic. So-called chronological inconsistencies can turn into an advantage. When the spectator to a reconstructed event or site observes the anachronisms, his or her ability to understand time itself is highlighted.

Our effort to reconstruct past times will always be anachronistic, and we shall be proud of this fact and turn it to our advantage. The past is not either good or bad, it is both. It is also what we make it be. The past is always used, and research on the past itself is filtered through present perspectives. Therefore there is no other option than to cope with anachronism in a conscious and explicit way. Make it method.

Acknowledgements

Thanks to Cornelius Holtorf for several years of project work developing approaches to the concept of time travel and thoughts on the method and its benefits for society. I would also like to thank students attending the courses on Archaeology and Time Travel at Lund University and Linnaeus University during the years. They have contributed with lots of enthusiasm and different, sometimes astonishing but always creative perspectives. This research would not have been possible without financial support from Crafoord Foundation and Hainska Foundation, from which I have received generous grants for projects concerning different kinds of time travel. Thank you for being brave enough to support this somewhat unconventional research. I also would like to thank Jes Wienberg, Cornelius Holtorf and Jerryll Moreno for constructive reading and commenting on drafts of this paper.

References

Björhem, Nils and Säfvestad, Ulf 1987. *Stenåldershus: rekonstruktion av ett 4000 år gammalt hus*. Malmö, Stadsantikvariska avd, Malmö museer.

Butler, Catherine and O'Donovan, Hallie 2012. *Reading History in Children's Books*. Houndmills, Basingstoke, Palgrave Macmillan.

Claeys, Gregory 2011. *Searching for Utopia. The History of an Idea*. London, Thames and Hudson.

Cramer, Michael A. 2010. *Medieval Fantasy as Performance: The Society for Creative Anachronism and the Current Middle Ages*. Lanham, Scarecrow Press.

Dell'Unto, Nicoló, Landeschi, Giacomo, Leander Touati, Anne-Marie, Dellepiane, Matteo, Callieri, Marco and Ferdani, Daniele 2015. Experiencing ancient buildings from a 3D GIS perspective: A case drawn from the Swedish Pompeii

Project. *Journal of Archaeological Method and Theory*. DOI 10.1007/s10816-014-9226-7.

Durant, John and Malice, Michael 2013. *The Paleo Manifesto: Ancient Wisdom for lifelong Health.* New York, Harmony.

Haynes, Bruce 2007. *The End of Early Music: A Period Performer's History of Music for the Twenty-first Century.* Oxford, Oxford University Press.

Howes, David (ed.) 2005. *Empire of the Senses: The Sensual Culture Reader.* Oxford: Berg.

Jensen, Bernard Eric 2015. At gøre fortider nærværende – fagfolks tilgange til reenactment. Tove Kruse and Anette Warring (eds.) *Fortider tur/retur. Reenactment og historiebrug.* Frederiksberg, Samfundslitteratur.

Kruse, Tove and Anette Warring (eds.) 2015. *Fortider tur/retur. Reenactment og historiebrug.* Frederiksberg, Samfundslitteratur.

Lowenthal, David 2006. From harmony of the spheres to national anthem. Reflections on musical heritage. *GeoJournal* 65:3–15. DOI 10.1007/s10708-006-0008-y

Magelssen, Scott 2007. *Living History Museums. Undoing History Through Performance.* Lanham, Scarecrow Press.

Martindale, Charles and Martindale, Michelle 1990. *Shakespeare and the Uses of Antiquity: An Introductory Essay.* London, Routledge.

Paardekooper, Roeland 2012. *The Value of an Archaeological Open-air Museum is in its Use: Understanding Archaeological Open-air Museums and Their Visitors.* Leiden, Sidestone Press.

Petersson, Bodil 2003. *Föreställningar om det förflutna: arkeologi och rekonstruktion.* Lund, Nordic Academic Press.

Petersson, Bodil 2008. Den hälsovådliga resan i tiden. Bodil Petersson, Kristina Jennbert and Cornelius Holtorf (eds.) *Arkeologi och samhälle*. Acta Archaeologica Lundensia: 97–111. Series in 8 No 58. Lund, Lund University, Department of Archaeology and Ancient History.

Petersson, Bodil 2010. Travels to identity: Viking rune carvers today. *Lund Archaeological Review* 2009/2010 (15/16), pp. 71–86.

Petersson, Bodil and Narmo, Lars Erik 2011. A Journey in Time. Bodil Petersson and Lars Erik Narmo (eds.) *Experimental archaeology: between enlightenment and experience.* Acta Archaeologica Lundensia Series in 8° No. 62. Lund, Lund university, Department of Archaeology and Ancient History.

Petersson, Bodil and Narmo, Lars Erik (eds.) 2011. *Experimental archaeology: between enlightenment and experience.* Lund, Lund University, Department of Archaeology and Ancient History.

Planke, Terje and Lars Stålegård 2014. Barcode 6 fra vrak til rekonstruksjon En utlegging av resultater og metoder. Elisabeth S. Koren og Frode Kvalø (eds.) *Hundre år over og under vann. Kapitler om maritim historie og arkeologi i anledning Norsk Maritimt Museums hundreårsjubileum.* Oslo, Novus Forlag, pp. 359–400.

Rentzhog, Sten 2007. *Open air museums: the history and future of a visionary idea.* Stockholm, Carlsson.

Roth, Stacy F. 1998. *Past into present: effective techniques for first-person historical interpretation.* Chapel Hill, N.C., University of North Carolina Press.

Samuel, Raphael 2012. *Theatres of Memory. Past and Present in Contemporary Culture* (revised edition). London/New York, Verso.

Skinner, Quentin 1969/1988. Meaning and Understanding in the History of Ideas. In: Tully, J. (ed.) *Meaning and Context. Quentin Skinner and his critics.* Princeton, Princeton University Press, pp. 29–67.

Slayton, Robert A. 2011. Reenacting Evil. *Commentary Magazine*, October 2011, pp. 43–45.

Syrjämäki, Sami 2011. *Sins of a Historian. Perspectives on the problem of anachronism.* Tampere, University of Tampere.

Wilk, R. 1985. The ancient Maya and the political present. *Journal of Anthropological Research* 41: 307–326.

About the Authors

Niklas Ammert is Dean of the Board of Teacher Education, Linnaeus University, Sweden. He is Associate Professor of History (History Didactics, History Education). Ammert's research mainly focuses on history teaching, history education and the uses of history – how individuals and groups encounter, interpret and use history at school, in higher education, in politics and in other cultural and societal contexts. Latest publications include: *History as Knowledge: Ethical Values and Meaning in Encounters with History*, Frankfurt am Main and New York: Peter Lang (2015); Ammert, Niklas and Heather Sharp, 'Working with the Cold War: An Analysis of Knowledge Types in Swedish and Australian History Textbook Activities' in *Journal of Educational Media, Memory and Society* 8:2 (2016).

Erika Andersson Cederholm is Associate Professor of Sociology at the Department of Service Management and Service Studies, Lund University, Sweden. Her research focuses on the intersection between commercial and intimate aspects of life, particularly in the tourism and leisure industries. Her recent research projects include studies on rural lifestyle entrepreneurship, gift economies, emotional work and the new professional roles in the meeting industry.

Laia Colomer is a Marie Skłodowska-Curie Individual Fellow at Linnaeus University, Sweden. She was educated in Barcelona (PhD in prehistoric archaeology, 1995) and in London (MA in Public Archaeology, 2000). She has extensive professional and academic experience in material culture and gender, archaeological heritage management, museums and public archaeology developed in the Netherlands, the UK, Spain, and Italy. Her current research concerns the uses of cultural heritage for the well being of migrant citizens in an increasingly globalised world.

Mads Daugbjerg is Associate Professor of Anthropology at Aarhus University, Denmark. He teaches in Aarhus University's programmes in experience economy and sustainable heritage management. His main research concerns social and material practices related to heritage, museums and tourism, especially in the context of former sites of war and conflict. His publications include co-edited special issues of *Critical Military Studies*, *The International Journal of Heritage Studies*, and *History and Anthropology*. His monograph *Borders of Belonging: Experiencing History, War and Nation at a Danish Heritage Site* was published by Berghahn Books in 2014.

Nicoló Dell'Unto received his PhD in 2008 from the Institute for Advanced Studies, IMT, in Lucca, Italy. He is currently Associate Professor at the Institute of Archaeology and Ancient History, Lund University. His current research focus is on the development of digital methodologies for the investigation and analysis of archaeological sites and landscapes.

Birgitta E. Gustafsson holds a PhD in pedagogy and worked at Linnaeus University, Sweden. Her research interest is in the field of learning as intersubjective meaning-making processes where the individual's understanding of oneself and the surrounding world are challenged and confronted.

Michaela Fenske, PhD, is a Heisenberg Fellow from the German Research Foundation and associated with the Institute of European Ethnology at Humboldt University, Berlin, Germany.

Niklas Hillbom received his PhD in 2005 in classical archaeology and ancient history from Lund University, Sweden. He is currently working as an archaeological guide in various countries around the Mediterranean and teaching at Lund University. His teaching includes several aspects on how new technologies can help us interpret the past and how to interact with our cultural heritage.

Cornelius Holtorf gained his PhD at the University of Wales, UK, in 1998 and was subsequently employed at the University of Gothenburg, the University of Cambridge, the Swedish National Heritage Board in Stockholm, and the University of Lund. Since 2008 he has lived in Kalmar, Sweden, where he is currently a Professor of Archaeology at Linnaeus University, Director of the Graduate School in Contract Archaeology (http://lnu.se/grasca) and the spokesperson of the Centre for Applied Heritage. He is also Adjunct Senior Research Fellow at Flinders University, Australia and Co-Investigator in the AHRC-funded project on 'Heritage Futures' (2015-2019).

Isto Huvila received his PhD in information studies in 2006 from Åbo Akademi University, Finland. He is a Professor of Information Studies at the Department of Archival, Library & Information, and Museum & Cultural Heritage Studies, Uppsala University, Sweden. His research focuses on information work and management, including archaeological information and knowledge production.

Britta Timm Knudsen, PhD, is Associate Professor of Culture and Media and Experience Economy at the Department of Culture and Communication, Aarhus University, Denmark. Her current research focuses on heritage, affects, tourism and citizen engagements. Her latest books are *Global Media, Biopolitics and Affect. Politicizing Bodily Vulnerability* (2015) and *Affective Methodologies* (2015). She currently participates in the research projects *Rethinking Tourism in a Coastal City: Design for New Engagements* (2016–2019, funded by Innovation Fund, Denmark) and *Permeable Green City Aarhus – Combining Life Politics, Biodiversity, Citizen Empowerment and Sustainable Urban Drainage to create an Ecologically and Socially Resilient City* (2015–2017, funded by Danish Centre for Environment and Energy).

Dawid Kobiałka is an archaeologist and cultural anthropologist with the Institute of Archaeology and Ethnology at the Polish Academy of Science in Warsaw, Poland. His work focuses on the archaeology of the recent past, public archaeology and heritage studies. Recent publications include articles in *Current Swedish Archaeology*, the *Journal of Contemporary Archaeology*, *Antiquity* and the *International Journal of Historical Archaeology*.

Magali Ljungar-Chapelon, PhD, is a senior lecturer in research methodology at the Faculty of Fine and Performing Arts and a researcher in digital representation at the Department of Design Sciences, Faculty of Engineering of Lund University, Sweden. She studies digital representation and interactive virtual reality-based performances that engage the audience as actor-spectator to investigate how to launch and analyse artistic processes and knowledge experiences for audiences physically immersed in virtual environments. She has a background in performing arts and social sciences, and her work is interdisciplinary and collaborative at the crossover between several art forms and disciplines: 3D art, dance, music, archaeology, architecture, interaction design, technical communication and social psychology.

Ing-Marie Nilsson[†] received her PhD in 2009 from the Department of Archaeology and Ancient History, Lund University, Sweden. She was a historical archaeologist at Sydsvensk Arkeologi, Ltd. Her research focused on church archaeology.

Stefan Nyzell, PhD, is Associate Professor of History at the Faculty of Learning and Education, Malmö University, Sweden. His main area of research is contentious politics studies. His most recent publication in this field is 'A Fight for the Right to get Drunk: The Autumn Fair Riot in Eskilstuna, 1937', in *Protest, Popular Culture and Tradition in Modern and Contemporary Western Europe*, edited by Ilaria Fevretto and Xabier Itcania, Palgrave Macmillan (2016). He recently began exploring the field of historical re-creation and embarked on the research project *Violently Medieval: Historical Re-Creation and Public Uses of History*.

Carsten Tage Nielsen gained a PhD from Roskilde University in 1996. Since the late 1980s he has researched applications of history in media, education and museums and now focuses on uses of pasts in everyday life. He is currently a part-time Lecturer at the Department of Communication and Arts, Roskilde University, Denmark, and a member of the cross-disciplinary research group Memory and Uses of History.

Roeland Paardekooper received his PhD in 2012 from the Department of Archaeology, University of Exeter, UK. He is currently director at EXARC, an international networking association on experimental archaeology and archaeological open-air museums (http://www.exarc.net).

Bodil Petersson, PhD, is Associate Professor of Archaeology at Linnaeus University in Kalmar, Sweden. She has researched and published on topics such as archaeological reconstruction and re-enactment, experimental archaeology, time travel, digital heritage communication, the history of archaeology and the role of archaeology in contemporary society. During the years 2013–2017 she was co-researcher in a project funded by the Swedish Research Council called ARKDIS, Archaeological Information in the Digital Society. Since autumn 2014, she has been Program Director of the Bachelor's Programme in Heritage in Present and Future Society at Linnaeus University. At present she is conducting a project on Experimental Heritage, a research field and a collaboration project involving researchers, artists and heritage workers, exploring the relation between art and archaeology/heritage in the local society.

Stefanie Samida studied pre- and proto history, classical archaeology and medieval history at the University of Tübingen and University of Kiel (both Germany). After obtaining her MA she completed a degree in media studies and received her doctorate in 2005. From 2012 to 2015 she was a researcher at the Centre for Contemporary History in Potsdam and collaborated on the research project 'Living History: Re-enacted Prehistory between Research and Popular Performance'. She is currently Junior Research Group Leader in the collaborative research project heiEDUCATION at the Heidelberg School of Education, Germany.

Thomas Småberg is Associate Professor of History, Malmö University, Sweden. He has published on political culture, power structures, social networks and friendship in the Middle Ages and is currently conducting research on medieval ritual and gender in Scandinavia. He also has a research interest in critical cultural heritage studies. Amongst his publications are: *Det stängda frälset. Makt och eliter i det medeltida lokalsamhället: Marks och Kinds härader i Västergötland ca 1390-1520* (doctoral thesis) and 'Mead and Beer and Cherry Wine and Wine both Red and White....' Feasts, Courts and Conflicts in Fourteenth-Century Sweden' (in *Rituals, Performatives, and Political Order in Northern Europe, c. 650-1350*, edited by Wojtek Jezierski, Lars Hermanson, Hans Jacob Orning and Thomas Småberg, 2015).

Per Stenborg is a Researcher and Associate Professor at the Department of Historical Studies, University of Gothenburg, Sweden, where he is also the Director of Studies in Archaeology. Over the last 25 years he has carried out several archaeological research projects in different parts of South America. Since 2008 he has collaborated with Denise Pahl Schaan on the archaeology of the Santarém Region in Brazil, and he has also been project director of the *Cultivated Wilderness Project* (2011–2014). Stenborg has conducted research about how archaeology and cultural heritage management may use digital and computer-based technologies in presenting and communicating their results and products and how – in turn – these technologies change the archaeological practice and the understanding of history. An outcome of this interest was the interdisciplinary research and development project *Digital Time-Travels* (2007–2010), which he directed. Since 2014 he has been a member of the *ArkDIS* (Archaeological Information in the Digital Society) project.

Cecilia Trenter received her PhD in 1999 from the Department of History, Uppsala University, Sweden. She is an Associate Professor at Linnaeus University at the Department of Cultural Studies. Her research focuses on the field of social memory. Trenter has been working with representations of the past in fiction and heritage adaptations, for example in her ongoing research on adaptations of memorials into fictional historical drama in films.

Ebbe Westergren is an archaeologist and Senior Curator at Kalmar County Museum, Sweden. He is also Honorary President of Bridging Ages, International Organisation in Applied Heritage and Time Travels. He has written numerous articles and edited several books in public archaeology/public history. He has led international projects in more than 15 countries around the world on applied heritage and the time travel method.

Jes Wienberg received his PhD in 1993 from the Department of Archaeology and Ancient History, Lund University, Sweden, where he is a professor and responsible for historical archaeology. His research focuses on church archaeology, monuments and heritage.

Index

List of index headings prepared by Carolina Jonsson Malm

11th century, 26, 33

12th century, 26–28, 39, 79–80

13th century, 39–40

17th century, 60

18th century, 143, 170, 235

19th century, 1, 6, 8, 17, 27–29, 138, 151

1920s, 142–143

1930s, 143

1940s, 16

1950s, 178, 278

1960s, 178, 285

1970s, 136, 178, 183, 204, 278

1980s, 4, 89, 91, 178, 301

1990s, 91, 104, 106, 135–136, 144, 178, 207–208, 230–231, 273

2000s, 273

20th century, 7–8, 17, 22, 91, 115, 140, 170–171, 290

3D analysis, 80; art, 54, 65; methodology, 25; modelling, 25, 34, 41, 63; scanner, 35; Studio Max, 41; techniques, 25, 80; visualisation, 25, 27, 43

acquisition techniques, 35

actor-participant, 47, 65

advertising, 2, 247

affective history, 141

Agnew, Vanessa, 136, 144, 149–150, 152, 158, 171

Ailnoth, 25

A Knight's Tale, 284

Alebo, Lena, 57, 60

Algotsdotter, Cecilia, 273

America, 8, 143, 171, 302

American Civil War, 17, 157, 160, 165, 172, 174, 188

Ammert, Niklas, 7, 113, 118–119, 121, 123, 125, 127, 129–130, 292, 299

amusement park, 196

anachronism, anachronistic, 7, 15, 281, 283–295, 297

Ancient Rome, 15

Anderson, Jay, 4, 19, 29, 43, 144–145, 152

Andersson Cederholm, Erika, 18, 257–259, 261, 270–272, 294, 299

Animation, animated, 62

antiquity, 17, 76, 175–176, 179, 187, 226–227, 233, 235, 296, 301

apartheid, 95, 130

applied heritage, 89, 91, 95, 300, 303

applied history, 107, 241, 243, 252

archaeo-appeal, 218, 224, 234

archaeological evidence, 5, 33, 57; excavations, 40; heritage, 3, 299

archaeologist, 50, 52–53, 57, 60, 66, 71–72, 75, 140, 158, 160, 179, 189, 192, 204–205, 209, 213–214, 216–217, 224–225, 227, 234–236, 301, 303

architecture, 25, 34, 38, 235, 301

Arn, 15, 273–275

Arntourism, 273

art, 33, 47–48, 50–54, 59, 61, 65–67, 70, 72–78, 90, 102, 117, 153–154, 170–171, 174, 209, 215–216, 220, 231–232, 285, 301–302

artefact, 178, 197, 207–208

artistic knowledge shaping, 54

artistic research, 48, 50, 52–54, 73–75

arts and humanities, 53

Asimov, Isaac, 81, 237

Asterix, 186

Ästhetisierung der Vergangenheit, 142, 155

Atlantis, 15, 128, 203, 235

audience, 6, 11–12, 17, 47–50, 54, 60–62, 65–71, 73–75, 80–82, 104, 135, 140–141, 147–148, 166, 168, 185–187, 191–192, 195–196, 229–231, 248–250, 283, 285, 288, 290, 301

audience survey, 49, 61, 65, 67–68

augmented realities, 2, 193, 223

Auschwitz-Birkenau, 16

authenticity, authentic, 13, 17, 20, 71, 123, 128, 130–131, 141, 150, 153, 158, 168–169, 172–174, 183–184, 188, 192–193, 197–198, 227, 242, 257–262, 267, 270, 272–274, 278, 281, 283–286, 289, 292–294

Back to the Future, 224–225, 230

Baltic mythology, 59

Baptismal Font of Dalby, 27, 31, 37

Barth, Fredrik, 250–251

Battle of Gettysburg, 169

Battle of Hastings, 191

Battle of the Nations, 16–17

Battle of Visby, 271

Belgrade, 105

Berlin, 45, 138–139, 151, 242, 253, 255, 300

Biedermeier, 242, 246

Blanchett, Cate, 272

bog body, 177

Bologna, 72

Bononiae, Imago, 72, 76

Borries, Bodo von, 249, 252

Braidwood, Robert, 178, 188

Brecht, Bertolt, 225

Bredarör, 50, 76–77

Bridging Ages, 9, 89, 91–92, 95, 97, 100, 107, 109–111, 303

Bronze Age, 4, 6, 47, 50–52, 55, 57, 59–61, 64, 68–69, 76–77, 81, 84, 119, 176

Brøgger, Anni, 52, 76

Butler, Catherine, 283, 295

C31, 105–106

Cape Town, 95

Cape Winelands, 95

Carnival, 13, 20

Carter, Howard, 177, 217

Ceremony, ceremonies, 54, 60, 64–65, 97–98, 103

Ch'ng, Eugene, 3, 19

Chamberlain, Joshua, 169

Chevalier, Tracy, 249, 252

China, Chinese, 15–16

Christianity, 61

chronology, chronologies, chronological, 5, 7

church, 25, 27–28, 30, 35–36, 38, 40, 43, 79, 83–84, 93, 95–96, 99, 138, 143, 273, 288–289, 292, 301, 303 civil war battle, 1, 163–164, 172

civil war moment, 1

Clarke, Arthur C., 3

Classical Athens, 15

climate change, 201–202, 230

Coleman, Simon, 162, 169, 172

Colomer, Laia, 229, 232, 299

Colonial Williamsburg, 143

commodification, 257, 262, 270

communication science, 11

community building, 89, 92, 98, 109

computer games, 2, 236, 271; graphics, 62

contemporary archaeology, 205, 217, 301

Cook, Alexander, 149, 152, 158, 172

corporeality, 6, 60–61

cosmological model, 59

Costner, Kevin, 201–203, 210, 231, 234

craft, 90, 158, 165

Crang, Mike, 158, 169, 172

credible pasts, 6

critical theory, 5, 7

crypt, 25, 27–30, 32–43, 79–80, 84

cultural economics, 19; festivals, 4

culture-historical archaeology, 220

cultural tourism, 2, 67, 174

curator, 147, 231, 303

curriculum, 90, 93

Cushman, Steven, 161, 164, 172

Dalby, 25–33, 35, 37–38, 40, 43–45, 79, 83–84

Damasio, Antonio, 75–76

dance, 52, 54, 56–58, 65, 99, 101, 103, 268, 301

Danish National Museum, 52

dark heritage, 263; tourism, 263

Daugbjerg, Mads, 12, 15, 18, 157, 159, 162, 166, 169, 172, 184, 187–188, 191–192, 195–196, 293, 299

decaf logic, 220

De Groot, Jerome, 2, 19, 150, 152, 162, 169, 172, 179, 188

Dell'Unto, Nicoló, 25, 36–37, 39, 42, 79, 83–84, 288, 292, 295, 299

democracy, 9, 93–94, 97, 119

Denmark, 25, 30, 33, 40, 43, 165–166, 175–177, 180–181, 186, 192, 195, 278, 299–301

Desjarlais, Robert, 159, 172

Detmold, 139

Dick, Philip K., 82

didactic, didactics, ix, 114–115, 129, 146

digital visualisation, 25, 43, 61

Disneyfication, 146

diversity, 94, 107, 126–127, 245, 285

documentary, documentaries, 27, 135–136, 165, 186, 216, 222

docu-soap, 242, 244, 248

Dover, 140

Dream Society, 1, 18–20, 216, 218, 226

Dresden Neumarkt, 10

Dryland, 202, 207–208, 210–211, 235–236

Dystopia, 201, 212

Early Middle Ages, 27–28, 30, 32, 34

education, 3, 5, 15, 20, 89–92, 94, 98–100, 102, 108–110, 116, 127–128, 143, 146, 150, 153, 155, 180, 186, 192, 228, 243, 250, 270–271, 274, 278, 299, 301–302

Egtvedpigens Dans, 52, 76

Egypt, 216–217

Eketorp Castle, 119, 123–124

embodied cognition, 197–198; experiences, 7, 15–16, 18, 277; minds, 197

embodiment, 49, 61, 75, 138, 217

emotional intelligence, 49, 75

empiricism, 51

enchanted zones, 244, 277

Enlightenment, 8, 155, 164, 173, 189, 212, 296

Entebbe, 93–94, 110

entertainment, 3, 12, 67, 73, 146, 150, 192, 229, 231, 241–243, 249–250, 254, 271–272, 274, 294

environmental sustainability, 89, 102, 129

Erfahrung, 159

Erlebnis, 159

Erlebnisgesellschaft, 147

escapism, 10, 164, 191

Estonia, 91

ethnoarchaeology, 145, 221

Etruscanning Project, 72, 78

EU, 72

evolution, 5–8, 209–210

exhibition, 47, 49–50, 54, 59–60, 67, 70, 73, 75–78, 81, 141, 147, 272, 278

existential authenticity, 259–262, 267, 272

experience economy, 22, 159–160, 171, 173–174, 216, 218, 227, 257–258, 277, 299–300; society, 147, 149, 193, 218, 257–258

experiencing the past, 1, 187, 258, 269, 271, 274, 278

experiential archaeology, 3, 19

experiment, 15, 34, 41, 47–49, 52, 60, 62, 64, 72, 75, 146, 154–155, 157–160, 165–167, 170–171, 181, 188, 191–192, 195, 197

experimental archaeology, 145–146, 148, 154–155, 157–158, 160, 165, 172–174, 188–189, 191, 212, 233, 242, 296, 301–302

Facebook, 124, 271

fantasy, 15–16, 166, 184, 191, 204, 213, 216–217, 222–223, 225, 233, 272, 295

Fenske, Michaela, 18, 145, 149, 152–153, 241–242, 244–248, 252, 271, 294, 300

film, 19, 201–217, 222–225, 227–237, 241, 248, 252, 260, 284–286, 289, 293–294

film and media studies, 19

Finland, 91, 300

folk culture, 141

folklore, 290

Forsgren, Margareta, 59, 76

Foteviken, 17, 127, 218

France, 138

Frauenkirche, 11

Fredell, Åsa, 55, 76

Freedom Charter, 98, 100–101, 110

Freedom Park, 97, 109

Freedom Tree, 93

Fund, 92, 105

Funkabo, 93–94

future anachronism, 285

INDEX 309

futureness, 10–11, 18

Gadamer, Hans Georg, 51, 65, 75–76, 84–85, 117, 127

Game of Thrones, 272, 274–275

Garden of Eden, 211

Gdańsk History Museum, 218

gender roles, 9, 17, 19, 244–245

geographical information systems, 80

Germanophiler Volksbildung, 143

Germany, 7, 20, 135–137, 139, 142, 144, 155, 195, 241–244, 252, 254, 300, 302

Gettysburg, 160, 162–164, 169, 171

Giannachi, Gabriella, 53, 71, 76

Gilmore, James, 18, 22, 159–160, 174, 218, 227

Girl with a Pearl Earring, 249, 252

Giza3D, 71, 77

Gladiator, 233–234

Gladiator effect, 233

Glasbacka, 54–55

Goldhahn, Joakim, 50, 54–55, 59, 72, 76–77

go native, 83

Gotland, 11, 14, 20, 40, 44, 253, 271

Great Britain, 140

Greece, 44, 233

group discussion, 49, 59, 67, 70-71

Guillou, Jan, 15, 273, 275

Guinevere, 271

Gumbrecht, Hans Ulrich, 278

Gustafsson, Birgitta E., 3, 7, 11, 20, 44, 113, 115–119, 121–124, 126–130, 244, 253, 292, 300

Gustafsson, Lotten, 3, 7, 11, 20, 44, 113, 115–119, 121–124, 126–130, 244, 253, 292, 300

Götene, 40

Halland, 54–55

handicraft, 261, 265

Handler, Richard, 146, 153, 159, 161, 165, 168, 172–173

Hansen, Hans-Ole, 33, 40, 44, 165–167, 180

Harrison, Harry, 81, 230, 232

Harvey Brown, Richard, 115

Haude, Bertram, 16, 20

Hawkman, 217

Hazelius, Artur, 141, 152

Hector Pieterson Museum and Memorial, 98

Heim, Michael, 62, 77

Herculaneum, 175, 235

heritage industry, 2, 7–8; pedagogy, 3; studies, 19, 172, 188, 232, 299–302; tourism, 262, 266

hermeneutics, hermeneutical, 84, 179, 190, 278

Hershman Leeson, Lynn, 53, 71

Hillbom, Niklas, 233, 300

historic environment education, 89, 91, 110, 127; sites, 3, 135–136, 143; themes, 6

historical consciousness, 12, 21, 116–117; context, 5, 7, 92, 268, 283; knowledge, 3, 35, 158, 248; novels, 3, 242; procession, 138; realities, 3; research, 11, 15, 251–252

Historische Festzüge, 138

history from below, 92, 149–150

history theatre, 145

histotainment, 241–242, 271–274, 294

Hitler, Adolf, 249

Hjemdahl, Kirsti M., 3, 20, 179, 181–184, 186, 188

Hochbruck, Wolfgang, 3, 15, 20–21, 145, 148, 153–154

Holocaust, 16, 172

Holtorf, Cornelius, 1, 3, 7, 11–14, 19–20, 145–146, 149–151, 153, 166, 173, 175, 179–181, 183–188, 191–192, 195–196, 212–214, 216, 218, 221, 224, 226–227, 257, 284, 293, 295–296, 300

Hopper, Dennis, 209–210

human rights, 94, 99, 130

Huvila, Isto, 83–85, 300

I, Claudius, 236

ICOM, 109, 127

image-based modelling techniques, 34–35, 37

imaginary pasts, 3

immersion, ix, 4, 11–13, 62, 157, 161, 175, 185, 191, 291, 293

Indiana Jones, 213, 220, 224, 234

industrial heritage, 266

interactive audience experience, 47

Internet, 85, 169, 184

intersensoriality, 47, 61

Ireland, 91

Iron Age, 2, 4, 119, 174, 176–177, 180–183, 185–186, 277

Isivivane, 97–98

Italy, 91, 176, 299

IT science, 11

Jackson, Stonewall, 169

Jadis, 247–248

James Bond, 215, 224

Jensen, Bernard Eric, 18, 20, 218, 226, 283, 296

Jerusalem, 137–138

Jesus, 31, 137, 154, 232

Johannesburg, 98

John the Baptist, 29, 31

Jones, Gordon, 15, 17, 21, 213, 220, 224, 232, 234

Jørgensen Thomsen, Christian, 176

Kalmar, 89–91, 93, 95, 97–98, 100, 102, 104–105, 107–110, 118–123, 127–128, 187, 228, 282, 292, 300, 302–303

Kalmar Castle, 119, 121–123, 282

Kalmar County Museum, 89–91, 95, 97–98, 100, 102, 104–105, 107, 109–110, 119–120, 292, 303

Kansteiner, Wulf, 12, 21

Kaul, Flemming, 50, 52, 54–55, 59, 64, 77

Kaye, Nick, 53, 71, 76

Keller Drescher, Lioba, 250

Keller, Ferdinand, 140, 250, 253

Kenya, 91

Kinect, Microsoft, 62, 67

King Arthur, 271

Kivik Grave, 47, 51–53, 55, 57, 59, 71–72, 75, 77, 81, 84

Kliptown, 98–101, 109–110

Kliptown Museum, 98

Knjazevac, 93–94

Kobiałka, Dawid, 15–16, 21, 183, 187, 189, 213–215, 219, 221, 224, 226–227, 230–231, 301

Kormann, Eva, 249, 254

Kragujevac, 106–107

Krippenspiele, 137

Kristiansen, Kristian, 3, 21, 220, 223, 227

Kronobäck Monastery Ruin, 93

Kulturnatten, 66

Lancelot, 271

Land of Legends, 2, 166, 175, 180, 182, 187, 195

landscape, 3, 45, 55–56, 60, 64, 69, 72, 93, 102, 158, 271, 290

Lara Croft, 213, 220, 224, 234

laser scanner, 25, 28, 34–35, 37–38

Latvia, 91, 110, 127

Lau, Meghan, 138, 140–141, 154

learning by doing, 92

Leeson, Hershman, 53, 71

Leipzig, 16, 127, 138

leisure, 2, 20, 145, 147, 155, 159, 174, 245, 252, 270, 299

Lejre, 2, 165–166, 174–175, 180–182, 184, 186–190, 192–193, 195, 275

Lekgotla, 98

Lethra, 180–187

lifestyle migrants, 257, 265–266

literary fiction, 2

literature, 117, 159, 165, 168, 231, 235–236, 260, 283, 285, 288–289

Lithuania, 91

lived reality, 13

Livia's Villa Natural Interaction, 72, 77

living history, 2, 4, 14, 19–20, 22, 119, 135–137, 141, 143–147, 149–150, 152–155, 157, 170, 173, 185, 195–196, 198, 241–242, 252, 254, 274, 287, 296, 302

Ljungar-Chapelon, Magali, 6, 47, 51, 54, 57–58, 61, 65, 67, 74–75, 77, 80, 83–84, 288, 292, 301

local historical societies, 91

local history, 89–90, 100, 104, 140, 152

locus celebris, 25, 44–45

London Charter, 73, 76

Los Angeles, 152, 208

Lowenthal, David, 3–4, 21, 159, 173, 249, 251, 254, 277, 289, 296

Lukas, Scott, 13, 21

Lund, 20–21, 26, 29–30, 32, 35, 43–45, 63, 66, 77, 118–120, 123, 127–128, 153–155, 173, 188–189, 212, 226–228, 237, 257–258, 270, 275, 295–296, 299–301, 303

Lund, Cajsa S., 60

Lund Cathedral, 29–30, 32

Lund University, 35, 63, 66, 77, 155, 173, 257–258, 270, 295–296, 299–301, 303

Luther, 249

Magelssen, Scott, 144, 146, 154, 158, 173, 284, 296

magic moment, 161, 191

Maier, Hans, 143, 154

Mariner, 202–203, 206–207, 209–211, 231, 235

mass media, 223

material culture, 4, 175, 177–182, 184, 187, 189–190, 196, 204, 211, 223, 229–230, 251, 293, 299

materiality, 20, 60, 172, 188, 196, 201–202, 204–206, 208–212, 218, 230–231, 234–236, 285–286

Matrix, 215, 222–223, 225–226, 234

McDevitt, Jack, 11, 21, 237

meaning-making, 84, 113–117, 122–123, 125, 127, 292, 300

media studies, 11, 19, 302

Medieval Week, 11, 14, 253

memory, 3–4, 12, 16, 22, 138, 152, 158, 167, 172–173, 188, 195, 197–198, 229, 231, 249, 277, 283, 297, 299, 301, 303

MeshLab, 38

metaphor, 9, 25, 32, 206

meta-story, 14

methodical anachronism, 287, 291

Meyer, Annemike, 152, 244, 248, 252–254

Middle Ages, 3, 11, 25, 27–32, 34, 41, 80, 137, 151, 228, 242, 244–245, 248–249, 251, 253, 271, 273, 277, 284, 287–288, 295, 302

migration, 94

mimesis, 214–216

modernism, 220

Montague, 95–97, 109

monument, 35, 71, 76, 81

motion-capture technology, 62

movie, 142, 196, 204, 208, 210, 234, 249, 273

Mozart, Wolfgang Amadeus, 288

multi-view stereo reconstruction, 38

mummy, 215–216

museum, 3, 20, 44–45, 47–50, 52, 54, 56–57, 59–60, 65–69, 71–75, 77, 80–81, 89–91, 93, 95, 97–98, 100, 102, 104–110, 119–120, 128, 135–136, 141–143, 145–147, 150, 152, 154–155, 159, 165–166, 172, 174, 176, 179–180, 182, 189, 196–198, 212, 215, 218, 228, 231, 235, 273–274, 278, 285, 287–288, 292, 296, 300, 303

Museum of Sketches, 66

museum pedagogy, 3; theatre, 136, 145

music, 54, 60, 69, 77, 117, 141, 284, 289–290, 296, 301

Napoleon, 154, 249

narrative, 13, 17, 31, 49, 71–72, 83, 93, 114, 116–118, 121–126, 128–131, 140, 153, 173, 205, 216, 248, 253–254

National Geographic, 207, 230

National Museum of Denmark, 176

natural sciences, 90

naumachiae, 137

Nazi period, 16

NeverEnding Story, 222–223, 225

New Archaeology, 178

New Market, 168

New Mexico, 91

Nielsen, Carsten Tage, 195, 301

Nilsson, Ing-Marie, 4, 25, 27–28, 31–33, 45, 79, 83, 292, 301

Norway, 33, 40, 179, 287

O'Donovan, Hallie, 283, 295

Oerlinghausen, 143, 155

Oesterle, Carolyn, 20–21, 147, 154

Öland, 118–119, 121

Old Testament, 28, 289

Olsen, Bjørnar, 33, 40, 45, 179, 189

open-air museum, 141, 147, 154, 179–180, 182, 189, 296

Österlens museum, 49, 54, 57, 66, 69

otherness, 220, 267

Outram, Alan K., 145, 154, 158–160, 173

Paardekooper, Roeland, 143, 145–146, 154, 160, 172, 180, 188–189, 191, 214, 227, 284, 296, 301

pageant, 138–140, 154

Pageant of Sherborne, 140

Parker, Louis N., 140–141, 154

participation, 68, 81, 98, 100, 128, 138, 244, 272

passion play, 137

pastness, 1, 11–12, 18, 20, 183, 186–188, 191, 257, 259, 267

performance, 11, 52–53, 67, 76, 81, 135–138, 141, 144, 146–147, 151–152, 154, 158, 172–173, 283, 292, 295–296, 302

performance studies, 11

performative authenticity, 183, 188

period rush, 12, 161

Petersson, Bodil, 3–4, 15, 19–21, 145, 151, 155, 160, 173, 180, 187, 189, 201, 204, 209, 212, 214, 216, 221, 227, 230–232, 234–235, 257, 281–282, 284, 289, 294, 296, 302

Petroglyfics, 74

Pfahlbauern, 140, 142

Photoscan, Agisoft, 38, 46

Pihlainen, Kalle, 15, 22

Pine, Joseph, 18, 22, 159–160, 174, 218, 227

played reality, 12, 102

Plimoth Plantation, 143

Poland, 218, 227, 301

politics of archaeology, 5, 188; of knowledge, 6; of the past, 5, 7–8

Pompeii, 175–177, 185, 188, 235, 288, 295

pop archaeology, 214, 227

popular culture, 1–2, 19, 152, 172, 179, 186, 188, 213–214, 216, 218, 224–227, 232, 234, 255, 260–261, 273, 283, 293, 301

positivism, 197, 220

post-industrial, 7, 218, 226, 266

postmodernity, 7

post-processual archaeology, 220–221, 233–234

post-structuralism, 179, 190

prehistory, 6, 82, 135–136, 139, 155, 176, 182–184, 302

Pretoria, 92, 97

procession, 6, 47–48, 50, 53–54, 56–57, 59–69, 71, 73, 75, 77, 80–81, 137–138

processual archaeology, 220–221, 233–234

psychology, 11, 19, 301

public archaeology, 21, 213, 226–227, 230–232, 299, 301, 303

Queen Elisabeth I, 272

racism, 17

radio, 90, 228

Raiders of the Lost Ark, 225

Ratelgat, 102, 104, 109

reconciliation, 89, 94–98, 109, 129

reconstruction, 1, 27, 29, 34, 38–40, 43, 46, 71–73, 78–79, 153, 155, 158, 160, 165–166, 168, 175, 196, 198, 250, 281–282, 285, 287, 293–294, 302

re-creation, 301

re-enactment, 2, 14, 16–17, 21, 107, 130, 137, 140, 144–145, 149–154, 157–158, 160–162, 164–174, 188–189, 191, 195–198, 213, 220, 223–225,

227, 242, 248, 271, 278, 281–284, 287, 291–294, 302

reflection in action, 196

Regolini-Galassi Tomb, 72, 78

religion, 52, 55, 64, 77, 90, 94, 147, 209–210, 236

Renfrew, Colin, 53, 78, 226

Rentzhog, Sten, 4, 22, 141, 143, 155, 284, 297

replication, 286

representation, 28, 49–50, 52, 54, 64, 69, 127, 138, 141, 143, 151, 174, 198, 215–216, 249, 283, 286–287, 301

Rio de Janeiro, 54

rite of passage, 64

ritual, 6, 29, 47–50, 52, 54, 56–59, 62, 64–67, 73, 77, 80, 84, 137, 141, 147, 236, 288, 292, 302

rock art imagery, 47, 51, 75

rock carving, 52, 64, 66, 69, 72–74, 80–81

Rockefeller Jr., John D., 143

role play, 2, 89, 109, 115–119, 123–124, 130, 248

Rolf Jensen, 218

Roman Empire, 137

Romanticism, 8, 174, 188

Rome, 15, 233, 236

Rosenzweig, Roy, 196, 198

Royal Armoury of Sweden, 272

Runia, Eelco, 167, 171, 174

Rüsen, Jörn, 116–118, 121, 126, 128

Samida, Stefanie, 3, 15, 22, 135–136, 143–145, 150, 152, 155, 191–192, 195, 293, 302

Samuel, Raphael, 3–4, 22, 283, 297

Saxton, William, 146, 153, 161, 165, 168, 173

Scandinavia, 25, 66, 77, 152, 218, 288, 302

Scania, 25–26, 30, 49, 57, 66

scenario, 3, 34, 41, 43, 80, 93–94, 96, 104, 110, 162, 202, 205, 223, 231

Schiffer, Michael, 221, 228

Schleif, Corine, 61

Schneider, Rebecca, 158, 164, 169, 174, 277

school, 5, 8, 49, 67, 70, 90–91, 93–94, 109–110, 114, 116, 118–119, 122, 126, 129, 162, 165, 170, 173–174, 186, 222, 227, 245, 265, 278, 299–300, 302

Schön, Donald, 196, 198

science fiction, 11, 81, 145, 227, 232, 241, 285

scripted battles, 167–168

sculpture, 25, 28, 30–31

senses, 6, 12, 34, 45, 48, 61, 65, 77, 81, 90–91, 95, 98, 122, 135–136, 157, 176, 183–185, 191, 195–196, 205–207, 233, 236, 241, 250–251, 261, 267–268, 271, 274, 278, 283, 288, 293–294, 296

Serbia, 89, 91, 93, 104, 106–107, 109, 129–130

service management, 257–258, 299

Shanks, Michael, 53, 71–72, 76, 78, 179, 189, 220, 223, 228

Shimada, Izumi, 160, 165, 169, 174

shopping, 2

Sibum, Otto, 170–171, 174

Silverberg, Robert, 81

simulation, 19, 27, 34–35, 37, 41–42, 175, 179, 214–216, 226

Skansen, 4, 141

slavery, 17

Slavs and Vikings Centre, 218

Småberg, Thomas, 271, 302

Snoop Dogg, 272, 274

social anthropology, 19

social cohesion, 9, 89, 92, 95, 108

social media, 124, 277

social sciences, 12, 90, 179, 250, 283, 301

social sustainability, 101, 263, 285

Society for Creative Anachronism, 284, 295

sociology, 19, 173, 257–258, 299

socio-museology, 278

soft power, 108

software, 38, 41, 79

South Africa, 89, 91–92, 95–102, 108–111, 129–130

Soweto, 98, 100–101, 110

Stanford Archaeology Center's Metamedia Lab, 53

Star Trek, 285–286

Star Wars, 231

staycation, 264

Stenborg, Per, 79, 302

Stockholm, 20–22, 43–46, 77, 128, 141, 153, 155, 188–189, 212, 272, 275, 285, 297, 300

Stone Age, 4, 90–91, 176, 192, 294

story, stories, 13, 20, 32, 82, 89, 93, 97, 116–117, 126, 140, 175, 192–193, 202–203, 206, 208, 217, 222–223, 225, 229, 232, 248–249, 255, 265, 284, 288–289, 293

story-telling, 175

structuralism, 179, 190

structure from motion, 38

study circles, 91

Sweden, 17, 25–26, 33, 40, 43, 47, 53, 79, 91, 95, 108–110, 114, 118–119, 122, 130, 187, 228, 269, 271–273, 278, 282, 285, 288–289, 299–303

Swedish Historical Museum, 285

Swedish Institute, 91

Syria, 17

Södra bruket, 118, 128

tacticals, 168–169

tangible history, 241, 247, 250

Taylor, Charles, 115–116, 125–128, 130–131

Tell, Wilhelm, 97, 100, 117, 122, 135–136, 140, 146, 167, 183, 192, 206–207, 233, 236, 265, 269, 292

theatre, 17, 52, 54, 65, 136, 145, 152, 174, 227–228, 231, 235–236, 288–289

theatre of memory, 3–4, 283

Thelen, David, 196, 198

themed environment, 2, 181; walk, 136

Thompson, Jenny, 3, 17, 22, 162, 174

Tilden, Freeman, 187, 189

Tilley, Christopher, 34, 45, 179, 190, 221, 228

Time Machine, 145, 230, 241–242

time travel paradox, 82

Timm Knudsen, Britta, 277, 300

tolerance, 89, 104–105, 107, 109, 129–130, 291

tourism, 2–3, 19, 21, 67, 144, 146, 160, 166, 168–169, 172–174, 184, 188–189, 243, 257–264, 266, 268, 270–271, 273, 299–300

tourism studies, 19, 258

tourism management, 67, 243, 271

tournament, 284

Trenter, Cecilia, 129, 303

TV, 2, 6, 15, 91, 186, 214, 233, 236–237, 242, 253–254, 271, 285–286

Tübingen, 76, 136, 142, 152, 155, 302

Turkey, 91

Tutankhamun, 177

Uganda, 91, 93, 110

United Kingdom, 179

United States, 91, 285

Urgeschichtliche Forschungsinstitut, 142

user experience, 71–72, 78, 81

utopia, 10, 295

Valhalla, 15

Vasa, 91

Venice, 54, 234

Viking, 4, 17, 131, 182, 218, 221, 227, 252, 271, 277, 287, 290, 296

Viking Age, 4, 182, 271, 277, 287

Vimmerby, 91, 110, 228

virtual acting, 3; virtual environment, 11, 27, 39, 53, 62, 65, 84; interpretation, 34, 39; reality, 14, 44, 47–49, 54, 62, 64–66, 71, 73, 77, 84, 287, 301

Visby, 14, 271

Västergötland, 15, 40, 273, 302

Wachowski brothers, 215

Wall-E, 223–224, 229

Wang, Ning, 168, 174, 259–260, 270

Warwick, 140

Waterworld, 201–208, 210–211, 230–231, 233–236, 293

Wells, H. G., 3, 29, 33, 145, 230, 241–242

Westergren, Ebbe, 9, 89, 110, 129–130, 214, 228, 292, 303

Wienberg, Jes, 4, 25–26, 44–45, 79, 83, 212, 282, 292, 295, 303

Wii, 67

world heritage, 102

World War I, 141–142

World War II, 16, 104, 107, 291

xenophobia, 97, 130

Yggdrasil, 59

Zander, Ulf, 205, 212, 215, 228, 233, 237, 275

Žižek, Slavoj, 215–217, 220, 222–223, 225, 228

Zürich, 140, 254